BRITISH PRISONERS OF WAR RELATIVES' ASSOCIATION

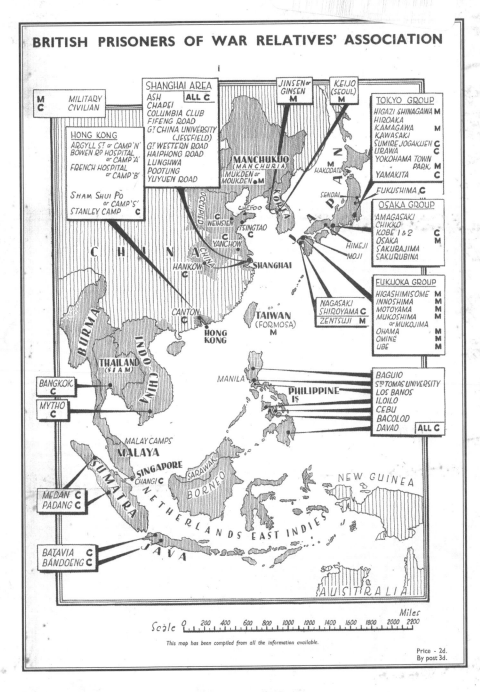

PRISONER OF WAR

PRISONER OF WAR

Voices from Captivity during the
Second World War

CHARLES ROLLINGS

EBURY
PRESS

1 3 5 7 9 10 8 6 4 2

Published in 2007 by Ebury Press, an imprint of Ebury Publishing

Ebury Publishing is a division of the Random House Group

The Random House Group Limited Reg. No. 954009

Addresses for companies within the Random House Group can be found at www.randomhouse.co.uk

A CIP catalogue record for this book is available from the British Library

The Random House Group Limited makes every effort to ensure that the papers used in our books are made from trees that have been legally sourced from well-managed and credibly certified forests. Our paper procurement policy can be found on www.randomhouse.co.uk

Printed and bound in Great Britain by Clays Ltd, St Ives plc

ISBN 9780091910075

CONTENTS

ACKNOWLEDGEMENTS

Thanks are due to the following for allowing me to reproduce material from private collections held in the Imperial War Museum, Lambeth: Adrian Abbott (Lieutenant Stephen S Abbott); Lawrence Bains (Corporal Lawrence Bains); Eric Barrington (Corporal Eric Barrington); the late Lieutenant-Colonel W M G Bompas (Lieutenant William Bompas); Lucinda Brooks (Lieutenant-Colonel Sydney Charles Fane de Salis, DSO); Mrs Jean Carpenter (Signalman John Stanley Walker); Mrs M Dalgleish (Midshipman J F Dalgleish); the family of S J Doughty; Jodi Fitzsimons (Lieutenant Dan Billany); Jane G Forsey (Lieutenant-Colonel P A Belton); Mrs Enid Innes-Ker (Sergeant W McD and Mrs Enid Innes-Ker); Miss M M King (Gunner Cyril George King); Erik Laker (Private Erik Laker); Sandra Luckett (Sapper Don Luckett); Richard Pelly (Major Sir John Pelly); Mrs John Pelly (Lieutenant John Gordon Pelly, RNVR); Celia Rambaut (Pilot Officer I P B Denton); Mrs Joan Rix (Flight Lieutenant Eric Williams); Susan Shearn (Pilot Officer E D Shearn); Mrs Audrey Sollars (Lance-Corporal Jack Sollars); Sebastian Stephens (Lieutenant-Commander W L Stephens); Mrs Dorothy Threadgold (Captain A G Threadgold); Patrick Toosey (Lieutenant-Colonel Philip Toosey); Major M S Wagner MBE (Lieutenant M S Wagner); Mrs E M White (Lieutenant H L White).

Every effort has been made by the Imperial War Museum to trace the copyright holders of the collections of the late Reverend G Bower, Mrs D B Crawford (Wendy Fleming), H E C Elliott, L E Morris, A F Powell, P Hall Romney, F H Thompson, E W Whincup and R S Young, but without success. Both the IWM and myself should appreciate any information regarding the current copyright holders so that they can be acknowledged in future editions.

I would also like to thank, very warmly, Roderick Suddaby, the Keeper of the Department of Documents at the Imperial War Museum, along with his able and attentive staff, for the assistance they have given during the past year.

I am also grateful to the following for allowing me to interview them and to use correspondence, diaries and unpublished manuscripts: H R Bewlay; Captain H H Bracken, CBE, RN (Retd); A C Bryant; the late M G Butt;

Edward Cadwallader; the late N E Canton; Mrs U Cole (G F Cole); the late H D H Cooper; Nicholas Craig (Squadron Leader G D Craig); the late H E L Falkus; the late Patrick Greenhous; the late Bill Greenaway; Mrs Vivien Johnson (T F S Johnson); the late J R Kayll; the late D M Lubbock and his eldest daughter Ann Pat Gooch; the late M H Roth; P G Royle; Sigrid Haase; Air Commodore D M Strong, CB, DFC RAF (Retd); Nigel Viney (Major Elliott Viney); the Public Record Office, for the escape report of the late J E T Asselin; and Duane Reed, of the USAF Academy Library, Colorado, for letters and diaries acquired from the estates of *Oberst* Freiherr Friedrich-Wilhelm von Lindeiner-Wildau and Major Gustav Simoleit, both of the Luftwaffe. Finally, I extend a hand to Robert Kee for kindly agreeing to write the Foreword.

For the use of drawings, photographs and maps I would like to thank: Adrian Abbott, H R Bewlay, the late Lieutenant-Colonel W M G Bompas, Mrs Jean Carpenter, Nicholas Craig, the family of S J Doughty, Jodi Fitzsimons, Enid Innes-Ker, Mrs John G Pelly, Mrs Joan Rix, Julie Summers, Mrs Dorothy Threadgold, the Toosey family, Mrs E M White, the Imperial War Museum and the British Red Cross Society.

I tender apologies in advance to any contributor I may have inadvertently overlooked, and to those whom I was unable to contact, despite all reasonable efforts, for leave to use their material. Among the latter are Charles and Elsie Bryant, Harry Crease, Maurice Driver, Ted Eames, Kurt Knierim, Gertrude Koppenhöfer, Hannelore Lewerentz, Jack Lyon, C J Lythgoe, Gisela Moody, Mrs Pam Milligan, Spenser Mulligan, Harry Swann and Harry Train. All have my gratitude nonetheless.

Finally, I thank my wife, Isabel; my agent, Charlie Viney; and my editors at Ebury for their encouragement and support.

FOREWORD

To have been taken a prisoner of war in the Second World War can evoke in those who were not themselves prisoners a personal sympathy which, to someone like myself who spent some three years in Stalag Luft III and other German camps, can sometimes seem rather overdone – though not of course in cases where people had been prisoners of the Japanese.

Yes, in German camps there was occasional anxiety over food, but Red Cross Parcels on the whole dealt more or less reliably with that; and, yes, there was boredom and occasional lonely wondering about when indeed the War was likely to end. But we had our secret radio, conjured skilfully by bribing some of the German guards and capable of receiving the BBC news. Quite apart from that there was the openness of the camp site, which allowed relatively as much physical exercise as one felt inclined for, including occasional cricket matches. Apart from that there was a theatre provided by the Germans in the camp which we prisoners could use as we wished, either for lectures on subjects on which fellow prisoners were so often extremely well informed, or for public readings, but also for the performance of plays well selected by prisoners with theatrical experience from former everyday life – Shakespeare's *Hamlet* or Shaw's *Saint Joan* for instance.

A former prisoner I met years later in London said: 'Sometimes I think they were the best years of our lives' – a comment which I noticed his wife seemed to have severe difficulty in accepting.

I met Charles Rollings, the author of this excellent book, long after the end of the War. He had so deeply immersed himself in the whole character of *Kriegsgefangenschaft* (German: literally, 'prisoner of war-ship') that I remember telling him that, despite his obvious youth, he could almost have been a prisoner of war himself. No one could have been found better capable of focusing attention on the whole constitutional nature of 'Kriegiedom', and his excellent selections of individual personal accounts, together with his reminder of how the Germans treated Russian prisoners as 'Untermenschen', makes it possible for readers to feel that they have been prisoners of war too.

Robert Kee

INTRODUCTION

PRISONERS-OF-WAR! That is not the least fortunate kind of prisoner to be, but it is nevertheless a melancholy state. You are in the power of your enemy. You owe your life to his humanity, and your daily bread to his compassion. You must obey his orders, go where he tells you, stay where you are bid, await his pleasure, possess your soul in patience.

Meanwhile, the war is going on, great events are in progress, fine operations and opportunities for action and adventure are slipping away. Also the days are very long. Hours crawl by like paralytic centipedes. Nothing amuses you – reading is difficult – writing impossible. Life is one long boredom from dawn till slumber. Moreover the whole atmosphere of prison is odious – companions in this kind of misfortune quarrel about trifles, and get the least possible pleasure from each other's society.

If you have never been under restraint before, and never known what it is to be a captive, you feel a sense of constant humiliation, being confined to a narrow space fenced in by wire, watched by armed men, and webbed in by a tangle of regulations.

I certainly hated every minute of my captivity – more than I have hated any period of my whole life. Looking back on those days, I have always felt the keenest pity for prisoners and captives.

Thus wrote Winston Churchill, Britain's Prime Minister from 1940 to 1945, of his experiences as a prisoner during the Boer War (1899–1901). Though his experience of captivity was brief – he escaped successfully after less than a month – his description in *My Early Life* was such an eloquent distillation of all that made up the plight of the prisoner of war that many of those captured in the Second World War copied it meticulously into their diaries.

But, despite Churchill's example, the various kinds of prisoners taken in the Second World War – ranging from disarmed combatants and 'protected personnel' such as doctors and nurses, through civilian internees and political hostages, to victims of the Holocaust – rarely warrant so much as a footnote in general histories, even the most notable ones. Given the duration and scope of the war, a conflict that raged for nearly six years across Europe, the Middle East, Asia, the Far East and the Americas, this is perhaps understandable. But it also makes it easy to forget that during this time the world was almost one vast prison camp.

Between 1939 and 1945 nearly half a million Allied servicemen heard the famous saying: 'For you the war is over'. For them, the fighting war might well have been over, but another was about to begin – a war in many respects no less hazardous than armed combat itself. Waged against boredom, despair, hunger, brutality, disease and, ultimately, death, this was a battle fought with no weapons other than one's own wits and character. Moreover, it was conducted against a fully armed captor who also had at his disposal barbed wire, searchlights, dogs, solitary confinement cells, cunning and brutal interrogation techniques, secret state police and the right to exploit prisoners for their labour.

Never before – not even during the Napoleonic Wars or the First World War – had so many men been made reluctant guests of the enemy. The total number of British and Commonwealth prisoners taken in all theatres in the Second World War was 353,941 (almost 9 per cent of the forces engaged), and for the United States of America 103,918 (or 2 per cent). Germany and Italy combined had taken 142,319 British Army, Royal Navy and RAF prisoners; Germany alone 95,532 American; and Japan some 320,000 Allied combatants of all nations (50,016 of them British, 21,000 Australian, 26,943 American). So many Axis prison camps dotted the globe that the location of many of them was unknown to the Allies until the end of the war.

The Western powers had slowly begun to realize, towards the end of the nineteenth century, that with modern warfare becoming more mobile the chances of large numbers of combatants being cut off and captured were increasingly more likely. Despite this – and although POWs were recognized and accorded some rights by the Hague Conventions of 1899 and 1907 – it was not until 1929, a decade before the Second World War, that an extensive body of international rules was put in place to govern their treatment.

The Prisoner of War Code of the Geneva Convention was signed in June 1929 by no fewer than 47 nations – including all future Second World War belligerents except the USSR. It contained 97 articles (compared with only 21 in the 1927 Hague Convention) that covered every aspect of imprisonment from capture to release. In practice, however, the application of its rules depended upon wartime conditions and the widely varying customs and attitudes of the various detaining powers. The chief obstacle to uniformly humane treatment of prisoners in the Second World War was the fact that four of the major powers involved – three Axis, Germany, Italy and Japan; and one Allied, the Soviet Union – ignored its provisions to a great or lesser degree.

Germany's attitude was ambivalent to say the least. The Nazis could quite plausibly argue that as it was the Weimar Republic, a regime they did not recognize, that had signed the Geneva Convention, they were not legally or morally bound by it. By and large, Germany's conventional armed forces did strive to adhere to the letter, if not the spirit, of the POW Code – at least on the Western Front – but did not always succeed. Completely the opposite applied on the Eastern Front, where Germany made no attempt at all to comply. This was partly because of Nazi racial theories classifying Russians and other Slavs as *Untermenschen*, but also because the Soviet Union, which had been more or less isolated from the international community since 1917, had not attended the Geneva Convention or signed the POW Code. In any case, Joseph Stalin expected his soldiers to fight to the death lest, as prisoners of war, they might become 'contaminated' by the West and be converted to non-communist ideas. The net result was that at least 3,300,000 of the 5,700,000 Red Army prisoners taken by Germany died in captivity – a mortality rate of 57 per cent, compared with a death rate of 3.5 per cent among British and Commonwealth prisoners and of 5 per cent among Americans.

In fascist Italy, the situation was somewhat more complex, due in large part to a conflict between the deep family and religious ties felt by most Italians, who harboured only a lukewarm commitment to Mussolini's military ambitions; the relative isolation of the peasant class, to whom enemy prisoners – especially the British – were an unknown and baffling quantity; and the aggressive and erratic nature of the fascists who were in charge of some of the camps. Much more than in Germany, the treatment of Allied prisoners in Italy was determined by the character of the individuals guarding them. Moreover, Italy was also unique, in so far as it was the only Axis power to sign an armistice mid-war and then became partially an Ally, helping rather than holding British, Commonwealth and American prisoners.

Japan, last but not least of the Axis triumvirate, had also signed the Convention. But soon after attacking Pearl Harbor on 7 December 1941 it announced that it would comply only loosely with its terms. In practice this meant hardly complying at all, although some Japanese camp commandants could on occasion be persuaded to recognize the Hague Convention. The intransigence of the Japanese was largely the result of dyed-in-the-wool attitudes about the value of their own fighting men should they become prisoners – attitudes they in turn projected upon the prisoners they themselves captured. A Japanese soldier's conduct in the field was governed by a warped version of the ancient rules of Bushido, 'the Way of the Warrior'. Bushido was first and foremost a code of honour, and involved fighting to the death. To lay down one's arms was shameful under any circumstances, and a cornered soldier should kill himself or charge weaponless against the enemy sooner than give himself up. So deeply was this embedded in the Japanese mind-set that, until the final months of the war in the Pacific, only a few thousand Japanese were taken prisoner by the Allies, and then only because most of them were wounded and unable to flee. During the 1944–45 campaign in Burma, only 142 Japanese soldiers were captured, whereas 17,166 were killed – a ratio of one to 120. Among the Western armies, by contrast, commanders expected an overall capture-to-kill ratio of only one to four.

Because they so rarely genuflected to outside influences, the Japanese abhorrence of surrender directly influenced their handling of prisoners from other nations. As far as the Japanese were concerned, by allowing themselves to be taken captive, these men proved themselves to be craven and worthy only of contempt. They were to be punished with starvation diets, hard work and physical abuse. Thus, prisoner-of-war existence in the Far East was as much a struggle for survival as was armed combat itself – probably more so. The number of men engaged in that struggle shrank tragically as the war dragged on. Nearly 30 per cent of Britons, Americans, Canadians, Australians and New Zealanders died in captivity.

In their treatment of the former Axis POWs the Western Allies generally adhered to the Geneva Convention. But, again treatment varied from nation to nation and at different stages of the war. The French did not treat their German prisoners well, either in 1940 or 1944–45, and allowed them to die by the thousand, usually of starvation and disease. Considering that many French captured by the Germans in 1940 were treated better than the British, and that most were released in 1941–42, this neglect seems inexcusable; however, it must be borne in mind that their country had been occupied and pillaged by the Nazis for five years.

When America entered the war at the end of 1941 it was initially unprepared to accommodate prisoners, but the Americans proved themselves quick learners in almost every aspect of war, and conditions in US camps improved, some camps verging on the luxurious. However, once Germany surrendered, Roosevelt and Eisenhower tore up the Geneva Convention, instead re-categorizing German prisoners as 'defeated enemies', denying them Red Cross parcels and the right to send letters, and sometimes handing them over to the French. Some of these prisoners were mere schoolboys, who had been conscripted into the army and surrendered without firing a shot. Having been transferred to camps run by the French, they were imprisoned for up to four years, during which time they were unable to write so much as a single postcard to their families or receive any form of relief. As a result of these policies, some 100,000 German prisoners had died of neglect by 1946 alone.

Lucky were those Germans and Italians captured by the British, although interrogation methods in London were tough and became really brutal towards the end of the war. Britain also violated the Geneva Convention by not segregating prisoners by service and sending most of them to Canada, where some camps were below par. But apart from harsh interrogation methods there was no deliberate ill-treatment or wanton neglect such as that perpetrated by the Americans, the French or, indeed, the Germans themselves. (Few accurate statistics are available for Italian POWs – the figure of 200,000 killed fighting the Allies includes those who died in captivity – but of those captured by the Germans when Italy changed sides in 1943, some 30,000 died of maltreatment because they refused to serve the Nazis). The fact that many Germans and Italians (25,252 of the former alone) elected to remain in Britain after their release between 1946 and 1948 is testimony not only to the effects of 'de-Nazification' but also to the pleasant memories they had of their experience as captives. Indeed, one former German POW recently donated £350 to have a plaque, with his name on it, mounted at the site of his former POW camp in Scotland.

Not suprisingly, the USSR treated its Axis prisoners abominably, which was really only giving the Nazis their just deserts. Of the 3,155,000 German POWs in Soviet custody, some 1,185,000 died, along with 300,000 Japanese.

Whether Allied or Axis, prisoners of war were in any case a nuisance, regardless of the captor's culture or ideology. The captor had to spend time, money and resources housing, feeding and guarding them, thus diverting manpower and material that could have been put to better use prosecuting the war. Thus the size of the daily food ration, for instance, and the quality of POW accommodation varied according to the demands made on the resources of the Axis at particular stages of the war and during certain campaigns. In Germany and Italy, treatment also varied according to whether they held more or less Allied prisoners than the Allies held Axis and which of these three services the captors or prisoners came from, as the army, navy and air force had different codes of chivalry.

POWs were almost as much an inconvenience to their own side. Their government and armed forces regarded them as living proof of their own tactical, if not strategic, failures and better kept out of sight and mind. Prisoners of war themselves sometimes felt chastened and humiliated at their capture, and the British in particular often believed (not always wrongly) that their government was not doing its utmost to ameliorate their conditions. But they were at least in the hearts and minds of their families and friends.

'Loss of freedom is hard to bear for those who have lived as free men in a free country,' wrote Queen Elizabeth in *The Prisoner of War*, a reassuring monthly magazine for next of kin first issued by the Prisoners of War Department of the British Red Cross in May 1942; 'and it is hard, too, for those who wait at home, to go cheerfully about their daily tasks in the knowledge that someone dear to them is in exile and a Prisoner. I hope that it may be of some small consolation to them to know that the Red Cross is striving by every means in its power to lighten the lot of British Prisoners of War and to make them feel that they are ever in the thoughts of those at home.' She concluded: 'They are often in my thoughts and in my prayers, especially the mothers and wives, the sisters and betrothed of those who have fallen into enemy hands.'

However, it was recognized by most warring nations, and by the Geneva Convention, that a prisoner had a right to try escaping. In fact, it was the duty of officers in particular not only to escape but also to harass and confound their captors in every way, thus pinning down troops who might otherwise be used at the fighting front.

But even persistent escapers made only a pinprick contribution to the war effort and, with very few exceptions, returning escapers had a negligible effect on the outcome of the war. So, in the great scheme of things, even the successful escaper was barely significant, and has been consigned to the margins of history.

Despite this, POWs – and escapers in particular – have become a sort of postwar cultural icon, a popular symbol of the will to survive against the odds and of defiance against tyranny and arbitrary rules. If one takes it as read that the public's interest is usually in what occurs at the point of maximum danger, then one can infer from the widespread fascination with Colditz, *The Wooden Horse* and *The Great Escape* a general recognition that to have been a prisoner of war (in the words of military historian Sir John Keegan, 'the enemy's chattel, not his opponent') was to have been in peril, while to have been free, even if a soldier, was to have lived in relative safety.

Prisoner of War stands in the unexplored terrain between, on the one hand, those general books which examine the experiences of the average POW and, on the other, the first-hand accounts that have appeared during the past sixty-odd years. It is based on interviews and correspondence I have undertaken with ex-POWs and their relatives since 1979; POW letters, diaries and wartime logs written and kept at the time; audio tapes and unpublished manuscripts in my possession and held at the Imperial War Museum, Lambeth; escape reports and Red Cross reports held at the Public Record

Office, Kew; microfilm records from the United States Army Air Force Museum in Colorado, and German documents from the Bundesarchiv in Freiburg im Breisgau.

I have also corresponded with and interviewed those on the other side of the fence – the camp staff who counted the prisoners on daily roll-calls, examined their Red Cross parcels, and censored their letters – and this will be the first book on POWs to include the point of view of the former captor. It is also unusual again in that instead of concentrating on one country, such as Germany, the net is cast wider and includes the experiences of POWs in the Mediterranean and the Far East.

Finally – and most importantly – *Prisoner of War* allows the Allied prisoner of war, his wife (or girlfriend) and his captor to tell their stories as they were written at or near the time or as they unfolded later in letters and interviews. The chapters are arranged thematically, in the order in which prisoners would typically confront events from capture, through interrogation, imprisonment and possibly escape, to final liberation and homecoming. Each chapter starts with an introduction, setting the context for the individual reminiscences that follow, which are then arranged by theatre of operations and preceded by a short preamble. For simplicity's sake, I have maintained throughout the ranks held by the men at the time of their capture, although junior officers received time-promotion after six and then twelve months, and would have ended the war two ranks higher. Thus a pilot officer captured in mid-1940 would be a flight lieutenant by the end of 1941.

As I have tried to tell the story of life behind the wire in the words of the contributors I have kept comment on individual reminiscences to a minimum, so it may be advisable to explain at this point certain aspects of POW life that readers may be unfamiliar with given the passage of more than sixty years since the events unfolded. The most important thing to bear in mind is that like the soldiers who went to the slaughter in the war of 1914–18, most of the British servicemen captured in Europe and the Mediterranean during the Second World War were not much older than schoolboys, and this to some extent defined their attitude towards their prison camps (third-rate public schools) and their captors (stuffy headmasters – indeed, not a few of the Axis officers guarding them were former teachers). Like schoolboys, they also developed their own particular argot: prisoners of the Germans were 'kriegies' (short for *Kriegsgefangener*, the German word for prisoner of war); prisoner-of-war life was 'Kriegiedom'; the German guards were 'goons', and making illegal liquor was 'laying down a brew'. Prisoners in Italy and the Far East likewise appropriated the language of their captors with humorous intent.

This youthful spirit was as much as anything else a reason why so many British and Commonwealth prisoners survived what was at the very best a sentence, of unknown duration, to boredom, privation and the loss of freedom and family, and, at worst, a dreadful ordeal that many did not survive.

1
CAPTURE

'I suppose there are circumstances where it can be a relief to be a prisoner of war. This was not to be one of them.'

— Far Eastern POW

It has often been remarked – even by former POWs themselves – that a prisoner of war is someone on the losing side who did not run away fast enough. This is as near to a bottom-line definition as one can get. But it is also a trifle harsh: one might say the same of a soldier who is killed in action. The fact is that as far back as history records, capture in battle was often unavoidable: the only other options were a quick death at the hands of oneself or the enemy, or a slow death from physical exhaustion, starvation, or lack of medical facilities.

For the first seven months of the Second World War – known as 'The Phoney War' – no British soldiers were captured at all (though one was killed in December 1939), as the army did not engage the enemy until the campaign in Norway in April 1940. Most British prisoners taken during this period came in fact from the Merchant Navy, victims of German U-boats and pocket battleships, which were sinking thousands of tonnes of Allied and neutral merchant shipping and either casting their crews adrift in lifeboats or cramming them aboard their supply ships. Technically, merchant seamen were civilians, entitled to be treated as internees and therefore exchanged for their German counterparts. Yet, the vast majority were escorted by circuitous routes to Germany, ending up in Milag Nord (Marine Internierten Lager), temporarily housed within Stalag XXA at Sandbostel, near Bremervorde in north-west Germany. They were later transferred to a new camp at Westertimke, 20 kilometres to the south, where some 4,500 of them languished behind barbed wire for the rest of the war.

Royal Navy (mainly Fleet Air Arm) personnel were likewise amongst the earliest captives: Germany took its first Fleet Air Arm prisoners on 14 September 1939. The first prisoners of any of the three services to be bagged by the Italians, who declared war against the Allies on 10 June 1940, were submariners. On the night of 31 July, the submarine HMS *Oswald* was rammed in the Mediterranean, and of a crew of fifty-five, three perished, probably drowning in leaking fuel oil; the survivors were taken to Italy. Altogether 5,529 Royal Navy officers and men were reported captured by Italy and Germany throughout the war. (The total number reported as taken prisoner by Japan was 2,304, of which 421 were killed or died in captivity.) Like the men of the Merchant Navy, they seldom had anything but Hobson's choice: freeze to death in the icy waters of the North Sea or the Arctic Ocean; drift for days in a leaky lifeboat with poor provisions; or be dragged aboard an enemy battleship or submarine.

Officers and men of the Royal Air Force, too, were among those captured soon after the outbreak of war. The first of them became guests of the Third Reich on 4 and 5 September 1939, although for almost six months the total number remained under 40. But in May and June 1940, as the German Blitzkrieg rolled across the Low Countries and France, the RAF suffered huge losses. When Fighter Command began sending fighter sweeps and escort formations over France in 1941, losses mounted again, as did those of the Middle East Air Force and the Desert Air Force after Italy entered the war. Allied infantry and tank offensives against the Deutsches Afrika Korps in Libya and Tunisia in 1941–42, the fall of Greece and Crete in October 1940–May 1941, and the raid on Dieppe in August 1942 also required air cover, and took a heavy toll on aircraft and their pilots. The mounting bomber offensive against Germany and the often suicidal daylight attacks on enemy airfields and other targets in occupied countries sometimes saw whole squadrons wiped out, with almost all personnel captured or killed. By the time that Germany surrendered, the number of British and Dominion Air Force POWs was 13,022 (4,480 officers plus 8,542 Warrant Officers and NCOs) – and that excludes those who had died in captivity, had been repatriated on medical grounds or had made successful escapes from Germany and Italy.

Soldiers tended to enter captivity en masse, and three major campaigns accounted for the bulk of army prisoners: the fall of France and the Low Countries in May–June 1940; the war in North Africa, 1940–43, and the collapse of Singapore and Hong Kong in 1941–42. But lesser campaigns played their part: Norway in April 1940, Greece and Crete in 1940–41. Small-scale operations by clandestine units such as the commandos, paratroopers, the Long-Range Desert Group, the Special Air Service and the Special Boat Service brought a steady trickle of specially trained officers, NCOs and other ranks to join their compatriots from the conventional armed forces.

Even when the Allies went over to the offensive and were patently winning the war, the highly mobile nature of airborne, amphibious and armoured operations could cause units to be cut off and captured. Between D-Day and VE-Day 1.4 per cent of Anglo-Canadians became POWs. In one operation alone, 'Market-Garden', Montgomery's bid to cross the Lower Rhine at Arnhem in September 1944, 6,500 officers and men of the 1st Airborne Division fell into German hands in nine days. Right up to the last minute, even as the Third Reich collapsed, aircraft were being shot down, and their crews joined the starving ranks of long-term prisoners. On the far side of the globe the Japanese, too, were still capturing RAF and Fleet Air Arm pilots, whose chances of survival at this stage were slim, as they were particularly loathed by the Japanese and quickly put to death.

However they were captured, the men were exhausted after days or hours of intense action, relieved at not being wounded, and thankful to be alive. Often, though, their feelings were mixed. For one man, to find himself a prisoner 'seemed like a terrible dream'; another found it 'very embarrassing' and felt 'highly confused' and 'frustrated and angry'. Others were 'fearful, depressed and bewildered' or simply 'stunned'. So numbed were they that it often took days for the reality of their plight to sink in. Meanwhile, families and loved ones back home waited days, perhaps weeks, for news: their men were missing, but were they dead, or prisoners?

WESTERN EUROPE AND THE MEDITERRANEAN

THE NORTH SEA, 1939

Royal Air Force personnel were among the earliest prisoners and once the 'Phoney War' was over and the fight began in earnest, they and their brethren in the Commonwealth air forces were taken captive in numbers large and small almost daily. They were mainly from Bomber Command and Coastal Command, which carried out operations round the clock.

Pilot Officer Laurence Edwards, a New Zealander in the Royal Air Force, No 206 Squadron, Coastal Command
POW from September 1940 to June 1945
On 3 September 1939, I was with No 206 Squadron in Norfolk and had just landed from reconnaissance over the North Sea. On the 5th I was sent on a similar trip and was shot down. I was picked up by a German seaplane

and taken to the island of Norderney. As the Germans put it, for me the war was over.

I had only recently arrived from New Zealand and had little knowledge of the people against whom I was fighting. Having watched the rise of Hitler, I imagined the Germans to be efficient and ruthless. I expected rough treat-ment at their hands. They surprised me. In the Luftwaffe hospital I was visited regularly by the aircrew and after operations ceased they would come and discuss flying matters with me. They were a fine group of fellows, much like the boys one found in any crew in the RAF. They were not particularly inter-ested in Hitler or Goering, but their faith in the German cause was unshakable.

But all the same I was pretty dashed lonely, and the fact that I had lost my crew of three did not help matters.

Later I was sent to a prison camp with prisoners pouring in from Poland. I encountered a different type of German – older; they remembered the humil-iation of the First World War defeat and its aftermath.

During my years as a prisoner, I never did come to understand the Germans.

FRANCE, 1940

Soldiers tended to enter captivity in much larger numbers, and three major campaigns accounted for the bulk of Allied army prisoners. The first was the German Blitzkrieg on France and the Low Countries in May–June 1940, which led to the capture of 34,000 British, 60,000 Polish, 630,000 Belgian and 1,500,000 French soldiers.

Private Alfred Charles Bryant, The Royal East Kent Regiment (The Buffs)
POW from May 1940 to May 1945
In September 1939 I went from 'somewhere in England' up as far as the Albert Canal in Belgium. We withdrew back into France and I went on leave at Christmas 1939 when I got married.

I had been married only 12 days when on 1 January 1940 the order came to embark for France, where I moved from one place to another. I had leave again and went back to France in April 1940.

We were going towards Germany while the others were going back, and we were under attack by the Germans from the air and the ground as we marched along the road.

Private Alf Bryant of The Buffs (to the right of the French officer) watches while George Formby performs for frontline troops in France, spring 1940 (*A C Bryant*)

At Doullens my battalion became part of 'The Sacrifice Army'. Our job was to hold up the German army there while the rest of our troops embarked at Dunkirk for England. Each company had only three Bren guns, three anti-tank rifles and one 2-inch mortar (with no ammo), and with these we were supposed to defend the area around the village. Our defeat was inevitable – we just didn't have the men and the equipment. On the morning of 20 May we were attacked by the crack 6th Panzer Division. We were overrun in about half an hour, but some of us managed to scuttle across the fields to Saint-Pol – only to find that being occupied by the 8th Panzer Division! After hiding up in the woods for the night we set off on foot back the way we had come, but ran into a heavily armed German patrol. There was very little cover – just a few trees – and they picked us off one by one, finally shouting at us to give up or be killed by machine-gun fire. My CO – a captain in his twenties – surrendered. We threw down what arms we had and walked out of the trees with our hands held high. Then we were lined up and searched. As they led us way they kept saying: 'For you the war is over'. They actually said it!

We were taken to some sort of HQ where our CO and another officer were separated from us. With thousands of other prisoners we were herded into cattle-trucks bound for the cage.

Elsie Bryant (*née* Bevis)
Wife of Private Alfred Charles Bryant
We never had a honeymoon. His leave was cut short and he went back to Canterbury barracks. He said he'd see me at the weekend, but didn't come back.

I was poking the fire in my flat when I felt that something was wrong. But my mother and my landlady told me not to be silly. Then I heard that both Alf and his brother Albert were on the missing list. On 8 July he was officially recognized as a POW.

He wrote to me and told me that what kept him going was the knowledge that I would wait for him and that I was setting up a home for us.

NORWAY AND GERMANY, 1941

Royal Air Force and Fleet Air Arm personnel found themselves entering captivity almost from the start of the war – Germany took its first Fleet Air Arm prisoners as early as 14 September 1939 – and continued to be captured in small numbers almost to the end. But large numbers were also bagged as a result of major daylight attacks on enemy ships, harbours and cities in all theatres throughout most of the war. Perhaps the biggest haul of FAA prisoners was the 19 men taken in one operation alone in July 1941.

Lieutenant David Lubbock, Royal Naval Volunteer Reserve, No 828 Squadron, HMS *Victorious*
POW *from July 1941 to April 1945*

I was 28 and newly married when World War Two broke out, and had been carrying out nutrition research at the Rowett Institute in Aberdeen for seven years.

I applied for the Fleet Air Arm. Two training courses of about 40 men each were started at Lee-on-Solent. Halfway through, one was embarked for Canada, but the ship was torpedoed and went down with all hands. The other, after being bombed out of Ford aerodrome, was sent up to Scotland to the half-constructed HMS *Condor* at Arbroath. I was posted to No 828 Squadron of Torpedo Spotter Reconnaissance (TSR) Albacores 'working up' on the Mull of Kintyre.

No 828 Squadron was destined to serve in HMS *Victorious*, an aircraft carrier then in the process of being built. After practising from Machrihanish with dummy torpedoes on a Clyde passenger boat provided for the purpose in the Clyde estuary, the squadron was posted to Hatston aerodrome, Orkney, to carry out anti-submarine patrols for Atlantic convoys coming east round the north of Scotland, until *Victorious* was ready.

At the end of July 1941, under the flag of Admiral Wake-Walker in a cruiser, the carriers HMS *Furious* and HMS *Victorious*, with a destroyer screen, set out from Scapa Flow to raid shipping in Kirkenes harbour and bomb Petsamo, right up in the extreme north of Norway near the Soviet border. Intelligence had informed us that the Germans were amassing shipping at Kirkenes to convoy troops east along the north coast to attack Murmansk from the rear. We dropped our fish [torpedoes] aimed at a ship in the harbour and headed back for the carrier. We were attacked by a Messerschmitt Me110, exchanged fire, possibly downed it in the sea (one was never accounted for) but were ourselves hit. My Telegraphist-Air Gunner (TAG), Jan Beer, was killed and I was temporarily blinded. We did not have enough wing surface left for my pilot, 'Skid', Lieutenant Lionel Bellairs, RNVR, to land on the carrier so we turned east to try and cross the German lines into USSR. We then had a dogfight with an Me109 until it ran out of ammunition, but by then we were so badly holed that 'Skid' had to put her down in the tundra, which he did with consummate skill. We were caught trying to walk through the German lines.

Incidentally, in 1990, almost 50 years later, the aeroplane was dug up and taken by the Norwegians to their war museum in Oslo. By the end of the war the territory in which we came down had fallen into Russian hands and they would not let the Norwegians have it until Gorbachev announced Glasnost.

Sergeant George Frederick Cole, Royal Air Force Volunteer Reserve, No 75 (New Zealand) Squadron, Feltwell
POW from October 1941 to May 1945
I was a wireless operator (W/Op) in a Wellington Mk IVC. Our squadron was among those who dropped the first 4,000lb bombs on Bremen on 10 October 1941. We brought back our blazing Wellington and were all recommended for the Distinguished Flying Medal, which none of us received.

Five nights later – on 15 October 1941 – we were shot down while bombing Cologne. At about 5,000 feet we got caught in a box-barrage with radar-operated searchlights and were coned by 30 searchlights. There was a tremendous explosion. I was hit by flak all down one side and in the head and back. Then fire broke out. Flames spread everywhere.

The pilot ordered us all to bale out. I pulled ripcord as I jumped. The next thing I remember was coming to in the middle of a lawn in Krefeld. An elderly German helped me into a house. I remember hearing an aircraft – ours? – hit the ground and explode. Whether any more of the crew had escaped in time I didn't know. I appeared to be the only survivor.

Then a Luftwaffe officer arrived in a car with three Gestapo. They took my hat [flying helmet] as a souvenir. All the locals stood watching, and they must have though I was French because they kept saying: '*C'est la vie, c'est la guerre*' as the Gestapo drove me off.

NORTH AFRICA AND THE MEDITERRANEAN, 1941–42

The Germans took their second major bag of Allied prisoners after entering the war in the Middle East and North Africa in aid of the Italians late in 1940. The subsequent fall of Greece and Crete to German ground and parachute troops was followed by the failure of repeated British offensives in North Africa. 'Operation Crusader', mounted in December 1941 with the intention of pushing the Afrika Korps back to the Mediterranean Sea, turned into what a German staff officer later described as 'one of the most extraordinary routs of the war', while the siege of Tobruk in July 1942 led to the surrender of 33,000 British, Canadian, Indian and South African officers and men.

Private Kenneth ('Kim') Stalder, No 189 Field Ambulance, Royal Army Medical Corps
POW from May 1941 to April 1945

I was called up in November 1939 and on 12 December joined No 189 Field Ambulance, Royal Army Medical Corps, based at Barnett.... First we served in Norway and then we boarded the RMS *Queen Mary* bound for South Africa. During the voyage I hit an officer and was chained to my bunk down below for a week. (The officer who was giving me so much grief was ex-Indian Army and in his fifties.) Then we went on to Ceylon [Sri Lanka], where I bought some cigars for my 'old man', not knowing then that we wouldn't see each other again for five years.

On a pilgrim ship coming out, cockroaches ate the cigars. Then to India, then up the coast of Africa, through the Red Sea, where again I was in hot water, this time for disobeying orders. I spent 14 days in the scuppers. Then Egypt and Palestine. Then I disobeyed orders again and spent a week breaking stones. New Zealand MPs oversaw us – they were enormous. Then, in November/December 1940, we arrived off Crete.

On Crete we were at first billeted in an olive grove. The CO pissed off to Egypt with all the booze and later became a colonel. But we had the time of our lives. Me and my mate set up the orderly room under a brothel in Heraklion, where we would get army pay sent to us. We lived on bully-beef and hard-tack biscuits and had booze and cigarettes.

In May 1941 the Germans invaded. By then I had dropped out of the RAMC and had tagged on to an army unit who had ammunition.

There were about four or five of us in a cave 15 feet up a hillside being mortar-shelled. The entrance was hit and started to cave in and we were low on ammo. German paratroopers closed in on us and we had to surrender. One of the paratroopers – a private, or *Soldat* – spoke English with a London accent, because he had run a tobacconist's in Tottenham before the war, and he sent me off to get cigarettes. The prisoners were a mixed bag – army, air force, British, French, New Zealanders, etc. They had tried to evacuate the island but were told they could only do so in batches of 50 men; they couldn't round up 50 men, so on Crete they stayed.

The back-up troops guarding us were Austrians, and were different from the frontline troops. One of them noticed my engagement ring and ordered me to hand it over. When I refused he threatened to cut my finger off to get at it, so I gave it to him.

COMITÉ INTERNATIONAL DE LA CROIX-ROUGE
Service   Palais du Conseil Général
Personnel sanitaire   GENÈVE (Suisse)

PS/BO   VO   ——   AIR MAIL

DEMANDEUR — ANFRAGESTELLER — ENQUIRER

Nom - *Name* _____ AM/49353

Prénom - *Vorname - Christian name* _____

Rue - *Strasse - Street* _____ Comité International de la Croix-Rouge

Localité - *Ortschaft - Locality* _____ GENÈVE

Agence centrale des prisonniers de guerre

Département - *Provinz - County* _____

Pays - *Land - Country* _____

Message à transmettre — Mitteilung — Message
(25 mots au maximum, nouvelles de caractère strictement personnel et familial) —
(nicht über 25 Worte, nur persönliche Familiennachrichten) – (not over 25 words,
family news of strictly personal character).

Private Kenneth STALDER, 189th Field Amb.,
R.A.M.C., is a prisoner of war at Stalag
III E, he is well.

Date - *Datum* _____ 22.9.41

PASSED P.16

DESTINATAIRE — EMPFÄNGER — ADDRESSEE

Nom - *Name* **Family STALDER**

Prénom - *Vorname - Christian name* _____

Rue - *Strasse - Street* _____ 190 Munster Road

Localité - *Ortschaft - Locality* _____ FULHAM S.W.6

Province - *Provinz - County* _____ LONDON

Pays - *Land - Country* _____

RÉPONSE AU VERSO   ANTWORT UMSEITIG   REPLY OVERLEAF
Prière d'écrire très lisiblement   Bitte sehr deutlich schreiben   Please write very clearly

Notification by the Red Cross of the capture, during the fall of Crete, of
Private Kenneth ('Kim') Stalder (*Kenneth Stalder*)

Lieutenant A F ('Junior') Powell, 13th Light Anti-Aircraft Regiment
POW from April 1941 to May 1945
El Mechili, Libya, April 1941. One of our guns was situated on a forward slope in full view of the enemy, who periodically machine-gunned it. So the crew took cover on the reverse slope and crept up to our gun to point it at the German machine gun and fire a few rounds now and again.

On the morning of 8 April 1941 an attempt was made to break out. Oddly enough the Division HQ drove west instead of east as I had expected it to do. One battalion of the Indian Brigade escaped to Tobruk, but the Battalion Commander came back to see what had happened to the rest and was captured. While we were driving west a Fieseler Storch – a German light reconnaissance aircraft – came into sight and one of our guns came into action and fired a few rounds. It was out of range – pity, because I think General Rommel was piloting it. The column then turned east and, shortly after, a white flag went up from the Divisional Commander's armoured command vehicle.

The Divisional Commander had surrendered and the battle of Mechili was over. We were not keeping our fifty yards between vehicles at that time and I was in the middle of a whole lot of other trucks. In no time at all there were German soldiers in amongst us calling for everyone to 'Come out' and 'For you the war is over'… We took a few things with us to a collecting point, where the officers were separated from the others, and settled down on the desert floor. There was no search and no taking of name, rank and number. We were tired from all the driving and a little relieved that we were not wounded. That first night I dreamt that we were still in convoy and sat up saying: 'The convoy is moving on'.

Private Stanley John Doughty, 12th Royal Lancers
POW from December 1941 to February 1945
We moved around the desert day by day, backwards, forwards and sideways in pursuit of Jerry, who was shortening his lines, sometimes running fast, at other times standing and fighting. Tobruk was the one outpost and port on the Mediterranean which had recently been captured by us, and from which much of our supplies came. Christmas Day came and went. Not even the bully and biscuits changed one iota, and on 28 December 1941 we were in the vicinity of Agedabia – a scruffy village surrounding a waterhole, south-west of Tobruk. As a village it was two or three mud-brick huts.

We were on our own as usual, but with another of the troop within sighting distance, when on putting our Bren away after a Stuka attack, there was an almighty bang. The interior of the car was full of smoke and both the gunner

Private Stanley John Doughty on the base of 57 Tank
Regiment, RAC, Warminster, February 1941 (*the family
of S J Doughty*)

and myself got out as quickly as we could, as the whole thing was going up in flames. Armour burns fast and furious, fed by petrol, rubber and explosives, and I shall remember always the screams of the driver who was trapped and couldn't get out. On reflection, it would have been hopeless to try to get him out, and I must admit that we didn't, a fact which has burdened my conscience ever since; instead we lay flat on the desert seeking cover behind a miserable little scrub-bush, shaking like a leaf in a state of abject shock.

Almost at once a German *Kübelwagen* came over to investigate, and before I knew what had happened I was sat on top of the car, with Frankie Gowland, the gunner, and taken to an interrogation centre in the back of a converted lorry.

Lieutenant Mick Wagner, 1st Battalion, The Welch Regiment
POW *from January 1942 to September 1943*

For me it really began, I suppose, at a place called Sceleidima, which lies at the edge of the escarpment leading up to the Jebel Akhdar and which is approximately equidistant from Benghazi and Agedabia. I was a platoon commander with B Company of the 1st Battalion, The Welch Regiment – then part of the 4th Indian Division. Our task, at the end of 1941, had been to mop up behind the advancing British armour and then perhaps to be part of the force that would make the 500-mile dash to capture Tripoli. In the process Rommel was to be defeated and, with luck, the Italians persuaded to abandon the war. Oh, vain hope! The reality was a vigorous, audacious, unexpected and highly successful counter-attack by the Afrika Korps [by this time renamed *Deutsche Panzerarmee*]. What had, in initial signals, been referred to somewhat euphemistically as a 'reconnaissance in force' turned out, in fact, to be a crushing advance that was to take Rommel's army back first to the Gazala line and later into Egypt, whence it was not finally to be dislodged until the British victory at El Alamein towards the end of 1942.

As the German attack gained momentum we were ordered forward to hold the pass up on to the escarpment at Sceleidima until our advanced armoured formations had withdrawn through our positions. We were then to follow. In fact, unknown to us at the time, our armour had been diverted further south and the approaching armoured column that we picked out across the desert, and which we could barely distinguish for dust and haze, turned out to be hostile. It was not until the shells burst amongst us that the truth finally dawned.

At the time I was discussing the interesting spectacle before us with our Headquarters Company Commander, Tom Pepper, when he fell badly wounded at my feet. From then on chaos and confusion reigned as all hell let loose. Some troops and transport eventually got away but a lot didn't. My group finally was reduced to a small number, including my company commander 'Wank' Evans and Tom Pepper, whom we half-carried during the next two or three days in our vain attempt to get amongst our own forces – wherever they might be. It was a pretty forlorn hope. Rommel's advance troops were by then far to the east and our small party was critically short of food and water and near to exhaustion. We had travelled by night and hidden by day in whatever sparse cover that part of the Western Desert had to offer. Even that proved insufficient. On about the third morning we ended a cold and wakeful night – much disturbed by the sound of vehicles – to learn the bitter truth: part of a German formation had also decided to laager in our chosen bit of cover, and, for one reason or another, capture was inevitable as darkness gave way to light.

Lance-Corporal Lawrence Bains, Middlesex Yeomanry
POW from June 1942 to August 1944

On 6 June 1942 shelling started early, our guns gradually withdrawing into the box. I moved my trucks, but we were still under fire. Had a scratch lunch in a huge vehicle pit. Shelling became worse, German tanks appearing on far ridge. I drove to Major Daniels, on top of the ridge, for information, but he was too busy, so we retired to the top of the ridge where my party scattered in slit trenches. I saw Colonel Selly's tank hit. Unknown officers told me help was coming in half an hour (1630 hours), but we next heard the Bofors gun crew being ordered to smash their guns. Soon after, German tanks arrived, and rounded us up at 1700 hours.

When 425 Battery surrendered, 107th Royal Horse Artillery box of the 22nd Armoured Brigade surrendered after a fierce fight lasting two days. My crew, together with Lance-Sergeant Onions' and Macdonald's trucks, were in the wagon lines. We were all together in a slit trench with our rifles, waiting for the German infantry, but the only enemy we saw were the tanks surrounding our men. We lay low till the last moment, hoping that nightfall would come and we could make an escape, but were ordered out of our trench by a German with an automatic rifle, so resistance was useless; but we were allowed to snatch a few belongings from our truck before marching off to join the rapidly growing main body of prisoners. I was dressed in summer kit, and in addition to this took with me my pullover, greatcoat, mug, knife, fork and spoon, water bottle, and three tins of fruit and a few packets of biscuits. These were all lying at the back of the truck and were easily accessible, but we were not allowed to climb in and get anything in case we sabotaged anything; nevertheless, I was able to smash our ammeter test-set.

Lieutenant John Pelly, Coldstream Guards
POW from June 1942 to April 1945

20 June 1942. The attack by the combined German–Italian armies on the fortress of Tobruk (Libya) began at about 0700 hrs. The Axis seemed to be concentrating their weight of artillery on one small sector of the perimeter of the defences, held by a battalion of one of the Indian regiments, the 5th Mahratta Light Infantry. Very heavy dive-bombing and shelling was kept up throughout the morning on this particular sector. At about 0930 hours the Coldstream Guards, less No 4 Company, were ordered to drive to a rendezvous with the 'I', or reconnaissance, tanks, and to put in a counter-attack, as some 300 German lorry-borne infantry were reported to be inside the perimeter. This counter-attack was never put through owing to some hitch on the part of the tanks.

No 1 Company (my Company) was then given a temporary position to hold in the area of the Sherwood Foresters. The shelling during the afternoon became heavy, and all round us, whilst the Stukas were never absent for more than 15 minutes throughout the day. German air superiority over Tobruk was absolute, and they dive-bombed and machine-gunned without opposition, not one RAF plane being seen throughout the whole day.

At about 1530 hours my platoon found itself only temporarily dug in and in the 'no-man's-land' of a furious duel between German tanks, which were plainly visible to our front, and our own 25-pounder and 6-pounder anti-tank weapons, to our rear. The machine-gunning and 75mm shelling from the tanks, which were by this time only some 400 yards from us, was very heavy, and it was nearly suicide to put one's head up over one's slit trench and watch out for enemy infantry. The tanks appeared to be in five waves, each wave led and directed by a Light Tank Mark IV. One Mark IV came right up to my Platoon HQ, its wireless being plainly audible, but we lay still and it moved on without seeing us. Two more waves of tanks went past, and by this time we were under shellfire from our own 25- and 6-pounder guns well to the rear. At about 1800 hrs we found the area completely surrounded by enemy tanks, and lorry-borne infantry, and were forced to give ourselves over to the Germans.

I had about ten wounded Guardsmen with me, whom I managed eventually to get out to the Main Dressing Station. About 300 officers and men of various units were collected on the junction of the El Adem–Tobruk–Bardia roads, where we spent an uncomfortable and hungry night.

Corporal Eric Barrington, Royal Air Force Police
POW June 1942 to April 1945
21 June 1942. Arrived back at the refuse creek in Tobruk at about 7 am and had just dismounted from the truck when we heard a few rifle shots and some South Africans shouted: 'The Jerries are coming!' I wondered what our captors would look like, blond German supermen no doubt. In another second another couple of shots passed close by me and I heard Phipps, who was standing just behind, say: 'I've been hit, anybody got a bandage?' and when I turned round again there was an ugly-faced, squint-eyed Jerry in a green peaked cloth cap (which we all envied) and carrying a businesslike machine gun with the business end pointing at us. 'Up, up, up,' he was yelling, 'war fini,' and of course we put up our hands. A young officer followed him, and several more Jerries, but nowhere could I see any of Hitler's blond giants.

THE FAR EAST

The third major theatre of war in which Allied servicemen were captured in droves was Singapore, which the Imperial Japanese Army invaded in December 1941. The fate of its garrison was sealed after the Japanese captured the McRitchie reservoir. When Lieutenant-General Arthur Percival, General Officer Commanding Malaya, formally surrendered on 15 February 1942, some 130,000 British and Empire troops became prisoners overnight, even though they constituted the biggest army in the world and outnumbered their foe by more than four to one. To this staggering figure can be added the 2,000-man garrison of Hong Kong, which surrendered on Christmas Day 1941. Yet more prisoners were captured in the Dutch East Indies and the islands in the western Pacific.

HONG KONG ISLAND

Lieutenant Harry L White (Canadian), Winnipeg Grenadiers
POW from December 1941 to August 1945
Around 2200 hours we were attacked, and while I was controlling the left and centre, the LMG [light machine gun] post on the right gave way and yelled that it was coming back. This meant I could be cut off from the bridge, so I retired the left and brought the centre down last, formed a rearguard and got back to the bridge, and signalled Captain Bardal, the CO's Adjutant, as per

Lieutenant Harry L White, Winnipeg Grenadiers (*Mrs E M White*)

arrangement. He immediately opened up with the two Vickers and three LMGs he had, with a terrific barrage, and I got my men across the bridge. There we stayed until morning, and didn't have much more trouble with the Japs.

Next day was 25 December 1941. Bardal and I were planning a counter-attack next morning when word came that a 'ceasefire' had been ordered at 1100 hours. We held our fire but the Japs kept it up – mortar, artillery, planes, etc. We wondered what was up. At about 1500 or 1600 hours we noticed white flags flying on the hospital buildings and at about 1800 hours word came through on the phone that the general had agreed to 'Unconditional Surrender'!!

At first we were quite stunned by the news – a relief that the fighting was over and we could now rest, but also a let-down feeling, when we realized that we had been beaten. We were ordered to stay at our posts, lay down our arms, and wait for the Japs to come and get us. We flopped where we stood. After a bit, about 15 or so men gathered around me. The spokesman was the senior corporal, Loval, I'd had over on the ridge. He said the men all wanted to say that they were glad they had been with me, that they felt they could trust me, I always told them what was up, what I had to do, and that they had confidence in me; they were prepared to do whatever or go wherever I said, and wanted to know if I thought we could escape. (If I had known what was ahead I would have certainly acted differently. As it was, I was full of the propaganda reports that had been coming through, 'Hold on, reinforcements are coming, the Chinese army is nearly here, etc, etc'.) That's the highest compliment I can ever hope to be paid and I felt very proud. However, I had to advise the men that I thought we should do as ordered, that in our exhausted condition and not knowing the country or the language, I didn't think we'd stand much chance of getting away.

SINGAPORE

Corporal Charles Kinahan, Field Engineer Company, Straits Settlement Volunteer Force
POW from February 1942 to August 1945
We were mobilized a few days before the invasion actually took place and were based in the Volunteer HQ in Beach Road, Singapore (opposite Raffles Hotel). Coincident with their landing in South-East Siam and Kelantan (a North-East Malay state) the Japanese did a night bombing raid on the Singapore Naval Base and on Keppel Harbour, west of Singapore City. So next day off we went to deal with our first lot of unexploded aerial

bombs – not having a clue what a Japanese bomb looked like! The Japanese had been bombing China for several years before they attacked Pearl Harbor, the Philippines and Malaya, yet British Intelligence had no details of the design of their bombs. We had been trained on German bombs with their booby traps. Fortunately for us unexploded Japanese bombs proved simply to be duds. No booby traps were found, though we could not assume this and had to take precautions. I was promoted to the rank of corporal and given control of one of the three small units – the others being in the charge of Ronnie Pullan (an Australian engineer in the Ford Motor plant) and Francis Thomas (deputy head of St Andrews School – an Anglican school run on British lines). My first bomb was in the yard at the back of a Chinese chop house near the civilian jail. To have dug it out would have involved the structure of the house so in the end we decided to leave it. The next was in a pigsty behind a Chinese *atap* [nipa palm; the leaves were used for thatching] house near the Tiong Bahru Housing Estate. Five piglets were running around in the bomb hole! We dug a shaft centred on the hole made by the bomb which we finally uncovered. I held the bomb whilst David Waters (our CO) extracted the fuse with the rest of the team at a safe distance. We then drove back to camp in triumph with me sitting astride the bomb.

Whilst the navy and RAF dealt quickly with unexploded bombs in their areas by putting a charge down the hole and blowing up the bombs where they lay, the army wanted bombs to be recovered intact for examination, which inevitably took a long time. The next bomb for my section was in swampy ground off the Thomson Road on the way to the Naval Base. The nature of the ground made this an extremely difficult task, which was finally abandoned after much waste of time. Our final bomb was in a rubber estate close to Tengah Aerodrome.

The last few days before Singapore surrendered were spent in collecting unexploded artillery shells. By this time the Japanese were closing in on the town. After extracting the fuses we dumped the shells in the harbour.

My little squad included two Czechs and a Dane, all of whom had civilian jobs in Singapore. Just before the surrender I managed to send telegrams to my parents and to Kathleen, my future wife.

The capitulation came as a great shock to us all. We had, I suppose, been victims of our own propaganda – that Singapore was impregnable. Right up to the moment of surrender we had never really believed that the situation could not be retrieved by counter-attack. In hindsight the result was inevitable once we had lost control of both air and sea. Our air force, such as it was, was completely inferior to the Japanese force; their Jap navy Zero fighters very soon shot our boys' Brewster Buffalos out of the sky. The sinking of the battleship HMS *Prince of Wales* and the battle-cruiser HMS *Repulse* by Jap planes on 10 December gave the Japs complete freedom of movement at sea and the ability to make landings on the peninsula behind our lines – a demoralizing experience for our infantry.

Much has been written about the First World War vintage naval artillery guns taken from battleships and installed on Blakang Mati and Pulau Brani Islands off the south shore of Singapore Island. These huge 15-inch and 9-inch guns were intended to defend the island from attack from the sea – which never materialized – and it was on these guns that the myth of impregnability was built. The 15-inch guns could only traverse through 180° and so were useless against attack from the north. The 9-inch guns could traverse through 360° and were therefore used to fire on the Japanese assembling in South Johore crossing to Singapore Island, and subsequent to their landing on the island. My understanding was that they did not do much damage as their shells were of the armour-piercing variety intended to attack warships at sea. Firing north to Johore the shells tended to penetrate deep into the swampy ground before exploding.

After surrender we assembled at the Volunteer HQ, where we stayed for several days without ever seeing a Jap. Perhaps foolhardy, Francis Thomas and I went for a walk around neighbouring streets – again no Japs in sight, but the general population very subdued and unresponsive to us, but not hostile.

Sergeant William McDonald ('Tam') Innes-Ker, Straits Settlement Volunteer Force
POW from February 1942 to August 1945

When the Nips landed on Singapore Island some of us, my company included, were pulled out of the beach and sent up to the suburbs round Tanglin Club, where a final defence line was being formed. Here we dug our foxholes for our machine guns and riflemen. I was by now platoon sergeant, and Phil Holt, a great friend of ours, was Company Commander. Here for days we were constantly dive-bombed, shelled and mortared, the latter being the worst. On one occasion a mortar shell exploded about 30 feet from where I was standing, but luckily the fragments must have gone the other way, for all I got was a great blast round my legs. By this time deserters, stragglers, wounded, etc, were pouring back through our lines, many of them lost and not knowing where to go. We directed some back and some we persuaded to join our line, which by now was the last line of defence round the city of Singapore; behind us was nothing.

Tam and Enid Innes-Ker: the last Sunday of peace before the war, August 1939 (*Enid Innes-Ker*)

One addition to our company was an Australian 25lb field gun, limber and some ammunition, and three of its crew – the other three pushed off looking for the harbour and boats to escape in. We had rearmed many of our riflemen with the Thompson sub-machine gun (the 'Tommy-gun' of the round drum type you must have seen in early gangster films of the Al Capone era), Bren guns and such like, taken off the men pouring through our lines. I, too, had picked up a Tommy-gun. Water became difficult and was at last shut off. We were lucky; just 100 yards away was Tanglin Club and its swimming pool, though its chlorinated water was not too nice at first. Later we were glad of anything.

No natives, Chinese or Malays, were in sight. They had all gone to ground – around us, anyway!

Mrs Enid Innes-Ker (wife of Sergeant William McDonald Innes-Ker)
On board a ship bound from Australia to England 16 February 1942
After dinner that evening we got the news on the ship's radio – Singapore had surrendered the previous day. I had never before seen men crying, and there were several near us in tears ... I think I had shed all my tears when leaving Tam and Singapore. The bad news was not unexpected, but I suppose up to the last minute we had had dim hopes that disaster could be averted by some miracle. Now I had to face the fact that, if Tam had survived the fighting, he would be a POW, probably for years, and I had no illusions that the Japs would treat their POWs well.

Sapper Edgar Whincup, 560th Company, Royal Engineers
POW from February 1942 to August 1945
We arrived at Singapore [at the beginning of February 1942] during an air raid by 29 Jap bombers, and because the island had very few aircraft based there, little or no opposition was encountered. We lost at least one troop ship, which was carrying all the equipment belonging to 560 Company. Consequently, we landed with only our own personal kit plus one rifle and 50 rounds each of ammunition.

We soon formed our first camp in a rubber plantation and almost immediately received our first orders. Viewed in the light of what we underwent later on, they seemed amazingly ridiculous. For instance, we were ordered to wrap empty sandbags around the rubber trees so that the barbed wire wouldn't damage the bark. Our own preservation seemed of secondary importance. We were formed into a Field Park Company and immediately began to collect, from various positions on the island, mines, ammunition, etc, which might prove useful in repelling the enemy. In other words, we, not the authorities, were trying to look after our own welfare.

Saragon Creek seemed to be a natural obstacle to the Japanese advance but it had to be made more of a problem for any army determined to attack us. Eric Wain, myself and one NCO were, therefore, detailed to take some navy depth charges, which we had salvaged from the navy base, prime them and lay them across the creek. It was quite a problem taking out each depth charge in a small native boat, dropping it overboard and then returning for the next one. It was inevitable that we should lose one or two. We completed our mission, all the depth charges were wired up and ready primed and all we had to do was wait, ready to blow up the Japs should they come sailing up the creek. An addition to our defensive preparations was a camouflaged 25lb field gun, whose officer was empowered to give us our orders and maintain discipline. However, waking up in our little tent after a peaceful night's sleep, we discovered that the RAs had pulled out, 25-pounder and all. Now, we were on our own!! – and wondering how long.

We waited all day for any sign of the Japanese or even of our own people. There was no sign of either, so, putting our fate into our own hands, we decided to try and contact our own company. Off we went, leaving everything behind except for our detonator plunge handle which we took with us, thus keeping to army regulations which stated that nothing was ever to be left which could conceivably be of use to an enemy. Bravely we walked for about 30 minutes through the rubber plantation when suddenly we encountered one of our own despatch riders coming towards us to tell us we were to fall back to our own company lines.

We were told that 560 Royal Engineers Company were now acting as infantry, that he (the despatch rider) had no idea where our line was and that we should just keep walking. This we did until eventually [we] found them at the Police Barracks, Mount Pleasant Road. It was at this stage that mortar fire was heard not far away, and soon it became only too apparent that the Japs had found our position, as it became increasingly and frighteningly nearer and nearer. It was then we suffered our first casualties, for Alec Southall, along with Driver Atkins and Sapper Mayling, were all killed by the mortar fire.

It is a matter of history now that all the guns defending Singapore were so positioned that they could only fire out to sea and so the Japs, coming over the Johore Causeway (ie, down from the mainland), cancelled out any fire the military authorities were hoping to bring to bear on them – a defensive disaster in planning!! Continually under fire, we were concerned with self-preservation, as we were painfully short of food and no rations seemed to be forthcoming. We therefore went scrounging around the residential area of the barracks, these upper-class houses belonging to police inspectors, etc. It was amazing what we found in one house – the remains of a meal which the occupants had left after departing in a hurry, and even some knitting on a chair in the lounge as if they had intended returning soon. We found stores of tinned food which we opened, filled any cooking utensils we found, warmed it up and took it back to our positions in the garden of the house. Needless to say, we were under continual mortar fire, which caused considerable apprehension to us and a large amount of damage to the area in which we were positioned. Something had to happen soon – and it did (two weeks after we arrived) for on 15 February, Singapore surrendered.

We wondered how this would affect us, and soon found out we were obliged to march into town where all troops were formed up and next day marched to Changi Barracks – about twenty miles away. Before leaving, we handed in our rifles minus the bolts, which we had thrown away. We were fearful, depressed and bewildered, and the fact that 130,000 of the British army had been captured did nothing to enliven our spirits.

The Dutch East Indies

Aircraftman (Driver) Frank Deakin Jackson, No 62 Squadron, Royal Air Force, Java, Dutch East Indies
POW from March 1942 to August 1945
I received an order on 5 March 1942 to take charge of four lorries and retrace our steps 20 miles to the small town of Garoet [Garut] where approximately 200 airmen were stranded at a school. They were to be brought to Tasikmalaja. There was a suggestion that the RAF were to regroup here before making for a tea plantation somewhere in the mountains. Maybe the intention was to hide up there hoping the war would be of short duration.

We found the small primary school and were not greeted as potential rescuers. Flight Lieutenant Simpson informed me that all British forces were now under Dutch command and the Dutch had surrendered that very day. As leader of this group at Garoet his instructions were that we all laid down our arms. I had disposed of my Tommy-gun in Malaya and my three companion drivers had not a gun between them. No problem, I thought, we will return to Tasikmalaja with empty vehicles. Simpson had other ideas. It was unconditional surrender and this meant no movement of vehicles, loaded or otherwise. I protested that we had left all our kit, little as it was by this time, with the main body of men at Tasikmalaja. 'No problem,' I was told, replacement clothing would be found for us. I did have an ulterior motive for wishing to return. At Tasikmalaja no mention had been made of the finality of surrender. However remote or hopeless, there was always a possibility of escape. Surrender meant any loophole was closed irrevocably.

I suppose there are circumstances where it can be a relief to be a prisoner of war. This was not to be one of them. There was a widely held belief that the Japanese only took prisoners for the purpose of interrogation and then 'disposed' of them. Reports had filtered through that prisoners had been taken at the fall of Hong Kong the previous Christmas and that they were being treated reasonably well, though Japan had not been a signatory to the Geneva Convention. I fervently hoped there was a basis of truth to these reports, unlike the baseless rumours that had had the misfortune to endure these past few months.

Then my mind was troubled by accounts that had been recorded by late escapees from Singapore. These concerned fanatical and crazed Japanese infantry occupying the Alexandra military hospital of that city. All patients of one ward had been systematically bayoneted to death. From there they proceeded to the operating theatre and repeated the ghastly process upon nursing staff and patients as they lay on the operating tables. The other horrendous incident concerned several Australian nurses shipwrecked off Banka Island. Survivors who had reached the shore were lined up at the sea edge and then machine-gunned. These events were among the mass of evidence at the postwar war crimes trial.

Pilot Officer Erroll David Shearn, Royal Air Force Headquarters, Java
POW *from* March 1942 *to* August 1945
Early in March [1942] the Japanese landed in Java, and Batavia [Jakarta] was declared an 'open city'. This meant that all troops had to vacate the precincts. We proceeded to Bandoeng and remained there for a few days. Before very long the Dutch capitulated, but Maltby, the RAF Air Vice-Marshal, and the general commanding such army units as were in Java got permission from the UK to conduct guerrilla warfare. Having had experience of the infantry in World War One, I found myself in charge of some 600 air force other ranks who were to take to the hills and fight the good fight. They had light shoes and about twenty of them would have been able to hit a haystack at 200 yards. I found this out by getting paper targets made, with a pinhole in the middle of the target, and having my 'marksmen' aim their rifles at the targets while I looked through the pinhole from the other side to see

how accurate was their aim. The experiment was not encouraging. I duly reported their state of efficiency to Maltby and was told I was to do the best I could with them. We then went to our battle stations in the hills. I drove with an unpleasant Wing Commander, commissioned from the ranks, who cheered me up with the assurance that 'nothing would happen and it would all fizzle out'. He was right. We had no sooner arrived at our destination in the hills, than we were told that the Japanese had threatened that unless we laid down our arms they would bomb Batavia. In consequence the British forces had also to surrender.

We were dispersed among a number of tobacco factories. [Sir John] Fletcher-Cooke, an RAF officer by name of [John Francis Fitzgerald] Gregg and I did not favour dossing down on the very dusty floor of the particular factory to which we were assigned, and after looking around a bit we found a garage behind the very pleasant house of a Dutch tobacco estate manager and obtained his permission to occupy it. Fletcher-Cooke and Gregg had a plan to get to the south coast of Java and try and get some sailing craft so that they could escape. With much secret reluctance and serious misgivings I accepted their invitation to join them when they pushed off. Before, however, this happened I was called to Maltby's HQ to look after the discipline aspect of the administration of the RAF in Java. The HQ was in a largish house in Tch Kajang. The Japanese had told Maltby that he was to be allotted an area and he was to ensure that the RAF under his command did not stray out of the area allotted. The plan then was that we were to build our own camps and the Air Vice-Marshal would be responsible for administering his area. As I spoke Malay I was sent round with a Wing Commander [Hector] Ross to select various sites for our camps. We visited a number of estates where the managers were most friendly and we consumed a lot of gin. We managed to select quite a number of suitable places for the camps.

Captain Arthur Geoffrey Threadgold, No 242 Battery, 48th Light Anti-Aircraft Regiment, Royal Artillery
POW from March 1942 to August 1945
My troops and the others in No 242 found ourselves defending Kemajoran [Java]. It was here at Kemajoran that I had my 21st birthday. (I was a big boy now!)

Shortly after this 242 moved again, to the military airfield at Tjililitan, where we had our first action against the enemy. Bombers first bombed the field and excited gunners showed me pieces of Japanese aircraft that had dropped out of the sky.

Captain Arthur Geoffrey Threadgold (*Mrs Dorothy Threadgold*)

Gun positions were quickly re-sited and dummies left in their place – a well-proved move, as during an attack by fighters the next day all the dummies were riddled by machine-gun fire – and again we were heavily engaged.

The news from Malaya was grim, and Singapore had fallen. We in the meantime had been reinforced by elements of Singapore regiments now acting in airfield ground defence roles, English Anti-Aircraft Regiments and Aussie Pioneers and machine-gunners – all without their main weapons but a welcome sight as there seemed to be very few Dutch or Indonesian soldiers around.

Batavia at the end of February 1942 was declared an 'open city' and we had to move. No 242 Battery were moved by night via Soekaboemi to Andir airfield near to Bandoeng, where we again were soon in action against the enemy air force. Here we heard that a battery of our 49th LAA Regiment on Sumatra had been surprised at Kalijati by Jap ground forces, which had landed at Erentanwetan on 28 February/1 March 1942, but that some of the men had managed to fight their way out.

We were not long at Andir, as orders came to move out to join 'Blackforce' (Brigadier Blackburn, VC) – but this event was cancelled and subsequent orders came to us to proceed to Tjilatjap, where we were to be evacuated by sea. This did not materialize and the Dutch capitulated on 8 March 1942. We were forced therefore to lay down our arms and to capitulate to the Dutch and Japanese demands.

This was near Gareot, where we lived under, in and on our vehicles, sometimes in tropical rain and alternatively hot sunshine – this state of affairs lasted about a week whilst we dismally awaited captivity. Which came all too soon and we found ourselves being moved to a railhead from whence we were sent by rail and under guard back to Batavia.

In Batavia we were crowded together with other troops into Koan School – a Chinese school in the native quarter – officers and men from a variety of units, even some Texan officers from 131st Field Regiment (Texas) USA. This was our first taste of being guarded in a confined area.

2
TRANSIT AND INTERROGATION

'It was here that I first came into contact with German service soap. The scented stuff almost turned my stomach. It was so sweet and yet somehow quite corruptly evil. I don't know why. Like an old tart trying to disguise her BO with scent. Repulsive. Never forgot how it permeated everything.'

— RAF prisoner at Dulag Luft

From the moment he surrendered until the day he arrived at a permanent prisoner-of-war camp, the new captive was almost as much at risk as he had been during the heat of battle. In the Great War of 1914–18 prisoners had sometimes been left in the front line, with all its attendant hazards, denied food, water and medical treatment, forced to march long distances, abused by enemy civilians and ill-treated during interrogation. As a result, the Geneva Convention of 1926 contained at least four Articles aimed at increasing his chances of survival at this early stage. The Convention also stipulated that a prisoner under interrogation was obliged to give only his name, rank and service number. However, other articles gave captors considerable latitude, allowing them to seek information about prisoners' next of kin and even their addresses back home. This put new POWs in an awkward and potentially dangerous position, as the interrogators used it as a pretext to withhold food, drink, sanitary facilities and comforts such as books and cigarettes, thus squeezing prisoners for further information.

Contrary to the impression created by popular films, however, little or no effort was made by the Axis forces to question the vast majority of British and Commonwealth prisoners. It would have been both impossible and pointless to interrogate the thousands of troops who fell into their hands, whether in France, North Africa or the Far East, as the ordinary soldier was not privy to Allied strategy, while NCOs and junior officers were unlikely to know much about the bigger picture. Even senior army officers generally met with little more than perfunctory questioning.

But all sides infringed the rules during transit, and these infringements ranged from causing prisoners minor discomfort and inconvenience to

42

committing outright atrocities, the former due as much as anything to the logistical problems involved in coping with large numbers of captives, the latter gratuitous and inexcusable.

GERMANY AND OCCUPIED POLAND

The greatest variety in the treatment of prisoners in transit was to be found in the Western European theatre of operations, where British officers, NCOs and other ranks were at first captured in small numbers. They were generally transported by staff car, lorry or train. German trains were much more comfortable than British, their third class being equivalent to our second, and civilians were nearly always ousted from a compartment so that it could be occupied only by prisoner and guards. This was clearly an effort by the Germans to protect prisoners from the public, as stipulated by the Geneva Convention.

Even in May and June 1940, when the Germans captured Allied troops by the thousand, most aircrew, especially officers, were evacuated to Germany using some form of vehicle. Some Allied aircrew prisoners were still being transported in passenger trains as late as 1944, but towards the end of the war aircrew were sometimes handed over to civilians to be beaten up, shot or hanged.

For soldiers, things were different. Almost all of them, including senior officers, were herded into *'Frontstalags'* (from the German *Frontmannschaftsstammlager*, or 'front-line other ranks' camp') and then force-marched through France, Belgium and Holland in blazing sunshine and denied food and water. Many of the wounded and injured were left untreated.

A number of atrocities were also committed, the most notorious on 27 May 1940, when the 3rd SS Infantry Regiment wiped out a company of the Royal Norfolk Regiment left behind in the Dunkirk evacuation. Major Lisle Ryder and his 80 men were cut off in a cowshed in a farm outside the sleepy village of Le Paradis and that afternoon chose to surrender. The SS marched them into a barn where machine guns had been mounted on tripods along the long, low wall opposite, and opened fire as the soldiers marched in. Most were killed instantly. When a signal stopped the firing, the Germans finished off the wounded with bayonets and small arms. Only two men survived, and they suffered serious injuries.

A similar atrocity was perpetrated at Wormhout in northern France, where on 28 May the SS *Leibstandarte* Division murdered all but 15 out of 100 officers and men of the Royal Warwickshire Regiment using machine guns and hand grenades.

While the Germans neglected to question the vast majority of its prisoners, an exception was made for naval and air force personnel, nearly all of whom were interrogated from the spring of 1940 onwards. Aircrew were the only source of information then available to the Germans about day-to-day conditions in Britain, but there was also a more immediate tactical purpose: the need for information that would help the Luftwaffe site its searchlight and flak batteries and thus defend German factories and towns from RAF bombers. As soon as possible after being captured, all air force personnel, and also naval flyers, were interrogated at Dulag Luft (short for *Durchgangslager der Luftwaffe*, or Transit Camp of the Air Force) at Oberursel, near Frankfurt am Main. German interrogation methods became more and more sophisticated as the war progressed, so much so that, after debriefing returned escapees in 1941 and 1942, the Ministry of Information produced a film called *Information, Please* to warn airmen what to expect.

As Pilot Officer Eric Williams – who later achieved fame as one of the three 'Wooden Horse' escapers – hints, the RAF were equipped with escape kits, and of course the Germans were keen to get their hands on these before prisoners could smuggle them into main prison camps, as they contained useful articles such as compasses and maps. However, compasses could be disguised as buttons and studs, and other items could be hidden up the rectum in a small cigar-shaped container and thus occasionally escape detection.

The *Deutsche Kriegsmarine* (German Navy) also had its own interrogation centre, in the naval base at Wilhelmshaven, and until such time as they could be questioned newly captured seamen were segregated from the older prisoners in a small *Dulag* (transit camp) at Sandbostel (and later at Westertimke). Peculiarly, however, the Kriegsmarine often left them there for weeks before calling them for interrogation, and then kept them in solitary confinement for up to a fortnight before questioning them. By this time the information gleaned was pretty near worthless.

Private Alfred Charles Bryant, The Royal East Kent Regiment (The Buffs) POW *from May 1940 to May 1945*

In France we were put on a train with thousands of men. We were conveyed to Germany in cattle-trucks – about 30 men to a truck with nothing to drink. Food was short, and when it was supplied consisted of one mouldy loaf between us. We could not see out of the wagon and had no clue where we were going.

After two days we were released from the wagons and found we were somewhere in Germany. At a small station we were given some coffee (if you could call it that). A lot of chaps did drink it but dropped down like flies and rolled in pain because the coffee burnt their empty stomachs.

We were put back in the wagons – again the destination was unknown. We were given five loaves between thirty men. The bread was green because it was so old. We were shunted backwards and forwards and at last the doors opened and we were told to get out. We were so weak we could hardly walk.

Gunner Cyril George King, 365 Battery, 92nd Field Regiment, Royal Artillery
POW from May 1940 to April 1945
In the daylight we found that we had stopped at a water pump and we were allowed to alight in two and threes in order that we may drink and have a very quick wash. A long line of guards watched us with care.

As we passed through Belgium and Holland the doors remained open, and if we passed through a station at a slow speed we were thrown small items of food which were scrambled for in the depths of the truck – many were the harsh words which were exchanged between French and Englishmen. It was now that my store of biscuits came in extremely useful, and now and then I would distribute a few, trying to put over in French that we were supposed to be allies. Frequent German troop and supply trains passed us and Jack [a sergeant in the Royal Engineers] and I would greet these with shouts of derision. This may appear pitiful, but it gave us some degree of encouragement and bravado. The slowness of the train at times meant that a few enterprising fellows leapt from the trucks and made for nearby houses, but their freedom was short-lived as they were shot down by the machine gun. These attempts meant that our doors remained closed all day long and we spent the rest of our four-day journey in semi-darkness. The half-loaf which we had each been given had gone and spirits were at a low ebb.

After two days of confined travel we arrived at Dortmund in Germany, where we were herded from the train and marched through the semi-deserted streets to an extremely large sports arena, having perhaps the capacity of our Wembley ground. I did not think that it would ever see so many prisoners, just thousands of dismayed men who had not the slightest inkling of what their future would be. Tired, hungry, filthy and completely at the mercy of their German conquerors. Jack and I struggled for a piece of ground on which to sit and we waited whilst interpreters gave their orders through loudspeakers and loaves of bread were distributed – one between five. Approximately two hundred of we British were segregated from the rest and we were moved back through the city towards the railway once again. There were few people in the broad streets and these only watched us pass in a rather uncomprehending manner as if we should not have been there. At that time there was no bomb damage at all and we gazed at the large blocks of flats and private houses, wishing all the time that we were back at home with all our own streets and roads. Back at the railway we boarded trucks once again, but this time our gloomy conveyances made up part of a goods train and we rattled on our way once again. Although we were now all of one nationality the general atmosphere was somewhat peculiar in that we came to divide ourselves into small combines or sometimes there was even a lone wolf. We watched to see that no one else received a larger ration of bread, more room for sleeping or was better off in any way. When I look back this was due to one thing only – the fact that each one of us had only one thing in mind – to reach home safely and in good health. In other words, except for one's immediate 'mate' or 'mates' there was not much consideration for the other men. Jack and I got on famously and there was never an argument between us, in fact all our efforts seemed to be directed towards keeping each other's spirits up.

After two more days' travel we were passing over vast plains with small villages and poor farmsteads. I could not imagine that this was Eastern Germany and so we must be in Poland – heaven help us if we were being shipped to Russia. However, during the last morning we stopped at a small station, were marched for about a mile down a road and there amongst the pine trees was our first prison camp – SCHUBIN.

Miss Margaret ('Peggy') King, sister of Gunner Cyril George King
Because my brother had been trying to make for French ports he was rather late in being captured. (He spoke French fluently.) Of course, this meant advice of his capture was late in coming to the UK. My mother and I were evacuated from our home, at Sanderstead in Surrey, to Northampton to stay with relatives, as the air raids were getting nasty. But my father had to stay in London. It was whilst we were there in Northampton that he received news – by phone, I think – of my brother being a POW in Poland. Such rejoicing! My mother could not get home quickly enough. Leaving Euston for Victoria there was an air raid well on and we were sent down to the Gents' toilet – quite something to a teenager! Eventually home to Surrey. Mother quickly made the bed up for me on the floor. I had been ill.

Main gate of Stalag (later Oflag) XXIB, at Schubin in German-occupied Poland (*IWM HU212022*)

Telegraphist Herbert Edgar Elliott, Royal Naval Volunteer Reserve
POW from August 1940 to May 1945
At 11 am [on 9 September 1940] we started off and travelled across Holland and into Wilhelmshaven ... we were able to see the country and passed through some flooded areas and parts where fighting had taken place. We had more than sufficient food for the trip and we eventually arrived at 11 pm in total darkness. Two were still on stretchers and it was as much as four of us could manage to carry them on our arrival. Our new guards did not realize just how weak we still were.

We had only been in our room five minutes when an air raid started and we were locked in the top storey of a high building. During the five weeks we were here, our aircraft were over every night with the exception of twice. The AA defence was very heavy, and, as we were alongside the dockyard, we were not very happy about things.

One night a small building opposite us was demolished and a bomb splinter came into the room. After this we were always taken to a cellar below the building. Our nerves were in a very bad condition and I was receiving attention for the wound behind my knee. We were allowed half an hour's exercise each day and we were regaining our strength.

The guards were mostly older naval men who treated us very decently and gave us tobacco and, occasionally, a cigar. They did not appear very enthusiastic about the war; the younger men, however, were full of the war and how they would win. Hitler was their God. Many Germans have spoken in glowing terms of him and there is no doubt in my mind that generally he was very popular.

The building we were in looked like an old school and we were once again questioned.

The Germans knew all the answers to the questions put to us and they certainly gleaned no information from me that I was aware of. We were questioned by a man who had lived for years in the Liverpool area and was very bitter against England.

The food was not very good, the bread being nearly black. I was never able to eat my ration. I met other men from the minelayers who had been picked up and found that altogether about 55 had been rescued by the Germans. There were only eight from my ship.

Lieutenant David Lubbock, Royal Naval Volunteer Reserve, No 828 Squadron, HMS *Victorious*
POW from July 1941 to April 1945
3 August 1941. Dulag Luft. It happened that Wing Commander Douglas Bader and I fell into enemy hands on the same day, he at Saint-Omer in

northern France and I in the Arctic Circle. We met up for the first time in Dulag Luft where, since I had a degree in natural sciences and was likely to be the nearest to a medical doctor that he would come across, he asked me to stay with him to help him look after his legs. Actually, the only doctor I came across as a POW was a gynaecologist! With one Flight Lieutenant Peter Gardner I naively started to tunnel from the hut we were in, but were soon discovered and in short order were sent with a draft of about 20 other POWs to a camp just outside Lübeck.

Pilot Officer Idrwerth Patrick ('Paddy') Bentley Denton, Royal Air Force Volunteer Reserve
POW from July 1941 to May 1945

The back flaps of the lorry opened and all we could see were some iron gates, heavily wrought. Through them we went, turned left and clang! clang! into individual cells. There seemed little to be done so I lay down on the rather unsavoury bunk and decided that a snooze would be a good thing.

How long this lasted I can't tell because I was woken by a banging of doors and keys and moved sharply left and then right down a corridor to a largish room with one barred window high up on the top left and a bunk, a chair, whitewashed walls and nothing else. All a bit queer. I decided, when left almost immediately alone, to continue my kip.

Then the most interesting part started, as a very well turned out bloke in the uniform of the International Red Cross came in and started talking in accented but perfectly fluent English. He was very sympathetic. 'Head OK? Not too badly burnt? What bad luck, old chap. I'm here, of course, to help you and your family. Where are you from, so that I can tell them? What squadron, so that I can get a message? By the way, where were you going to, what aircraft?' Smooth as a piece of silk. But a fearful blunder. My mother always smoked Gold Flake and he produced a packet. They were [not the same brand but] a very good resemblance, but somehow the mere gesture and the memory of them triggered something off. So I did the old routine name, rank and number. I thought that he was going to burst into tears.

Didn't I trust him? He was only there to help. 'Come on old chap.' I said I was rather tired and could we talk again later. This pantomime went on for a few days at intervals of hours, sometimes minutes, during any period of 24 hours. He seemed to be getting a bit fractious towards the end and actually confessed that he knew my blasted name, rank and number and don't blame him if my whereabouts didn't reach my nearest and dearest and the squadron.

Dulag Luft, Oberursel, where new air force POWs were interrogated, November 1941 (*author's collection*)

I felt rather sorry for this forlorn figure so pretended to break down on the promise that he would help me. To this, of course, he agreed. I told him that the aircraft was a Hartford, powered by the new Wright Whitworth Cyclone engines and that our destination was Cologne. Quite fascinating to see this basically nice chap solemnly writing all this bull down in his little book with a look of childish satisfaction on his face.

Shortly after this we were again loaded into a truck with Luftwaffe guards and set off. This time, instead of leaving by the wrought-iron gates, we were taken out on the other side of the building where a narrow causeway ran alongside the canal. We turned left over a bridge and then along a road of *pavé*. After a few miles, as the back flap was open, we were most encouraged to see a very pretty girl on a bicycle wearing a pink polka-dot frock. It was quite evident that her legs stretched up to her shoulders. Very good for morale.

The goons behaved impeccably, giving us the odd cigarette and almost creating a feeling of camaraderie.

After some miles we were unloaded and put into a railway carriage. This was the beginning of a journey which eventually took us through the Ruhr to Dulag Luft outside Frankfurt. I was surprised and perhaps rather disappointed to see how little damage we had done at this stage despite fairly strenuous efforts. I recall the Germans pointing out Cologne Cathedral in all its grandeur. There was a great temptation to tell them that in our book this did not constitute an industrial target. I decided not to.

At the odd station where we stopped the populace indicated quite forcibly that we did not rate too highly in their popularity ratings. *Terrorflieger*, *Kindermörder* and other catchphrases came to their lips and our ears. We maintained a dignified silence and merely contracted British phlegm and a look of utter contempt. I don't think that this attitude endeared us to them particularly.

We eventually arrived at Frankfurt and transferred to a coach but with a larger posse of guards. On the way to Oberursel we passed an aerodrome with some 109s at dispersal. I found out afterwards that some of the blokes from Dulag Luft had lobbed out [escaped] and actually had one of these running and ready to move before the Germans shot them up a little. I think the Messerschmitt also suffered as a consequence. Nobody died but the security at the aerodrome was much increased, so the effort was not wasted.

Oberursel is a pretty little village and the interrogation camp did not impose too much on the surrounding area. We went through all the standard bull and then we, as crew, were separated. After a while a charming chap, again in Red Cross uniform, came in to jolly me up and, damn me, offered a

Gold Flake. We had a friendly chat and he departed leaving the cigarettes as, he said, a gesture of goodwill and friendship.

This palaver went on for about eighteen hours and then we were transferred across a narrow lane to the transit camp.

It was here that I first came into contact with German service soap. The scented stuff almost turned my stomach. It was so sweet and yet somehow quite corruptly evil. I don't know why. Like an old tart trying to disguise her BO with scent. Repulsive. Never forgot how it permeated everything.

The transit camp was an almost frightening experience as it was filled with recently shot down Royal Air Force personnel. The cross-questioning that went on put any German interrogation into the pale. Luckily I found one friend there who had been with me in England and Canada so eventually I was accepted as genuine. There was good reason for this, as in the interrogation centre was a well-known RAF man [Flying Officer Benson Railton Freeman] who transferred allegiance. He was found out and not too soon. He brought great shame on our British family and did us and the nation gross disservice.

A couple of days after this we were moved; this time, after a truck ride, to a railway and into wooden-seated carriages. Another long and hot journey which was obviously to the south. Eventually we were delivered to a camp which we found was at Biberach, Bavaria. We were in no way expected by the resident German staff and spent some hours locked up in the barracks. An English private was, for some odd reason, sent to see if we were OK and bring some ersatz coffee. I knew that a friend of mine of prewar days had been grabbed during the Dunkirk episode so managed to ask the soldier if anyone of his name was in the camp. The answer was yes. So, much to my pleasure, some hours later when we were popped into the camp, I was met by one mate and some remembered names.

The first question quite startled me. 'Are we mad?' To this I could honestly answer that the one I knew was no nuttier than when I had known him previously. Then there was 'When were you last in England?' 'What's going on?' 'What happened to you?' 'What happened to your clothes?' All great fun and an enormous relief and relaxation for us all.

This respite didn't last for long, as the goons, having discovered their blunder, loaded us up again onto a train and we then travelled, laboriously, hungry and monotonously from Bavaria to the Baltic. Gross incompetence and most aggravating.

We finally arrived at about 10 pm in a station which was barren of people except some Wehrmacht characters with a singularly unpleasant-looking officer. The station looked as inviting as a small version of Manchester Central on a wet Sunday night. We stumbled out and the officer then indulged himself in a typical fit of German hysteria. '*Mörderschwein, Fliegermörder, Kindermörder*' and so on. It was bad-mannered and quite unnecessary.

We were then marched off from the station, with rather a heavy guard, to what was to be the climax of the evening for the good citizens of Lübeck and their teenagers and children since, on the command of the officer, they started to throw brick ends, stones and epithets at us. They were pretty inaccurate so we only suffered a small sense of resentment at this undignified behaviour.

Sergeant George Frederick Cole, Royal Air Force Volunteer Reserve
POW *from October 1941 to May 1945*

After driving me and the Luftwaffe officer to their HQ near Krefeld the Gestapo interrogated me under a spotlight and eventually I fainted. Apparently I alone had got out of the aircraft and all the rest of the crew had bought it, but the Gestapo didn't believe it. As it happened another did survive, I found out later.

The Luftwaffe officer was a gentleman who spoke perfect English. He tried to persuade them to let me go into hospital and eventually got me into one run by nuns. There they put me on a slab. The officer looked at me, pressed my hand and said: 'You must be very, very brave'. Then my back and neck were probed and the pieces of flak removed – I was given no anaesthetic. Afterwards they took me to a room with a guard outside. Whenever I peed I passed blood. I was suffering from internal bleeding.

They took me to Stalag VIJ – still in Krefeld – and gave me POW number 6438. It was a camp for foreign slave workers. All those in my compound were Russians and no Germans dare enter. The only food we had was water and swedes. Later I was taken to the *Lazarett* – military hospital – where they put a bandage on my shoulder and left me lying on a palliasse. The next morning I was covered in flea bites. Some of the wounded and amputees had flees under their bandages, and they couldn't reach underneath to scratch.

The Red Cross finally whisked me away after an argument with a Frenchman. I asked if I could use his chamber pot, and do you know what he did? He spat at me! Spat at me! So I spat back. The Frenchman brought his officer along and I spat at him as well. He went and fetched the German *Kommandant*. When he heard my story he stood and harangued the Frenchman.

But one Frenchman, an Anglophile called Paul Lombard, actually did try to get me repatriated to Vichy France on the pretext that I had TB. He even doctored the X-rays. Instead, I was sent to a gaol – it was a very old gaol, and heavily guarded and patrolled by dogs. My cell had a wooden bed, a bucket and a tiny window. I was given bread and sausage for breakfast, and then they took me to the train station. There the guard brought me black bread and soup. In the train, the German soldier sitting next to me gave me his white bread, which was a rarity in Germany.

At last I arrived at Dulag Luft. The German officer in charge of interrogating prisoners was a *Hauptmann* von Mueller of the Luftwaffe, who turned the radiators up in the cells to make prisoners talk. After my dose of this heat treatment, Mueller came in and told me to take off my clothes in front of him. I was covered in flea-bites. There were so many you couldn't get a pin between them. I told him about other RAF prisoners who had been left behind at Stalag VIJ, Basil Cotton and 'Bunny' Rigley and others.

I then requested that I be sent straight away to the prisoners' communal compound. Squadron Leader Elliott was the SBO. An Irishman called Paddy Byrne and an RAF sergeant named Joyce were also there at the time, both of whom were suspected of being stool-pigeons. In the compound I met Rupert Davies – later to become famous as TV's Maigret – and was later presented with a bottle of good brandy by Mueller, who also got Basil Cotton, Bunny Rigley, etc, out of Stalag VIJ. They were later repatriated. In the meantime they were purged to Stalag VIIA at Moosburg, but I missed the posting because I was sick with a discharging eardrum, as it had burst in the explosion over Cologne. In the camp hospital I met Henryk Kowalski, a Pole who had been so badly burnt when he was shot down that you could no longer see the features on his face. I was there for a month, and spent the time trying to teach him better English.

After leaving the camp hospital I was sent to Stalag VIIIB, Lamsdorf, and then many of the prisoners – about 120 – were transferred to Stalag Luft III by cattle-truck. One of the prisoners, Anthony Shrimsley, was too slow to march from the train to the new camp and was bayoneted in the leg just before we arrived at the gates.

Squadron Leader George Dudley Craig, Auxiliary Air Force, No 607 Squadron, Hawkinge
POW from 4 November 1941 to 22 April 1945
I was taken to the mess of a Luftwaffe unit, and there given a meal and treated with extreme courtesy. This was about the time when [Rudolf] Hess had flown to Britain in his crazy attempt to stop the war, and as I was leaving I asked the commanding officer, an *Oberst* [colonel], if he had a visitors' book. The *Oberst* deplored the lack of one, whereupon I replied: 'You should get one. Who knows when one of our leaders will be dropping in among you some day soon?'

The *Oberst* laughed like hell and smacked his pipe so hard against his wooden leg (a relic of the First War) that it broke it in two.

Squadron Leader George Dudley Craig in Stalag
Luft I, Barth, 1941 (*Nicholas G D Craig*)

Pilot Officer Eric Ernest Williams, Royal Air Force, No 75 (New Zealand) Squadron
POW from December 1942 to October 1943

On my arrival at Dulag Luft, I was searched by a *Feldwebel* [senior sergeant] who was very thorough, making me strip to the skin and going through every article of clothing with care. He then gave me a Polish tunic and breeches, taking my own, as he said, to be X-rayed. I managed to retain the silk maps and compass from the escape kit. After the search I was locked in a cell three metres by two metres and kept there for nine days. The window was of obscured glass protected by iron bars and throughout the nine days was never open. I protested but with no result. My guard expected me to sweep out my own cell, but I refused. I repeatedly asked to see an officer, but was not allowed to do so for two days. When at length an officer appeared to interrogate me I asked for cigarettes, a book, exercise and a bath, but was refused all these unless I would give my squadron number, bomb load and target. I refused and the officer walked off, saying that he would come back in a day or two to see if I had changed my mind.

I was interrogated by three people in all, each adopting a different approach. They were as follows:

(a) *Bogus Red Cross Representative.* This man had a form which he wanted me to fill in. The form started off perfectly innocently with name, date of birth, mother's and father's names, whether dead or alive, and suchlike personal questions, but gradually led on to the date of joining RAF, where trained, for how long, where stationed, station commander's name, etc. The whole form was rather cunningly done and might easily lead one to say more than one should. When I ran my pencil through the form and handed it back, the 'Red Cross' man lost his temper. I imagine that he had experienced this reception too often for him to see it as a joke. He informed me that unless I filled in the form my people would not know that I was a prisoner.

(b) *Operational Type.* This officer told me he was an operational pilot on rest. He tried to gain my confidence by telling me that he was not an intelligence man and hated doing the job. His attitude was 'knights of the air' and he did not carry paper and pencil, but continually tried to lead the conversation round to my target. He told me that one of my crew had already told him all he wanted to know and when I told him that I did not for one minute believe him he said that I was a stupid man. On his next visit he produced a book containing the names of a lot of stations in England and told me that we were from Newmarket. I told him that if that was what he thought I was quite content.

Pilot Officer (later Flight Lieutenant) Eric Ernest Williams (*Joan Rix*)

POW barracks, Stalag VIIIB (*author's collection*)

(c) *Confidential Type*. This man I consider to be the most dangerous. He would talk for a long time on social matters, on art, national characteristics, and of how Germany did not hate the English, but was surprised and hurt when we declared war.

He, also, did not produce paper and pencil or attempt to interrogate me. His line was that the interrogators and interpreters were university professors who had copious forms and reports which they had to fill in. He said: 'It's all red tape, you know, just a matter of form. Just tell them what they want to know. They will then lock the form away and be happy. Then you can go. There is too much form-filling in Germany, but these chaps have single-track minds and I'm afraid they will not pass you through until all their nice little forms are completely filled.'

During the whole time I was in the cell I had no exercise or fresh air and nothing to read or smoke. My diet consisted of two thin slices of bread, one dry and one thinly smeared with some sort of spread, and ersatz coffee for breakfast; a plate of thin soup for lunch; and the 'breakfast' again for supper. The cell was intolerably hot, the heating being controlled from outside the cell. When I complained the guard turned the heat on still more.

After being released from the cell I was taken across to the transit camp, where I waited for about 12 days before being taken to Schubin in Poland.

Sapper Don Luckett, Royal Engineers
POW from July 1941 to May 1945
Stalag XVIIIA, Wolfsberg, Austria

We were eventually ushered through a gate in the inner compound, and made to form a queue at a table, at which three German soldiers were seated with official-looking paper in front of them, together with bottles of ink, metal and rubber stamps and a box full of identity tags complete with strings. The identity tags were of metal with a serration along its length in the centre. Each man gave his army number, rank and name to one of the Germans, who duly entered it on the official form in front of him. His colleague gave each man an identity tag that was stamped with a four-figured number on both halves of the tag, with the wording 'Stalag XVIIIA' also stamped on it, this number also being duly recorded on the forms. We were told to wear the tag at all times and never be without it. Our existence was now known to the International Red Cross Organization in Geneva, who would in turn inform the War Office in London, and so our relatives eventually would know at least that we were prisoners. Many people at home did, in fact, learn their

Stalag XVIIIA, Wolfsberg, showing rustic German administrative buildings in the background (*author's collection*)

relatives' whereabouts from enemy propaganda radio broadcasts by 'Lord Haw-Haw' at that time, but were discouraged from believing it by the authorities from a security point of view. The enemy was up to all kinds of tricks to glean information, no matter how trivial or from any source available, so caution was the watchword. Having given the necessary information to the three English-speaking German soldiers at the tables, we were led to a huge pile of clothes that were made up of remnants of the various army uniforms of the many countries that Germany had overrun.

NORTH AFRICA AND THE MEDITERRANEAN

Conditions in Greece, Crete, North Africa and Italy were generally worse than those in Western Europe, owing partly to the heat, the inhospitable terrain and the endemic disease, but also to the capriciousness of the Italians. Despite the terms of the Geneva Convention, the German Afrika Korps almost always handed their prisoners over to the Italians. There were several reasons for this, all of them plausible. First and foremost, North Africa was part of the Italian Empire and therefore Italy's theatre of war: Nazi Germany had stepped in mainly to save its ally from further embarrassing defeats. Second, up to 1941 the Italians had taken few Allied prisoners. Indeed, the boot was very much on the other foot. This reduced Italy's bargaining power over conditions for her prisoners in England. Third, it was good propaganda, as the more the prisoners Italy had the more Mussolini could create the illusion that he was winning.

Soldiers captured in Libya were evacuated on foot and by lorry to transit camps – no more than hastily thrown-up collection points – situated along the Mediterranean coast, and from there shipped by sea to only slightly less rudimentary transit camps in Italy. The Italians at the front line tended to treat their prisoners brutally, much to the annoyance of the German troops, who had often to intervene. The Italians also made little distinction at this stage between officers, NCOs and other ranks or between army, navy and air force prisoners, simply herding them all together in columns, lorries, collection points, submarines and ships' holds. It was only in Italy itself that their rank-consciousness came to the fore. However, the Afrika Korps occasionally held on to RAF personnel, flying them to Greece or Italy and then taking them to Germany either by air or, again, by train.

Prisoners taken in Greece and Crete remained the property of the Wehrmacht, and after being held locally in requisitioned buildings were taken to Dulag 185, a converted army barracks in Salonika (Greece) about which no one who was held there has a good word to say.

Again, most prisoners captured in North Africa and the Mediterranean escaped interrogation. However, officers and men of the special forces were questioned, often quite brutally, and army and air force officers captured in North Africa were occasionally taken before Field Marshal Erwin Rommel.

CRETE AND GREECE

Private Kenneth ('Kim') Stalder, Royal Army Medical Corps
POW from May 1941 to April 1945
After being captured on Crete we were put on an Italian cargo ship to Greece and docked at Salonika. I was the last out of the hold, which was full of faeces, so I was told to stay behind and clean it up. When I finally got out on deck an SS officer in a belted raincoat and highly polished boots called me a bastard and punched me in the jaw.

I spent only a few days in Salonika, where there was a former Greek army barracks which was now being used as a Dulag for both army and air force prisoners, whether officers or men. There was no warning-wire in front of the walls or fences to keep prisoners away from the perimeter, and whenever we strayed too close the guards took potshots at us.

Every one of us had the runs, but if we wanted to go to the bog at night we had to sidle along the outside walls of the huts with our hands held up high. Many prisoners were shot at night trying to go to the toilet.

After a few days several thousand of us were moved by train to Germany, ending up at Stalag IIID at Berlin-Steglitz.

NORTH AFRICA

Corporal Eric Barrington, Royal Air Force Police
POW from June 1942 to April 1945
El Gubbi, Libya, 21–23 June 1942. On our march out of town truckloads of German infantry passed quickly by and the men looked at us in wonder and some pity. I don't suppose we looked too pleasant a spectacle. Most of the Germans were stripped to the waist taking full advantage of every breath of wind, but we were still hurried along as fast as we could go. At long last the bulk NAAFI stores at El Gubbi came in sight and then we turned off the road and were shepherded inside a hastily erected single-wire fence to await further

marching orders. That was another scene which will always be engraved on my memory. The store buildings were a mass of twisted ironwork and smouldering remains. Scores of German tanks, trucks, guns and all kinds of vehicles were parked nearby, but most impressive and perhaps most heartbreaking of all was to see a seething crowd of our own chaps, Imperials, South Africans, Indians, Negroes, all kinds and conditions from the world over, officers of all ranks with majors as common as flies in summer, standing or lying about in a dense mass, occupying many acres of ground and many times outnumbering their German captors. For the first time I realized the seriousness of our loss and the immense blow to our national pride and prestige; there must have been over 2,000 men that afternoon in El Gubbi prison cage, and many more were arriving.

Once inside the 'cage', our first prison camp, we were left to our own devices and allowed to wander anywhere within the barbed wire. All we wanted was to rest and to drink, but drink there was none, so using my kitbag for a pillow I lay down on the spot and, covering my face and neck with my tunic, fell into a doze, or more apt a coma, being absolutely exhausted, more so than ever before. Soon, however, the flies and blazing sun made me uncomfortable and I decided to see if it was at all possible to get a drop of water – my throat was swollen and lips very sore. The guards at intervals patrolling the boundary wire were besieged with crowds of men almost praying for a drink, but all the guards could do was shrug their shoulders and say 'Kein Wasser' [no water], showing us that they also were on short rations. For half an hour I wandered round seeking a drop of water and sometimes I saw a crowd of chaps rush to a spot where some fellow more fortunate or more farsighted than the rest of us had a two-gallon petrol tin of water and was generously giving it away. Once or twice some attempt at organization was made and a German water wagon would drive up, only to be surrounded in seconds by a crowd of men acting more like wild beasts than human beings until the Jerries were sick of the disgusting spectacle and refused to bring any more of the most valuable thing in the desert, only to see it fought for and practically half of it spilled and wasted in the process. They actually were very short of water themselves and could not supply more than 2,000 men out of their own rations. The fault lay in the destruction of almost every water point in Tobruk by our own men on the previous day, not thinking then that they were preparing a halter for their own necks. Disappointed and very miserable, I threw myself down between two officers who lay in the shelter afforded from the sun by two tar barrels with a blanket spread over the top and weighted down by flat stones. Three other men from my unit, Dick, Mac and McCleod, were somewhere near in a similar condition and until sundown at half past eight we all lay not caring what happened to us.

We were hustled up the gangplank of the *Rossolino Pilo*, surrounded by guards and naval officers, with no time for a look around. We had not expected berths or hammocks, but the accommodation reserved for us was something of a shock. Down a perpendicular 20-foot iron ladder one by one into a gloomy hold about 12 yards square. There were 200 chaps already in the hold when we arrived, but the ladder did not empty until there were at least 500 men crammed into that small space and it was impossible for most of them even to sit down, and certainly no room to move in any direction. Mac and I were lucky and got jammed against a wall down which we slid until we were sitting with knees hunched up.

Private Stanley John Doughty, 12th Royal Lancers
POW *from December 1941 to February 1945*
The German officer didn't need to ask us anything. We carried our AB64s [army paybooks], which gave details of our army careers, and our cards were well known to them since they had captured so many in France. Before long we were, with others, in the back of a 15cwt truck under guard, off to the town of Misrāta on the Mediterranean coast. There I was singled out from the other prisoners and taken, under escort, to a town jail, a *Beau Geste* sort of place on the waterfront.

This, on top of my recent experience, made me certain I was in deep trouble. Why otherwise was I selected? I feared the worst. Instead I was put in isolation in a cell, and left there on my own overnight. Early the following morning I was joined by another British prisoner and an RAF sergeant, who immediately engaged us both in conversation in good English, asking about how, where, and why, etc. Unfortunately for him, I think I must have been still in shock because I remember wishing him to Jericho, and didn't want to talk to anyone, being full of my own thoughts of my plight. Later that day all three of us were taken out – you can imagine my thoughts at this time – but were separated. The other squaddie and myself joined a huge group of some 50 to 70 British and Commonwealth prisoners in the back of an Italian diesel lorry and trailer, under Italian guards, and the RAF type just disappeared. Subsequently I decided he was a plant, but if so, the whole exercise was poorly done, and no pressure used.

Lieutenant Mick Wagner, 1st Battalion, The Welch Regiment
POW *from January 1942 to September 1943*
For me the next couple of months were the dreariest of my life. But before the real deprivation and depression set in, there was one most interesting episode.

After capture we were taken to a German field headquarters (of the 23rd Panzer Grenadier Regiment, I think) for preliminary interrogation where name, rank and number only was the customary order of the day.

I spoke reasonable German and in the course of things I used this to impress on our captors how imperative it was for Tom Pepper to get medical attention. Some time later, to my astonishment, I was led away and told I was to meet a most important person. This turned out to be Rommel himself. He was clearly too occupied to waste much time with a junior subaltern and his only utterance that I can recall was to repeat in German the hackneyed phrase 'For you the war is over'. As things turned out he was wrong.

We were soon handed over to the tender mercies of the Italians and taken to a transit camp (a concrete-floored warehouse) in Benghazi. A week or so of misery there was followed by a week-long ride crowded into the backs of open lorries as we made the laborious 600-mile journey to Tripoli. Food and water were almost non-existent: the days were burning hot, and the bitterly cold nights were spent crowded into desert forts that had seen the coming and going of soldiery of one sort or another for hundreds – perhaps thousands – of years. These forts, occasionally used, it appeared, by wandering Senussi tribesmen, were uniformly derelict and my principal memories are of hunger, cold, thirst and filth. We became lousy beyond belief and our meagre blood supply was avidly sucked from us by lice whose ancestors had probably feasted on the troops of a more ancient Roman army.

Our immediate destination turned out to be another temporary staging camp, this time just short of Tripoli itself. I now recall its name – Trig Tahuna. It was a green and pleasant place, and though we remained louse-infested and miserable, my salient memory is of three days of glorious food – just bread, dates, lemons and water; not in abundance but a feast in comparison with the last two to three weeks. Sadly it was not to last. In a matter of days we were again herded into lorries and taken to the port of Tripoli for embarkation for Italy. Three Italian cargo ships were loading prisoners for the journey and we were finally battened down in holds in conditions of extreme discomfort and overcrowding. Pray God the sea would remain calm. It did, for mass sea-sickness would have been the last straw! We were allowed on deck in small groups once each day of the voyage and we noticed that the German soldiers manning the relatively primitive anti-aircraft guns were openly contemptuous of their Italian allies who were guarding us. They, the guards, wore their life jackets continuously and were always without boots lest we were bombed or sunk. In this they were wise. Though I was never certain about this, we gathered from what we heard when we reached Naples that ours was the only one of the three ships that set off from Tripoli at that time to reach Italy safely.

THE FAR EAST

Little or no provision was made for newly captured Allied servicemen in the Far East. They might rot for days, weeks, months or even years in the town or on the island where they were captured; they might be continually transferred from one collection point to another and from camp to camp at short notice; they might even end up in Japan itself. Few of the prison camps were specifically transit camps or permanent camps. More often than not, they were both – and labour camps as well. Generally, throughout Siam (Thailand) and the Philippines, a new camp was opened whenever a new job arose, and was then closed down when the job was finished. Prisoners were moved from their place of capture and from one camp to another either on foot or by goods train or by sea. Conditions were almost always appalling, with no food, water, rest or hygiene. You walked – or ran – until you dropped, were crammed into metal train wagons and squeezed into the damp holds of oil tankers. If you died, you died.

Sometimes the treatment of prisoners in transit went beyond mere indifference to their fate. One instance of this was the beheading of 200 wounded Indians and Australians left behind during the retreat from the Muar River, in Malaya, in January 1942.

The Japanese were even less punctilious about interrogation than the Italians. Questioning prisoners was the preserve of the Military Police, who produced a comprehensive manual on interrogation techniques, and later the Kempeitai, often referred to as the Japanese Gestapo, except that they were much worse. However, interrogation seldom served much tactical or strategic purpose. More often than not it was carried out after an unsuccessful escape and was the pretext for brutality, torture and killing. The following note on interrogation methods comes from the Japanese Military Police Training Manual:

The essential points to be secured by the interrogation of POWs are, in general, as follows: Unit and mission, location, administrative organization, new equipment and material, recent orders, whereabouts and names of Senior Officers of related forces, bivouac area of preceding night, combat and marching conditions, special training, food situation, morale and cooperative spirit, terrain features of operational areas.

The questions to be asked will be properly chosen according to the situation at the time. However, the name of the Unit and its location must be asked even when time is short. In interrogating a POW, successful results can be achieved by using previously acquired information as the basis for supplementary questions.

HONG KONG ISLAND

Lieutenant-Colonel Peter Allison Belton, Headquarters, Eastern Command, Hong Kong
POW from December 1941 to August 1945
Friday, 26 December – Tuesday, 30 December 1941. This – the day after capture up to the end of the month – was taken up in trying to restore the water supply, the handing over of arms and ammunition, the re-clothing of troops, sending out of burial parties, commencement of casualty lists and collection of personal effects. Some 150 envelopes containing personal effects of those killed were forwarded by a visiting party of Staff Officers, including Colonel Andrews Levinge, Colonel Simpson, Major Robertson, and were received at HQ but were subsequently lost ...

At 9 am on the morning of 30 December we marched off to North Point Camp under escort of a company of Japanese and Major Agashire. Brigadier Wallis was offered a seat with Major Agashire in his car but refused on the grounds that he preferred to march with his men. The Japanese major also marched with his men. It was an interesting march – we saw damage done by our shells at Tytans Gap, many bodies and few Chinese. The streets were cleared for us, 'the Stanley Army'.

Lieutenant Harry L White (Canadian), Winnipeg Grenadiers
POW from December 1941 to August 1945
On 26 December 1941 we moved up to Wan Chei Cap where the Japs were waiting for us, and a tough-looking crowd they were – ragged uniforms covered with netting for camouflage, black running shoes with separated big toe, short, squat, dirty apes. They looked at us. They yelled, grunted, or hit us with their rifle butts to get us to do what they wanted. Captain Walker and I and 50 men were segregated and loaded with equipment of all kinds (our own) – telephones, rifles, bayonets, etc – and we had to climb Mount Cameron. We rested while the Japs had their lunch where they had been attacking us on 22 December. I pointed out to Walker two shell craters, also about 20 manholes about two feet across and three feet deep. The Jap captain in charge of us seemed rather decent when he realized that Walker and I were officers. He had his men bring something for us to sit on, and a tin of milk each. We had nothing to eat with us. The men also got some milk (it had been our own once).

We were kept on the go up and down the hills from one place to another until 0400 next morning, until we could hardly drag one foot after another, and still with nothing to eat. I got one look at the Jap captain's map while trying to help him find his way, and it was a far better map than any of ours – all our positions were marked, roads, paths, etc. We finally ended up at Hong Kong University, where we spent the night and all next day. Then we were moved on to Victoria Barracks, where we found the rest of the Battalion.

The next day the Japs held their Victory Parade, and I shall never forget an incident that happened. We were up overlooking one of the main streets about 20 feet up and there was a stone wall around the place about four feet high. Everyone was at the wall looking at the parade which had just started to go by. A large air force came over, and the big shots were coming by at the head of mounted artillery. I was in the room we were using for the officers just near, when our mess sergeant came up to me, white as a sheet, and said: 'Mr White, what shall I do with these?' He had two live grenades in his hands! Imagine my consternation and excitement. There were gendarmes and sentries all around. If they should see the grenades, God help all of us! I took the grenades and went into the 'can' and stood on the toilet and put them in the water bowl above. I was sure trembling, I can tell you.

Next day they started to move us across to the mainland. So far we had been living off the odd tin of stuff some of us had picked up here and there. What a dismal, down-hearted group we all must have looked – British troops, Canadians, Hong Kong Volunteers and some Indians, all carrying what bits of clothing, etc, we had been able to pick up, which in most cases was very little.

We were taken across by barges to Kowloon then lined up, and the long trek to Shamshuipo began. What a come-down for the proud British troops, five abreast, straggling for over a mile, led by the General and his staff, interspersed by the odd Chinese coolie. Some had taken a chance to give help carrying their kits. They never pass up a chance to earn something. The streets were lined with Chinese; some who seemed sorry for us, some who obviously felt the opposite, a few of the despised little yellow men [acting] as sentries along the column. Japanese flags were flying from the buildings.

We arrived at Shamshuipo prison camp on 28 December at about 1700 hours. The place already seemed jammed, as the barracks, which usually held 2,000 troops, was now to hold 8,000. We finally got some organization. Had over 50 men in a hut that normally held 30. We officers ended up in a room with six, where there was normally one, and so to sleep on the concrete floor.

Commander R S Young, Royal Navy
POW from December 1941 to August 1945
Our small naval party were moved to a much-shelled old British camp at North Point in Hong Kong Island. This had been a small military outpost

Allied prisoners of war marching to Shamshuipo camp after the fall of Hong Kong (*author's collection*)

crammed with our soldiery, mostly Canadian. It was in a dreadful state, having been much shelled and used as mule lines. Everywhere was covered in dung and debris in the bombed building with no sanitation at all for several hundred troops. A hasty latrine was dug literally overhanging the water of the harbour. It seemed an easy escape route if one could attract the attention of a Chinese sampan or boat. All one had to do was to show the Chinese sufficient money and drop down into the mud of the harbour and then the boat. An attempt was later successfully made this way by an English ex-Hong Kong businessman, Lieutenant-Colonel Lindsay Tasman Ride [commander of the Hong Kong Field Ambulance], who had lots of money and could speak sufficient Chinese. Personally I had nothing except a dollar or two in my pocket and no Chinese language at all. Also where was one to make for? It was true that there were rumours of a Chinese Chiang Kai-shek army coming to the relief of Hong Kong. But this was very unreliable. In fact the army did not exist at all. The Japanese at that stage conducted no roll-call, and one could have walked out at night, but to where and how?

SINGAPORE

Sergeant William McDonald ('Tam') Innes-Ker, Straits Settlement Volunteer Force
POW from February 1942 to August 1945
After the surrender of Singapore we had to stand fast for three days while the Nips reorganized themselves, and during that period we prepared ourselves as well as we could for marching off to a POW camp, which we were told would be at the east end of the island, in the Changi Military Barracks area. All the bungalows round our area had already been pretty well looted before we got into position; the particular one we used as Company Headquarters had all the furniture ripped, beds defiled, books thrown all around, and all the lavatories choked with excrement. It looked as though a gang of mad vandals had roared through. This was common throughout the suburbs; done by Malays, we thought. They had turned over to the Japanese en masse, unlike the Chinese.

In due course we piled our arms and, carrying what we could, set off on the 12-mile march to Changi. Here eventually some 20,000 British and Australian troops were penned in an area designed for 1,000. All the Indian troops, some 10,000, were kept separate from us whites and went into different camps, where [we heard] many of them turned their coats and joined the Japanese cause.

Aerial view of Changi Prison, Singapore, used as a POW camp by the Japanese
(*author's collection*)

Lieutenant-Colonel Sir Philip Toosey, c 1942 (*reproduced by permission of the Toosey family*)

The courtyard at Changi Prison (*author's collection*)

Lieutenant-Colonel Philip Toosey, 135th Field Regiment, Royal Artillery
Prisoner from February 1942 to August 1945
POW Camp 330, Changi Barracks, Singapore
We had our own rather mixed battalions. My particular bunch consisted of my own regiment – the 135 Field Regiment, part of the 2nd Battalion of the Gordon Highlanders, and part of the 2nd Battalion of the Argyll and Sutherland Highlanders – and my team in the early days was myself, Captain H S Wood from the RASC, Captain Northcote, my Adjutant, and Major Peacock, one of my Battery Commanders. We had our own medical staffs and sick parades and rudimentary hospitals, our own Adjutants, and Orderly Rooms, Quartermasters and Cookhouses, working party arrangements and so on. We ran the camp with our own army methods and discipline and there was another thing which made our experience different from that of most other prisoners of war. Our groups, varying from a few hundred to a few thousand, became quite nomadic. They moved about, in small parties up to quite big groups, with sometimes quite a semblance of freedom, along undeveloped waterways and new jungle roads over some hundreds of miles. The Japanese obviously relied on the colour of our skin to give us away if we tried to escape; they also knew the Siamese were more than ready to sell us for a fair sum of money.

Corporal Charles Kinahan, Straits Settlement Volunteer Force
POW from February 1942 to August 1945
After two or three days we received orders to proceed on foot to Changi Military Cantonment at the south-eastern corner of Singapore island – about 12 miles away. The civilians were put in Changi Civilian Prison. This meant carrying such personal belongings which we possessed – not much more, in my case, than what we stood up in at the moment of surrender. All our personal belongings had been looted from the house in which we had left them on mobilization. I was able to supplement these from the stores at Volunteer HQ. Items which proved valuable – mosquito net, trousers and long-sleeved shirt – were acquired at this time and possibly account for the fact that I never had malaria during the whole period of my imprisonment whilst many died of the debilitating effects of persistent malaria combined with undernourishment, beriberi, etc.

Although ordered to march to Changi (which most did), my unit risked Japanese wrath and took a lorry with such kit as we had. We scarcely saw a Japanese en route and those we did simply waved us on. We were thus saved an exhausting march under tropical conditions.

Company Sergeant-Major P Hall Romney, Malaysian and Singapore Volunteer Forces Machine-Gun Company
POW from February 1942 to August 1945

On the morning of 31 March 1942 we learned that all British and Australian troops, numbering nearly 50,000, were to move to Changi, about 15 miles away on the north-east part of the island, and that we were to march there, carrying our kit, in the heat of the day.

We began marching at two o'clock in the afternoon, through streets lined by unsmiling Asiatics, with a few armed Japanese posted at intervals. I wondered what thoughts lay behind the unsmiling faces. Most were Chinese, and those who still retained affiliations with China had no reason to love the Japanese for what they had done in their homeland. But the uppermost thought in the minds of most Malayans, Chinese, Malays, Indians, Eurasians, was probably one of apprehension now that British 'paternalism' had given away to Japanese domination.

Other troops were making their way to Changi from a number of directions, as civilian internees were moving similarly to Katong.

SIAM (THAILAND)

Sapper Edgar Whincup, 560th Company, Royal Engineers
POW from February 1942 to August 1945
From POW Camp 330, Changi (Singapore), to POW Camp 241, Ban Pong (Thailand)

Things soon changed when, one day in November 1942, the Japs told us that we were to be moved. They persuaded us that our destination would be a camp which would provide us with all the amenities and comforts we had gone without at Changi – almost a holiday camp in fact.

Disillusion was not very far away. We were transported back to Singapore station, where a train was awaiting us, comprising steel vans with sliding doors on each side. Twenty-five men were allocated to each truck. You can imagine how inconveniently uncomfortable we were, travelling under such conditions in the intense heat. We tried to give ourselves some relief from the energy-sapping heat by taking it in turns to sit by the doors, our legs dangling over the side. Whenever we stopped at a station, the Japs allowed two men out to make some tea by taking hot water from the engine.

It was the fact that we sat by the door with our legs dangling that led to an incident which came back to memory time and time again after it happened.

The Red Cross had provided us with one pair of boots and a trilby hat. Halfway through the journey it was my turn to sit by the door, and soon after I had taken my place, the train slowed down to negotiate some points. It was travelling slowly enough for a hand suddenly to grab my hat, when my head was turned away, and the recipient to disappear into the fields at the side of the track. I had been day-dreaming at the time – and so lost my headgear!

The three-day journey was almost impossible to bear, because of our cramped spaces and the intense heat beating down on the steel exterior but, eventually, we arrived at Ban Pong – a small uninteresting country town which housed a transit camp (soldiers came from Singapore and stayed just a few days before moving on).

THE DUTCH EAST INDIES

Pilot Officer Erroll David Shearn, Royal Air Force Headquarters, Java
POW *from March 1942 to August 1945*
From Tch Kajang to Batavia (Jakarta), Java
Before we got cracking with the building of our camps the scheme was changed and the order was that we were all to march to Batavia, some two or three hundred miles or so. I was filled with dismay, as I reckoned that unless I was lucky enough to be at or near the head of the column I would probably die, with hundreds of others, from dysentery. Maltby, however, managed to get the orders changed by the Japanese and they decreed we should have to move by train from a railway junction called Tasik Melayu. The main body moved off to this place but I remained with some two or three hundred others as a rearguard. We were to tidy up the estates where the men had been accommodated. Again, because I could speak Malay, I was chosen to go round the estates and ask the respective managers if they were satisfied with the way their estates had been left. The general attitude was 'Why worry? I have many coolies and they can do any further tidying up that is required. Have another gin'.

The day came when we were to join up with the main body, which was waiting in Tasik Melayu to entrain for Batavia. Our column was on the road a little way from the HQ at Tch Kajang waiting for a pass which would allow us to go through the Japanese lines. Time passed and the pass did not arrive. The officer in charge of the column told me to go back to HQ and telephone for it.

Now the extraordinary thing was that I had dreamed, not once but two or three times, that I was entirely alone and hordes of Japanese were coming towards me. This exact condition of affairs seemed possible in actual life.

Leaving the column on the road and going back alone to the deserted HQ, I was in fact going towards the main Japanese forces coming up the road towards Tch Kajang. I got into the sidecar attached to the motorcycle ridden by an orderly, and off we went to HQ. As I left this orderly and entered the deserted HQ I turned and said to him: 'Stay exactly where you are and don't move an inch no matter what occurs'. To my relief, after I had telephoned to the main body in Tasik Melayu, I found the orderly waiting for me on his motorbike. The pass, I had been told, was on its way. It had arrived by the time we got back to the column.

We went off by road to Tasik Melayu and I went into a house there with the rest of the HQ staff. The men of the main body marched past us en route to the station to entrain for Batavia. As the Australians came along they were singing 'Waltzing Matilda'. In the dark the tramp of feet and the sound of the song were very impressive. When I hear that song I frequently think back to that evening in Tasik Melayu.

For some reason best known to themselves, the rearguard with which I had come from Tch Kajang was not entrained but was marched off to an aerodrome a few miles from Tasik Melayu. The HQ, including myself, remained in a house in the town. We were given passes allowing us to go into the town between 11 am and 12 noon, and anywhere outside the town between 4 pm and 5 pm. Among the others in HQ I found an Air Commodore [Benjamin James] Silly (his actual name). We discovered that we both had been members of the UPS (University-Public Schools) Brigade in World War One. After a while all officers above the rank of Wing Commander were sent away. I believe their destination was Taiwan [Formosa].

We remained in the house in Tasik Melayu for some weeks. We had ASC supplies and food was quite reasonable. On, I think, 18 May we were ordered to occupy a hangar in an aerodrome close to the town. There we stayed for a while and eventually marched from the aerodrome to Tasik Melayu railway station to entrain for Sourabaya [Soerabaja], which is at the north-eastern tip of Java. The march, some six miles or so, in the blazing sun, carrying about a hundredweight of luggage – ie, all my possessions I thought of use, and which I could manage to carry – was an ordeal. I arrived soaking wet with sweat as if I had jumped into a pool of water. The train journey took two days or so and we travelled *fourth* class. I hung my shirt out of the window to dry.

3
IMPRISONMENT

'The prison looked most depressingly grim, but the sight of the Japanese prison commandant, perched on a wooden box, was most unnerving. Hatred and contempt distorted his features ... No one would ever be able to reason with this maniac. Was this exhibition to be a foretaste of things to come?'

— Far Eastern Prisoner of War

Permanent accommodation for prisoners of war could range from converted fortresses to hutted and fenced camps. But whatever form the living quarters took, they must, according to the Geneva Convention, be hygienic, free of damp, and adequately heated and lighted. The dormitories had to be the same size, and have the same minimum cubic air space, as those provided for the detaining power's own depot troops, and have comparable fittings, bedding and conditions. Whether housed in a fortress or a hutted camp, prisoners of different services, races and nationalities were to be segregated.

Arriving at a permanent camp could either be a shock or a relief to a new prisoner – depending, first, upon how he had been treated up until then, and, second, on his first impression of his new quarters. As will be seen, Allied combatants captured in the Western theatre in the middle period of the war, particularly air force, generally went to 'better homes' than those captured in North Africa in 1940–41; and all were accommodated in less appalling conditions than those captured in the Far Eastern theatre.

GERMANY AND OCCUPIED POLAND

In the 'Greater Reich' – Germany, annexed Austria and occupied Poland – almost all prisoner-of-war camps were run by the German army. The army tended to requisition old buildings – castles, fortresses, citadels, reform schools, disused barracks, even farms and country houses – and surround them with barbed wire and sentry towers equipped with searchlights and fixed machine guns and typically manned by two guards armed with sub-machine guns and rifles. In such camps were housed thousands of Poles captured in 1939, a sprinkling of French soldiers captured in skirmishes on the Franco-German border, and officers, NCOs and other ranks of the French Air Force and the Royal Air Force and Fleet Air Arm captured during the 'Phoney War' of late 1939 and spring 1940. There were also some British troops captured in Norway. Officers were held in an *Offizierslager* (Oflag for short) and NCOs and other ranks in a *Mannschaftsstammlager* (Stalag). For administrative purposes the German High Command, or *Oberkommando der Wehrmacht*, divided the Greater Reich into military districts (*Wehrkreise*). POW camps were numbered according to the district in which they were located and suffixed with 'A', 'B', etc, according to when they were opened. Thus Oflag IXA (at Spangenberg) was the first officers' camp opened in Wehrkreis IX, and Stalag VIIIB (at Lamsdorf) was the second other ranks' camp to be opened in Wehrkreis VIII. A camp might also have a secondary Lager or a series of branch camps. In this case the main camp would be known as a *Hauptlager* and the suffix followed by an 'H' (as in Oflag IXA/H). A secondary camp was called a *Zweitlager* and its full name ended with a 'Z' (as in Oflag IXA/Z at Rotenburg). Just to confuse the issue, a branch camp (of which there could be several) was known as a *Zweiglager*.

It was not until the summer of 1940, with the Blitzkrieg in the west, that the German POW authorities began to reopen camps that had been used in the First World War. At this stage the Luftwaffe started to assume more control over aircrew prisoners and finished constructing the first purpose-built POW camp of the war, Stalag Luft I. The Kriegsmarine did not open its first purpose-built camp for naval prisoners until 1941.

As the war progressed and the population of these camps swelled, the Germans continued to open more and bigger camps. However, with the exception of labour camps, few were purpose-built, and even during the middle and later periods of the war the German army persisted with conversion jobs. Needless to say, these camps were often badly equipped and unsanitary. At various times the army tried to concentrate as many prisoners as possible in as few camps as possible. The Luftwaffe also aspired to one camp for the RAF and USAAF, but it, too, had to admit defeat and return some prisoners to the uncertain mercies of the army camps. Consequently, prisoners were repeatedly moved from camp to camp – some long-term POWs as many as nine times.

Oflag IXA/H, at Schloss Spangenberg, Germany, was one of the first POW camps occupied by British prisoners in 1939 (*IWM HU20593*)

GERMANY

Flying Officer Michael Heriot Roth, Royal Air Force
POW from May 1940 to May 1945
Oflag IXA/H, Spangenberg
The charabanc from Dulag Luft dropped us in Spangenberg village. After several check counts, a green-coated Wehrmacht NCO agreed we were all present and signed the Luftwaffe's receipt. We were sorry to see the Luftwaffe go: they at least behaved like human beings – liberal in outlook and light-hearted in their relations with us. The Wehrmacht soldiers were by contrast a miserable, mentally constipated bunch: they were still fighting the war of 1914–18. Garrison troops, underpaid, ill-fed, they had little to be cheerful about. Older men, with meagre pensions ahead and no chance of promotion, they loathed looking after young and spirited RAF officers. As we trudged from the village towards the castle road, they kept shouting for us to hurry.

After 40 minutes' more slogging, sweating, cursing and stumbling, we reached the top. It started to drizzle. Enshrouded by cloud, the castle loomed bleak, gloomy: a far cry from the romantic picture we had glimpsed on a faded prewar tourist poster in the village below. As our names were called, we crossed the drawbridge and entered the castle through its wicket gate.

Pilot Officer Idrwerth Patrick ('Paddy') Bentley Denton, Royal Air Force Volunteer Reserve
POW from July 1941 to May 1945
Oflag XC, Lübeck
We walked on, for about three miles, to a typical barracks camp which is common to all nations worldwide.

We were taken into a bare building and to the great hilarity of the goons had to strip naked and parade. I had a silver watch which was a 21st birthday present from an uncle. It was chased and rather good. That went. I also had a birthstone signet ring from a great grandparent. That went. All this while standing naked and cold tended to make one feel irritable, if not actively hostile, but there was not much one could do.

Eventually, the Germans having had their fun, we clambered back into our bits and pieces and entered the compound of Oflag XC. Quite one of the nastiest camps, not from an environmental point of view, as the barracks were new, but because of the commandant and hence his staff. It would not be an exaggeration, I think, to describe them as antipathetic to the Allied cause. Not that we had many allies then.

Flight Lieutenant Harry Crease, Royal Canadian Air Force
POW *from October 1941 to May 1945*
Stalag Luft I, Barth-Vogelsang

Our march took us down a gravelled road that looked like any other road in farming country. On one side was a patch of woodland and on the other, a freshly ploughed field. When we came to a small lane that intersected our road, the patch of woods ended. A few yards further on was a fenced field containing several nondescript wooden buildings. It could have been a run-down farm but for the tall gun towers that stood at each corner.

'Welcome to Stalag Luft One,' *Hauptmann* Pieber said. 'For you the war is over.'

During my stay at Dulag Luft I had been so grateful for being alive that I hadn't given much thought to what it really meant to be a prisoner. As long as I had been on the move, or about to be on the move, my captivity hadn't felt permanent.

During the train ride from Dulag to Barth, movement had ceased. The horror of having to sit in the same place for two days and nights, without the liberty to even stand up and stretch, had killed my light-hearted approach to this novel prisoner-of-war experience. This was a grim game and the Germans played it ruthlessly.

The wash of cold fresh air that had bathed me as I had stepped out of the evil-smelling coach had been as refreshing as a shower bath and I had felt a sudden elation of freedom. Now, as I entered what Pieber had called 'our new home', I felt trapped. The fences appeared stronger than the ones we had left at Dulag Luft. The guard towers looked uglier and more heavily armed. In the distance, beyond the camp's barbed-wire fence, I could see the barns and outbuildings of a farm. The joy of freedom within sight but out of reach.

I lined up for my issue of two army blankets and a set of eating utensils. As I turned away from the counter with my bowl and mug in one hand and my blankets over my arm I heard Pieber's voice.

'Do not break them,' he said. 'They will not be replaced.'

I felt insulted. I had been proud to fly with eagles and now my captors were trying to take away my dignity.

The feeling of being caged got worse when the men waiting for us inside the camp crowded around us. I heard a voice in the crush say: 'You're the first people from outside we've seen in over a year.'

Squadron Leader David Malcolm Strong, Royal Air Force
POW from September 1941 to April 1945
Oflag VIB, Warburg

Most of the men in the camp were British army officers taken in the Greek and Cretan campaigns, but there were also a number of RAF prisoners, and we formed a battalion at Oflag VIB where we met up with all the army POWs taken at Saint-Valéry and Dunkirk. The journey there from Lübeck was in French horse-trucks, over 60 POWs to each truck. The journey took the best part of two days.

Oflag VIB was a lively camp because the army officers who formed the majority had learnt in their 18 months of captivity how to make themselves comfortable, and, more importantly, how to handle the Germans. We were divided into five battalions of which four were army and the remaining one was RAF/Fleet Air Arm. As far as I can recall we were 12 to a room in double bunks, and occupied five huts at the northern end of the camp. The German army were our gaolers and told us that all British officers were being held in one camp so that we could be easily repatriated at the end of the war, which they maintained would soon happen as the German army was about to take the surrender of the Russian army and there would be no point in the British holding out any longer.

Lieutenant-Commander William Lawton Stephens, Royal Naval Volunteer Reserve
POW from March 1942 to October 1942
Marlag und Milag Nord, Sandbostel

Many of our men, who had spent the entire journey in their cattle-trucks, were in very poor shape and were suffering from cramp. Forty men in one of those trucks is no picnic. However, despite all that their spirit was perfectly amazing and they amused themselves making wisecracks at our guards – it was a good job they didn't understand them. After a long wait some trucks arrived and we were piled in and driven off to our camp under a strong escort. It was quite a short trip, about five or six miles.

There was a great opening of gates and array of sentries when we arrived and then more gates and sentries, and finally we were inside. It was about lunchtime and not knowing the Hun, I fully expected to be given something to eat before anything else happened to us. I was quite wrong, because although we were taken into the camp dining room we were certainly not given anything to eat; instead, they commenced to search us one by one. The most revolting man was in charge of the proceedings; he was a Commander

Allied air force prisoners lining up for roll-call, Stalag Luft I, Barth, winter 1941–42. Lieutenant-Commander James Buckley, DSC, RN, the first leader of the famous 'X Organization', on right talking to German officer (*Victoria Buckley*)

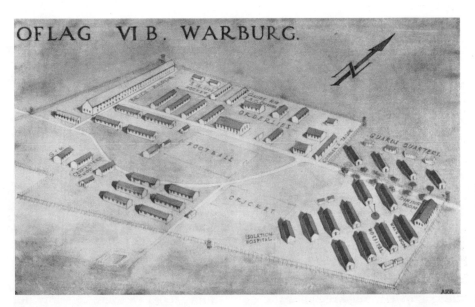

Birds'-eye view of Oflag VIB, Warburg, drawn by officer for inclusion in the camp magazine *The Quill* (*author's collection*)

in the German navy, and though I have forgotten his name, I certainly haven't forgotten his face – if we ever meet again. He shouted loudly at us, gave us hell generally and then took everything we might have left on us in the way of letters, photographs or money, away from us. I will say this, however, he did give us receipts for everything. Eventually, the search over, we were led along to our hut, which stood in a small wired-off compound quite by itself, looking rather like an isolation ward, which indeed it was.

I think I must just say a few words here about the layout of the average prison camp. First of all the most desolate possible places are nearly always chosen. Places where the country round about is fairly flat and where there are no trees nearby to give you cover if you escape. Most camps are 'wired camps', that is to say one is surrounded by barbed wire usually doubled and about fifteen feet high; inside the wire there is a deep trench and inside that again a single tripwire. If one ventures beyond this tripwire the sentries are liable to shoot; these are usually of two kinds, the mobile ones who simply walk up and down a beat on the outside of the wire and the immobile ones who are housed in wooden towers two to three hundred yards apart and who have searchlights and a machine gun at their disposal. It behoves one to be very wary of the latter; they often have a very light trigger finger.

The camps vary enormously in size, but generally the wooden huts in which the prisoners live are laid out in rows and when space allows, there is a clear place set aside for recreation and games.

Such was our first camp, which was called Milag Nord and was really a camp for British Merchant Navy officers and seamen.

Private Kenneth ('Kim') Stalder, Royal Army Medical Corps
POW from May 1941 to April 1945
Stalag IIID, Berlin-Steglitz
When we got there we were offered big pots of boiling spuds – and afterwards had the shits!

Then one day an orderly came in and said I was to move to Stalag Luft III. He didn't know why and neither did I. But the camp turned out to be Stalag IIIE at Kirchhain.

Flying Officer Harry Roland Train, Royal Australian Air Force
POW from July 1942 to May 1945
Stalag Luft III, Sagan (Żagań)
Marched from Sagan railway station to Stalag Luft III, which is near goods yards. Thoroughly tired, hungry and dirty. Searched etc in Reception Block, which is

in a separate compound to the camp proper, and then removed to the prisoner's compound. Met Tim Mayo [from my squadron] at the gate. Needless to say he was very surprised but I suspect pleased to see me. We had a long yarn and I had a meal in their room. Poor old Tim got it at Saint-Nazaire – his first trip.

The facilities here are much more primitive than Dulag. The camp consists of eight living blocks and canteen and kitchen in another block. The lavatory and washrooms are outside and not water-flushed. Being now early summer, they are not too wholesome. There is a small kitchen range at the end of each living block which is used by the (approx.) 80 officers and 10 orderlies living in the hut. Communal meals are not served but cooked. Reich food rations are brought from the kitchen at 1200 hours and hot water is available at some other periods during the day.

Oberst Freiherr Friedrich-Wilhelm von Lindeiner-Wildau, German Air Force Kommandant, Stalag Luft III, Sagan, from May 1942 to March 1944
The biggest problem during the initial layout and construction of the camp was the procurement of personnel and material. This problem increased until the end of the war and, with the expansion of the camp, could never be solved satisfactorily. If we succeeded in getting people and material, they were withdrawn sooner or later by higher authority for projects deemed more important. It wasn't until March 1942 that the first RAF officers and sergeants could be transferred from the Luftwaffe POW camp at Barth in Pomerania to Sagan.

When I took command in May 1942, Stalag Luft III consisted, aside from the 'troop compound' for the German administration and guard personnel, of an East Compound with 401 officers and a Centre Compound with 873 NCOs and sergeants, all members of the RAF. Their number increased in the next three months, due to new arrivals from Dulag Luft, the air force POW camp at Barth, and from army POW camps at Spangenberg, Bad Sulza, Kirchhain, Warburg and Lamsdorf. The humane housing of all these people proved rather impossible.

Stalag Luft III lay south of the town and occupied an area of about 59 acres, with a circumference of about 6.25 kilometres. Each compound was strictly separated from the other, and could only be entered with a special pass. All the compounds were surrounded by two parallel-running fences, three metres high, about two metres apart, and tightly strung with barbed wire. The space between the fences was filled up with coiled and tangled barbed wire, about one metre high. This was called the 'Lowengang' ('Lion's Walk'). In the actual compounds, and about ten metres from the inside barbed-wire fence, were affixed small stakes with wire, circling the compound. This marked the so-called 'warning line'. The crossing of this line was expressly forbidden; it was comparable to the first 'Halt' shout of the guard, who was authorized to shoot after giving two more warnings. This practice was protested at first by the POWs, but because of the state of affairs at that time, their protests were ignored. Outside of the prison camp, watchtowers were located every 75 metres. They were manned night and day by guards who had been issued with binoculars. Also positioned on each of these towers were one machine gun and a searchlight to sweep the fence and interior of the compound at night. The towers were connected to the watch room by telephone.

Sapper Don Luckett, Royal Engineers
POW from July 1941 to May 1945
Stalag XVIIIA, Wolfsberg, Austria
We trudged away from the railway siding in a long column, and out onto the main road that was bounded by a hedge on either side. A few houses could be seen a little way off with the usual signs of habitation around them. Well stocked allotments could be seen behind the hedge on one side, one of which had a good crop of runner beans growing on stakes, which drew forth a comment from someone in the ranks that 'at least they are civilized enough to grow beans' – everything looked so fresh and green.

Quite soon a large barbed-wire fence came into view that marked the perimeter of the camp. Sentry towers were much in evidence spaced out along the fence, furnished with searchlights and po-faced guards who were looking down at us. We turned into the massive double gates that marked the main entrance, and halted near a long low tent, where straw could be seen on the ground outside. At some distance away, another high fence was visible with many of our own men watching our arrival through the wire, who gave us a wave in greeting. We had arrived at the outer compound of Stalag XVIIIA at Wolfsberg, in the county of Karnten, in Southern Austria.

A strangely clad character, dressed in the oddments of various foreign uniforms, told us to make ourselves comfortable in the tent. He went on to say that his role in the camp was that of an interpreter, and tomorrow we would all be given a hot shower and have our clothes disinfected, and that shortly a meal would be given to us. He himself had been in the place for a few weeks, and said that providing you didn't upset the guards, they in turn would not upset you, and having been documented on the morrow, we would be quartered in the huts in the main compound.

Pilot Officer Paddy Denton, Royal Air Force Volunteer Reserve
POW from July 1941 to May 1945
East Compound, Stalag Luft III, Sagan
One day in 1944 an influx of recent boys came in, one of whom was allocated to a nearby block, the Officer Commanding of which was a rather tedious plump Wing Commander. He proceeded to interrogate the newcomer and asked him what he did before the war.

'I was a professional dancer, sir,' was the reply.

'Ah, a bloody gigolo I suppose?'

'Yes, sir. I suppose you could say that.'

'When you are talking to me put on your battledress jacket instead of standing in your shirtsleeves.'

'Very well, sir.'

The battledress jacket displayed a DFC and bar. Collapse of the Wing Commander who couldn't have run a piss-up in a brewery even if he had been given the key.

POLAND

Gunner Cyril George King, 92nd Field Regiment, Royal Artillery (Territorial Army)
POW from June 1940 to April 1945
Stalag XXIB, Schubin
The main building was of stone, half of which housed approximately 50 Polish army officers. The remainder was filled with tiers of wooden beds – just three shelves without divisions, sprinkled with dirty straw. In the compound itself were recently constructed low wooden huts, which could contain a double shelving of beds. The main atmosphere of this camp was of despair. There was no British leader and the men lay around in the sunshine all day gazing at the sky or watching the road for some sign of civilian life.

Private Alfred Charles Bryant, Royal East Kent Regiment (The Buffs)
POW from July 1940 to May 1945
Stalag XXA, Thorn (Toruń); Stalag XXB, Marienburg (Malbork)
When we did get to the POW camp we found it was a place called Thorn in Poland. A short distance away along the road was a fort that was used by the German troops to guard the POWs. The camp was made up of tents in a big field and we could see sailors working inside some of them. The camp was called Stalag XXA.

We were put into tents and had all our hair cut off. Our photographs were taken and we were each given a number. My number was 10871. We stayed for about ten days while we regained our strength. While we were there the Germans put up an effigy of Mr Chamberlain, who had been Prime Minister when war was declared, and when the guards passed the main gate they would turn their heads away from the effigy, but when a guard cycled by he would hit it with his hand.

The next five years of my life were a constant struggle against fatigue, starvation, heavy labour and a general desire to lie down and die; at least that way I would get it all over with. From my capture in 1940 and up to the latter part of 1944 I spent most of my time working on various farms near whichever prison camp we happened to be stationed in at the time. The best five years of my life were wasted.

Some time later the camp was divided and I was sent to Stalag XXB in East Prussia, to a large camp at Marienburg. The camp was on top of a hill with the river Nogat below. There were thousands of Poles, Czechs, French, etc, there. We were put into huts with about 60 bunks. They were in tiers of three, the bottom ones being about six inches off the ground. It was almost Christmas then – my first one in a POW camp. It was very cold and we had hardly any clothes to wear. A lot of the prisoners had frostbitten toes and fingers, and we were made to attend roll-calls in the snow twice a day. The unfortunate prisoners who slept on the bottom bunks did not get any sleep as the rats could be heard running about. Some men were bitten by the rats. We stayed at Stalag XXB for about two years, from 1940 to 1942.

The guards at the camp were hardly the cream of the German army. Because the Reich needed men for the dreaded Russian Front, the high command tried to contain its prisoners with the minimum of guards, usually reservists or veterans of the Great War.

Telegraphist Herbert Edgar Elliott, Royal Naval Volunteer Reserve
POW from August 1940 to May 1945
Stalag XXA, Thorn (Toruń)
Thirty-five of us were roused from the transit camp in Wilhelmshaven early on 19 October 1940 and marched in darkness to the railway station where we were placed in a cattle-truck and locked in with armed guards. Rations for 36 hours were given to us but we spent nearly 72 hours travelling without any further rations. The truck we were in was filthy and had about an inch of dirt on the floor. There were no seats and we had to sit and lie in this filth.

22 October 1940 found us at Thorn arriving 2 am. We had not washed for three days. We had a wait of eight hours at Posen in a siding and Polish people found out we were there and pushed food and cigarettes through to us.

Thorn lay on the Vistula River and in the next few weeks I crossed this river several times. One bridge had been badly damaged by the Poles, but the Germans had built a good temporary bridge over it.

Our home now was Fort 17, an old Polish fort which overlooked the station. The town was well built and large. Names of streets had been altered to 'Adolf Hitler Strasse', 'Hermann Goering Strasse', etc. The roads were mostly cobblestones and not good to walk on. Outside of the town, people were living in ramshackle huts and nondescript dwellings. Roads were just cart tracks and hopeless.

The Fort itself was grim and damp, and vermin were everywhere. Between 40 and 50 of us were placed in a long narrow room with a school desk as the only piece of furniture. Here we had our meals and slept. We lay on the floor in our clothes and had one blanket of a 'very sorry nature' each. The rations were far from adequate. I was very pleased when I was told I was being moved with 500 others.

We moved off in the morning of 20 November 1940 and once again travelled in cattle-trucks, arriving Bromberg [Bydgoszcz] about 7 pm the same day. We had to march through this old city, which was similar to Thorn. Some German children spat at us but the Poles here were sympathetic, as we always found them. Polish women and children helped us a great deal in those days. They would throw small parcels of food to us as we walked through the streets. I have seen women knocked down by German soldiers and men chained together. Yet these same German soldiers showed us many kindnesses.

We reached our new camp at 9 pm and much to our surprise found new wooden huts, two tier beds, springs, sheets, etc, hot showers and a nice stove in each room. Sixteen men in my room, which after the Fort was like heaven.

ITALY

In Italy, as in Germany, all POW camps were under regular army control, although they also came under the jurisdiction of *Carabinieri* (military police). The country had been divided into six military districts (*posta militare*, or PM) and at one time contained as many as 72 prisoner-of-war camps, although there might have been more, as the Red Cross did not know the location of every camp. Most of the camps were converted barracks, castles and monasteries. Little attempt was made to segregate officers from NCOs and other ranks, although some camps had separate compounds and another, Campo PG (Prigionero di Guerra) 12, was created especially for senior officers. Although often architecturally attractive and surrounded by breathtaking countryside, Italian camps were often sub-standard – even more so than the worst German camps – and the commandants and guards were generally much more capricious than their Axis counterparts in the Greater Reich.

Private Stanley John Doughty, 12th Royal Lancers
POW from December 1941 to February 1945
Campo PG 52, Chiavari
Eventually, in the autumn, we were taken by train up the length of Italy to a hutted camp just outside Genoa, at a place called Chiavari. I remembered that the name reminded me of the sub-title of *Punch* – 'The London Charivari' – but what its meaning was I knew not. The camp itself was superb after Capua. It was numbered 'PG 52', was entirely of new wooden, two-storeyed huts, containing wooden slatted beds, one above the other, and had a brick-built washing trough with cold running water from a series of stand-pipes. Lavatories were of the usual Italian type, a deep trench in the ground over which one squatted and tried to avoid falling in. The camp was situated in a fold in the hills with a steep ascent on one side and encompassed by a river on the other three sides which took a 'U' bend around the site.

After a welcoming speech by the Camp commandant in good English, telling us that if we were good boys it would be a home from home, we really thought we had arrived.

Lieutenant Dan Billany, 4th Battalion, East Yorkshire Regiment
Captured North Africa, June 1942, killed some time after October 1943
Campo PG 66, Capua
When we went in through the big gate of the camp, into the ring of barbed wire, we wondered for how long. How long before the gates opened on us again. We seemed simply to be marching out of the world, marching into storage till the war was over. We guessed at six months before we went back along the road to the station. It was June when we came in; the hot trees along the road were heavy with leaves. It would be winter before we re-passed them, going the other way.

So we marched, out of step, out of the world.

We were inside the main fence, but outside the officers' compound. There

Lieutenant Dan Billany (*Jodi Fitzsimons*)

was the grating sound of the wooden gate as it closed and sealed us in. At the sound one quailed very slightly, deep down. And we went on grinning our easy, tolerant contempt for the Italians – the specified British attitude, more or less laid down officially.

Lance-Corporal Lawrence Bains, Middlesex Yeomanry
POW from June 1942 to August 1944
Campo PG 66, Capua
It would be difficult to analyse our feelings as we entered this camp [5 August 1942], they being a mixture of relief, curiosity and trepidation. It seemed a vast place, with many wire compounds, some with tents and others with huts, both wooden and stone, ours being one of the tented ones near the main road. The POWs in our party sat down on the grass and awaited the preliminary search; this was fairly thorough, although I had nothing to lose: knives, forks and Italian mess tins seemed to be the chief attraction. This over, we were allowed to sit about in groups, draw water and hand in any money for safe keeping or exchange, but money had become quite valueless.

So we hung about for several hours until the senior Regimental Sergeant Major organized us into groups of 90, subdivided into three, with a sergeant in charge of each; this done, each group was allocated five tents. These were constructed from Italian groundsheets and were about ten feet high at the centre and sufficiently roomy to give good sleeping room for their 18 occupants.

Most of the fellows were feeling very hungry, and I gave away two of my biscuits but ate little myself; we had almost given up hope for any food that day, when in the early evening we were assembled in groups and given a very thin macaroni and vegetable stew, about a pint. Our mess tins having been confiscated made it difficult, but I was fortunate in retaining my enamel mug and a spoon so was able to draw my ration, and quite enjoyed it, as it was our first warm meal for five days.

Later that evening I saw a queue forming outside a stone hut and promptly joined it, being rewarded with a thin, short and rather worn blanket, and so with this and my old cavalry greatcoat around me, I settled down for the night on the dusty ground of our tent.

Lieutenant John Pelly, Coldstream Guards
POW from June 1942 to April 1945
Campo PG 21, Chieti
This camp is new, and has only been going three weeks. It consists of six large bungalows with two wings each, one bungalow (wired off) being used by the Italian guards, another for the hospital and the Commandant's Offices, etc,

while the remaining four are for Officer POWs. There is a central road running through the camp, there are three bungalows on either side, while the cookhouse is at the end of the road. Surrounding the whole camp is a 20-ft wall, with sentry posts, searchlights etc, at regular intervals along the top, and with *Carabinieri* patrolling continuously inside the walls. Outside the walls is a mass of wire, and there are supposed to be more sentries. So it looks a tough proposition for an illegal exit. Chieti village is right up above the camp on a high hill, and looks very attractive, while to the south and east are some high mountains usually shrouded in cloud. The whole place looks far more attractive than the transit camp at Bari, although there is still no room for recreation.

Lieutenant William Bompas, Royal Artillery (Field)
POW *from December 1942 to April 1945*
Campo PG 21, Chieti
As I walked in the gates and saw the camp for the first time my feelings were, firstly, of pleasure at the size of the camp, the air of cleanliness, and the permanence of the buildings, which were large brick bungalows; and, secondly, of amazement, because everyone was walking round on a cold January morning in shorts or blankets, the latter worn like a cloak, and in some cases like a skirt as well. After the usual search, I learnt the reason when I joined the inmates. They had all been taken at Tobruk, in desert kit, and had no other clothes sent or given to them. I, in battledress trousers, shirt, pullover and vest, felt extremely overdressed.

There were four bungalows, each U-shaped, and each side of the U having six rooms, bathrooms, etc. Each room had 15 double – or two-decker – beds, so that there were 180 or so in each half-bungalow. Lieutenant Horace Wright [also of the Royal Artillery] went straight off to hospital for two months, and I had the job of settling down with 30 strangers of a different army, whose talk was of Cairo, Alex, Mena House, Mersa, the Harbour barrage, and bottles of whisky. They were all extremely interested in new equipment, prices of drinks in England, and when the war would end; my handicap was my temporary deafness, which did not clear up for a month, so that I said 'What?' to practically everything.

Lieutenant Mick Wagner, 1st Battalion, The Welch Regiment
POW *from January 1942 to September 1943*
Campo PG 35, Padula
After about six weeks a fairly large group of us was on the move again. This

time by train, I think, but it could have been a lorry, up into the uninviting and arid hills and mountains of central southern Italy. We were heading, we soon learned from our guards, for a newly opened camp in a disused monastery in a village called Padula, which I subsequently learned is in the Vallo di Diano close to the eastern border of Campania where it abuts the Basilicata region. It felt like a new adventure. What would it be like? Would it be reasonably warm and would the food be better? It could hardly be worse than we had been getting at Capua; and would there be the Red Cross food parcels we had heard vaguely about?

Perhaps most important of all just then, would there soon be letters from home? It seemed ages since we had filled in the various Red Cross forms and we still didn't know whether our relatives knew we were still alive; and nagging away, because it would be our duty to try, would there be opportunities for escape, and if so what sort of terrain would we have to cope with at the outset? On the last score we were soon disillusioned. At that time of year that part of Italy looked harsh and inhospitable; it was rock-strewn and there was little cover – or so it seemed from that train. Anyway, we certainly didn't feel like trying to escape just then; first we would need to learn a bit of Italian, accumulate food supplies and obtain maps, clothing and the other requisites of an escape attempt. But all that was for the future; first there was Campo PG No 35 at Padula to contend with.

Then at last we were there, marching through gates that we were not to see again for 18 months when we were hurriedly moved north to Bologna. By then British and American troops would have conquered Sicily and Mussolini would have been deposed. My first impression of Padula was of relief. At least it wasn't rows of dreary Nissen-type huts; and furthermore we new arrivals got an enthusiastic and hospitable welcome from those already there.

Aesthetically, Padula didn't let any of us down. It was, and still is, magnificent. Perhaps the finest cloisters in the world? The longest? More noteworthy than those at St Peter's itself? All or some of that may be true. It certainly seemed impressive at the time, though we were never, in our captive days, to see more than the main cloistered area. Beautiful it remained even after adaptation as a prison camp for some 500 British officers. Inevitably, from the Italian point of view, we must have seemed a pretty unruly lot, and no doubt we did not really do our bit as conservationists of this superb bit of medieval religious architecture while we were at Padula. In fact, later on, in our search for fuel for fires, we ransacked the roof voids for anything combustible and on occasions removed timbers that were part of the roof structure. Luckily, nothing ever fell down.

THE FAR EAST

The camps in which Far Eastern POWs were held were makeshift from the start. For the first three or four months after the fall of Hong Kong, Malaya and Singapore there was little or no Japanese POW administration and prisoners were accommodated near their place of surrender, usually in former British military barracks, such as those in Shamshuipo and Batavia. Changi, on Singapore Island, also boasted a convenient civil gaol, which had been designed along the same lines as the notorious American penitentiary, Sing-Sing, as well as an army barracks built by the British.

By March 1942 the Japanese *Rikugunsho* (Ministry of War) had set up a separate office for POW affairs. This office divided the occupied territories into three administrative districts, each run by its own section. District One comprised Japan, China, Korea, Manchuria, Formosa and the Philippines, along with the territories known as the Nan 'yo-cho (the Southern Region), such as Hong Kong and Saigon. The second district included the Celebes, Borneo, the Moluccas, Timor, the Lesser Sundas, New Guinea, Rabaul, the Bismarck Archipelago, and Guam and Wake Islands. Although District Two was under the jurisdiction of the Imperial Japanese Army, there was some overlap, as certain parts were controlled by the Tokei-tai (Naval Secret Police). All other territories held by the Japanese, such as Malaya, Burma and Siam (Thailand), came under District Three.

The largest POW camps were located in Districts One and Three, particularly the Philippines, Singapore, China and Japan itself. However, throughout the war the Japanese opened as many as 176 camps in their home islands and another 500 in the Occupied Territories, an area stretching across five time zones and some 4,000 miles from opposite points of the compass. Allied prisoners were therefore accommodated in camps scattered as far apart as Manchuria, south-east Asia and the south-west Pacific. Many of these consisted of no more than a few bamboo and atap huts often built by coolies or even by the prisoners themselves.

Officers of field rank were normally separated from the men under their command, but not so junior officers, who often shared the same standard of accommodation as their troops. Almost all of the camps in which they were held were indescribably wretched. Even the most unsanitary Stalag in Poland was a holiday camp compared to the disease- and vermin-ridden bamboo-and-wire cages holding the British, Dutch, Australian, New Zealand and American troops captured in Burma, Singapore and the Pacific islands. Death was their constant companion.

HONG KONG

Lieutenant-Colonel Peter Allison Belton, HQ Eastern Command
POW from December 1941 to August 1945
Camp 203, North Point, Hong Kong Island
Our arrival at North Point Refugee Camp was one of my worst experiences. We were lined up in the road outside and I was told to allot accommodation – eight huts at 250 men in each. The huts were little more than 30 yards long, some were damaged by shellfire and were indescribably filthy. The whole camp was just a muck-heap, and like all muck-heaps, covered with millions of flies. We made representations to the Nipponese on the inadequacy of this accommodation and were given the rest of the camp, as it was no longer required. This was helpful and reduced numbers in huts to Officers 50, British Troops 150–170, Indians 190. We also asked for brooms, soap, etc, and what rations would be forthcoming. The former were supplied immediately and the latter were already in the camp – some pig carcasses, some green vegetables and bags of rice – our first taste of POW rations.

In this situation Brigadier Wallis was magnificent and showed great resource and set an example to other senior officers to make the best of a bad job. The whole area had to be cleaned up before we could settle down and the time was now mid-afternoon – fires were started for rubbish – squads made up for clearing drains and latrines, a party detailed for the cooking shed, etc, etc, and by 7 pm in the evening we ate our first meal of pork, rice and vegetables (greens) all cooked together in a *congee* or porridge, amidst the smoke of our rubbish fires, which was slightly less nauseating but certainly more healthy than the stench that had overhung the place on our arrival. Our other difficulties in the camp were, no water supply except from a brackish well, no lighting, no proper cooking pots except kongs raised on bricks, no drugs or chemical cleansers.

Commander R S Young, Royal Navy
POW from December 1941 to August 1945
Camp 204, Shamshuipo Barracks, Kowloon, Hong Kong
Shortly most officers and men were moved across the harbour to our old army barracks on the mainland at Shamshuipo in Kowloon. We had to march, of course, to the ferry and get to the other side, carrying what gear we had. The Japanese made this into a sort of Japanese Victory March, and encouraged the Chinese onlookers to jeer at us, not very successfully. In fact on the way we passed many Chinese who had been tied up to lamp-posts and beaten for some unknown offence, and were left starving to death.

Shamshuipo Barracks in Kowloon had been much shelled and bombed early on. It had also been looted of all contents, but though mostly a ruin and barely habitable was luxury compared to North Point. Here the army took charge, and some sort of discipline was enforced. The main thing was to distribute the rice ration, which only came in by lorry very occasionally, as fairly as possible. Starvation looked highly probable.

SINGAPORE

Sapper Edgar Whincup, 560th Company, Royal Engineers
POW from February 1942 to August 1945
Camp 330, Changi Barracks
Changi Barracks was a peacetime British army camp and, very soon after our arrival, it was obvious that the Japanese had no idea what to do with us and [we] were left to our own devices, to fend for ourselves in a comparatively normal atmosphere. We underwent kit inspections, and frequent roll-calls were carried out, both meant as attempts to lift our morale. Some troops were sent to the docks every day to clear up the damage caused by the bombing and fighting. These working parties came back at night with quantities of essentials they had been able to scrounge – almost anything you could think of they 'acquired' – without the Japs realizing what was taking place. This went on for some time until it became obvious that the Japs' suspicions were being aroused at the extent of the pilfering. Extra care now had to be taken to allay their fears that we were putting something over on them.

During this interim period, quiet and full of foreboding for us, we took over the Sikh Temple in 'India Lines' and made it into a C of E Church which we named St George's. With very primitive tools, Ken Wilson and I made the altar rails for the church.

SIAM (THAILAND)

Corporal Charles Kinahan, Straits Settlement Volunteer Force
POW from February 1942 to August 1945
Camp 241, Ban Pong
I was sent on the first group of 2,000 prisoners. Although at the time we had little knowledge of what was in store for us, in retrospect I was indeed fortunate to be sent on this party to an area where we got lots of nourishing food.

In other war zones officers and other ranks were put in separate camps, but in our case, except for the last few months, they were not separated. It helped the morale of other ranks to have their officers with them.

Ban Pong lies in a flat plain with rice fields in all directions. Much other food was produced in the area – fruit, egg, peanuts, etc. We were in this area for about three months. Adequate food restored my health. The main horror of the camp was the annual flood following monsoon rain and the snow melt many miles north in the Himalayas. The cookhouse area was on higher ground but in the prison huts we were wading around in filthy water up to our knees – the latrines having overflowed!

The prisoners were housed in long huts built of bamboo and roofed with atap palm fronds. There was a passage down the middle and platforms on either side made of split bamboo on bamboo framework. Each man had a space 7 ft long by 2 ft 6 inches wide on these platforms. The split bamboo became inhabited by lice and bedbugs – caused by the lack of personal hygiene amongst some of our fellow prisoners.

The camp guards consisted of Japanese officers and NCOs (mostly elderly). The other ranks were Koreans who were not fond of the Japanese. They were mostly pretty slack in the performance of their duties.

THE DUTCH EAST INDIES

Captain Arthur Geoffrey Threadgold, 48th Light AA Regiment, Royal Artillery
POW from March 1942 to August 1945
Koan School (Bandung) and POW Camp 354, Boei Glodok, Java, Indonesia
In Koan School, we soon found out about face-slapping and kickings, and also what a diet of rice began to taste like. Rice with tinned apple stew, sometimes a few vegetables, weak Chinese tea and a small sugar ration, although for a time we did bake all our own bread in one of our mobile field bakery ovens, but this titbit was soon to disappear.

Outside working parties commenced from here and these were to Kemajoran to fill in craters on the blown-up runways.

Our stay in Koan School was not long, as we were moved into the gaol in Batavia at Boei Glodok – a dark grey, high-walled stone compound, with inner compounds, and the Japanese guardroom at the main gate; our only sight of the outside world now was when we went outside on working parties.

Flying Officer Erroll David Shearn, Royal Air Force
POW from March 1942 to August 1945
Tasik Melayu (Tasikmalaya) and Sourabaya, Java

At Sourabaya it was pouring with rain when we arrived and we marched some miles through the downpour to a school called the Lyceum. This school normally accommodated some 300 or so scholars. The Japanese packed about 2,000 RAF into it. I shared a largish classroom with about 19 other RAF officers. The school had only recently been constructed and there was a quantity of builders' material hanging around. I secured a fair-sized wooden frame and I cut a length of rope from the rope in the school gym. With these I made myself a very comfortable bed and rope mattress. A fellow officer who had been a yachtsman gave me valuable advice and assistance.

Aircraftman (Driver) Frank Deakin Jackson, No 62 Squadron, Royal Air Force
POW from March 1942 to August 1945
Camp 354, Boei Glodok, Java

It was as we lined up outside the prison that I felt the first tremors of fear and apprehension. The prison looked most depressingly grim, but the sight of the Japanese prison commandant, perched on a wooden box, was most unnerving. Hatred and contempt distorted his features. His use of an interpreter was hardly necessary to convey his malice towards his new charges. He proceeded to harangue us in an increasing frenzy. In acrimonious terms he stressed the Nippon soldier did not allow himself to be captured in battle. We were to be despised and could consider ourselves fortunate to still be alive. Then, this madman indignantly screamed at us the information that our people had deliberately flattened (steamrollered) Nippon prisoners in New Guinea. Incredibly, he had overlooked his earlier assertion that his countrymen did not allow themselves to be captured. It was no time to reason with him but to accept his venomous tirade. No one would ever be able to reason with this maniac. Was this exhibition to be a foretaste of things to come?

4
SURVIVING THE DAY

'Many were the schemes thought up to annoy the sentries. We had time to think up these things and it was the only way in which you could restore any degree of self-respect.'

– British army private in Italy

A prisoner of war's quality of life as day followed monotonous day was not determined only by the philosophy of the regime under which he was held and by the caprices of his captor. The inspiration provided by the authorities back home and his superiors within the POW camp itself was almost as important. Article 18 of the Geneva Convention ruled that the internal administration of each prisoner-of-war camp should be under the leadership of a responsible officer prisoner. This principle was amplified in Article 43, which stipulated that, wherever they were held, prisoners could appoint representatives to negotiate with their captors and with the Protecting Power and a compatriot to assist as an interpreter. These representatives would also be in charge of distributing such vital necessities as food, clothes, letters and parcels.

Such well-intentioned resolutions were easier made than implemented. During the first two or three years of the Second World War servicemen were discouraged from dwelling on the possibility of captivity just as they were discouraged from contemplating death in action, as the War Office considered it bad for morale. In spite of this, the RAF instigated escape and evasion lectures for operational aircrew as early as 1940, as well as instructing them on how to behave in the event of capture. But it was only when losses in Bomber Command mounted and soldiers were captured in droves in North Africa and the Far East that the three service ministries, with an eye to producing a 'Camp Leaders' Guide', began to draw up guidelines on how those already 'in the bag' should conduct themselves and to advise them on the terms of the Geneva Convention. However, most prisoners, even the most senior amongst them, never so much as clapped eyes on a copy of the POW Code – even though Article 84 made it clear that copies should be displayed for all to see – while the projected leaders' guide never materialized.

As it was, many prisoners – especially army 'other ranks'– had little confidence in their senior officers, who they felt had achieved their rank more by privilege than ability and who in any case had let them down on all major battle-fronts. It took officers of fine calibre and great character to transform defeated, dispirited men into an effective internal organization that could ensure a decent standard of living among the squalid conditions typical of most camps.

Their well-being depended not only upon the efficiency of this organiza-tion, but also upon the camp leader's relationship with the commandant and his staff, with the Protecting Power and with the authorities back home. These factors could determine whether the amenities in the camp were good or bad or even existed at all; they could make a difference whether you had a good camp theatre, a bad theatre, or no theatre at all; whether or not you ate today; whether or not you stood outside your barrack in the rain or snow all day; whether or not you had wood for the stove when the conditions outside were sub-zero; whether or not you received medical help when you were ill – in short, whether you lived or died.

In camps where strong leadership was lacking or where conditions were particularly harsh, deprived prisoners – most of whom were barely in their twen-ties and found prison camps different from school only in degree – found an outlet for their frustration in mocking the enemy. Officer prisoners in German camps, where the captors were know as 'goons' after a low-browed apelike cartoon creature of little intelligence featured in the *Daily Mirror*, soon had tormenting the enemy down to a fine art. It was known as 'goon-baiting', and many prisoners, such as the famous Wing Commander Douglas Bader, made a wartime career out of it. Baiting the enemy was, however, something to be done judiciously, as the enemy had the advantage of solitary confinement cells, rifles and sub-machine guns. The 'goons' put up with a lot and generally only gave their tormentors a week or two in the 'cooler'. (Nevertheless, some Senior British Officers (SBOs) banned such activities on the grounds that they disrupted escape activities and were, in any case, unnecessary.) The Italians were much more touchy and inclined to be trigger-happy. Baiting the Japanese was generally unwise: they needed little or no provocation to kill out of hand. As in everything else, the benefits of baiting the enemy depended largely upon who he was.

GERMANY AND OCCUPIED POLAND

British and Commonwealth Air Force personnel captured by the Germans were fortunate to the degree that the first RAF officer of any seniority, Wing Commander Harry 'Wings' Day of No 57 Squadron, was captured as early as

The legendary Wing Commander Harry 'Wings' Day with his cat at Dulag Luft
(*author's collection*)

October 1939 and was given a copy of the POW Code by the commandant of Oflag IXA/H, who was a veteran of the Great War. By virtue of his seniority according to the Royal Air Force List, Day automatically became the Senior British Officer, and when he was transferred to another camp, his interpreter, Squadron Leader Sydney Murray, took over the task of *Vertrauensmann* (literally 'Man of Confidence'), liaising with the Germans. Although higher-ranking Royal and Merchant Navy officers arrived shortly afterwards, Murray continued to be the buffer between the prisoners and the guards. Day and Murray, both of immense character and both widely respected, set the tone for relations between prisoners and commandants in most camps in which the Allied air forces were held for the rest of the war.

Army prisoners were less fortunate in that, as most of them were captured in large numbers in hard-fought campaigns, the situation in which they found themselves was chaotic and their morale likely to be low. Neither their German captors nor the Prisoner of War Directorate of the War Office had foreseen that thousands of men would be taken prisoner in France and the Low Countries, Crete and North Africa. In summer 1940 – when supply lines across Western Europe were cut off by the Blitzkrieg and there was a hiatus in the flow of food parcels, clothing parcels and letters – prisoners of all nationalities and services suffered terrible hardship. But new prisoners suffered the most, owing to lack of internal organization and a lack of confidence in their senior offices, whom they saw – not altogether unfairly – as being largely responsible for their plight. While a few of the army SBOs were highly regarded by their subordinates, the bulk of army prisoners in the period 1940–42 felt they had been badly let down by their leaders both on the battlefield and in the camps.

Strength of character was even more essential for senior NCOs. In camps for RAF other ranks, the prisoners' *Vertrauensmann* rarely appointed himself according to seniority; mostly, he was chosen, either by ballot, or by cabal, or organically by some form of 'emergence'. However, in the army Stalags, camp leaders were appointed according to seniority, like SBOs, and came in for a great deal of criticism, as a large number appeared more interested in feathering their own nests than looking after their men. Whatever the validity of such accusations, they had plenty of time to fester in camps where the enemy provided few facilities and all prisoners had to look forward to was yet another day of mind-numbing, soul-destroying boredom.

GERMANY

Flying Officer Michael Heriot Roth, Royal Air Force
POW from May 1940 to May 1945
Oflag IXA/H, Spangenberg, May 1940

Whatever did you do all day is a question asked more than any other of POWs. Do? There wasn't anything to 'do' in the sense of doing as used by those living in a free, working society. We had no jobs to keep. Time was ours. And at first we didn't find anything to 'do', except wait for the next meal.

Initially, even the simple demands of the German regimen were blessings – responsibilities to be met at definite hours: first *Appell* (roll-call) at 7.30 am, followed by sick parade, breakfast, parcel call, gym parades, lunch; a second *Appell* around 4 pm, then supper; lights out at 10 pm. Six days a week *Hauptmann* Gross took the *Appell*. Gross was a tiny man, under five feet. His legs, still bowed from his Great War service in the cavalry, made it difficult for him to stand straight. He had risen from the ranks and was proud of his officer status; yet he was still a sergeant at heart and tried to make us as smart as a squad of his own troops. On *Appell*, his short pointed waxed moustaches twitched with dismay at our sloppy drill. He chattered like an angry squirrel: someone was talking, not standing erect, moving their head, shuffling their feet, unshaven, or had forgotten their cap.

Hauptmann Gustav Simoleit, German Air Force
Temporary Commandant, Stalag Luft I, Barth-Vogelsang, 1941–42

The commandant of the camp had the commanding and disciplinary power of a colonel (regimental commander), and I was only a captain of the reserve.

I had to take over my new duties and responsibilities in a very difficult time. Rumours had spread over the country, especially in the neighbouring military units, that in the camp of Barth there were unbelievable fraternizations and even drinking bouts with the prisoners. We never had so many visitors in our camp than at this time, majors and colonels and even generals. They all wanted to see that strange camp where such things could happen.

First of all they were astonished to find a little captain as commandant of the camp. It was always a very hard piece of work to convince them that, leaving out the unhappy and uncorrect [sic] beer gifts to the prisoners, all our work and our whole humane attitude were not a kind of treason but the real and correct execution of the Geneva Convention. Somehow I succeeded in convincing my high-ranking visitors.

Hauptmann Gustav Simoleit, briefly commandant at Stalag Luft I, Barth, and subsequently adjutant at Stalag Luft III, Sagan (*IWM HU21007*)

But in the relations with our High Command, when I defended the interests of the camp and the prisoners, it was not easy for a captain to quarrel with officers who all were higher in rank. My disciplinary and commanding power of a colonel did not help me very much. Therefore I demanded again and again to appoint a higher officer for the post of commandant, whose rank would make it easier to work for the benefit of the camp. At last Major Burchard for a short time was appointed commandant before the history of Stalag Luft I came to an end.

Lieutenant David Lubbock, Royal Naval Volunteer Reserve
POW from July 1941 to April 1945
Oflag XC, Lübeck, 1941
End of August 1941. Lübeck. The commandant was a Nazi army officer who shrieked at us of 'guns, not butter' and gave us a starvation diet. We had no Red Cross parcels or letters from home. The clever camp cat, eventually caught with difficulty in his ninth life, was consigned to the pot.

Flying Officer Michael Heriot Roth, Royal Air Force
POW from May 1940 to May 1945
Oflag VIB, Warburg, 1941–42
On 8 October 1941 we left Lübeck bound for Warburg, Oflag VIB, but not before the camp received a surprise visit from two officials from the American Embassy in Berlin. Despite [the commandant, *Oberst* von] Wachtmeister's precautions we were able to sneak them a written statement of our complaints and the many violations of the Geneva Convention. We hoped they'd lay it on thick so that the next bunch of inmates would fare better than ourselves.

Wachtmeister and his gang didn't let us go without a last 'squeeze', however. On 7 October they called a special *Appell* with orders that we were to bring all our blankets on parade with us. At pistol-point they then took two blankets away from all who had two. They insisted that we'd been issued with two blankets, but the fact is they'd only issued one blanket per man in the first place, and the ones they took belonging to us were clearly Red Cross issue from Geneva.

Our Wing Commander – not having himself an extra blanket – told us to give up our blankets without making a 'fuss'. Asinine creature. Squadron Leader Roger Bushell, a great goon-hater and superb linguist, got into a terrific shouting match with Wachtmeister's loathsome adjutant, who yelled out that all Englishmen were liars and told 70,000 lies. Bushell replied we were not liars and demanded that the adjutant produce the papers we had signed on our arrival for the original issue of one blanket per man. The adjutant refused. I believe that some kriegies forestalled the adjutant's plan by tearing a single blanket in half, folding it, and then handing in two halves as two whole blankets. It was a very unpleasant fracas, and our hatred for everything German became written on our faces.

Certain that the war would be over by Christmas 1941, the German High Command wanted most of its Allied officers prisoners in one camp before then. As a result, there were 25 nationalities among the POWs at Warburg: officers from many parts of the Empire – Indian officers (Viceroy's Commission) captured in France and North Africa, Arabs, Maoris, men from Australia, New Zealand, South Africa, Canada, and far Fiji. There were Polish, Czech, Dutch and French Air Force officers who had got to England before Dunkirk. There was a Greek general and his aide. And besides these and more, officers from the British Navy, Air Force, Fleet Air Arm, and army officers from Laufen, Biberach, Tittmoning and Spangenberg. In all, 3,000, under the command of Major-General Sir Victor Fortune, KBE, CB, DSO. The British army types were in the majority. They were a courageous bunch with terrific morale. They had the knack of finding something positive in the grimmest situation. At first the RAF felt superior and pooh-poohed their 'Let's get organized, chaps; let's improvise; let's put on a good show so the goons see we don't give a damn for their bloody-mindedness.' But eventually, even the cockiest RAF types had to admit this attitude paid off. For example, one could either moan about the midday soup ration, or one could look forward to drinking it in the main dining hall to the music of the camp dance orchestra. Within ten days of their arrival, the army put on a professional variety show. The General had bullied the goons into giving us wood and lighting equipment for improving the skeletal stage that the French had left behind. Soon after this, new shows were planned every two weeks. I recall the first full-length musical, *Behind the Scenes*, about the trials of a producer in rehearsal. It was a zinging success due to the extraordinary talent of one officer who when on stage virtually became a woman. Offstage, he was a visual nonentity, but on, he blossomed into a personable and totally believable female – a fine actor. Among the shows at Warburg were *George and Margaret*, *Coriolanus*, *Henry V*, *Rhapsody in Blue*, *The First Legion*, a Christmas pantomime and several revues, as well as symphony concerts.

The army types organized everything to the nth degree. Apart from entertainments and lectures by competent teachers in more than 50 subjects, they bullied the goons into letting us run our own chapel, barber's shop, tailoring and shoemaking establishments, hot shower hut, library, piano and music practice rooms, gymnasium, hospital, dental clinic, and carpenter's shop. One most valuable contribution was an organization that called itself 'Foodacco' – a barter market. Practically all our everyday needs (except food) could be taken care of from inside the camp. We were a self-supporting society.

Gunner Cyril George King, Royal Artillery (Territorial)
POW from June 1940 to April 1945
Oflag VIB, Warburg, October 1941

Once again we were persuaded into the usual cattle-trucks and commenced our journey [from Oflag VIIC, Laufen] to the Army Officers' camp at Warburg, which was roughly near Kassel. The camp was established in that there were widely dispersed wooden huts for accommodation, the usual three bands of barbed wire and the sentry towers with high-powered lights to sweep the interior and mounted machine guns. What made the big difference was that the camp was already occupied by large numbers of air force officers, sergeant pilots, etc. Now these men had no regard whatsoever for German discipline, they did not wish to keep their uniforms in a tidy condition, were not willing to appear at regular times for roll-call, and clashed on many occasions with the opinions of the higher-ranking army officers. Quite frankly it was a very large, ugly camp and there was no unison of spirit amongst the men whatsoever.

Pilot Officer Maurice George Butt, Royal Air Force Volunteer Reserve
POW from August 1940 to May 1945
Oflag VIB, Warburg

When I first heard of Douglas Bader in spring of 1940, I just didn't believe the story that there was a legless man flying in the RAF. However, the story appeared in a Sunday paper, and none of my flying training course believed it either. Heaven knows, we found flying demanding enough without any handicaps.

One day at Warburg, in spring 1942, there he was, walking towards us with the characteristic kick action with which we were to learn to associate him. Even then, we initially accepted him as another airman who had landed a bit too heavily – there were a few about. Incredibly, we soon learnt otherwise and his three stripes stated his Wing Commander rank.

He went round the camp giving talks on happenings in the Battle of Britain, the tactics and strategy of the Luftwaffe and the counter-tactics by the RAF, and an assessment of the navy's rule in assuring there would not be a successful floating crossing of the Channel by the German army in summer

1940. It was stimulating to listen to, and the enthusiasm with which he was involved in hacking the black crosses out of the sky was quite infectious.

Bader was a natural goon baiter – he provoked mischief and fun with the Germans at every opportunity. On parade (*Appell*), when we were being counted – at least twice a day and more often during the escaping season – spring and summer, particularly after an escape – he would stand on his pins swaying slightly to maintain stability, and then when the German officer or the NCO came within range, he would manage to fall all over him, much to everyone's glee, except the Germans'. After two successful pull-downs, the goons insisted on his having a chair to sit the count out. All Germans steered clear of him to avoid a pull-down whenever they spotted him about the camp.

Consequently Bader became prime material for being moved away from the camp, along with other troublemakers of escaping tendencies.

There came a rumour or 'latrinogram' as we called them that there was to be a purge or draft of some of the RAF to a new supercamp – Hermann Goering's Holiday Camp, it was called.

It transpired that about 80 RAF officers were to be transferred to this new camp somewhere well East, probably in Russia. In the event, it turned out to be Sagan (Stalag Luft III) in Upper Silesia, an eastern province of Germany.

The day before departure at morning roll-call *Appell*, we were told that anyone on the 'purge' who felt they were unable to walk to the station for a disablement reason should report to the German MO (*Arzt*) immediately after that *Appell*. It was a two-mile walk, as we had learned on the way in, back in October 1941.

In a flash I realized there was a possibility of wearing the Germans down a tiny bit, assuming they would be providing alternative transport to Shanks's pony. In fact, it transpired they clearly had Bader in mind. Nevertheless, a dash over to the barrack block for a scrubbing brush and a quick abrasion of my left leg to simulate inflamed flesh, followed by another dash to the MO room and another application of rough brushing just before the German MO appeared, and his glance at my medical record sheet assured him I needed a lift to the station, a two-mile march. Up to that time, my leg problem had only broken out once in Germany.

So, to the derisive calls of the marchers, a pony and trap carrying Bader and three others passed the main column to reach the station first. We were amazed to find a plush first-class carriage had been arranged, quite different to the ordinary rigid wooden slatted seats, which we called travelling 'hard-bottomed'. This was a touch with the hand of Herman Goering behind it, we deduced. Goering had a keen sense of chivalry from the First World War, and thus the special treatment for Bader, an 'equivalent' man.

There were six [of us] only in the compartment and one *Postern* (guard) posted outside in the corridor to watch two compartments. Came the usual riot act, 'You will not attempt to escape, otherwise you will be shot without warning. You will not stand up in the compartment. If you wish to go to the *Abort* (loo), make a request to the guard. Do not approach the window, or you will be shot' and so on. We had heard it all before, but one never really knew how trigger-happy the particular guard on duty might be – a lot depending on his own problems, bombing of his home, lack of leave, possible posting pending to the Eastern Front, all of which would affect his interpretation of his duty.

Well, we settled down after boisterous banter, and Bader did a review of the war situation. Two days later, unwashed, unshaven and bottom sore with sitting, we were feeling quite jaded. The carriages at that point had been shunted off at a junction prior to the last leg of the journey. A careful series of questioning had revealed from the guards our ultimate destination, and the diagrammatic railway map above the seats had enabled progress to be charted.

No sooner had a steam engine coupled up to the carriages than Bader, noting our cheesed-off state, sprung up and said: 'How about a cup of tea chaps?' We looked up in amazement and some concern as he reached for his kitbag and dug a teapot out followed by a packet of tea from a Red Cross parcel. Putting back the kitbag onto the luggage rack, to our horror he turned round to the window and immediately opened it wide, waving the teapot about outside. The goons erupted into activity, shouting, rifles primed and in a high state of agitation. The *Unteroffizier* (sergeant) appeared, followed by the *Feldwebel* (senior sergeant) and after a while a *Hauptmann* (captain). Revolvers were being waved around quite wildly and several rifles were pointing at the open window from the guards standing outside in the marshalling yard. Calmly Bader explained that he wanted a brew of tea and wished someone to take the teapot to the engine driver in order to have the necessary boiling water added from the engine. The officer saw that discretion was the better part of valour and did not want an immediate posting for himself to the Eastern Front just because his distinguished guest might cause a major incident, and so the order was given, and the teapot taken to the engine-room by a guard who was as amazed as the rest of us. A cup of tea in the middle of Europe in the middle of the war! The Bader magic had worked again.

With our spirits rekindled, we set to work to prepare for the end of the journey. The boys in the next compartment distracted the guard with a long-winded dialogue about food, displaying items of Red Cross parcels and, to keep him really fixed, sparing an occasional knob of chocolate. 'You like that, yes?' etc. Thus a diagrammatic rail map was taken from its frame on the wall of the carriage, and sewn under the lining (a Scottish plaid) of the leather jacket I had re-confiscated from the enemy at Thorn. It required much skill and determination to push a needle through the leather, hence only four penetrations were made, so that a single diagonal stitch about one inch long retained the map (stiff cardboard-backed) from its top two corners.

The map measured about 24" x 12" and the idea was to walk through the search with it sandwiched behind the coat lining. The only snag was that the two diagonal stitches of white cotton were visible on the outside of the black leather jacket.

Bader, as usual, had the searchers in a turmoil. '*Herr Hauptmann*, make sure you look inside my tin legs – they are full of contraband,' he provoked. This froze the goons, and the officer in charge had already had his leg pulled and suffered some face loss from the tea on the train incident. He let Bader through complete with his tin legs stuffed with contraband.

Realizing that hesitation was a loser, I threw myself at my searcher, suggesting that I stripped everything off. He was a little man in stature, but with a keen watchful eye. He seemed to sense that it would be ludicrous to doubt my innocence, and let me by, after feeling with both hands between the leather jacket and my shirt, with us facing each other. Even the stiffness of the enclosed map on the back of his hand escaped his sensitivity. Then came the awkward walk away with the two white diagonal cotton strands shouting for attention. A prearranged diversion was in progress further along the line, which focused attention away. Thus the re-confiscated black leather jacket got into yet another camp, this time carrying a bonus diagrammatic rail map.

Flying Officer Percy Frank ('Red') Eames, Royal Air Force
POW *from July 1940 to April 1945*
Stalag Luft III, *summer 1942*

The two former fighter 'aces' Wing Commander Bob Tuck and Wing Commander Norman Ryder used to walk around the circuit reliving their glory days in the Battle of Britain. They would pretend one hand – say, the left – was an enemy bomber or fighter and the other hand, the right, a Spitfire or a Hurricane, and the two of them would run, jump and spin about after their own twisting, winding hands, like two cats chasing their tails, and blow raspberries to imitate the noise of machine guns.

When Douglas Bader arrived from Warburg, he joined in. There was a certain amount of rivalry and even antagonism between the bomber types, who were in the majority, and the fighter types who were fewer in number but more flashy.

One day Bader was sitting in my room describing one of his aerial dogfights. As he reached the climax he asked: 'And d'you know what I did next?' And one of his audience butted in: 'I know, sir. You pissed in, gave him a squirt' – and here he licked his index finger and chalked a '1' in the air! All guffawed except Bader, who, glaring at the wag, rose from his chair and stomped off without a word, laughter ringing in his ears.

Lieutenant-Commander William Lawton Stephens, Royal Naval Volunteer Reserve
POW from March 1942 to October 1942
Marlag Nord, Sandbostel, 1942

The daily routine was a fairly simple one. We were called at nine by our servant – a Marine who had been taken at Calais – and after washing and dressing went across to the communal dining room, where we were all fed in small messes of eight or ten. I must say here that the feeding at Marlag was better than any other camp I was in. This was partly because the German navy cooperated with us and partly because of good internal organization in the camp. Breakfast was always a gamble; if the Red Cross parcel situation was good, which it seldom was in those days, one might get sardines on toast and tea or one might only get a slice of toast and butter. Sunday was nearly always a 'Gala Day'; we had porridge and a slice of toast and occasionally – very occasionally – someone was able to bribe a sentry, with cigarettes, to bring in some eggs; that was always a big event.

At ten o'clock we had roll-call, and the commandant, a funny little man who was almost as broad as he was long, used to come in and watch us being counted. This didn't last long and by 10.15 or so one was free with the whole day in front of one and absolutely nothing to do. A state of affairs I used often to long for before I was captured! Actually, practically everybody did something; you can't just go on doing nothing for months and years in that sort of environment – you would go mad. I started to learn German, as it seemed essential to be able to speak and understand it a little before one could even consider a successful escape. I used to work at this from 10.30 till 12.30, when we had lunch. This was always a poor meal and consisted of German soup, a slice of toast and jam, and some tea. The soup, although cooked in our galley, was actually made from the rations issued by the Germans, and was, therefore, of very poor quality.

After lunch most people had a siesta for an hour or so. I used to sleep until about two and then do some more German until teatime, 4.30. Tea was just tea and sometimes, if you were lucky, a Red Cross biscuit.

Then we had another roll-call at five o'clock and after that we always had a football match or some kind of sport that one could either watch or participate in.

Supper, which was much the best thing in the whole day, was at seven o'clock. We used to really 'go to town' on these suppers. There was always some sort of meat or fish from our parcels, potatoes, and sometimes dried or even tinned fruit for a sweet; this was rounded off by the inevitable bit of toast and jam and tea.

After supper we used to play bridge or read or sometimes just talk about all the things we were going to do when we got home again. Then at 10.30 lights out and one crawled into bed thinking – 'Another day gone, thank God!'

Pilot Officer Theo Faire Storrier Johnson, New Zealander in the Royal Air Force
POW from August 1940 to May 1945
Letter home from East Compound, Stalag Luft III, Sagan, 1943
27 April 1943
Dear Dad,

Here I am at last settled in at Stalag Luft III. After the best part of three years spent in moving from one wire-bound enclosure to another throughout the length & breadth of Germany, we've at long last arrived at a 'lager' which is under the Luftwaffe Administration and where I very sincerely hope we will remain until the end. Our barrack blocks are the most comfortable we've yet had, there being only eight men to a room. This room consists of three Aussies, four New Zealanders, a Canadian (Bob Coste by name who completes his fourth year as a 'kriegie' in a few months' time) and 'Charlie' [the skeleton]. The last member who supports himself on a nail beside the window definitely leers at us from the moment we rise in the morning until the minute we retire at night. He was imported by one of our Aussies who is a budding medico. Our furniture is two tables, two forms, one chair, four stools, four lockers, four of the usual double-tier wooden bunks and two bookcases which we have managed to knock up out of an old packing case. Andy Sutherland is in the sergeants' compound which is just over the fence on the western side, but unfortunately no intercourse is permitted between the two compounds. Owing to the constant upheavals which are always attendant upon a change of camps I fear that my work hasn't been going too well of late, but what worries me more is that I can't make up my mind what I really want to do anyway! Fondest love to all,

Cheerio, Theo.

Pilot Officer Paul Gordon Royle, Australian in the Royal Air Force
POW from May 1940 to May 1945
Stalag Luft I, Barth, and Stalag Luft III, Sagan
The weather seems to have been always cold, and the heating stoves in our rooms were starved of fuel, as were we. The morning and afternoon roll-calls were miserable in winter.

We spent our time talking, reading in our own language when books arrived, and German newspapers after I had learnt to do so. I translated German news bulletins from the *Völkischer Beobachter* and pinned them up on a noticeboard daily. The German bulletins, I think, were factual and presented the operational events accurately. Our information was augmented by the BBC when reception became possible. We played ice hockey introduced by the Canadians, after equipment was received from home. We studied, in my case maths and physics, and passed an examination set in England. We walked round and round the compound. We saw many excellently produced plays, some featuring Rupert Davies and Peter Butterworth who after the war distinguished themselves on stage and TV. We were sometimes taken to see German news films, in the early days. We wrote the two letters that were permitted each month and mourned the frequent lack of reply. We attempted to convince the Germans of our certain victory, and their stupidity in continuing the war to no avail. But our major preoccupation was attempting to escape, over the wire, under it or through it, but with limited success.

The Americans were great churchgoers. We had a Scottish padre in camp. He was kept busy by them but less so by the rest of us.

The administration of the camps by our senior officers was as we would have expected, and so was the response. I think that complete discipline was maintained, perhaps a little less so by the Americans. For example, they seemed unable to share the barrack cooking-stove without an element of disagreement. We had such matters sorted out and there were few problems among us. The entrepreneurial spirit was satisfied by the establishment of 'Foodacco', by which food and cigarettes were priced by points and traded.

Our German camp officer from the beginning was named [Hans] Pieber, an excellent and fair-minded officer. He it was who took many photographs of our camp life and took us on occasional walks around Barth on parole. He helped us where possible within the limits of his duty to his country. The regard with which he was held was shown by his appearance as a guest in the BBC TV show *This Is Your Life* some years ago.

There were guards in elevated boxes at the corners of the compound, and others inside and outside and at the gate, and 'ferrets' who spent their time looking for tunnels. Some of the guards were known to 'shoot on sight' and eventually paid the price. Most were, I suppose, fairly neutral. Some were blackmailed and did our bidding, but the details were not advertised as we quickly became aware of the need for silence for security's sake.

By the end of the war there were officers from many countries in the RAF: the UK, Ireland, Australia, the USA, Canada, New Zealand, South Africa, France, Jugoslavia, Rhodesia, Norway, Czechoslovakia and others; a few naval

Lieutenant (later Captain) William 'Bill' Bompas (*W M G Bompas*)

and army officers and in addition members from the air forces of other countries, for example RAAF, RCAF, RNZAF, USAAF – and cooperation was exemplary.

Lieutenant William Bompas, Royal Artillery (Field)
POW from December 1942 to April 1945
Oflag VIIIF, Märisch-Trübau (Legnickie, Czech Republic), 1943–44

At 8.15 the roll-call bugle goes, and at 8.29 I pull on trousers, a greatcoat and slippers, and stagger into the corridor. Roll-call takes about ten minutes, then a wash, and breakfast comes up at nine. After tea of coffee, sardines or meat-roll or prunes, and bread and jam, a walk round the camp to shake it down. Possibly a rehearsal, or read, till lunch, at one o'clock, of soup. Then read or a game of rugger till tea (of tea only) at three o'clock. After tea, another walk, play cards, read, talk, shave, and possibly rehearse till roll-call at six. Supper of bully and potatoes, and then, unless in a show, cards (bridge, vingt-et-un, etc) till lights-out at 10.30. Talk till twelve or so, and sleep. There are other occupations, such as swimming or skating when the weather is suitable, snowball fights, blowing a trumpet, darts, making models, sunbathing, or doing nothing – all useful.

Pilot Officer Jack Kenneth ('Tiger') Lyon, Royal Air Force
POW from June 1941 to May 1945
North Compound, Stalag Luft III, Sagan

One POW I remember was Jules Silverston. He was Jewish, and also above normal recruiting age, but had volunteered for air gunner duties, the only aircrew category open to him. But he was shot down 1940. Played the cello. Not everyone's cup of tea, could be exasperating at times. He came to me one day, almost in tears, begging me as senior officer in my room to accept him as he was being persecuted in his own room by a certain officer mainly on account of his race. Anti-Semitism was not exclusive to the Germans.

POLAND

Telegraphist Herbert Edgar Elliott, Royal Naval Volunteer Reserve
POW from August 1940 to May 1945
Fort 17 (Stalag XXA), Thorn, 1940

I met up with the army lads captured in France for the first time and they were in pretty bad shape then. They looked anything but soldiers and I must confess I got rather annoyed at some of them for not showing Jerry more of the traditional British spirit. The Germans certainly seemed to have more respect for the naval prisoners. This has proved the same throughout the whole time I was a prisoner.

Gunner Cyril George King, 92nd Field Regiment Royal Artillery (Territorial)
POW from June 1940 to April 1945
Stalag XXIB, Schubin, 1940

All my life it has been my opinion, even now, that one's existence is not really divided into days, but into periods of time during which one looked forward to something, no matter what. Experience has taught me that very often the golden objective is never reached, but never mind, a further space has been covered in good spirits. In my predicament, therefore, I decided to use that method and commenced by looking forward to the morning with its quietness and colours of the rising sun. Next, came midday with the arrival of the main food – such as it was. Lastly, there was the evening when the Polish officers gathered outside their building and sang their folk songs with such vigour and spirit. Thus, I could not look forward to the end of the war, or even a home-coming – but at least I was edging myself in that direction.

ITALY AND THE MEDITERRANEAN

CRETE

Sapper Don Luckett, Royal Engineers
POW from July 1941 to May 1945
Frontstalag, 7th General Field Hospital, Maleme, Crete

The future looked so bleak and an awful feeling seemed to creep in amongst us all. The officers had long since been removed to the mainland, having been flown there in Junkers Ju 52 aircraft, and were never placed in the same camps with Other Ranks. There were quite a few senior NCOs amongst us, with lesser ranks right down to the humble lance-corporals, but in such a situation rank meant nothing at all. Those who tried to pull rank were very quickly put in their places, with some even finding themselves ostracized, the character of the individual counting for more than qualifications. Captivity can be a great leveller.

ITALY

Lieutenant A F ('Junior') Powell, 13th Light Anti-Aircraft Regiment
POW from April 1941 to May 1945
Campo PG 17, Rezzanello

The first prisoners in the castle were from those captured at Mechili – the HQ of the British 2nd Armoured Division, a motorized Indian Infantry battalion, one RAAF fighter pilot (who had been shot down) and a Sudanese officer. There were also some who had been captured elsewhere; from the 9th Australian Infantry Division, commandos, and RN aircrew. I don't know how the Italian authorities decided who was to go to which camp but we were the first large 'bag' so they may not have had much choice. The Divisional Headquarters included officers from most services, such as Engineers, Ordnance, Medical, Dental, Signals, Armoured Corps, Service Corps, Chaplains and us gunners. So we had a good mix of talents and there were Regular, Territorial and conscript officers. The ranks were from Brigadier to Private but no non-commissioned officers. Since the Divisional HQ and the HQ of one battalion of the Indian Brigade were the core of the prisoners, most knew each other well and things settled down quickly.

Later some officers left and others arrived, including some South Africans captured in Tobruk and a Canadian. At any one time there were about 100 of us.

In each camp the senior British Officer was in charge regardless of service or country. At first the commander of the Indian Brigade, Brigadier Vaughan, was our SBO, and he had his Brigade Major and Staff Captain with him. Other ranks could be put to work, so some of them were our cooks and batmen. Duties, such as Messing Officer, Officer-in-Charge showers, O/C canteen, O/C parcels, were allotted and changed periodically. Other officers organized exercise classes and games. There was also an escape committee to coordinate and help would-be escapers.

Private Stanley John Doughty, 12th Royal Lancers
POW from December 1941 to February 1945
Campo PG 52, Chiavari

Many were the schemes thought up to annoy the sentries. We had time to think up these things and it was the only way in which you could restore any degree of self-respect. They were all old, or handicapped, guards, men who had little interest in the war and were only waiting, like us, for its end. The sentry boxes formed a cordon around the perimeter of the camp, and at night they used to call to one another, when instructed by the guard commander, in turn, I suppose to see if they were awake. Number One would call 'Allerta Sentinello Una', then Number Two would sing like someone out of an Italian opera, 'Allerta Sentinello Duo', and so on round the camp. You can imagine a whole camp-full of men or, more subtly, only one prisoner, calling a number out of sequence. Funnily enough, although this infuriated them, it was a month or more before the practice was stopped; meanwhile, chaos ensued.

Lance-Corporal Lawrence Bains, Middlesex Yeomanry
POW from June 1942 to August 1944
Diary kept in Campo PG 66, Capua
The next day [6 August 1942] we were woken early and formed up outside our tents to draw our early morning coffee, which as usual was issued at some unearthly hour. It was fair stuff, by POW standards, an issue being in an Italian bully tin, and welcome in the cold of the morning. Having gulped this down, we completed our dressing and dawdled out to roll-call.

At Capua, roll-calls were always after coffee, at about 0700 hours; each group formed up three deep and was checked by an Italian sergeant or interpreter, and apart from standing to attention when the officer entered the compound, very little discipline was observed, fellows sitting down till they were actually counted, wandering about at the back and hanging about in the tent-lines till the last moment. This latter caused much uneasiness, as it gave them an opportunity for stealing, so we used to take our 'valuables' out on roll-calls with us, and in the end left an official orderly in the lines till the last minute. These daily checks tended to be rather a farce, as fellows could slip from one group to another, and everyone seemed very unconcerned about it. Our group, being number 18 out of 21, and being one of the last to be checked, used to return to bed after coffee and only get out on parade at the last minute; I was surprised at the general laxity allowed.

Corporal Eric Barrington, Royal Air Force Police
POW June 1942 to April 1945
Diary kept in Campo PG 73, Carpi (Modena)
1 January 1943. A sunny though frosty day. Up at 11.15 am. After playing a rubber of bridge in our International Match which lasted from 12.30 am to 2.30 am slept well after silencing the usual lice. Tea, bread and cheese at 11.30 am, then to Canteen where Mac and I spend our remaining lira on a kilo each of onions, apples, oranges. I had also half a kilo of celery in exchange for some

apples. Continued our bridge till skilly time 4.30 pm, then another two rubbers against Scotland. Prepared my usual addition to the stew of raw onions and celery and had indigestion again. Tea up at 6 pm, and to celebrate the day we finished off our Christmas parcels by scoffing the last tin of Lusty's Braised Steak and Macaroni, much superior to the Eyetie macaroni, though as we had missed the olive oil issue we had to have it cold; however, my last piece of Christmas cake more than made up for it. For once I feel satisfied. Bridge again till 12.15 am with a break for a mug of cocoa at 9.30, brewed up in the wash-house over a parcel box. The Eyetie orderly officer interrupted an interesting hand when on his rounds, ordering us to *dormires*! Of which, of course, we took no notice. The usual P[iss] parade during the night.

Lieutenant Dan Billany, 4th Battalion East Yorkshire Regiment
POW from June 1942; killed some time after October 1943
Memoir written Campo PG 17, Rezzanello, near Piacenza
We did not hurry to get out of bed the first morning at Rezzanello, because it was the first spring mattress we had slept on for many months; and also the air outside the blankets was icy. There were no bugs in the bedsteads. The sheets and mattresses and pillows were very clean.

The room we were in was big enough to contain 15 beds, with cupboards, wardrobes and a long table and still plenty of vacant floor space. The walls looked, in the morning light, clean, cold, and slightly damp. The ceiling was covered with formal painting executed with great care and no taste. It was a smooth, plain ceiling, but it was painted to give an illusion of relief and modelling. From every bed all round the room a nose pointed at this ceiling, as we all speculated how much of the carving was three-dimensional and how much was illusion. Subsequent examination established that it was all illusion.

At half-past eight a bell rang. We had been forewarned of it. It was the roll-call bell, and within five minutes of its sounding we must all be in the courtyard, formed up in fives in alphabetical order.

We got out of bed to begin our new life. It could not, in any case, be more primitive than Capua, and it looked like being much more civilized: but it was cold, and we might have *less to eat*. Already we knew that during the winter we should have only one Red Cross parcel a fortnight, instead of one a week, because of transport difficulties. That was bad enough: but it was said that the syndicate system was to be abandoned, and all food centralized: we would not be able to divide the crumbs and lick out the tins.

Roll-call did not take long, because there was at Rezzanello an American-Italian interpreter who ripped out our names like a machine gun. The Senior

British Officer then formally announced that all the Red Cross food would be centralized and not issued to individuals as at Capua. Meals would be prepared in the cookhouse: no cooking at all would be done by officers: and we should have four meals a day – breakfast, lunch, tea and dinner. The apprehension caused by this announcement was alleviated when the Senior British Officer added that breakfast would be ready in fifteen minutes. Everybody thought of meat roll, sausage, beans, porridge. The SBO then said that breakfast this morning would be one biscuit and a cup of tea. This proved standard for the future, except that sometimes we did not have the biscuit.

We hurried off to wash before breakfast; it was freezing, so this was no time for half-measures: plunge to the waist in icy water, be hearty, get a glow on, etc. The bathroom was solid with half-naked, bad-tempered, short-spoken men, all shivers and gooseflesh and bristly chins, queuing for a chamber pot, the only available vessel which would hold water. There were six washboards and six taps, but the water had gone off, and all that was left was a bath half-full. Some people had brushed their teeth in it, too. You waited your turn, dipped a chamber-pot-full of water out of the bath and poured it into one of the bowls, first plugging the drain with your handkerchief because there were no plugs. Then you washed and shaved as quickly as ever you could before all the water ran away.

We have learned this about all large buildings in Italy: the water depends on a pump. The pump depends on the electricity. The electricity depends on overhead wires which break whenever there is a high wind, thunderstorm, Act of God, or political crisis. If the wire does not break, the original electricity depends on mountain rivers and waterwheels, so in the long run the water depends on the water. The result of all this is that the water fails approximately three times a day. But there is always somewhere in the building a tap nearer to the pump, or the ground, or Nature, which keeps on running when the others have stopped. You have to know where this tap is, and as soon as your own tap begins to hiss and gobble, you whip up your shaving-tackle in both hands and run for this tap before anyone else gets there. In the nature of things, you are never first, but you may be early in the queue.

We understood there was a garden round the building, and that we were allowed to walk in it. In fact we had seen it from one of the windows, a few yards of lawn, some empty flower-beds, and a path, all enclosed by the little circle of barbed wire which surrounded the building. So immediately after breakfast we hurried down the little slope which led to the garden. The path was hard and white with frost. As soon as we got out into the garden, we slipped and fell very hard on our bottom. A sentry outside the wire folded up with mirth.

From the garden we could see the outside of the building and walk round it on three sides. Beyond any doubt the place was a castle: rather bogus, but still!

Imprisoned in a castle in the foothills of the Apennines. Romance, Richard and Blondel.

> *Beneath was stretched, like a green sea,*
> *The waveless plain of Lombardy**

and winding across it we could see the wide river Po, reminding us of a Witty Jest by Kit one day when the water failed at Capua:

ITALY MUST MAKE MORE WATER!
The battle of Italy will be won on the Po.

The castle was set in a landscape of beautiful wooded hills, like the Derbyshire country north of Ashbourne, but with dark thickets of fir which now on the north side were grey with frost, but on the south were already touched by the sun to dark green. The air was clear, clean and piney. It was said that on clear days the Alps could be seen from the castle.

The castle was a square stone building with a turret like a Christmas cake standing up at each corner. The batmen had a story that it was built 150 years ago by a Scotsman who married an Italian heiress, and certainly there was something dimly Scottish about it. It was like 'Lucia di Lammermoor' – as Scottish, and as Italian. It was perhaps the scene-painter's impression of the stage-manager's impression of Donizetti's impression of Walter Scott's impression of the late seventeenth century; and the arch which led into the garden was faced with white marble as if the local funeral furnisher had been called in to finish the job. This arch was guarded on either side by two life-sized plaster lions, one of which had an expression of unshakable piety; and in the marble of the gate were carved the words:

ARS LABOR

which caused dispute, the popular opinion being that both words were misspelled: but it was maintained by a minority that the words represented a Latin form of the motto LABOUR AND WAIT, and this was taken as evidence that the entire building had been supplied to order by the Co-operative Wholesale Society, Scottish Branch. There was much in the general structure of the castle which lent probability to this view.

---

* Writing from memory, Billany slightly misquotes the line 'Beneath is spread like a green sea', from Shelley's 'Lines written among the Euganean Hills'.

Within, the castle was cunningly designed to prevent anybody getting anywhere in a hurry. There were perhaps four rooms you could get into without passing through any other rooms. At the other end of the scale, there were rooms which could only be gained after opening and closing half the doors of the castle. During the first day there was a good deal of writing out of notices, in English and Italian:

PLEASE CLOSE THIS DOOR

Lieutenant John Pelly, Coldstream Guards
POW from June 1942 to April 1945
Diary kept in Campo PG 21, Chieti
Everything here appeared well organized. Room orderlies, Mess orderlies, English cooks, small home-constructed theatre (stage of beds), education programme, sit-down meals with proper cutlery, better food, in fact things looked good, from the outside anyway. All the Battalion are in the same room, and have a spare bunk, spent all the morning trying to arrange a transfer from my present bungalow to theirs. Had tea with Peter and hope to transfer tomorrow. There was an out-of-doors concert after supper.

THE FAR EAST

Whereas in Germany and Italy the enemy made some attempt to adhere to the POW Code, making it possible, even in the worst camps, for good leadership and good organization to make a positive difference to living conditions and hence morale, this was not so in the Far East, where the Japanese had more or less torn up the Geneva Convention. Thus, in Singapore, Burma, Siam, the Dutch East Indies and Japan there was very little any SBO or Man of Confidence could do to protect prisoners from a bad commandant.

As it was, events in the Far East proved that the worse the conditions under which prisoners suffered, the less confidence they had in their senior officers. Lieutenant-Colonel Philip Toosey, Royal Artillery, has only belatedly been recognized as one of the most inspirational SBOs in the Far Eastern camps, rather than the dolt portrayed by Alec Guinness in the film *The Bridge on the River Kwai*. However, as the Japanese systematically starved and overworked their prisoners and instigated next to nothing in terms of provisions or facilities, it was seldom possible for camp leaders to make great improvements to ameliorate the lot of their men, who more often than not had to fall back on their own ingenuity, physical stamina and mental and emotional resources.

HONG KONG

Lieutenant Colonel Peter Allison Belton, HQ Eastern Command
POW from December 1941 to August 1945
Notes kept in Camp 203, North Point, Hong Kong Island
Wednesday, 31 December 1941 – Saturday, 24 January 1942. The first part of this period was pretty bad but gradually we had the camp cleaned up, huts repaired and with the permission of the Nipponese had improved our rations so much that we were eating a normal half-loaf of small British ration milk-bread – all obtained from foraging parties which went out daily under the direction of Colonel Fredericks, who did a magnificent job. Disease was our greatest menace, but this was kept to low levels, considering conditions, by Sandy Warrack, who joined as Medical Officer from Bowen Road and by outside assistance from Dr Selwyn Clarke, who brought drugs and had the local rubbish dump, which was right next to the camp, sprayed with petro-leum and burnt. In spite of this, however, flies continued bad and it was nothing to kill off over 200 in half an hour.

Commander R S Young, Royal Navy
POW from December 1941 to August 1945
Argyle Street Camp, Kowloon
On 18 April 1942 all officers, with one or two exceptions, were transferred to Argyle Street POW camp, also in Kowloon, leaving the main lot of ratings and other ranks behind at Shamshuipo.

This place was a well-barbed wire enclosure, surrounding some eight or so wooden huts. There were sentry towers and a guardroom, etc. It had been used previously by us in peacetime as a sort of barracks, but not a prison camp, to house the many Chinese refugees who fled from China before our war. These had been escaping from the Japanese onslaught against China in 1937, the Japanese drive to South China with the Japanese occupation of the Canton area a year or two before the attack on Hong Kong itself.

We were some 500 officers, Naval, Military and Air Force, crammed fairly tightly into the huts. A sleeping place on the ground, or a camp bed if one managed to bring one, touched the next. Each hut had a very small room at the end, with a two-bunk wooden bed. The more senior officers, Major-

General Christopher Maltby, MC, Commodore A C Collinson, Royal Navy, and the brigadiers, got these. Each hut had a cold shower, and an Asiatic lavatory. The Japanese thought they were housing us in relative comfort, which we didn't deserve. Perhaps we didn't! They thought our defence of 18 days only was not at all glorious.

Anyway, there we were in Argyle Street, surrounded by lots of barbed wire, watchtowers and sentries, in overcrowded and verminous huts on a really starvation diet, probably for the war's duration. In fact most of the officer personnel did stay there for two years, until May 1944, facing death and disease, the remainder being moved back to Shamshuipo until the end of the war in August 1945.

SINGAPORE

Sergeant William McDonald Innes-Ker, Straits Settlement Volunteer Force
POW from February 1942 to August 1945
Camp 331, Changi Prison
Changi Jail was very well organized and we Volunteers were lumped with a lot of Royal Artillery gunners in D1, a large, ground-floor ex-workshop room, where some 150 or so were quartered on the floor – 6 feet by 4 feet per person and a 2-foot alley between ranks. This was much better than being on the three higher floors, which consisted of cells and where they were crammed three to a cell, with long flights of steel stairs to go up and down. This was particularly tiresome at night, for one of the effects of a practically pure rice diet is that your bladder works overtime and nearly everybody found a need for a leak at least four to six times a night! While each cell had a native 'squatter' lavatory hole in it, these were naturally not allowed to be used as there was no running water, apart from a few shower taps out in the exercise yards, and then there was only water for certain hours, twice a day, morning and evening for an hour at a time. There were no lights anywhere, of course, and our days were therefore governed by sunrise and sunset, ie, about 5 am to 6 pm.

Changi Jail had been constructed before the war, on the lines of Sing-Sing in the USA, and was meant for something like 600 prisoners in single cells. We had to cram some 10,000 British and Australian troops into this, but were given an area round about the jail on which we erected dozens of bashas, each holding about 100 troops. A basha was a long hut 100 feet by 25 feet, built of hardwood uprights, bamboo laths, and roof and sides covered with atap, made of plaited palm leaves. Sleeping/living platforms ran down each side and these were raised about 3 feet off the ground, which was floored with split bamboo, rather like a closed venetian blind. On these platforms men lived and slept, 6 feet by 4 feet being the usual space allowed each man.

Our officers were quartered in what had been the jailers' houses, outside the main blocks, of which there were four. The whole was surrounded by a 30-foot-high wall, and inside this surrounding wall were the four blocks, Admin Block, Cookhouse Block, etc, and four exercise yards. The latter were turned into latrine areas; troughs for urinals and boreholes 30 feet deep for the other need. Each block held about 60 men; the remaining 8,000 or so were outside in the bashas.

'Tenko' (roll-calls) were held, under Japanese supervision, at dawn and dusk, and also at any other time the Nips wanted it, if bloody-minded. This, however, so confused everyone, for there were many working parties away out on their jobs, gardening, firewood gathering, and the main job – that of airfield construction nearby at Changi Point – that no one could ever balance the books satisfactorily.

Here, after a time, I got a job in the POWs' Camp Office on the card-index filing desk, where a couple of us kept a card-index roster of every POW in the place; where he was quartered, what he was doing, whether in hospital or on a working party, or what have you. This index was, of course, altering daily, as men were moved here and there, died, or in one or two cases just vanished. One man was murdered and pushed head-first down a borehole, where his body was later found! On this office job we were allowed one day a week off to join an outside working party in order to get some sunshine. I always chose a garden party, for here one worked away outside or down by the seashore, planting, digging and weeding, growing greens to mix with our rice – rather like working on allotments at home. Following Chinese practice we generously fertilized these gardens with the products of our latrine areas, particularly urine, which, diluted, is very good for green stuffs. This was collected by special gangs in wheeled army water tanks, and spread on by us with bamboo pipes every morning.

Sapper Edgar Whincup, Royal Engineers
POW from February 1942 to August 1945
Camp 330, Changi Barracks, Singapore
All the time we felt we were caught in a trap from which there seemed to be no escape. The food deteriorated in quality and quantity, the days stretched into weeks with monotonous regularity. Camp life followed a regular, boring pattern and the only real evidence of the fact that we were in enemy hands was the occasional sight of a Nippon guard slowly riding through the camp on his bike. Soon our supplies of bully beef ran out and the Japs even rationed our rice.

Atap huts at Tarmakan POW camp on the Burma–Siam Railway (*author's collection*)

SIAM (THAILAND)

Lieutenant-Colonel Philip Toosey, 135th Field Regiment, Royal Artillery
POW from February 1942 to August 1945
Camp 249, Tamarkan

When we arrived in the camp there was already a small party of anti-aircraft gunners, led by Major Roberts, and I was subsequently joined by most of the 2nd Battalion of the Gordon Highlanders and the 2nd Battalion of the Argyll and Sutherland Highlanders, Captain Boyle of the Argyll and Sutherland Highlanders, Captain H S Wood, RASC, and again my Adjutant, Captain Northcote. Fortunately for us David Boyle had learned some simple Japanese when he was in prison in Kuala Lumpur. For the rest of the duration of our prisoner-of-war existence he acted as my interpreter and did a most wonderful job. At one stage, when he told them exactly what I thought of them, in Japanese, he had one of his arms broken, and two ribs, by the butt of a rifle. But he was a very brave man. He had in fact won an MC during the campaign itself.

THE DUTCH EAST INDIES

Pilot Officer Erroll David Shearn, Royal Air Force
POW from March 1942 to August 1945
Camp 356 ('the Lyceum'), Sourabaya, East Java

On my arrival at the Lyceum, soaking wet (it was pouring with rain), Humphrey Douglas Wightwick, who afterwards became a valued friend, took pity on me and lent me dry clothes so that I had a more comfortable night than I otherwise would have done. I dossed down on a tiled verandah, which I found uncommonly hard and unyielding. A wooden floor, I discovered later, was apparently much more yielding and in consequence less uncomfortable. We organized ourselves as best we could and arranged that one officer each day should clean up the room we occupied. The 'order of batting' was arrived to by drawing names out of a hat. A colourful Australian, Pennifold, always called 'Penny', was the first to have to do the chores. He made a tremendous fuss and groused like anything. He, so he said, wasn't used to being a 'bloody skivvy', and so forth. I offered quite seriously to do his work for him. In reply I was assured that he could adjectively do the job as well as anyone else and if I thought he wanted to 'scrimshank' or dodge the column I was making an adjectival mistake. After that relief to his feelings he gave up grousing and got on with the job.

Captain Arthur Geoffrey Threadgold, Royal Artillery
POW from March 1942 to August 1945
Camp 354, Boei Glodok, Batavia

Behind these walls one began to feel like a convict, but concerts, church parades and room inspections reminded us that we were still British soldiers and airmen. (There were a lot of RAF in Glodok.)

About September 1942 the Japs called for a draft of troops to go overseas – where we knew not as yet, but together with over 800 others I volunteered, mainly to get out of this damned prison. Together with two other officers of 242 Battery, Lieutenants Bill and Nicholas, we left Glodok with elements of other artillery regiments and RAF personnel.

We left Java on the *Nagara Maru* bound for Singapore, where we docked on 25 September 1942, then after disembarking were marched to Selarang Barracks, Changi, a place of ill fame as it was here that the Japs forced their captives under duress to sign the oath of allegiance to the Imperial Japanese Army (Dai Nippon Gun) – promising to obey all orders, not to escape, etc.

JAPAN

Gunner Frederick Hawkes Thompson, Royal Artillery
POW from March 1942 to August 1945
Wakayama Camp, Japan

Random thoughts written on 7 August 1944 while in POW Japan. Today is Bank Holiday Monday and our 'Yasme' [Rest] Day – we have just finished our midday meal. Outside it is pouring with rain. Last night we had a terrific gale – consequently there are lots of slates off the roof – and so the roof leaks. At present I am sitting on my bed space. On either side of me are great pools of water – my own little domain getting away with a steady drip – and I am keeping my fingers crossed that I shall have a dry bed tonight. The atmosphere is intensely depressing – everyone seems to be numbed and too fed up to speak.

The water has been off all day – so we have had no tea (green leaves in hot water) since this morning. The soup, almost devoid of vegetables, amounted to a small mug – the rice a very small bowl.

The food – never good – is steadily deteriorating. For weeks we had only pumpkin for vegetables and our meals have been just rice, soup and boiled beans, all steadily declining in both quality and quantity.

Somehow we manage to cope, but we have all been asking ourselves the same ominous question. How long before complete physical collapse? For two-and-a-half years we have lived on a diet consisting almost entirely of rice

– which is quite OK as long as you have other food to go with it. Here you just don't get the other food. Consequently almost the entire camp is sick. We feel that the Nip QM is robbing us, as things are getting desperately scarce.

Speaking for myself, my mind just feels dead – I have long ago given up worrying and fretting over food and conditions. This life teaches one not to hope for or expect anything – it avoids disappointments – and one must take things as they come.

I feel desperately hungry – but somehow it doesn't hurt anymore – it's the natural feeling.

Today I don't even feel depressed. I just can't attempt to explain my emotions – they are just non-existent.

Although there are officially about 60 sick in the camp of 400 men, there is only 10% who are reasonably fit. They are the cooks and permanent staff.

Tomorrow when we go out to work (night shift for me) we will walk there in a dream and, generally speaking, just plod our way blindly through the shift. What little good our food does us just about halved through stomach troubles and diarrhoea, which every one of us suffers from. It is one of the biggest problems and curses in the camp.

I am just going to write home and tell them a pack of lies – I'm in excellent health and spirits – What a joke! Then I will smoke half a 'tailor made' to make me dizzy and put my hunger off. Tomorrow I hope to do well with dog ends and so help my ration of fags out.

The next thing to do is to get one's head down and try to sleep. One can forget so much asleep – it's the best thing to do – then wake up for the next tiny meal – a walk round – then 'tenko' and bed.

What a life. Not a life – mere existence. But why worry? – things will turn out OK I know, and as long as I can get through with no lasting ill-effects I'm content to wait on patiently – and even under these hellish conditions, I can sympathize with the inhabitants of this poverty-stricken country. They must stop here – I can and will go back to LIFE!

Lieutenant Stephen Abbott, East Surrey Regiment
POW from February 1942 to August 1945
Official Debriefing Report on No 7 Despatch Camp, Chi, Japan
As compared with what I have heard from other camps, treatment of officers here since January 1944 has been good. On three occasions the Japanese authorities have threatened to place officers on half rations if we refuse to do a certain amount of light work such as gardening. On each occasion we refused to do so. They did actually put us on half rations for a period of two

weeks. When they saw, however, that we did not intend to submit to this kind of treatment they once again increased our rations. When they did this we volunteered to carry out spare-time gardening work. During the later months it was the practice to hold a conference each month with the Nippon camp commandant and his sergeant. At these conferences matters of general routine and treatment were discussed fairly and fully and very good results were obtained. The atmosphere at these conferences was most friendly and I honestly believe that the opportunity which they gave us to explain our point of view round a table was one of the best and fairest moves the Japanese made in this camp.

5

FOOD, DRINK, CLOTHES AND TOBACCO

'I was in Germany for nearly nine months; during this time there were only two occasions when I was not actually hungry'
– Royal Navy POW

While the question always uppermost in the mind of prisoners was when the war would end, and with it their captivity, the major determining factor in POW existence – 'kriegiedom', they called it in Germany – was food. 'FOOD' in capital letters, quotation marks and italics, underlined, and in Technicolor, wide screen and stereophonic sound. The reason for this was not greed, but continual hunger. Article 11 of the POW Code stipulated that the food given to prisoners of war should be equivalent in quantity and quality to that given to the depot troops of the captor. In other words, they should eat as well (or as badly) as the men guarding them. The responsibility for cooking the rations in communal kitchens, and for distributing them, was to be shared between captor and captive, but prisoners were also entitled to some means of preparing themselves any extra food they had. They were also to be given adequate drinking water and allowed tobacco. All collective disciplinary measures affecting food were prohibited.

The Articles that followed laid down that clothing, including underwear and footwear, should all be supplied by the captor and that prisoners on working parties should receive whatever kit the nature of their employment required. Clothes should be regularly replaced and repaired. All camps should have canteens where prisoners could buy, at local prices, food, drink and useful articles such as toiletries. The profit made from the canteens should be used for the benefit of the prisoners.

For the vast majority, however, little of this came to pass. While they were in transit, army prisoners rarely received enough food and water, partly because the supply lines of the advancing armies that overran them were not geared towards feeding prisoners on the move, particularly when they were captured in large numbers; but also, as some prisoners reasoned, because keeping them hungry and thirsty made them easier to manage and less likely to escape, as well as diminishing their morale. However, air force and navy prisoners captured in small numbers tended to receive better rations (though that isn't saying very much). The amount and quality of food increased once they reached a permanent camp. But even these terms are relative, and in any case supplies fluctuated as the fortunes of the detaining power waxed and waned.

What was happening, in effect, was that the detaining powers were feeding their prisoners on the lowest scale of rations, those of a non-working civilian, though even the most bone-idle could not have survived on them for long. Lucky were those prisoners who worked on farms for good employers, as generally they were better fed – although, again, that wasn't saying much. After the war, having for years fed their prisoners as cheaply as possible, the former Axis powers made astronomical claims for POW food and accommodation, expecting to be fully reimbursed.

In practice, Allied prisoners of war were charity cases, with the bulk of their food (at least in Germany and Italy) coming from Red Cross parcels when really the contents of these parcels were only intended as a supplement to their standard rations – in other words, a luxury rather than, as it turned out, a necessity. After the war, most ex-POWs from the European camps readily admitted that they owed their lives to the Red Cross, and not to the efforts of their captors or, indeed, of their own government. Even so, prisoners in Europe had it much better than the Far Eastern POWs, most of whom never saw a Red Cross food or clothing parcel in three and a half years.

GERMANY AND OCCUPIED POLAND

The basic food ration for prisoners in the Greater Reich was soup – soup yesterday, soup today, and soup for ever more. It consisted mostly of hot water with (and often without) dehydrated soup mixes. There were, of course, local variations. Sometimes a little potato or kohlrabi could be detected drifting near the bottom, more rarely a few pieces of meat. (When there was no meat the Germans would tell their prisoners it was 'a meatless day', but as meat was the exception rather than the rule the excuse was regarded as some kind of German joke, and not a very funny one.) This unappetizing and unsatisfying concoction was cooked in the communal kitchens and distributed with other rations, if there were any, at mid-morning, lunchtime or mid-afternoon. The staple ration in German camps otherwise consisted of black bread, 'eating fat' (a lard-like butter), artificial jam and root crops, usually blighted or rotten. These were always given out grudgingly and the scale could be reduced at any time, sometimes to zero.

During the summer of 1940, when Germany took Allied prisoners in droves, the rations were so exiguous that prisoners could not even walk up and down stairs without blacking out, and hundreds collapsed during roll-calls. Thousands of prisoners – officers as well as NCOs and other ranks – began to show the first signs of malnutrition. Lying on their bunks, they tortured themselves by imagining the wonderful dishes they would eat on returning home. Cigarettes and tobacco were also in short supply (apart from thousands of Player's captured by the Germans at Dunkirk the only smokes available were almost-hollow Polish cigarettes and rancid French cheroots), and the only clothes they had were those they stood up in.

The camp canteens were also a swindle, charging prisoners extortionate prices for such basics items as combs, hair tonic and non-alcoholic beer and levying a form of VAT.

The cost of all these items – food, accommodation, canteen purchases – was being automatically deducted from the prisoners' pay back home, so that the detaining powers could be reimbursed after the war. But the amounts deducted were greater than the value of any services that the prisoners received, and in any case the former warring governments each decided to waive their claims. HM Treasury did not, however, pay the prisoners back; it simply kept the money.

POLAND

Private Alfred Charles Bryant, The Buffs
POW from July 1940 to May 1945
Stalag XXA, Thorn (Toruń)
When we had rested from being processed after our arrival about 300 of us were given work to do, which was the building of the Danzig–Berlin road. We started work just after daybreak and worked until it was nearly dark. We had very little food. At twelve each day the water wagon would come round (it was called 'The Soup Cart') and we were given a small amount of soup consisting of greasy water with swedes floating on the top. When we returned to the camp we were given a slice of bread and a small piece of fat about the size of a postage stamp. If you did not eat it immediately someone else would steal it. When the harvest was ready some men were sent to work on the farms.

Gunner Cyril George King, Royal Artillery (Territorial)
POW from May 1940 to April 1945
Stalag XXIB, Schubin

Meals at that camp were very simple. Breakfast consisted of a bowl of ersatz brown coffee without sugar or milk. At midday the previous year's potatoes were loaded straight into large cauldrons where they were boiled in their own dirty scum along with the large black flies which often settled on the top. As far as possible the skins of these potatoes were eaten, for they provided more bulk for one's stomach. The pint of thin vegetable soup which accompanied them certainly did not. In the evening we were issued with two each of the large Polish army biscuits, which contained caraway seeds. They were coarse and hard and eaten along with a very small piece of sausage meat. Such was our daily diet.

It must be remembered that it was to be a long time before Red Cross parcels were received or parcels from family – a limited amount could eventually be sent to us through the Red Cross, but of course many of these never arrived.

Some men, who had been shell-shocked or rendered slightly simple by the conditions in which they were living, insisted on hoarding potato peelings, cabbage stalks or anything else which they could lay their hands on in the vicinity of the cookhouse. Their beds smelled foul, as did the clothing of their owners, and no doubt was one of the causes of the appearance of lice. I was disgusted and filled with loathing at first, but soon learned to sit with the others and rid myself temporarily of the vermin, which lurked in my sweat-sodden shirt and trousers.

After perhaps two weeks the authorities of the camp began to call for volunteers for working parties, and although the suggestion appeared at first to be repugnant I could see quite plainly that it would be better to make some kind of choice rather than be forced out. In any case Jack (the Royal Engineers sergeant who had accompanied me since France) was an NCO and was not obliged to work, so that it would be of no use attempting to stay with him. Accordingly I attached myself to a party some 40 strong which was to be commanded by a Pipe Major and destined for a village called Windhoek, Polish name Bartchin. Jack was disappointed with my decision but could see my reasoning and in due course we parted company.

Before our departure it was necessary to provide us with certain items of kit. There were very few of us who owned a complete uniform and so there were many who were issued with Polish army jackets, trousers, very light overcoats and caps. My boots had completely worn through and so I received a pair of Dutch wooden clogs. It took some time to get used to these as I had no socks, only rags to wrap around my feet, and the rough edges of the clogs rubbed one's insteps until it was found that there was a certain way to lift one's feet.

Pilot Officer Maurice George Butt, Royal Air Force Volunteer Reserve
POW from August 1940 to May 1945
Fort 15 (Stalag XXA), Thorn, March–July 1941
The level of diet was, in accordance with the Geneva Convention, to be on a scale comparable to garrison troops. In reality, the German army could not possibly have depended on the fighting ability of their men on this diet – unless it was devised to ensure they resorted to their own initiative to supplement supplies.

The food situation was a dominant thought in most minds. Hunger concentrates the mind on its own relief. The low diet was a cause for concern and indeed it is a well-known fact that Red Cross parcels saved the lives of so many, and, too, avoided the abject misery of prolonged starvation. Like most problems, the human being adjusts to a situation until such time that changes can be made. The phases of change to starvation are initially over-consciousness of hunger for which the only compensation is excessive intake of fluid, after everything in sight has been consumed. Some individuals exercised supreme restraint and managed to save part of the bread ration (a fifth of a loaf a day) overnight for breakfast. Most didn't, and some of those who did, got up in the night to finish it off in case mice intervened, or even in case there was no tomorrow.

The next phase of hunger, after any accumulated fat on the body had been consumed, is a considerable weakening in both physical and mental capacity. The warning signs are a tendency to black out when getting out of bed or standing up from a chair. These are nature's warning signs to throttle back, as it were, on excessive movement. Hence relaxed postures become a necessity which developed into habits of resignation and in some cases despair. The real answer at that point is regular but short sessions of simple walking in fresh air to maximize a 'ticking over' of one's engine, and so avoid atrophy of muscles.

At Toruń, or Thorn as it was then on the British atlas, the prospect of Red Cross parcels ever arriving to relieve the situation was almost ruled out. What accentuated the food problem was the potatoes which had come out of winter store (it was late February when we arrived) and were delivered in bulk into a magazine, an unventilated underground store room – and having been poorly harvested, the potatoes were half rotten from exposure to frost and green from light exposure too. The swedes were similarly frostbitten, and together these stank to permeate half the rooms in the camp. This obviously caused a natural revulsion to these two vegetables which often formed the basis of a speciality soup served up by the cookhouse each lunchtime.

One day we were given a ration of dog biscuits, the three-and-a-half-inch square type, and this proved a great psychological boost, an inversion to incredulity that we should have these instead of bread. The war must be ending, the last crusts of bread being reserved for the VIPs of the Fatherland. Much merriment sponsored these wild speculations, until we considered what would be the next step when the biscuit supply was exhausted. Some people actually broke teeth biting these rocklike bricks of rye. The best way of consuming them was found to be by soaking them and then boiling up the mess – mixing anything available with the mash such as sugar or jam, though availability was the key.

Boiling up had to be, as all water was suspect and highly chlorinated. The Medical Officer (MO) was hot on that. To generate heat for boiling up was another problem as the fuel supply was briquet coal, strictly rationed. Several methods of breaking up dog biscuits were tried, including rolling a glass bottle to crush up the bits. This took an incredible time, of which we had spare. However, on reflection, it was some days before soaking was considered a feasible proposition, which highlighted our culinary ignorance.

Then one day, the rumour came through from the *Kommandantur*, the office which controlled the camp, a building a mile away with huts for interpreters, etc, that Red Cross parcels were on the way. Our spirits soared. Our lethargy forgotten, there were smiling faces to be seen all around. It was indeed a breath of spring.

Rumour became reality on this score, and within two days a wagonload of parcels arrived and crossed the bridge over the empty moat to the cheers of all on hand. We slept better that night.

The farm wagon's first appearance previously was two days after our arrival, to collect the spoils of the arrival search, the items of clothing and other possessions considered contraband. Whenever we left a camp, it meant a search of our possessions on departure, and that didn't take too long in the earlier years, and another more thorough search at the new camp. There were different standards of security at the various camps. Often the searchers didn't seem to know what they were looking for. It became a game of some skill and ingenuity to get obvious items through the search. Compasses, maps, the camp radio, tools acquired from workmen or fashioned from bits and pieces found lying around, printing ink, civilian clothes, anything of use to escapers, all had to be smuggled out, and into the new camp. The drill was to be organized, the theory to wear the German searchers down and detect the easiest one to get things past. Hence the first group to be searched never had anything important to get past, and so the form of the searchers was tested.

Fort 15 at Thorn in Poland: one of several underground fortresses used as a *Straflager* by the Germans in 1941 (*author's collection*)

On Day One at Thorn, we were all herded out for roll-call to be counted and searched. Immediately we found that Irvin flying jackets – the fleece-lined sheepskin leather jackets – were being confiscated. I well remember the remonstrations of one young navigator who was most reluctant to part company with his.

Realizing I was next on call, I decided to test the *Abort* (lavatory) arrangements as a means of avoidance, and in no time was being escorted by an armed guard (*Postern*) down the long tunnel. I realized the only hope was to leave my flying jacket in the loo. Before reaching it, the heads of two army orderlies appeared around the door of what transpired to be the cookhouse. 'Everything all right Sir?' they asked – having heard the marching feet of the goons and I approaching it had primed their curiosity. 'Can you hide my jacket?' I asked, and they laughed with joy to be doing something against the enemy. Hence, on the way back from the loo, I outpaced the middle-aged guard, dashed into the kitchen and flung the jacket into the helping hands of a cook orderly. Just in time, before the alarmed guard came in rifle at the ready, I pretended to be trying to scrounge a drink, and the guard was so relieved, he didn't notice my jacket had gone – into an empty cold oven in fact. I collected it later, having managed to wangle a large metal file and a crossbow saw through the search.

The following day, the farm wagon made its first appearance to collect a whole heap of flying jackets, tools, and so-called civilian clothing. I was lucky to be on hand as the wagon was leaving with its load down the long sloping tunnel towards the bridge over the dry moat. A quick appraisal showed a driver with three armed guards. Just by the exit from the tunnel was a staircase either side leading to the semi-underground rooms. Without a diversion to distract the guards, I managed to grab two jackets, having walked alongside the wagon for ten yards or so, and dashed down the staircase amid a roaring of enraged guards. In no time a search was mounted, but it was rather half-hearted, and so I became a baron of jackets – two flying jackets and a black leather belted motoring coat confiscated from an army type by the Germans. The latter jacket I hung on to through all subsequent searches, and eventually gave it away to the driver who took us to the airfield in Belgium on our way home four years later. The history of getting the three jackets through many searches would make a chapter of reading. The main ploy was always to study the searchers and spot the one who was either tiring of his task or rather cursory and disenchanted with his remit.

Of course, the really important things like radio, civilian clothes, maps and tools were being got through by the responsible escape officer of each hut or group, and this was done with much resolution by way of arranged diversions or even bribes. The most helpful asset was to apply a stance of calm and relaxation to the point of boredom. Casualness was the key to all successful escaping activities, particularly when challenged.

Later, when we left Thorn, the problem of the jackets was simply resolved by the Germans providing crates for our heavier items of equipment, record players, library books and personal clothing. This latter item came about because after nearly a year in prison following the fall of France, the longer-stay or 'older' prisoners had received clothing parcels from home via the agency of the Red Cross and quite clearly could not carry all their possessions. Perhaps it was the influence of the American Ambassador's visit earlier on, but by requesting provision of packaging, the Senior British Officer got the request granted. By luck, the three jackets were placed at the bottom of a wooden crate to be filled by another older prisoner, and whilst we made use of the fact that the packing of the crate was not supervised, we needed another diversion to get the coats into the next camp.

GERMANY

Flying Officer Michael Heriot Roth, Royal Air Force
POW from May 1940 to May 1945
Oflag XC, Lübeck, July–October 1941
By far the greater number of kriegies at Lübeck were British army officers, some captured on Crete, others in Albania. Their train journey to Lübeck had taken days and days in overcrowded cattle trucks, with so little food or water that many had died. After the ordeal of that terrible journey, to them Lübeck was a paradise. To us, after Barth, it was hell. They told us that a few days before we'd arrived an RAF bomber had dropped a stick of incendiary bombs right along the outside perimeter of the camp, completely destroying the German officers' mess, and wounding a few kriegies in the camp hospital. This incident accounted for the extreme personal hostility of the local goons. The day after the raid the commandant had posted sentries inside the camp with fixed bayonets and orders to shoot kriegies on the slightest provocation. Happily for the kriegies, a German inspecting general came to report on the damage, saw the guards inside the compound, and immediately threw them out. He then gave the commandant, *Oberst* von Wachtmeister, a terrific raspberry. Wachtmeister was a senile, hateful old basket – he had to stand to attention at the salute for twenty minutes while the general gave him his 'cigar' (the German expression for a severe reprimand) right in front of the kriegies. Served him right. He was the most hated man around. He always

shuffled about in his First Great War uniform trailing a nickel-plated sword scabbard. On one day entering the compound, he caught the flukes of his scabbard in the barbed wire, wrested it free, then got it between his own legs and tripped and fell to the round. He was livid, since he was seen by dozens of grinning kriegies. Morale rose a point – a long malicious laugh enjoyed by all. One of life's highlights at the time.

Aside from the bloody-minded attitude of Wachtmeister and his goons, the worst thing about Lübeck was the hunger trouble, made more intense by the lack of books. Wachtmeister had confiscated them as a personal reprisal for the RAF raid; what had angered him most was the total destruction of his wine cellar. Wachtmeister further refused to inform the Red Cross at Geneva of the existence of the camp, so we were denied this source of possible supplementary rations. The official German rations were about half what they should have been: the *Feldwebel* in charge of the cookhouse and our rations was a thief who, aided and abetted by the administration, kept back half for his own trading operations on the Lübeck black market. The weekly sausage and margarine ration for 500 kriegies – small though it was when divided – made a sizeable amount for barter when in one piece. We complained about this to the German officer in charge of our company (the RAF were quartered apart from the army). He investigated our complaint, found it true, and said: '*Es ist ein Schweinerei,*' meaning literally it was the sort of conduct one would only expect from a pig. He at once protested on our behalf to the commandant and quoted German Army Regulations. Wachtmeister had to yield. From then on, our own kriegie representatives divided the rations and took over the operation of the cookhouse.

In some small way we benefited from Wachtmeister's corrupt administrative staff. It sold us – at fantastic prices – through the canteen items such as fig biscuits, gherkins, pickles, ersatz tomato and Worcestershire sauces, plus German mustard made by the Popp and Popp Chemical Company in Hamburg. Obviously our *Lagergeld* was still backed by genuine currency, and the middlemen were making a packet. Along with the meagre bread ration and daily spud, these condiments became part of the monotonous diet. Each kriegie had his own eating plan: I ate one very thin slice each of potato, with gherkin, mustard and ketchup; cutting each so-loaded slice into four, I would literally chew each mouthful thirty-two times – a health hint of Prime Minister Gladstone's. Some kriegies bashed their daily rations at one swoop, leaving nothing to look forward to for the next twenty-four hours. Others got so hungry they were not above pinching each other's grub – inevitable under conditions of extreme hunger. Some kriegies foolishly swapped their bread for cigarettes: their craving for smokes being greater than their hunger.

Even though cooking in the huts was forbidden, a few made small stick fires in the latrines (we actually had flush toilets at Lübeck), on which they tried to make their bread rations more palatable by frying them in fat. I recall seeing one poor sod drop his bread into the urinal by accident; he quickly retrieved it, shook it off, refried and then ate the soggy mass. Three others, prompted by a streak of sadism as well as hunger, stalked and captured what was believed to be the commandant's cat. They battered it to death in the latrine with heavy stones and then tried to cook it – a cruel and horrible débâcle. It was a tough brute and defied all efforts to make it edible. Its executioners were not hungry enough to eat it raw.

Private Kenneth ('Kim') Stalder, Royal Army Medical Corps
POW from May 1941 to April 1945
Stalag IIIE, Kirchhain, and Stalag VIIIB, Lamsdorf
In my years as a POW – that's four years – I only ever got two parcels of fags and one clothes parcel. When I came out of hospital in 1946 I weighed only 5½ stone – the effect of long-term starvation. I was still skinny and was allowed to draw three times the normal rations.

Pilot Officer Idrwerth Patrick ('Paddy') Bentley Denton, Royal Air Force Volunteer Reserve
POW from July 1941 to May 1945
Oflag VIB, Warburg, October 1941–September 1942
We had a bit of a party one night in one hut, which was divided from the famous *aborts* by a rather dirty, slushy ditch with a very narrow planked footbridge over it. One good friend enjoyed his liquor and decided that come what may nature must take its course. It was a cold night and for one reason or another he slipped and fell on the little bridge and into the muddy water. Quite undeterred he walked, having pulled himself together, somewhat damp and muddy, to the bog where he sat in pensive mood. After some time his absence was noticed by one of the more observant of the party. Thinking that he might have gone astray two or three of us, in Samaritan fashion, went to find him. This we did, still sitting paralysed, quite unable to move and claiming that he had gone blind. He did recover his sight in about 24 hours but we were a little disturbed next morning to find that our chateau-bottled booze had attacked the galvanizing in the container in which we had made it. A salutary lesson, as otherwise we might have made ourselves ill on further occasions.

Red Cross parcels store at Stalag Luft III (*author's collection*)

Lieutenant-Commander Hugo H Bracken, Royal Navy
POW from July 1941 to April 1945
Dulag Luft, Oflag XC, Oflag VIB, Stalag Luft III

The Red Cross claim that parcels were released from stock at the rate of one per week gives the impression that the prisoners received parcels at that rate in the camps. That is absolute nonsense. I got part of a parcel in Dulag Luft [in August 1941] and then nothing while I was at Oflag XC, Lübeck, until I reached Oflag VIB, Warburg, at the end of October. After Stalag Luft III was evacuated at the end of January 1945 until we reached the United Kingdom in June I never saw a Red Cross parcel. In between those dates the issue of Red Cross parcels never exceeded one per room per week, or between one-eighth or one-twelfth of a parcel per man per week. I have checked this with a number of POWs, who are in general agreement with this. Had we received one parcel each per week we would all have needed a long course with Weight Watchers when we got home. Also I can recall only seeing one or two British Red Cross parcels; virtually all were either Canadian or American in Stalag Luft III.

There were from time to time rumours that the Germans had pinched some of them. These were investigated and proved to be unfounded. On the other hand, to our shame, it is a fact that Red Cross parcels were subject to a certain amount of pilfering by dockers in this country and elsewhere.

Sub-Lieutenant Maurice Driver, Royal Navy
POW August 1940 to April 1945
East Compound, Stalag Luft III, Sagan

Wine making and spirit distilling were carried out by many people in the camp. I first attempted to produce alcohol by chewing potatoes and fermenting the chewed pulp. This is a procedure well known to anthropologists and which can be explained through the presence of a starch-splitting enzyme, ptyalin, in saliva. I remember the attempt quite well – Rupert Davies and I sat outside one of the huts chewing and spitting to produce a large bowlful of frothy liquid. I don't remember that we fermented it by itself – probably we mixed it with raisins and then distilled the fermented mixture. I tended to produce a more potable distillate than many of those engaged in this activity as I took precautions to minimize the presence of poisonous alcohols in the final product. My most abiding memory of this business is the loss of much of what I had distilled through the German guards' thievery while we were outside the huts during roll-call.

Lieutenant-Commander William Stephens, Royal Naval Volunteer Reserve
POW from March 1942 to October 1942
Marlag und Milag Nord, Sandbostel

Boredom is one of the things from which one suffers most of all. Each day is exactly the same as the preceding one, and one really lives almost entirely for mail and food. To anybody who has not been a prisoner of war this is probably difficult to understand, but you are always hungry, which means that you spend most of the time thinking about your next meal; and you are always longing for news and parcels from home, which keeps you wondering when the next mail is going to arrive.

I was in Germany for nearly nine months; during this time there were only two occasions when I was not actually hungry. The first was when I escaped with fourteen days' rations on my back and was recaptured after five days; I ate the remaining nine days' rations between the time of being captured and arriving at the local police station – this lasted about half an hour and the results were disastrous. The only other occasion was when I had my birthday. It was a great tradition amongst all British prisoners that anyone having a birthday should be given a really enormous supper; to this end the table at which one normally fed would save as much as they could for the big night.

All this talk about food, or rather lack of food, is not intended to be in any way an unfavourable criticism of the Red Cross, who do the most wonderful work and without whose aid we should undoubtedly have all starved.

Lack of cigarettes was for many of us even worse than lack of food, but here some French colonial troops, who were in the next compound, helped us a lot. They used to throw packets across the barbed wire to us – much to the fury of the guards. The procedure was quite a funny one. The two compounds marched with each other for about twenty-five yards, and one sentry was on this beat, fortunately for us on the French side of the wire. One of the Frenchmen used to start the game by chucking us a packet when he knew the guard could see him but when he was also far enough away to make sure he wouldn't get a rifle butt in his head. The guards invariably rose to this bait and gave chase; just as they started to run someone else would throw another packet over and the Hun would change his mind and dash for the new miscreant. Complete chaos reigned, and cigarettes poured over the wire to us. The party usually ended by the sentry firing his rifle in the air and everybody running in all directions. Once we nearly had a tragedy when an infuriated sentry did manage to get someone on the head with the butt of his rifle. Although I think he will carry the mark for the rest of his days, his head must have been a thick one, because it didn't kill him and neither did it stop our supply of cigarettes.

Sapper Don Luckett, Royal Engineers
POW from July 1941 to May 1945
Stalag XVIIIA, Wolfsberg, Austria
The cry of 'Grub up' brought the men tumbling out of the tents in double-quick time to form a queue in front of two large containers. The people who were ladling the food out looked like German kitchen staff, and they gave to each man a fair ration of mashed potato and boiled cabbage, the food being dumped into whatever sort of container we possessed, be it tin plate, mess tins, or as one man was using, the shell of his tin helmet, this to the chagrin of the guards who stood nearby. As each man received his share, he went into the tent and settled into the straw to eat of the meal. All seemed to agree that if this was the standard of food and accommodation it augured well for the future. Owing to the sort of diet we had existed on over the past months, the sudden influx of solid food proved to be too much for our shrunken stomachs, so the food had to be left and put on the side, to be consumed later. This meal was one of the two we were to receive as a solid meal during our entire stay, as the type of food to come was of a 'sloppy' nature, and only required a spoon to devour same.

Major Elliott Viney, Oxford & Bucks Light Infantry
POW from June 1940 to May 1945
Oflag VIIB, Eichstätt, Bavaria
Till nearly the end we were living comparatively well, getting one Canadian Red Cross parcel a week, not individually – they were all pooled – and each small group organized its own cooking. The Germans still issued rations as provided by the Geneva Convention, usually a mug of acorn 'coffee' at 7 am (I often used it for shaving), soup and a fifth of a bitter brown loaf. I wish I had a list of the contents of a standard parcel; although all tinned, it had been carefully devised to give a balanced diet and on the whole we kept very fit with plenty of exercise. Every room had a small stove for heat and cooking, but coal was infrequent, consequently the many references to wood and fir-cone collecting.

ITALY

As in the Third Reich, the main ration for POWs in Italy was soup, served with bread, and either with or as an alternative to rice (in the north) or macaroni (in the south). 'After the war, I never want to see macaroni again as long as I live,' wrote one British prisoner. In some camps, especially during the summer, prisoners were able to buy local produce, including fresh fruit, at reasonable prices (although the prices became less reasonable as time went on, rationing was introduced, and both sides took advantage of the opportunities for corruption).

On the whole, however, POW rations in Italy were slightly more generous and nourishing than those in Germany, owing to the Italians' own passion for food and their reluctance to see anyone starve. The hunger that prisoners endured sprang largely from enemy incompetence and a reluctance to be hurried, although a vengeful *commandante* might cut, withdraw or tamper with rations as a reprisal for escape attempts – a practice far more common in Germany.

Private Maurice Newey, Royal Army Ordnance Corps
POW from June 1942 to April 1945
Campo 54, Fara Sabina (Rome)
The Eyeties were having trouble getting the parcels to the camp, so we were rationed to half a parcel a week. Although receiving three letters a month, that January [1943] was very miserable. The heavy smokers were reduced to drying tea leaves and rolling them in paper (sometimes leaves from the Bible) to try to assuage their craving for tobacco. I was very thankful I was a non-smoker. When I did have cigarettes I used them for bartering purposes. Some chaps preferred cigarettes to food. One entrepreneur set up an exchange and mart business, where tins of food could be bought for cigarettes or a straight exchange could be made.

Lance-Corporal Lawrence Bains, Middlesex Yeomanry
POW from June 1942 to August 1944
Campo PG 66, Capua
We had coffee at 0630 hours and our first issue of dry food was bread and cheese at 1000 hours; the loaves were pitifully small, varying in weight, and the slice of cheese was only a taste, and we did not get any on meat days, ie, Thursdays and Sundays. At 1130 hours we drew our midday soup – very thin stuff whose main constituent was olive oil, with a little mixed vegetable floating about, and sometimes flavoured with tomato puree. On meat days this was supplemented by a bully tin full of good meat and vegetable stew, very tasty, although often the former was noticeable for its absence or rarity. On meat days the normal soup would be issued first, and then we would queue again with our mess tins to receive a small share of stew, and much speculation was aroused – whether we would strike lucky for meat or not. After several weeks the two 'courses' were combined and the lottery became even more adventurous.

The evening meal, issued between 1600 and 1630 hours, was the usual rice or macaroni vegetable stew, but was very liquid at times; this reached such a pitch that one fellow caused much amusement by finding one piece of macaroni in his issue. There was always plenty of vegetable, varying with the different seasons – eggfruit was one of the most popular – and new to us – and tomato puree helped to add flavour to the meal. We used to get between a third and a half of an Italian mess tin, but the majority of this was 'gypo', which we used to drain off first and then tackle the remaining rice and vegetables as a second course, occasionally sprinkling it with our issue cheese, grated.

The above was the total rations we got from the Italians, with the exception of fruit and vegetable issues. These took place every day or so, and we got several apples or a peach or a handful of tomatoes. These last were very plentiful at times and formed an important part of our diet, and I became very fond of cheese and tomato spread, finding it tasty and satisfying.

The evening meal was brought to our tent lines in small square dixies, and our group sergeant, Cutting, used to ladle it out. It was soon found that those first in the queue got mostly vegetables and gypo, whilst those at the back had nearly all rice or macaroni, with the obvious result that people began to hang back so as to draw a more substantial meal. This eventually reached such a pitch that a rota was drawn up and we drew food answering to our names. The rations never worked out exactly; there were usually five or six buckshees, and these also were worked off the rota. As far as our group, and most of the others, was concerned, the rations were issued fairly and without fiddling on the part of the sergeant.

A word about the cookhouse staff would be in season. In all previous camps, with the sole exception of Trig Tarhuna, the cookhouses had been the scenes of the worst and most open corruption I have ever seen, so all eyes were turned most anxiously towards the cooks in this camp, particularly when it appeared our stay might be prolonged. Fortunately corruption, though it existed, was, as far as I could see, mild. The cooks, of course, had as much thick rice and cheese as they desired, but, after all, the amount that 20 to 30 men can eat out of 2,000-odd men's rations is small, and they were the only ones doing any physical work; this included those aristocrats of prison life, the wood choppers. One or two others also had generous rations, such as the Regimental Sergeant Major (RSM) and favoured Sergeant Majors, interpreters, etc, and some of that low type which always hangs around cookhouses and pals up with the cooks. The concert party and organizers, on show nights, drew buckshees, as did boxing entrants … Summing up, one could say that there definitely was graft, but on a far smaller scale than at any other previous camp.

The chief racket was in connection with the bread. In Africa loaves were counted on our strength, but in Italy the bread, always slightly underweight, was weighed, so a surplus number of loaves resulted. In all fairness, I think employed men ought to draw larger rations, but here the cooks and their associates could have just what they chose, and large numbers of loaves were sold each day for cigarettes, the price varying between ten and 20 Player's.

There was some connection, though I could never get to the bottom of it, between the senior Regimental Sergeant Major, Holdsworth [of the Northumberland Fusiliers], and the Italians, and one could purchase bread with cigarettes from a small power house which controlled our water supply. Towards the end of our stay, after repeated protests on all sides, 'buckshee bread', ie, that above the number of POWs and the extra for employed men, was issued in turn to groups, but this turn of events must have hit someone badly for the system was dropped before it had even reached our group, No 18. There was a change to potato bread in September, which met with universal approval, as although coarser and less tasty, the loaves were larger and none of us would have refused more food at any time.

On the first Monday of our arrival, 5 August 1942 – a date never to be forgotten – we grouped ourselves together in 'parcel groups' of five, I joining with Bombardier Sadler of South Notts Hussars and three corporals from the 1st Royal Northumberland Fusiliers, Buchanan, Alexander and Anderson. We were told that one parcel would be issued to these groups on Mondays, Wednesdays and Fridays, and we were all agog with excitement, as several labels had been discovered advertising such tantalizing things as sausages, bacon, jam and other foods we had not expected to meet again for some time; several Player's packets were also found.

On the veranda of the canteen, etc, a long trestle table had been erected, and behind it were stacks of mysterious cardboard boxes. We queued up in groups, one representative from each parcel group, and filed forward to draw a box and 50 cigarettes. We then formed up in front of the table and handed our precious cargo to one of the 'stabbers' behind (it was an Italian order that all tins must be stabbed to prevent hoarding with a view to escape). The stabber removed the lid and we saw for the first time what was in our parcel, as he tipped the lot out on to the table, stabbed each tin, and replaced it in the box. On the OK being given by the Italian supervising, we once again stepped forward, took our parcel, and made for our lines at top speed. Once inside our tent we were surrounded by our parcel-mates, and excited discussions as to how we should plan our menu, as the parcel had to last till Wednesday. Different groups adopted different systems, but ours was the usual so I will confine myself to that.

As parcels usually came up before midday soup, we used to combine bread and cheese, soup and something from the parcel in one meal. I remember in our first parcel we had a tin of salmon, so that had to go first, particularly as the weather was very hot in the afternoon. It was only a normal-sized tin and between five was little more than a taste, but to us, who had had nothing but macaroni, rice, biscuits, bread and vegetables for two months, it was the last word in perfection, and most of us used our share as a spread on our bread, for which we also had margarine and jam, to which we helped ourselves from the common tin. In the evening, with a very welcome cup of sweet tea, we had a pound-tin of meat and vegetable between us, leaving us, I believe, bacon and tomatoes for our Tuesday's lunch. In addition to these main items we had three ounces of cheese, half a pound of plain biscuits, a quarter-pound of chocolate and a dozen sweets, all of which we divided up and had when we wanted them. The excitement and enthusiasm over these parcels had to be seen to be believed; they seemed perfection itself and gave us new life and hope, quite apart from the great physical benefit they were to us.

We did not draw these parcels regularly at the rate of three between five a week; sometimes we only drew two, depending on the stocks in hand and probability of fresh supplies. This, of course, gave rise to many weird rumours, and a day never passed without someone on our tent bringing in some 'parcel griff' [rumour].

Private Stanley John Doughty, 12th Royal Lancers
POW from December 1941 to February 1945
Campo PG 66, Capua
The days passed with depressing similarity. The small loaf of chestnut flour bread, and something that passed for coffee in the morning, with a dixie full of cabbage water in the evening. The cooks were British, and by common consent all rations other than bread were put into the stew, since the quantities involved were so small that they couldn't have been divided out fairly otherwise. Officially we were entitled to butter, meat, sugar and macaroni as well – the Italian army ration – but in what quantities we knew not, but presumably they appeared in the stew.

Lieutenant John Pelly, Coldstream Guards
POW from June 1942 to April 1945
Campo PG 21, Chieti
25 August 1942. The 'new boys' are drawing their parcels tomorrow and also cigarettes. Each Bungalow has a Parcel Room here, which is kept locked by

the Italians. In the room are all the parcels that have been issued to the Bungalow, and each officer has his own number on his parcel. The room is opened for an hour each day, during which time one may take out anything, but this must be punctured by the supervising *Carabinieri*, thereby stopping officers from having unopened tins in their possession for escaping. It is a far better system than puncturing all the tins and just handing over the complete parcel all opened up, as in that case one must finish the contents quickly or else it goes bad.

Corporal Eric Barrington, Royal Air Force Police
POW June 1942 to April 1945
Campo PG 73, Carpi (Modena)
Thursday, 7 January 1943. Cut up a large and very strong onion to put in my stew, but it proved too much for me and made my eyes stream, burned my mouth and gave me stomach-ache. We still go on buying the onions, though, in absence of anything better. Fruit seems to have disappeared from the canteen lists and is very dear when it does arrive.

Lieutenant A F ('Junior') Powell, 13th Light Anti-Aircraft Regiment
POW from April 1941 to May 1945
Campo PG 17, Rezzanello
Food was a big item in our lives. At first we got the army ration, but there was no rationing in Italy and the camp could buy extras from a local contractor, Signor Brusamenti. The messing officer could order what was needed to supplement the army rations, but rationing was soon introduced and, for example, our bread ration was decreased from five rolls a day to one and a half. The Red Cross aimed to provide each prisoner with a ten-pound food parcel each week and these came from various sources – England, Scotland, Canada, New Zealand and the British residents in Argentina. I kept a record of the parcels received between September 1942 and May 1945. In those 137 weeks we received 115 parcels, which was a very good record.

All parcels were opened in the presence of an Italian officer. We did not see the parcels or know what was in them, and the meat, fish and vegetable cans were kept by the mess. Any wanted at once were punctured so that they could not be stored for an escape attempt; the others were removed to a store outside. The jams, butter, spreads, etc, were divided up and issued to individual officers for use whenever they wished. Some prisoners received private food parcels but these were few and far between. I received four while in Italy.

Allied prisoners in Italy often reached their new camp to find it not yet built: typical was Campo 73, in Carpi, near Modena, where they had to live in tents (*author's collection*)

Campo 73, once completed, was not much different from any other hutted POW camp (*author's collection*)

THE FAR EAST

In the Japanese camps the basic ration was rice, rice and more rice, often heaving with maggots; one had to shift for oneself and scavenge in the surrounding jungle for ingredients that would make this rice palatable and provide real sustenance.

Mealtimes in the Far East stretched one's ingenuity, and prisoners tried mixing the rice with grass, leaves, molasses, insects, scavenged meat, black-market eggs – anything that would excite the taste buds and, more importantly, prevent, or at least delay, death through starvation and disease.

When food and clothing parcels did arrive, courtesy of the American or Indian Red Cross, they were opened by the Japanese, who blatantly ransacked them and either ate the food themselves or sold it at inflated prices on the black market. Most Far Eastern prisoners had to wait until the Japanese surrender before seeing a food or clothing or tobacco parcel.

HONG KONG

Commander R S Young, Royal Navy
POW from December 1941 to August 1945
Camp 203, North Point, Hong Kong Island, and Shamshuipo, Kowloon
25–30 December 1941. Food was already getting scarce. A little rice was brought in by the Japs daily. Some of us had a few left-over ration tins which friends shared. The Canadian troops would willingly give up any food in exchange for a few cigarettes. Eventually when the latter gave out, they picked bits off the asphalt road to use as chewing gum. By that time they were generally very demoralized. Also dysentery was setting in, and many other diseases, for which no treatment was available.

Incarceration at North Point had seemed an eternity and vastly humiliating. Really we had been marched to Shamshuipo after only five days. We actually stayed at Shamshuipo until 18 April 1942. There were strong feelings about the distribution of the extremely meagre food ration and poor-quality rice supplied. What little there was, was doled out as fairly as possible. Looking out over the harbour it was plain that no Japanese supply ships were arriving. The Japanese themselves must have been pretty short in this non-self-supporting ex-British colony. On 15 February 1942 the fall of Singapore took place. A lot of frontline Japanese troops used in the attack on Hong

Kong had been sent to take part in that campaign. We learnt that millions of the civilian and Chinese population who couldn't flee from Hong Kong were starving, perhaps worse than us.

Lieutenant Harry White, Winnipeg Grenadiers
POW from December 1941 to August 1945
Shamshuipo Barracks, Kowloon
The camp, in the short time that we had been away, had been stripped by the Chinese; the wiring, light fixtures, doors and windows were gone. In fact, anything moveable, and if they'd had another two weeks, they'd have taken the huts too.

There were no cooking facilities. We had very few dishes or cutlery, etc, using tin cans, or a fork or a spoon. We had a few tins of food that we had brought in with us and the Japs brought in some rice. For the first week we had two meals a day – boiled rice with a few greens and a bit of bully beef thrown in, no salt, and tea 'without'.

SINGAPORE

Corporal Charles Kinahan, Straits Settlement Volunteer Force
POW from February 1942 to August 1945
Camp 330, Changi Barracks
My memory of these months in Changi is dominated by hunger. One could think of little else; I dreamt of nice tasty dishes – sausages and mashed potatoes with tomato sauce. We had brought a certain amount of tinned food with us but this did not last long. After that we had little but plain rice. At surrender [in February 1942] I weighed about 170 pounds. By the time we left Changi in early July for Siam I had gone down to 105 pounds and was almost too weak to climb stairs.

The British camp commander's office had collected together odds and ends of food which were not enough to issue as group rations. They used these foods to establish a 'diet centre' to which they sent a few of the most debilitated to give them a few square meals for a few days. I was one of those selected. I subsequently found that the place allocated to me had in fact first been offered to my great friend Maurice Gulliford, who declined it in my favour. Such noble self-sacrifice when we were all starving hungry was an act of friendship of the very highest quality and could have saved my life.

Sapper Edgar Whincup, Royal Engineers
POW from February 1942 to August 1945
Camp 330, Changi Barracks

Real wholesome food was at a premium and the following list will illustrate what 200 men were allowed to live on over selected periods of three days:

28/4/42: flour 46 lb, sugar 25 lb, milk 29 tins, tea 7 lb, salt 8 lb, ghee
(fat) 5 lb, rice 16 oz per man per day
17/6/42: flour 90 lb, rice 1.2 cwt, salt 5 lb, ghee 5 lb

We had no meat of any kind, but as a special treat for the Emperor's birthday we were given 60 tins of pineapple.

However, our meagre rations were increased by virtue of an incident which came upon us quite by chance. One day, one of my comrades found out where the Japanese rice store was situated. Our only problem was how to get the rice away from this store, but ingenuity (always a major part of a prisoners of war's existence) came to our rescue. We were wearing the short-sleeved army vest, and by tying the sleeves and the necks together we provided ourselves with a container. Over the fence at night we went and regularly returned with a vest full of rice. This continued for some time until one day a sleeve became undone and a small trickle of rice from the store should have betrayed our secret – but the Japs never noticed! Lucky us!

As you can imagine, hunger was never far away and we were continually trying to find ways of augmenting our meagre diet.

It was about this time that little cooking fires were springing up all over the camp and the Japs, seeing these, realized that we were getting food from somewhere, and immediately stopped all fires. We weren't going to be beaten, and small secret fires started up as we made our cooking equipment out of small and old cans which burnt small amounts of wood and charcoal. Trying to disperse the smoke was a problem, so we built a tiny flue in such a position that the smoke could go through the fly sheet of the tent (inner linings) but, much to our dismay, it found its way out on all four sides.

THE DUTCH EAST INDIES

Pilot Officer Erroll David Shearn, Royal Air Force
POW from March 1942 to August 1945
Camp 356, Sourabaya, East Java

After some weeks at 'the Lyceum', where the food consisted every day of a meagre amount of boiled rice with weeds and vegetables, and a minute amount of meat, mostly offal, we all lost weight rapidly. I went down from about 11 stone to 8 stone.

Gunner Frederick Hawkes Thompson, Royal Artillery
POW from March 1942 to August 1945
Camp 353, Xth Battalion Barracks, Batavia (from his diary)
August 1943. Once more we have a blitz on in camp. No more fires or books at present, but we still have parcels – another half [per man] today. Maybe our air raids are upsetting them – anyway, let them come and worry us and mess us around. As I say, we are too used to it [for it] to make us really uneasy.

Captain Arthur Geoffrey Threadgold, Royal Artillery
POW from March 1942 to August 1945
Notes kept in Camp 354, Boei Glodok Batavia
Rice and weak vegetable stew the main meal of the day in the evening, and bubur for breakfast. Bubur – a rice *congee* or rice porridge – looked like bill-posters' paste only thinner. Meat? Eggs? What do they taste like? Almost forgotten items of diet nowadays.

Contact with local population was prohibited. Woe betide you if caught bartering – but it did go on nevertheless.

Aircraftman (Driver) Frank Deakin Jackson, Royal Air Force
POW from March 1942 to August 1945
Liang Camp, Ambon (Amboina), the Moluccas
The food consisted largely of rice and bean soup that contained, at times, a trace of goat meat. Later, the large flower from the banana tree was added to the stew but this I found unpleasant to the taste but at least gave some bulk.

Sugar in minute quantities was issued with the breakfast rice. Consequently no sugar was used for tea-making, neither was milk, as this latter was never available. Tea without these commodities we found very acceptable in the tropical climate.

Our cooks lived and worked at Liang kampong [rather than in the prison camp] and were only seen when assisting with the food deliveries.

JAPAN

Lieutenant Stephen Abbott, East Surrey Regiment
POW from February 1942 to August 1945
Official Debriefing Report on No 7 Despatch Camp, Chi, Japan
Although towards the end of our stay clothing was naturally becoming very much worn, I think nevertheless the Japanese did all in their power to supply us with essential kit. The only real shortage was that of boots and socks.

SIAM (THAILAND)

Sergeant William McDonald Innes-Ker, Straits Settlement Volunteer Force
POW from February 1942 to August 1945
Sonkurai No 2 Camp, Thailand (from his diary)
18 June 1943. To feed 1,200 men we have 20 buckets, so feed in relays – some get breakfast at 5.30 am and some at 11! Ditto for supper. Rations are now reduced, as trucks cannot get through to us either way from Burma or Thai. We actually draw from Burma and now every other day 100 men have to drag bullockless wagons through knee-deep mud to another camp five kms away for rice and beans. Takes them all day and exhausts them, and this before the monsoon has really started.

6
WORK

'The truck stopped and we clambered out, and were taken a short distance through the olive trees to some mounds in the ground. It then dawned on us what the task ahead was. We had to dig the bodies out of the shallow graves, wrap them in the white cloth and place them in the wagon. As expected, the bodies were in an advanced state of decomposition ...'
— British sapper captured on Crete

With millions of their young men in the armed forces, all nations involved in the Second World War found that despite employing women in factories and on the land they still needed conscript labour to keep their economies running. Even Nazi Germany, a nation with a ready-made slave-pool of millions in its concentration camps, experienced a dire manpower shortage. So prisoners of war became a convenient source of labour.

This had been foreseen by the Geneva Convention, which devoted no fewer than eight Articles (numbers 27 to 34) of the POW Code to this question. Under the terms of the Code captors could put only physically fit prisoners to work. Even then not every prisoner, whether fit or otherwise, could be compelled to work. There were also other restrictions. Non-commissioned officers were to undertake only supervisory duties unless they specifically asked for paid work. Officers could not be made to work, but if they wished, suitable employment might be found for them.

No prisoner of war could be employed on work for which he was physically unsuited. In the event of accidents at work, he was entitled to the same medical treatment, legal benefits and compensation as the detaining power's own employees. The detaining power was also responsible for the welfare and pay of prisoners working for private individuals. Their hours, including the time spent travelling to and from work, should not exceed those permitted for civil workers employed locally on the same job. Each prisoner should be allowed a rest of 24 consecutive hours each week, preferably on Sunday.

None of the labour undertaken by prisoners should be directly connected with the prosecution of the war. In particular, the POW Code forbade captors from employing them in the manufacture or transport of arms, munitions, and any other material destined for combat units. It was also forbidden to employ prisoners on unhealthy or dangerous work and to make working conditions harder by imposing disciplinary measures.

Every labour detachment had to be attached to a main POW camp, whose commander was responsible for the observance of the provisions of the Geneva Convention. Conditions should also reflect those of the prisoner-of-war camps themselves, with a similar standard of hygiene, sanitation and medical care, similar food, and provision for the reception of food, clothing and personal parcels and for sending and receiving mail.

The Convention also acknowledged that prisoners would have to be employed within the main POW camps in order to ensure their smooth running. Thus NCOs and other ranks could be detached from their own camps to serve in officers' camps as batmen or orderlies.

Soldiers were to receive wages for all work they undertook, enabling them to buy extra food and articles from the canteen. Officers, however, would have to be paid by the detaining power. Equivalent sums of money would be docked from their service pay at source, to ensure sufficient funds to reimburse the detaining power after the war.

As can be imagined, in practice things worked out a great deal differently.

GERMANY AND OCCUPIED POLAND

In Nazi Germany, even before the outbreak of hostilities, the High Command of the Armed Forces drew up a list of which terms of the Geneva Convention it believed it could violate with impunity, along with a list of jobs an enemy might give POWs and on which Germany therefore decided it, too, would employ them. Nor was there any shortage of potential POW labour. By late 1943 Stalag VIIIB, Lamsdorf, accommodated some 13,000 prisoners, while Stalag XXB at Marienburg (Malbork) was bursting apart with almost 25,000 men. These camps fed detachments of prisoners to various satellite camps throughout their respective military districts (such as the *Zweitlager* and *Zweiglager* previously mentioned, as well as the 'building and works camp', known as a *Bau-und-Arbeitslager*, or BAB). All an employer wishing to exploit POW labour had to do was obtain a permit from his local labour office, then approach either the main POW camp or the branch camp and draw up a contract with the commandant.

Work detachments generally consisted of about 20 men, but were sometimes bigger. In August 1944 Stalag VIIIA at Görlitz was providing no fewer than 46 working parties, their complement ranging from as few as nine men working in a clay pit to as many as 173 working down a coalmine. Each detachment elected a 'Man of Confidence', usually an NCO who had volunteered for work, and he would be responsible for the well-being of the prisoners and liaise between them and their employer. If the place of work was remote from the POW camp, the employer had to provide secure accommodation (although the Wehrmacht's administrative office would reimburse his costs and provide sentries), but if the site was nearby the men were transported to work every day, returning to the camp at the end of their shift, often with stolen food or some other form of contraband.

The scale of pay worked out at only 60 per cent of the German wage, minus a levy for board and lodging and, sometimes, income tax. It averaged out as 70 pfennigs a day. Even then the pay was in *Lagergeld* – specially printed camp money that, like Monopoly money, had no purchasing power in the real world. It could only be used in the camp canteens (or at selected local shops) to buy beer, lemonade, combs, hair oil, razor blades, and so on. These goods were also subject to taxation. Half a litre of beer cost 30 pfennigs. A single pack of razor blades could cost a month's pay. Having one's clothes laundered just once a week cost almost two days' wages. The Germans also devised other ways of parting the prisoners from their money, such as charging them for receiving mail and parcels from the main camp or for sports equipment and musical instruments.

The only advantage in working was that it at least got them out of the soul-destroying confines of the prison camp and gave them access to food and women. But the fact that by doing this they were helping the enemy caused a crisis of conscience, especially amongst NCOs supervising working parties. For even if they were not engaged directly in 'war work', in total war all work done by POWs aided the enemy's war effort, even if they only replaced German farm labourers so that they could wear army uniforms at the Ostfront. As the war went against Germany, however, this dilemma became largely academic. In 1944 the OKW, the Wehrmacht's High Command, on Himmler's orders, ceased to recognize those articles of the Geneva Convention that enshrined the right of NCOs and protected personnel such as Royal Army Medical Corps staff (including stretcher-bearers, orderlies and drivers) to refuse to work. In fact, as early as June 1943 as many as 200 RAMC personnel were employed in one labour detachment alone, and on 15 December 1943 the OKW had established a special punishment camp, Stalag 383 at Hohenfels in Bavaria, for recalcitrant NCOs.

From the OKW regulations for foreign workers in Germany:

Every prisoner of war liable for work and able-bodied is expected to exert himself to the full. Should he fail to do so the guards or auxiliary guards are entitled to take rigorous action. Guards who fail to take such action will themselves be held responsible and severely punished. They are entitled to enforce their orders by force of arms.

GERMANY

Telegraphist Herbert Edgar Elliott, Royal Naval Volunteer Reserve
POW from August 1940 to May 1945
Stalag VIIIB, Lamsdorf, and Bau-und-Arbeitslager 21, Blechhammer
On 23 August 1942, 87 of us were taken by charabanc from Lamsdorf to this working camp at Blechhammer where we made the 48th Arbeitsbataillon up to 600 strong. The facilities were good but we had to work long hours.

We were on our legs from 4.30 am until about 8 or 9 pm. We usually arrived back from work at 6 pm, then had to bath, roll-call and cook a meal. There must have been a million workers of all nationalities here, all employed on the same site. A large oil-from-coal plant was being erected which included power house, railway station and sidings, roads and anything that could be thought of.

Women were employed on navvying work, also German servicemen under punishment. Thousands of Jews were here too. Two committed suicide to my knowledge. On the fourth day here I reported sick and did not go to work any more.

2 November saw me once more on my way back to Stalag VIIIB, where the German doctor passed me as sick.

I spent six months here in convalescence after which I was graded fit for sitting work only. I have always considered this a good accomplishment on my part.

I had nothing to do and made many new friends. Also did a course on Industrial Organization.

The winter was bitterly cold and we had practically no firing at all for the stoves. We had one alight from noon till 6 pm in a room holding 120 men.

I met men who lived a few minutes' walk from my home and we were able to discuss the latest news from our respective homes.

Men captured at Dieppe, Crete and North Africa were here and I had many an interesting talk on our various experiences. I made friends with men from Canada, Australia and New Zealand, some who were in quite good positions. An Australian warrant officer who slept next to me was a factor for the Standard Oil Company and we passed many an hour on the subject of oil.

In April '43 a party of unfit men were needed as orderlies at a RAF officers' camp and I managed to have my name put down for this work although I was not supposed to go out of VIIIB.

Flight Lieutenant Harry Crease, Royal Canadian Air Force
POW from October 1941 to May 1945
Stalag Luft I, Barth-Vogelsang, November 1941

An army corporal came to the door. He was one of the NCOs who had been assigned to our block as orderlies.

'There's bales of wood straw outside, gentlemen. You can fill your new palliasses.'

'Palliasses?' I asked. 'What's palliasses?'

'Mattresses, sir. There's a pile of new covers out by the door. You'll have to fill them with wood straw.'

'Wood straw?'

'The Canadians call it excelsior, sir.'

The excelsior had been packed into bales, like hay. It was compressed so tightly that it had to be pried off the bales like thick planks. Then it had to be shredded into a fluffy mass. The sandy stretch of ground between our block and the next was like one of the rings of a circus. We were the clowns, clumsily shredding and packing straw into burlap-like mattress covers. Some of the old kriegies stood in a circle watching our antics.

'Fill them up really full,' one of them said. 'It will pack down in a few days. If it's not thick enough the cold will come up through the bottom of the bed.'

The mattresses were like blimps when we struggled with them back into the building.

We positioned our bunks in the corners of the room on opposite sides of the door. With the open-ended framework of the bed, the wall was needed as a backrest.

Eric [another new arrival] had heaved his big-boned body up over the bloated bulk of his mattress and seemed to be clutching at a deflating balloon.

'I think it's rising,' he said. 'I'm getting closer to the ceiling.'

Gunner Cyril George King, Royal Artillery (Territorial)
POW from June 1940 to April 1945
Oflag VIIC, Laufen, Bavaria

Naturally enough there was always some job which could be found for we orderlies, but I think that I can truthfully say that whilst I was at Oflag VIIC I was never given any work which caused me acute discomfort. The summer

Oflag VIIC at Laufen in Bavaria, winter 1940–41 (*author's collection*)

months passed easily – the diet was monotonous, with its soups, dried fish, black bread and vile-tasting cheese, but there was always the Red Cross to help us out with their little parcels and how they were blessed for their oddments of luxuries.

I carried jugs of hot water and tea to the officers' rooms, scrubbed their floors and passageways and when the day's work was over just dreamed my time away in the sun or argued about the outcome of the war in our own quarters.

There were never any new prisoners to our camp and so we knew nothing of our growing air force or of operations in any sphere. In October of that year 1941 there were rumours of a move for all officers and men and by the end of the month there came the final orders. We learned later that Oflag VIIC was used for the housing of civilians from the Channel Islands.

Sapper Don Luckett, Royal Engineers
POW from July 1941 to May 1945
Stalag XVIIIA, Wolfsberg, Austria
The man in charge of the hut, the leader or '*Stubenführer*', was a jovial sort of character from an Australian unit, who welcomed us into the hut, taking our POW numbers and names, which were duly entered into a large book he carried. He had been captured in Corinth and had been in Wolfsberg for several weeks prior to our arrival, and gave us all the information about the day-to-day activity and answered our many questions, or as many as possible.

This system did, in fact, lead to some men promoting themselves so that they would not be sent out to work. It was commonly known as 'Stalag Promotion' and was carried out amongst the earliest arrivals at Wolfsberg, the 'ghost' rank being given at the initial documentation and later by the respective record offices back home, the rank forgotten on returning to the UK. Similarly, some senior NCOs volunteered to go out to a working camp in the hope of landing a plum 'staff' job, but usually ended up disappointed, as they took their chance the same as everyone else.

The actual allocation of any staff job within the camp depended upon the qualification required, and sometimes the personality of the man himself, the position being sanctioned by the majority of opinion also. Those who could speak German reasonably well were in the forefront as an interpreter, or *Dolmetscher*, or as an intermediary – a go-between, 'man of confidence' or *Vertrauensmann*, and as such was set a little apart from the common herd.

POLAND

Private Alfred Charles Bryant, The Buffs
POW from July 1940 to May 1945
Stalag XXB, Marienburg (Malbork), November 1940–June 1942
I helped repair the railway after the RAF bombed it. I remember the RAF
made a raid on the Messerschmitt factory at Marienburg about three miles out
of town, hitting a workshop, and six months later, after we had repaired it, the
RAF came and bombed it again. We had to do all sorts of jobs, including
sweeping the roads.

The camp guards were older men – mainly reservists and First World War
veterans. The Gestapo would come every week and search the huts, occasionally stripping them down. When working parties were returned to the
camp, they were searched.

The food was still very bad and our Red Cross parcels were stopped for
several weeks because of RAF bombing.

Six of us managed to stay together and we were put on a farm with six
more men. Each day the guards would come and take us to the farm and
return at night to the cottage.

ITALY AND THE MEDITERRANEAN

The Italians, too, utilized foreign labour, largely following the German
pattern. However, they used POWs a good deal less, employing them
mainly on farms in the central and northern provinces during the sowing
and harvesting seasons. Usually working parties were accommodated in
satellite camps attached to a main camp in the same region. Thus, for
instance, Campo PG 78 at Sulmona had a sub-camp at Aquafredda desig-
nated Campo PG 78/1, while Campo PG 103 at Marciano had at least six
satellites. Within the camps themselves, prisoners took on the same
administrative responsibilities as their brethren in Germany and Poland,
and in some cases were dragooned into building their own accommodation
and latrines.

The German presence in the Mediterranean theatre from the end of 1940
onwards, shortly after which they occupied Greece and Crete, inevitably
brought Nazi forced-labour policies in its train, and British and Commonwealth
prisoners in 1941 found themselves occupied on a variety of unsavoury tasks
before being transferred to permanent POW camps in Germany.

Sapper Don Luckett, Royal Engineers
POW from July 1941 to May 1945
Frontstalag, 7th General Field Hospital, Maleme, Crete

A dozen of us were detailed off on this particular morning, and we marched out along the road to collect some picks and long-handled shovels and rolls of white cloth that were stored in a small shed. We climbed into the back of one of our own vehicles, driven by a German driver, and were taken to the foothills some way from Canea. The truck stopped and we clambered out, and were taken a short distance through the olive trees to some mounds in the ground. It then dawned on us what the task ahead was. We had to dig the bodies out of the shallow graves, wrap them in the white cloth and place them in the wagon. As expected, the bodies were in an advanced state of decomposition, and on lifting them out brought forth such a pungent smell that we could not help retching and baulking in the process. Something like 20 bodies were recovered, and eventually taken to a barnlike building not far from Canea. Their identities were not known, apart from the fact that they were our men, they wore remnants of khaki clothing, their pockets were empty and as they had no identity discs their number, rank and name were unknown. It was a grim task to perform and its memory was to last for a long time. We were each given two cigarettes for our toil, and vowed that we'd not wait around the gate again for further work.

Private Maurice Newey, Royal Army Ordnance Corps
POW from June 1942 to April 1945
Campo 54, Fara Sabina (Rome)

Once we were kitted out, we were visited by Red Cross officials who came to inspect the camp. I think that they must have been disgusted at the state of our model camp and the toilet facilities (or lack of them), for the Italians were requested to build brick huts and a brick-built latrine.

Volunteers were called for to do the labouring work, extra rations promised to the workers. A lorry arrived in the camp carrying building materials. The driver left his vehicle unattended to attend to some business and when he returned, the naive fellow found that all his tools had vanished, together with everything moveable including his driving mirrors. They had all been appropriated. (POWs don't steal, they appropriate.) Dire threats were issued if the property was not returned, all to no avail. No more lorries were left unguarded after that. More materials arrived and were carefully guarded, but in spite of this, things still mysteriously disappeared.

The work progressed slowly, the workers spinning it out as long as possible so that they could continue to draw extra rations. Three huts were nearing completion when gale-force winds swept the camp. Because they were built at the top of the compound, they were getting the full blast of the wind. The top hut began swaying. The news spread like wildfire and we all hurried out to see the fun. The top hut swayed to a dangerous angle and we held our breath, but damn, it righted itself. Another fierce gust and it slowly toppled over to the accompaniment of our concerted cheering. The Eyeties rushed in, bayonets fixed, thinking that we were deliberately pushing the huts over.

We stood our ground as the next hut, left unprotected by the first hut, started swaying, until it, too, toppled over to more loud cheers. The guards stayed until the third hut collapsed, then left with our mocking laughter ringing in their ears.

THE FAR EAST

Imperial Japan's policy on POW labour, like that of Nazi Germany, was determined before the war, and was reaffirmed in September 1942 during a meeting of prison camp commanders in Tokyo. Lieutenant-General Mikio, the chief of the Prisoner of War Control Bureau, made it clear that 'war prisoners should not pass a single day eating the bread of idleness'. His intention was to use POW labour to increase Japan's productivity. But he insisted that the demands on them should be reasonable, they should be used efficiently, and force was to be avoided. All the same, it still meant 'no work, no food'. This programme enable the Japanese to build railways, bridges, airfields, shelters and warehouses, and to have labour permanently on call on docks, down mines and in factories. But it is the 'Death Railway' which has become the most notorious symbol of the abuse of POW labour and with which the name Far Eastern POW has become almost synonymous.

SINGAPORE

Sergeant William McDonald Innes-Ker, Straits Settlement Volunteer Force
POW from February 1942 to August 1945
Camp 330, Changi Military Barracks
Water was scarce, food what we had carried in, and everything chaotic. For two or three weeks these conditions prevailed until some sort of order was set up by

our Higher Command. Quite early on the Nips sent out working parties to help clear up the devastated city, which really was a shambles after the weeks of bombing, shelling and mortaring. It will never be known how many Asians were killed, but it is said to be 10,000. The stink of putrefying flesh at times and in places was ghastly. I was in a party of 200 under Captain L V Taylor, a Shell Company assistant ...We were all SSVF men, and we were first quartered in a small palm-hutted camp at the foot of Bukit Timah in the old Rifle Range. Here we were formed into a Mobile Recovery Unit, with some ten patched-up army lorries, and our job was seeking out and recovering all sorts of oil, petrol and other drums, thousands of which had been secreted by our army in hidden dumps here and there all over the island. We collected loads of these and took them to a huge dump the Nips were organizing near the Singapore Harbour Board.

After a few months here we were shifted to another camp at Pasir Panjang, an old Shell oil depot, and this time we were quartered in concrete coolie lines [where native employees had slept], five of us to a room. Our job was the same as before, plus loading ships at the Harbour Board on occasion, but there were precious few of these, and the Harbour Board area had been fairly badly damaged by their own bombing. There was one Blue Funnel ship sunk alongside in the Empire Dock more or less blocking the entrance, resting with deck and upper works awash, and this remained here till the end of the war.

Here we stayed until Christmas 1942, when all outside working parties were withdrawn back into Changi. There were many of these working parties dotted about the island; for example, Ted Shrubshall was in a party on Blakan Mati Island loading and unloading bombs and shells. Blakan Mati was one of our fortified islands guarding the harbour and was a honeycomb of underground tunnels, gun emplacements and store houses built in the rock; a veritable treasure house for the Nips, for it had not been very badly damaged, bar the guns being made useless.

THE DUTCH EAST INDIES

Pilot Officer Erroll David Shearn, Royal Air Force
POW from March 1942 to August 1945
Camp 353, Xth Battalion Barracks, Batavia
From this camp drafts of officers and men were sent to the adjacent islands to carve out landing strips almost with their bare hands. When work was finished for the day, the almost exhausted prisoners were permitted to erect such shelter for themselves as they could from any material they might find available. The death roll was, I was told, around 50 per cent of those sent on the draft. The

condition of the survivors was deplorable. All suffered from deficiency diseases of one sort or another. Blindness, 'dropped feet', pellagra, beriberi, and so forth.

I found myself paraded to depart on one of the drafts. The interpreter called out: 'Fall out anyone who has been wounded.' I promptly fell out. Asked where I had been wounded, I pulled up my shirt and showed the pretty noticeable scars on my right side and back. The interpreter asked: 'Where did you get that?' I replied: 'France.' 'You can send the bill in to the Germans,' was the rejoinder. I was then told to fall out. I was thus spared what doubtless would have been a very unwelcome experience.

It was at this camp that I decided to occupy myself in the 'works' contingent. Chiefly we made brushes from bamboos, and very painful it was on one's hands until one got the knack. Later on I became pretty expert and at another camp started my own brush factory helped by two other ranks. I remember offering finished brushes to some Dutch who thought I wanted to sell them and were not at all interested. When it dawned on them that there was no charge, they couldn't get them quickly enough.

Aircraftman Frank Deakin Jackson, Royal Air Force
POW from March 1942 to August 1945
Liang Camp, Ambon (Amboina), the Moluccas
The first working party was a very large one and revealed the purpose behind the shipping of our draft to Ambon. Our task was to clear and extend an airfield abandoned by the Dutch Airlines. The short strip was so overgrown and neglected it had obviously not been used for some considerable time. The airfield was little more than half a mile from the camp, but to reach it meant a detour of two miles because thick jungle intervened.

We would turn right leaving the camp and then follow the Liang road until a secondary road appeared at a right-hand fork leading to the airfield. This road was rather steep, and sharp coral broke its surface while magnificent teak trees soared towards the sky as they lined the route. So impressive were the trees I often gazed up in wonderment at their majesty. At least I still had an eye for the beauty of nature.

The road terminated at the airfield, which ran parallel to the eye-dazzling white beach. Looking across the Banda Sea a much larger island than Ambon could be seen close by, and we were to learn it was named Ceram [Seram].

The first day was occupied in clearing debris and scrub from the ends of the runway and I think the intense heat was our only problem at this stage. Sweet potatoes were found and gathered from one end and treated as quite a windfall. Before work ceased, wood for cooking these vegetables was hastily collected for use back at camp as we were able to make small fires among clumps of coral. The Nips did not interfere with these activities taking place during *yasumes* (rests) but would not allow contact with the locals seen hovering at the jungle's edge. Work ceased a little before dusk.

In this remote corner of the world, and I felt it could not be much remoter, I had been surprised, that first day at the airfield, to see an old Sentinel steamroller. I remember being emotionally affected seeing this relic from home standing idle and forlorn. I never saw it put to its proper use but there were men who later told me they manhandled it up and down the runway.

The working parties usually comprised about 300 men accompanied by a handful of our officers. These officers had the onerous task of interpreting just what the Nips required of us, conveying these instructions to their charges and then ensuring the work was carried out most diligently. Of course we could never put heart and soul into our efforts but had to make a show of really trying. Often the Japanese would scream 'buggero' or 'speedo' in an effort to get the best out of us. (These expressions came so naturally to the Nips I rather suspect they also formed part of their language.)

After a few days of working here I came to realize our health was really beginning to deteriorate. There had been those days on the prison-ship, the excruciating march, a night exposed to the rain and a near starvation diet. The rice ration had been reduced since arriving on the island, possibly due to shipping difficulties, as Ambon possessed no rice fields. To be hungry day after day was endless torture. These circumstances were now taking their toll. Working a full day in temperatures of around 90°F would be trying at the best of times; to men in our condition it was sheer purgatory.

JAPAN

Lieutenant Stephen Abbott, East Surrey Regiment
POW from February 1942 to August 1945
Camp 13B, Aomi, 1943
In the early part of the year our first Camp Commander, Lieutenant Yoshimura, was asked by the local factory authorities to honour them by opening a new sector of the quarry. The first blast was to be carried out with British dynamite, captured at Singapore. He duly went up there with three of the chief factory managers and let off the charge. Far too much of the dynamite was used, and most of the hill was brought down. Lieutenant Yoshimura and the three managers were all killed, and their bodies have not yet been recovered. We were given a new Camp Commandant.

Gunner Frederick Hawkes Thompson, Royal Artillery
POW from March 1942 to August 1945
Notes made at Wakayama and Icuno camps, 1945

1 April 1945. There has been a great change during the last week. On 26 March we were told that we would be moving camp. On the 28th we were away. Everything was very sudden. After leaving the camp we had a three-mile walk to Wakayama station. Luckily our heavy packs were taken for us by lorry. On our arrival at Osaka we were marched to a nearby camp – a four-storey warehouse in the thick of the city, a terrible place for human habitation – but the Yanks who were there looked far better than us human wrecks, owing to them being able to get food from their place of work. After a comparatively good meal of rice and soup we slept a sound sleep, as we were all more or less exhausted. After breakfast the next day we moved again to the station and after a seven-hour (approx.) journey we arrived at our new home in the hills. What a marvellous place this seems at present. We are in a valley entirely surrounded by pine-clad hills, and for Japan the camp and accommodation are really good. After cleaning the place up (it needed it badly), the camp looks similar to what I imagine a Canadian camp in the Rockies would look like. Food is very poor, however, but like everything else we must be patient and wait for things to improve.

Two hundred of the men have gone out today to the local mines, and we are all eager to hear what they have to say when they arrive back. I am in Grade B (not fit enough for the heavier work) and I expect to be out tomorrow.

BURMA–SIAM: THE 'DEATH RAILWAY'

Sergeant William McDonald Innes-Ker, Straits Settlement Volunteer Force
POW from February 1942 to August 1945
Sonkurai No 2 Camp, Thailand, 1943

In Changi life was a bit more grim and restricted. We were quartered, 50 of us, in what had been a junior officer's bungalow. In March 1943, with conditions, food, water, getting very bad, the Nips 'advertized' a move into Siam for the 'sick'. There were also parties being organized for Borneo, and I put my name down for that place, but was not picked, and instead was posted to 'F' Force in a party of 1,200 so-called 'Sick, old and those not for labour'.

This party, 'F' Force, followed various other groups or 'forces' which had been sent to Siam and Burma to build for the Nips a short-cut railway line to link Bangkok and Rangoon, by which they intended to support their army, which was attacking India through north Burma. Due to naval activity, chiefly American

The first, wooden, bridge at Tamarkan nears completion, January 1943 (*reproduced by permission of the Toosey family*)

The steel girder bridge at Tamarkan after aerial bombing by the Allies in 1945 (*reproduced by permission of the Toosey family*)

submarines, the route round Singapore and up to Rangoon was very hazardous and time-consuming; also, their ships were so stretched all over the south-east Asia area they simply had not enough sea power to support these vast, lengthy and diverse lines of communication. Hence the idea of the railway, to be built within one year, and through mountainous jungle for some 200–300 miles. The line was to follow mainly along the Kwai Nong River and thence over the Three Pagodas Pass, down into the flatter, more cultivated, lands of South Burma to link up at Moulmein with the existing Burmese system. It was a route which had been thought of and surveyed years before by both British and Siamese authorities and abandoned as not practical. The Nips, however, with some 50,000 white prisoners and a similar number of impressed Asians – Tamils and Chinese from the Malayan plantations and mines – pushed on, using this slave labour foolishly and ruthlessly. So foolishly that half their labour died and those who survived did a fraction of the work they were capable of had they been properly fed. It was an appalling example of cutting off your nose to spite your face.

That the railway was ever completed was a miracle, and what a ramshackle affair it was, aided by sloppy, sabotaging work – by all the white prisoners, at least. Derailments were constant (when we came back down it from Thanabaya in December 1943, trucks from our train ran off, and each time the offending truck was simply uncoupled and pushed over the side), and it is said that the traffic it carried before being bombed into uselessness by the Allies was probably only 5 per cent of what it should have been capable of. An appalling blunder by the Glorious Nippon!

I have not yet described our journey to Siam. We were loaded into covered steel goods trucks at Singapore; all steel – roof, sides, floor – and with sliding steel doors. Something like 30 men to a truck measuring 18 feet long by 10 feet wide, plus all our kitbags, cooking gear and so forth. We could not all lie down at one time but had to take turns half at a time. At first our doors were locked shut, but it was so suffocating that the whole trainload kicked up such a row, beating on the side and howling like beasts, that they permitted us to have the doors open. Our Nip guards travelled in civilized coaches, one at each end of a train containing 1,200 prisoners, all British.

The journey took something like five days and nights, by which time several men had died and been pushed out of the trucks on to the track. We had one meal a day, of rice and weak vegetable water, and half a water bottle of boiled water. We stopped frequently in the Siamese portion to load wood for the engines. At these stops we just burst off the train into the undergrowth, for many had dysentery and the trucks were becoming filthy. It usually took the guards quite a time and a lot of firing of rifles to get us back on the train.

We arrived at Ban Pong, a big junction, at evening time and there we were moved to a transit camp for the night, leaving behind all our gear except what we could carry. We never saw our gear again. At the transit camp we could wash in a stream, and did, being pretty mucky, as you can imagine. Next evening at dusk we were formed up and told we would march to our camp that night. This we did for ten nights, covering 20 kilometres a night, and any who fell out were just left in the darkness – to die. We were given a rice and water meal at dawn and dusk at each staging post, and these posts were usually staffed by half a dozen Australian troops, who were permanently there. For ourselves, we just fell down where we were, and it was seldom there was any cover, so that when it rained – and it did – we just lay in miserable huddles.

After a couple of nights the road, which was really only a sandy track, petered out and we continued on beaten jungle tracks passing established work camps, half-completed bridges, blasted cuttings, and all the signs of the railway in its early stages.

All the time, as we grew weaker, goods and clothing were abandoned at the trackside, as we found we could not carry them. I threw away a cherished Los Angeles telephone directory, which made excellent smoking paper and from which I had hoped to barter many a meal from men who cared more for a smoke than a meal (meal?!). One night I collapsed and lay on the trackside, absolutely done. In the dawning along came a Nip officer and two men in a minibus, collecting such dropouts. He was a Kempeitai (Jap Gestapo) captain, but a very educated man. He spoke excellent English and was reasonably friendly. He brought us bananas from a village – a few atap huts where all the inhabitants kept fearfully out of sight till we went on – and I often feel those bananas saved my life. Later in the morning we caught up with our party and I rejoined my pals. This sort of back-track pick-up only lasted as long as the wheeled vehicles could follow; after that any who fell out were just left, and I guess many just died where they lay.

We marched at night for two reasons: one, so that the local inhabitants in the early and more populous areas would not see us slaves and the condition we were in; and, two, for coolness, it being very hot during the daytime, which we spent as best we could in our staging camps.

As I said, after about ten nights' marching we came to a fairly large river, about 50 yards across, and here we were stopped in the ruins of what had been an older Indian coolies' camp. It had long bashas [huts] of about 150 feet, with a central pathway and on each side an elevated sleeping platform; all made of bamboo and already falling to bits and roofless. When dawn came we found our task was to build a bridge across this river. To picture the scene just cast your mind back to the film *Bridge on the River Kwai*, and that is exactly it. Exactly, countryside and all; towering bamboo jungle steep up one side, falling away with the river Kwai to the flatter lands (all jungle-covered) below. There appeared to be no villages or inhabitants and we later learnt that the nearest village was some 20 kilometres away.

The rains had started and for weeks we were never dry. For roofing material nipa palm leaves were cut from the valley area some miles away and dragged to our camp, where we set to to cover the tottering bashas. Railway work was supposed to start immediately, but in fact it was some days before we could say the camp was even remotely habitable.

I was drafted, together with other 'older men', to a Bamboo Hut Repairing Gang and seldom worked on the bridge, though at times I was sent out as numbers of men able to do anything were so scarce. I believe out of 1,200 men we seldom were able to send out a workforce of more than 10 per cent; all the rest were sick. You have seen sketches of men being carried to work, beaten on by raving Nips – all true, so true. In our gang, and I was sergeant-in-charge, was 'Ding Dong' (Irving-Bell); he was a good deal younger and was a corporal.

Once the bridge building started, overseen by a dozen or so raving lunatic Jap Engineers, our troubles really multiplied. These Engineers were ruthless maniacs and would come tearing into our bashas, beating dying men to their feet and endeavouring to get them out on the work gangs. Our own Jap guards, who had come with us from Singapore, were helpless against these Engineers and could do very little to help us.

In the camp were stationed six or eight elephants, with Siamese or Burmese *utis* (mahouts), and these elephants were used for hauling logs to the bridge site. At one time I was 'hooker-onerer', that is, I followed behind the elephant and hooked on the chains for hauling the logs. Another time Irving-Bell and I were put to work cutting short lengths of bamboo with slots and cappings to be filled with the ashes of our dead. This rather useless project died out pretty soon, for we could not keep up with the demand. I said ashes, for we burnt our dead in a great burning *ghat* every evening or so; we had no tools and were too weak, anyway, to dig graves, and I must say it takes a hell of a lot of bamboo to burn five or six human bodies.

Corporal Charles Kinahan, Straits Settlement Volunteer Force
POW from February 1942 to August 1945
Camp 241, Ban Pong, and POW Camp 250, Chungkai, Thailand
The journey from Singapore to Ban Pong (the base for the railway) took four days. We travelled in boxcars – each holding 28 men. Fortunately the guards allowed us to keep the cargo doors open, otherwise the heat would have been

intolerable. For this concession we were on our honour not to attempt to escape. As we settled down I was delighted to hear a Northern Irish accent amongst my fellow passengers, Frank Reid, a Queen's Law graduate who had been in a legal practice in Ipoh, Malaya, and in the local volunteers there. We struck up a firm and lasting friendship, and were together for the rest of our imprisonment; Frank later became godfather to our youngest son Timothy. Our friendship was tried under severe conditions and was not found wanting.

Conditions in the boxcars were extremely cramped with no room for all 28 men to lie down at the same time, so we took turns to lie down whilst others stood in the doorway. To defecate you had to stick your bum out of the cargo door, whilst your mates inside held your arms – quite a performance! There were numerous stops all along the line. At several stops at small stations in Johore we were acknowledged by large numbers of employees on rubber estates in the area. Somehow the word had got out that a trainload of POWs was to be in the area. They had come probably hoping to see their old *tuan* (manager) and to offer him (and the rest of us) food such as bananas. It represented a considerable sacrifice by people already short of food and was a boost to our morale.

The railway construction started at Ban Pong, about 40 miles west of Bangkok where the north/south railway from Singapore turns east to Bangkok. This was the base area in which plant, materials and equipment were assembled.... The first section of the railway was due north to Kanchanaburi, about 20 miles over flat rice-field country; it was built by the Siamese. The POW work started at Kanchanaburi, the crossing of the river Kwai. A wooden bridge was built by Japanese engineers using POW labour. Subsequently the Japs built a steel bridge on concrete piers; they had dismantled a bridge in Java and brought it from there, but it was at least two years before that was completed, so the temporary wooden bridge was essential for moving materials up the line as it [the line] was pushed towards the Three Pagodas Pass and South Burma, about 200 kilometres.

...We were moved from Ban Pong to Chungkai, which was sited on the riverbank a mile or so upstream from the bridge in a rice field area. I was to spend the next 30 months in this camp.... As camps go it was better than most. We got reasonable food and were able to supplement our diet with peanuts, bananas and duck eggs with the money we earned by working – a mere 15 cents per day. We were able to bathe in the river after work each day and to wash our clothes there.

In my first few months at Chungkai I was one of a party working on cutting through a rock face. We drilled holes by hand for explosives and then removed the resulting rock. It was hot work with the glare off the rock. I was also involved in this period with embankment building, manually passing baskets of earth along a human chain.

My greatest good fortune was to be appointed NCO in charge of a ration party which went every day by river to Kanchanaburi to load rations on to barges and lorries for transit to our own and other camps. The officer in charge was Captain Murdock of the Manchester Regiment, who died from an abdominal complaint (possibly cancer) before our release. This was heavy work. Bags of rice weighed two piculs (about 266 pounds). These were lifted by four men (one on each corner) on to the shoulders of a fifth man. I learnt the knack of load-carrying the hard way, but was soon able to perform as well as the others, several of whom had been manual labourers, dockers, etc, in civilian life.

Working parties were detailed by the Senior British Officer in the camp – in our case Lieutenant-Colonel H C Owtram from a Lancashire Territorial Unit, followed by Colonel Williamson of the Indian Army. The Japanese took no part in selection, but merely told him how many men they wanted for particular jobs or for transfer to another camp.

Sapper Edgar Whincup, Royal Engineers
POW from February 1942 to August 1945
Camp 241, Ban Pong, Thailand
It was from this camp that the arduous, back-breaking and thoroughly unpleasant task of building a railway into Thailand was ordered by the Japanese. Because we the REs [Royal Engineers] were supposed to be a specialized company we were required to build the trestle bridges over which the railway would run.

The first journey we made from the camp was in the nature of a reconnaissance during which, accompanied by four Korean guards with Lee-Enfield rifles, no ammo, one handcart, one Japanese surveyor and a Japanese sergeant, Lieutenant Pringle, George Watson, Sergeant Sherran and I surveyed the area along which the railway would run. With us we took two sacks of rice and a tent. We measured relevant distances and the probable positions for sleepers and rails, etc, hacking our way through malodorous, virgin jungle, pegged out these measured distances as far as the Pagoda Pass (on the Burma–Thailand border), and all this on a meagre diet of rice. We did manage occasionally to obtain a scraggy chicken, etc, from any kampongs we passed. It was a long and extremely exhausting several-day stint, and walking there and back did not exactly improve our tempers or the condition of our feet.

We returned to Ban Pong having completed our survey of the area on which we were to work. From then on, daily we set out to build embankments, level the ground, fix the rail-layers and straighten our previous peggings to accommodate the width of the trains that were to run. We were taken to the railheads on flat, open bogies pulled by a diesel engine manned by Japanese engineers. When we arrived at the point where we had finished the previous day, the Japs up front would shout 'Brake', which we on the bogie duly did.

Our working day lasted from dawn to dusk, a day often 12 hours long and, of course, as we proceeded further from the base camp, we made our own camps as we went along. The most difficult part of the job was when we had to round cliff edges or pass the sleepers over ravines. For the latter, we had to build wooden trestle-bridges, and it was at these times that the moments of greatest danger occurred, especially when we had to drill holes in the cliff face. These drillings were one metre deep and were a stint for two men, working the whole of one day but completing only one hole. One disturbing and degrading feature of the work was [that] when the Japs suddenly took an intense dislike to any one man, or if they thought we were not working hard enough, they just pushed then over the edge of the ravine – two men died in this way.

Our next camp was Tonshan, just the usual huts and stores. As the railway progressed up through the jungle, so new camps were built at appropriate intervals, appropriate that is to the progress we were making.

Our next camp was at Kanyu, situated near to the area where we were beginning our next job, that of blasting and cutting through a large hill, around which the river ran. We were formed into gangs of two; one man was the hammer man, the other the chisel man. Each pair had to drill a hole of one inch diameter, one metre deep into the granite rock, one man holding a one-metre-long chisel, the other man using his hammer. Three holes had to be drilled each day before we were allowed to return to camp. After the holes had been drilled, charges were then inserted and the whole area detonated. Of course, afterwards the whole area had to be cleared of debris.

7
CONTACT

'Only in title were we military. In fact, we were human beings in exile. The real world we had left behind was no longer real to us; there were no practical possibilities of rejoining it. Our isolation was complete.'

– British officer POW in Italy

If food was the major defining factor in a POW's existence, almost as important were his relations with other prisoners and some kind of contact with the outside world. Unlike common criminals, prisoners of war had no idea when their sentence would end, and anything from eight to 20 officers might be squeezed into the same room, and up to 400 NCOs and other ranks be cooped up in the same barrack block, for months or even years. Thus it was vital that they strike up relationships with fellows who were at least compatible if not necessarily the best of friends. By virtue of service ties most men who entered a prisoner-of-war camp during the first half of the war did so either with the remnants of their unit, or with the certainty that they would spot a familiar face among the old lags who lined the fence to gawp at newcomers.

Friendships and partnerships were also formed by common interests – those who ran the camp administration, for instance, were a race apart from the common herd; likewise the theatre, the camp newspaper or magazine, the library and education 'eggheads' and the escaping fraternity had their little cliques. Sometimes these cliques were accused of obtaining concessions to which the general run of prisoners were not entitled. Sometimes self-interest and fear of losing privileges would prevent one of these cliques from helping another. But by and large the camps were run honestly and with reasonable efficiency.

One of the worst aspects of long-term imprisonment was the sense of remoteness from the outside world – a remoteness that made prisoners appreciate more than ever the simple things like walking on fresh green grass, watching the sun set over the sea, catching a bus, riding in a car, using a telephone, sleeping in a proper bed, seeing one's family, and pursuing a career. It was therefore a godsend that the Geneva Convention provided for the sending and receiving of letters, postcards and photographs.

POW letter-card from Flight Lieutenant Alf Thompson, a Canadian in the RAF imprisoned at Oflag VIB, Warburg, 1942 (*Nora Crete*)

Article 36 left the warring parties to settle between themselves the number of letters and postcards that prisoners could send, although the norm in Germany and Italy seems to have been one letter (of a page in length) and three or four postcards a month. Not later than one week after his arrival at a POW camp a new prisoner was entitled to send a postcard to his family notifying them of his capture and informing them of the state of his health.

All the Axis powers allowed their prisoners access to newspapers and radio broadcasts, but the news bore as much relationship to reality as chalk does to cheese, since the leaders could not even tell the truth to their own citizens, let alone to prisoners of war. Both Germany and Italy produced a regular monthly propaganda newspaper especially for POWs, who soon put them to a more useful and immediate purpose – although it has to be said in all fairness that the German one, *The Camp*, at least enabled prisoners to contact relatives in other camps and claim misdirected Red Cross parcels, which were stored at Stalag XIIA, Limburg, in north-west Germany. In most camps, even from the beginning, POWs created their own newsletters, newssheets or newspapers as a substitute for news from home. As the war progressed prisoners began building their own radio receivers. Almost every camp in Germany and Italy could receive the BBC news by the middle of the war. Far Eastern prisoners of war were even more ingenious, building radios from the parts of abandoned vehicles and other components smuggled in by friendly natives. However, possession of a radio receiver carried the death penalty, so it was vital to keep knowledge of its whereabouts secret to all but a select band of 'boffins', who then relayed the news throughout the camp. Some camps also had transmitters, but these were never used.

FRANCE, GERMANY AND POLAND

Despite the injunctions in the Geneva Convention against undue delays in forwarding mail, and the pious resolutions made by the warring parties, prisoners in German hands experienced long gaps between letters, as did their next of kin, and it was not uncommon for letters to take up to three months to reach their destination – as the following prisoner laments. When letters did reach camp, they were a welcome boon. During times of no mail the immediate company might lift the spirits. Those on working parties might even find the local population not entirely hostile, especially as the war went in the Allies' favour.

FRANCE

Lieutenant Commander William Stephens, Royal Naval Volunteer Reserve
POW from March 1942 to October 1942
Rennes Transit Camp, France
It was extraordinary how high our morale was during those early days. The fact that we knew that the Saint-Nazaire job had been successful must have helped us; in fact, our only real worry at that time was that our families would not know what had become of us. Then after we had been in captivity four or five days came the great moment when we were told we might write a letter and that it would take about a fortnight to get to England. We were simply thrilled, and it was just as well that we didn't know that most of those letters, which were written on 2 April, didn't get to England until about the middle of July!

GERMANY

Mrs Vivien Johnson (née Symonds)
Pen-pal, later wife, of Pilot Officer Theo Faire Storrier Johnson, Royal Air Force (Prisoner from August 1940 to May 1945)
At the end of 1940 the Red Cross started a scheme for POWs to be 'adopted' and sent money for food. As a result of a Red Cross appeal my family 'adopted' four and one of these was Theo Johnson. So we wrote to each other for four years before we eventually married on 7 January 1947; although the story seems to belong to a very mushy romantic novel the reality was an extremely happy marriage.

This meant that we didn't meet until we had exchanged mail for nearly five years. Our letters were very infrequent on Theo's part as his were, obviously, rationed by the Germans and he could only spare me a few postcards because he had family members in both New Zealand and the UK.

I wrote as often as I had time to spare from a 12-hour working day on a dairy farm without weekends off and only a few days holiday each year. All parcels were sent by the Red Cross, which received our monthly cheques for the four POWs that my family 'adopted'.

When the news broke in 1944 that the Gestapo had murdered 50 officers from Stalag Luft III, I was very concerned that he might have been one of these as I didn't know if he was into the escape mode.

Flight Lieutenant Allen Roy Mulligan, DFC, Australian in the Royal Air Force
POW *from August 1940 to April 1945*
Letter to his fiancée in England from Stalag Luft I, Barth, 27 June 1941
Dear Pam, I am sorry to hear that you have had so few letters from me so far. I have been writing twice per month and letters should be getting through more quickly now as it is all going by airmail. Your last letter was dated 4/4/41which was quite good. They have heard at home from me now and received my first letter during Xmas week but I suppose you have heard that in letters from home five months is the average time for letters to reach me from Australia. The weather during the last week has been super and lying in the sun all day seems to help the time pass. Medical comforts parcels are very good things for these conditions. If at all possible could you send some through the authorized chemists or stores? Thanks a lot for your letters Pam, we work the little news we get to death and you would be surprised at the commotion the arrival of letters causes here. I have received 22 from you so far as I have had 22 letter days up to now. Please remember me to Bob and Nona and all and I do so hope everything is well. We are OK but of course looking forward to the day we get back. Sorry that news here is nothing to write home about – cheers for now Pam and all the best to Bruce and the family. Yours, Mull.

Flying Officer Michael Heriot Roth, Royal Air Force
POW *from May 1940 to May 1945*
Oflag XC, Lübeck
One of the kriegies was a Flight Lieutenant Gosman, who had been acting Adjutant of my squadron in France. We had never been particularly warm acquaintances; nevertheless he suggested I could take the one empty bunk in his small room. It was a gesture and I appreciated it. There were seven other occupants: two embittered Fleet Air Arm lieutenants, Messrs Ross-Taylor and 'Skid' Bellairs, shot down flying torpedo bombers in Norwegian waters. They'd been operating off a carrier commanded by a Rear Admiral who, in the face of contrary advice from his Air-Commodore Advisory Officer, had sent off squadrons of slow-flying Swordfish aircraft in broad daylight, without air cover, to their certain destruction. There wasn't a cloud in the sky. The operation was a predicted disaster – a 90 per cent loss of men and machines to German fighters and without any results to show for it. Ross-Taylor and Bellairs were already preparing some choice remarks for the Admiral after the war. Others in the room included two lean and scrawny Scotch types, pals, but who never smiled. There was an Irishman we called 'Sex' – his real name

was Organ – who before the war had been the actor-manager of a Shakespearean touring company, and as such had developed stomach ulcers. He was a hilarious mimic and impersonator, and entertained us with parodies of bosomy aging operatic females he'd met in his travels. One of his best was from *Samson and Delilah*, in which the actress playing the young and seductive Delilah was actually a 60-year-old bird who sang with hands under the chin: 'I am young, am I not?' Ludicrous. Organ had a vast, fascinating store of managerial anecdotes, most of which had to do with eluding the duns (bailiffs), or getting across the border in or out of Scotland without paying his company's bills. Organ filled our days with laughter, bless him.

Kurt Knierim
German schoolboy, Elbersdorf village, near Spangenberg (Oflag IXA/H)
Letter to author, 1999
In the years between 1939 and 1945 I was only a child. Castle Spangenberg and the former regional agricultural estate in Elbersdorf were prison camps for English POWs from 1939 to 1945. The buildings located within the former agricultural estate in Elbersdorf were called the *Unterlager*, that is, 'lower camp', whilst castle Spangenberg was called the *Oberlager*, that is, 'upper camp'.

Several hundred Englishmen were kept in the camps. They were guarded by so-called *Landesschützen* [literally, land-guards, or country guards]. The camps were surrounded by thick barbed wire, so that there could be no contact with the local population.

Once a year, on the so-called *Tag der Wehrmacht* ('Wehrmacht Day') the local population had the opportunity to visit an exhibition in the hall of the hotel 'Zum Goldenen Löwen' ('The Golden Lion').

Objects that had been manufactured in the upper and lower camp were exhibited here. Amongst the exhibits were oil paintings, aquarelles, embroidery, woodcarvings, as well as costumes from Shakespeare plays, objects made of glass, etc – all of high artistic and aesthetic value.

The local (German) population enjoyed visiting this exhibition, which lasted several days, very much, because it demonstrated what kind of an artistic life was possible behind barbed wire.

One quite often heard of escape attempts. For example, prisoners would don the clothes of (local) tradesmen/craftsmen working within the camp and try to escape.

There was also talk of 'subterranean passages' (ie, tunnels).

Relations between the French, Polish and Dutch prisoners and the German population were very good. They would sometimes live under the same roof as the German population; they would eat at the same table with the Germans, and helped work the land. Prisoners who died were buried in a religious ceremony on the Old Cemetery, and the bell of the hospital chapel was rung on such occasions as well.

Sometimes, when the prisoners were playing football on the local football field – under German guard, of course – they would drop much-sought-after chocolate onto the grass for the German children. It was vital that the German guards did not notice this, because when they did, the chocolate would be taken away from us.

Major Elliott Viney, Oxford & Bucks Light Infantry
POW from June 1940 to May 1945
Oflag VIIB, Eichstätt, Bavaria

Our one radio set gave us the nine o'clock news every day for five years; it was given to one representative from each room at 9.30; he had to memorize it and give it to his room after lights out. The Germans were sure we had a radio, but they never found it. The risk was on moving to another camp, but the sports apparatus came with us and the set was sewn inside a basketball.

Squadron Leader George Dudley Craig, Auxiliary Air Force
POW from 4 November 1941 to 22 April 1945
East Compound, Stalag Luft I, Barth-Vogelsang

John Gillies and I were highly involved with the Intelligence and Coding Team. The first letter with Intelligence information we ever sent was, I think, through a Swedish representative of the YMCA who smuggled it out of Germany for us. We also sent and received messages in photographs: the front would be separated from the back, a message written on the inside, and then the two parts glued back together. I remember the messages being discovered because the photographs came unstuck. Luckily nothing very important was inside. We also used what was known as a Square Code, whereby the first letter of certain words (say, every fifth) would be transferred to a grid by RAF Intelligence back home (we always referred to them as 'Control') and which, if read from left to right or from bottom to top or diagonally, would form a message. But after a while we ceased using this system, which the Germans also discovered when the clot of a Military Adjutant in Stockholm gave it away.

I well remember John and I later devising a code in which to receive transmissions on our secret camp radio and composing a masterpiece of a letter in Squadron Leader Torrance's name to Torrance's wife. It took about five pages of foolscap – and therefore several letter-forms – and dealt mainly with advice to Torrance's wife to sell certain stocks and shares. I gather when she received the first letter she panicked somewhat as she did not realize that the ostensible content of the letter was a phony.

I remember how terribly exciting it was when we got an acknowledgement of it from 'Control' and they said they would start transmitting. If I remember rightly the coding of the first message was slightly corrupt but later on it worked smoothly.

Lieutenant William Bompas, Royal Artillery (Field)
POW from December 1942 to April 1945
Oflag VIIIF, Märisch-Trübau, Czechoslovakia
Language definitely alters in the bag, and if you think somebody is a dirty bastard, although it really means very little, you have no hesitation in addressing him as such. If you're fed up with someone's company, you merely go away – and why not?

Gertrud Koppenhöfer (née Böttcher)
German mail-censor at Stalag Luft III, Sagan, from October 1943
Since the 'Total War' was declared by Goebbels (March 1943) the German citizens were not free in choosing the field of activity they wished to do. In consequence our studies were reduced to six months and we were running the risk of being forced to work in an armament or ammunition factory until the end of the war. I already had the experience during my mandatory time in 'War Labour Service' in 1942 when I was forced for five months assembling shells for big guns under awful conditions in factory and accommodation. This time was the most terrible experience I had in my young life.

Sigrid Moritz, Inge Klocke and I myself studied in Dresden and lived in the same boarding house. We were glad to hear of an offer of the German Air Force to work as a censor in camps for prisoners of war. Officers of the German Air Force visited colleges all over Germany to encourage trained interpreters and correspondents to volunteer, after examination, as civilian employees. So we volunteered for Sagan Camp in October 1943 and in retrospect we did not regret that decision ever since.

We came to Sagan when the Post Control Office [Postüberwachung] had to be enlarged. Owing to the increasing air raids and more pilots being shot down over Germany there was lack of censors in camp. Until summer 1943 active soldiers of the German Air Force with knowledge of foreign languages and a few

German mail-censors at Stalag Luft III: Gertrud Böttcher
(later Koppenhöfer) to the left, Sigrid Moritz (later Haase)
to the right (*Sigrid Haase*)

German girls trained as interpreters and translators censored the mail for all prisoners shot down and in prison all over Germany and in occupied Poland.

We got short instructions and introduction how to work. In separated rooms for about three to six persons we had a supervisor (one of the Luftwaffe soldiers) whom we could contact in case we did not understand some idioms in the letters or were suspicious something was mentioned which had to be blacked out. After few weeks' introduction in our task we had to read independently all the incoming and outgoing mail we had been assigned to by alphabetical letters, our contingent to that time was about 100 letters per day, even more when it was incoming mail only.

The instruction was to black out everything which would discredit the German government or the German people; any reference to the locality of the camp or indication of air raids or bomb alarm; description of camp life, for example lack of food or coal, of other miserable conditions in camp, bad treatment by the Germans etc.

Our attitude towards the prisoners was of course reserved. We were not allowed to meet them, speak to them or write a note. As we knew of spot-checks we didn't dare to put a note in the censored incoming letter, nevertheless some did. We only met prisoners once or twice, but it was dark and we could not see each other. This was in the cinema-room in the camp after we finally had success in being allowed to attend one of the American or British movie shows.

When we walked around the camp sometimes prisoners tried to get in contact with us by shouting a few words across the barbed wire. We answered if possible in a reserved manner as there was always a guard watching and listening, and we did not know whether he would report his observation to the Camp Leader or the administration office where the Political Supervisor (a member of the Nazi Party) anyway suspected the censors and all the other members of 'Postüberwachung' of doing 'conspiration and fraternization with the enemy' – as they called it.

Hannelore Lewerentz (née Zöller)
German mail-censor at Stalag Luft III, Sagan, from January 1943
I was dealing mainly with the 'Mac's'. Although we were forced to stick to strict rules and regulations with regard to censorship most of us tried to handle letters carefully and to delete as little as possible. I remember that at the beginning I myself felt quite uneasy when reading letters of strangers with all their private and confidential contents. But with time going by we became acquainted with the individual family history of many of our 'clients', getting to know the good and bad news. And we naturally developed preferences, and when we received

our lots of mail we very often had a quick look through whether there was a letter for one of our favourites, which we then gave priority.

One little story is still in my mind. One of 'my kriegies' very anxiously awaited news of a happy family event. When eventually I had the letter with the news before me I was so delighted myself that I added my own 'congratulations'. Unfortunately, this letter underwent a control examination with the result that I was called before the German colonel in charge who punished me for this forbidden expression of sympathy by cutting out my home leave and by giving me a stern warning.

Pilot Officer Theo Faire Storrier Johnson, New Zealander in the Royal Air Force
POW from August 1940 to May 1945
East Compound, Stalag Luft III, Sagan, September 1943
My Dear Aunt Loui,

I do hope you are receiving my mail, for although I've nothing about which to write I like you to know that I am keeping in the best of health. Realizing how dislocated our lines of communication probably are, I really don't expect to receive much more mail from England but as I've received only one letter from you since May, and that dated early March, I do trust that all is well with you. Here life has recently been all that even we could ask – fine weather, plenty of exercise, regular parcels and just enough work to fill in the odd evenings. Last month we ran a very successful sports meeting and if the times for the track events can be accepted as a criterion we are all pretty fit. A short while later a marathon relay of about 27 miles was run round and round the compound by 50 runners from each barrack; each of the eight barracks completed the course in a little over two hours. In one or two cases I've asked people to write to me care of you again and if any letters should arrive I'll be very pleased if you would hold them for me. In the highest of spirits I once again send my love to you all,
    Theo

POLAND

Telegraphist Herbert Edgar Elliott, Royal Naval Volunteer Reserve
POW from August 1940 to May 1945
Arbeitslager, Bromberg [Bydgoszcz]
On 20 January 1941 I received my first letter from home and was generally very excited. I was the first of the 'Minelayers' Crews' to receive a letter. The few that were with me were as excited as myself and I could hardly call that

first one 'personal', for all read it. On this day we received news that all naval men had to return to Thorn.

Margaret ('Peggy') King
Sister of Gunner Cyril George King, Royal Artillery (Territorial Army)
POW at Stalag XXIB, Schubin, June 1940
Mail was erratic and, of course, he could not tell of work he was doing. The Red Cross was wonderful and we were able to make up parcels for him and take these to London. We could also send letter cards.

ITALY

Prisoners in Italy awaiting letters and parcels from home experienced much longer delays than those in Germany, because things were changing fast in the Mediterranean and forced the Italians to make frequent mass transfers of prisoners to camps farther north. This was particularly hard to take when the war news was depressing, and perhaps accounts for a greater tendency than in Germany for some of our Allies to get involved in 'rackets' and even to throw their lot in with the enemy. When Italy changed sides in September 1943 there was further disruption to the mail service, as next of kin had no idea where their prisoners were and did not know whether to address letters to Italy or Germany.

Lance-Corporal Lawrence Bains, Middlesex Yeomanry
POW from June 1942 to August 1944
Campo PG 66, Capua
A bone of contention in the camp were three Syrians, who were determined to get on the right side of the Italians, giving fascist salutes whenever possible, always springing to attention, etc. As a result they became most unpopular and once or twice were mildly maltreated. They had special food, which they cooked themselves, and occasionally this was tipped over by angry POWs; all very petty and rather a pity.

Lieutenant David Dowie, 4th Battalion, East Yorkshire Regiment
POW from June 1942 to September 1943
Written in Campo PG 49, Fontanellato
Fontanellato has been in every way the steady breaking down of our isolation; our personal isolation and our prison isolation. We have seen the outside life

of the world flow in towards us in successive stages, like an increasing tide. At Rezzanello we were occupied entirely with personal problems: how best to live in a small community cut off from the world. Only in title were we military. In fact, we were human beings in exile. The real world we had left behind was no longer real to us; there were no practical possibilities of rejoining it. Our isolation was complete. We were isolated also as individuals. Conversation was in most cases the exchange of signals between friendly craft. There was seldom an invitation to come aboard. Each was aware of his own life as a course which he followed alone, each concerned only with his own salvation. The daily prison routine was ultimate reality to us. Yet around these self-interests grew a superficial comforting sense of living within a friendly community, pursuing your own aims in a favourable environment.

Private Maurice Newey, Royal Army Ordnance Corps
POW from June 1942 to April 1945
Campo 54, Fara Sabina (Rome)
The great day came when the bugle-call signalled the arrival of the first batch of mail.

I always considered myself fortunate that I was single and that I hadn't left any girlfriend waiting for me, so that I had only myself to worry about. I knew that my parents would be worried about me, but I didn't let that weigh too heavily on my shoulders. For the married men it must have been a great strain, and to see their eager faces as they listened for their names to be called was quite sad for, knowing the Eyeties by now, it would be too much to expect them to get all the mail, so somebody was bound to be disappointed. A joyous whoop and a smile of relief would be given by those who received a letter. The poor chaps who didn't, looked as miserable as hell. The mailman tried to reassure them by telling them that there was more mail at the station, but it was small comfort and they would walk disconsolately away.

For some unknown reason, there is always someone who gets five or six letters at once, while others either get one or none at all. This proved to be the case again and the fortunate chap was the object of many envious looks.

Christmas [1942] arrived, but no extra rations to celebrate with. The Pope sent each man a calendar-cum-diary, with a Christmas message from him inside and a Papal utterance for each month. I was not too thrilled with this gift; a couple of loaves per man would have been a damn sight better in my opinion. It wasn't spiritual food we needed. We had a Padre in the camp to supply this, but this idiot used to spend a lot of his time chasing lizards, for when he put his foot on their tails, they would shed them. This seemed to fascinate him. He could have spent his time better going round the tents and giving comfort to any of the lads who needed it.

Lieutenant A F ('Junior') Powell, 13th Light Anti-Aircraft Regiment
POW from April 1941 to May 1945
Campo PG 35, Padula
During most of 1942 the war news was most depressing; the German army was nearing Alexandria and Stalingrad, while the Japanese were spreading over the Pacific and into Burma. But as we were brewing up one morning we were surprised to hear Big Ben sounding the hour over the new radio speaker the Italians had installed. Then an English voice announced: 'This is the BBC News', and proceeded to tell us of the great victory at Alamein. This was the last time we heard the Allied news – at least officially.

Corporal Eric Barrington, Royal Air Force Police
POW June 1942 to April 1945
Campo PG 73, Carpi (Modena)
Saturday, 9 January 1943. And the best duly arrived, a long-awaited letter from my wife, posted on 4 November and re-addressed from Campo 66 to 54 to 73. My first postcard from Benghazi in June arrived home in November! May the Eyeties roast in hell. To think my folks had to wait five long months before they knew I was a prisoner, and what in heaven's name happened to all my Capua mail? Over 40 letters and cards and moreover three telegrams have I sent since arriving in Italy. However, now they know and I am more at ease. I was encouraged to have a grand cleanup by this good news from home, so shaved and then carried on with the dobying [laundry], but it was not a success, the Italian soap making practically no lather in the cold hard water, and I suppose the things will take at least three weeks to dry in this weather.

Miss Christine Knowles, OBE
Chairwoman of meeting of Next of Kin of Officers
Speech to members, London, 6 October 1943
The government say if you have an address in Italy you will do better to write to where you last knew your prisoner was. I think that is logical, because the Germans are very logical people. They would receive the mail, and they would forward it on to where they have moved the prisoners. If the prisoner has joined up with our own people so much the better, and if a letter goes

astray that does not matter. I think we can only be guided by what we are told to do. I cannot think we understand all the ramifications of it, and I do not think anybody can, but we have been told to continue to write to where we know the men were until we know they are anywhere different. That is what has always guided prisoner-of-war correspondence up to now. You will realize that a letter card gets through in under three weeks now to certain camps.

THE FAR EAST

The next of kin of prisoners in Far Eastern camps perhaps suffered the greatest mental and emotional turmoil, as the Japanese were extremely reluctant to allow any POWs to have contact with the outside world apart from receiving 'the news' from the Japanese Broadcasting Corporation, which they believed contained all the truth that was needed. Even the best efforts of the Indian Red Cross were unable to alleviate the situation.

However, there were at least some local resistance members in Burma and Thailand in touch with the British authorities in India, and they did their utmost to bring aid to Allied prisoners.

One such was Boon Pong Sirivejjabhandu, who became a legend to the prisoners working on the Death Railway. Boon Pong was a captain in the Free Siam Army and an underground agent of the 'V Organization', which had been founded in Bangkok. Its members smuggled money, food and medicines to sick and starving prisoners. Boon Pong himself risked his life countless times, cashing cheques, delivering medical supplies to camp hospitals, and supplying batteries for the secret radios.

Japanese Ministry of War, Formula for POWs writing letters

1. We prisoners are permitted to write home by the generous government of Nippon.
2. I am in a Japanese Prisoner of War Camp in —
3A. My health is excellent.
3B. My health is not excellent.
4A. I am now in hospital on account of sickness.
4B. I was in hospital but now I have recovered my health.
5. I hope you are all healthy, and are living well. Are the children well? Have you enough money for food to keep yourselves?

6. My daily work is easy. We are being paid according to the number of days we work.
7. We officers are being paid the same salary as that of the Japanese officers (according to the ranks per month).
8. I am always wishing that this miserable war will be over and that I should return home again.
9. At present I am not working.
10. I am constantly thinking of you. It will be wonderful when we meet again.
11. Our camp is well equipped and the accommodations are comfortable, our daily life is very pleasant.
12. The Japanese treat us well so don't worry about me and never feel uneasy.
13. Would you kindly look after Mr or Mrs —
14. Goodbye. God Bless you. I am waiting for your reply earnestly.

Three of the above can be used. The number of each to be placed opposite No. on the sheet of paper supplied.

SINGAPORE

Sergeant William McDonald ('Tam') Innes-Ker, Straits Settlement Volunteer Force
POW from February 1942 to August 1945
Camp 331, Changi Prison
Of course, we had many expert electricians and engineers, and it was said that at one time there were ten secret radio receivers operating. One, I believe, was hidden in a sack of rice each day. Some were operated by hand-driven generators, one actually tapped into the Nip office electric light line, and others were powered by batteries extracted from lorries. Anyway we troops got a good deal of what we called 'Borehole Griff', said to originate from one operator who hung his radio halfway down a borehole and then sat on top, in the dark, listening in at BBC Overseas News time! I must say that all these 'Boreholes', which were passed by word of mouth, got fearfully exaggerated and twisted and very often had no word of truth. I do not know how many times we were told the Americans had landed in the north and were sweeping down towards Singapore.

During all our POW time we were only allowed to send five postcards of no more than 24 words each, and these went to Europe via Russia I believe, taking a year or eighteen months in transit. On the other hand, letters from home were more frequent, and at first from the UK they were unlimited in length, though later they were cut down to postcards of 25 words. These would arrive in huge batches and be taken by the Nip administration for censoring. Here they would lie for three or four months, a few samples here and there being actually censored (none of mine were). Then they would come to us in Camp Office for distribution, and for weeks afterwards people would be huddled in corners reading and re-reading their letters. God, how we looked forward to them. The Australian Red Cross permitted photos to be sent and any of likely-looking wives and sweethearts were pinched by the Nips and hung up in their quarters for leering at.

Mrs Enid Innes-Ker
Wife of Sergeant William McDonald ('Tam') Innes-Ker
[February 1942.] One very good thing that came out of this evening was that Sir Harry Battersby, the British High Commissioner in New Zealand, told me it was now possible to send letters to Far Eastern POWs, told me how to address my letter and that I must only send one sheet of paper, written on one side only. The very next day I perched on my bunk writing awkwardly on one corner of the dressing table. There was so much I wanted to say I did not know where to begin, or how to compress it. I could not give any indication that we were on a ship bound for home, in case the censor would not pass the letter, so I gave our address c/o Mrs Youngs, and just said in the letter that we were 'unsettled', hoping that Tam would make the correct inference.

This first letter was the only one he received before he went up to Siam, and I am so thankful that he had that message to take with him. Tam wrote a very sad note on the back of my letter, at a time of great misery and suffering for him, when he was sure neither of the date nor where his camp was. In my letter I said that my greatest comfort was the thought that Tam was so sane and balanced. I mention this because it was quoted later by one of Tam's friends in a most moving letter just before Tam went up to Siam.

[In England] I floated into two more temporary jobs with the BBC, both in the Overseas Division, before finally settling down ... I first went to the Pacific Services Director, whose secretary was away nursing a sick mother. There was a very good scheme in operation whereby copies of inter-departmental memoranda were circulated to the various Heads of Services, and through reading these memos as they came round I learned that it was possible to send a radio message to Far East POWs, through the Indian Service Director. I dashed off in great excitement to his secretary to find out the procedure. She received me in a very off-hand, cool manner and said it was only for next of kin and the message must only be 25 words. I assured her that I qualified and hastened to my office to compose a message that would compress everything I wanted to say into just 25 words. When I handed her my typed effort, she took it without looking at it and casually flicked it into a basket on her desk. It gave me no feeling of confidence that my message would be treated with loving care or that it would ever reach Tam – but miraculously it did! If I had not happened to be floating round the Overseas Division I do not think I would ever have heard of this opportunity to send a message; certainly none of the official organizations, like the Red Cross or the Colonial Office, ever mentioned to me this possibility. These messages were relayed at All India Radio, then put out by them and picked up by brave men in Changi camp operating illegal receivers. When Tam got back into Changi after being some weeks in a working party out of camp, he was told there was a message for him and where to go to find out about it. So before he went off with 'F' Force for that appalling journey and those terrible months in Sonkurai rai and Tanabaya [Thanbyuzayat], he knew that I was safely in England and he had my first letter, written in New Zealand. It was little enough, but it was something to hold on to.

... I did try gently murmuring to Tam's mother that he was in the army and, if alive, must be a POW, but she was deaf and it did not seem to get across, so I thought it was a pity to press the point. She was an old lady and if she liked to think he was living in a bungalow it was kinder to let her go on thinking that. It did, however, slightly inhibit me when talking to her about Tam.

... The Christmas of 1942 was very quiet and muted. There was nothing for us to celebrate and still no news of Tam, but at least we were in our own home and I had come to rest in a pleasant job at the BBC. For the first time since that far-off February we felt settled in tolerably comfortable circum-stances, to wait, however long and weary the years might be, till the end of the war and, all being well, Tam's return.

... The highlight of 1943 was undoubtedly the receipt of Tam's first post-card, which arrived on the 14th July – the first news of him for 18 months. Thank goodness he was alive and well – or at least he had been a year ago; the card had taken that long to arrive.

It was little enough, just a few words written 12 months ago, but I cannot find the words to describe what it meant to me. I dashed down to Golden Acres in Elstead that weekend to show the card to Tam's mother, his father joined us from Exmouth that weekend, and we had a somewhat emotional reunion. I left the card with Tam's mother, so that she could feel she had something from him. It may sound daft, but I felt this was a real sacrifice on my part, and I was not quite easy in my mind until she had returned it. How ironic that just at this time, while we were so relieved and delighted, Tam was enduring a hellish existence in that infamous camp at Sonkurai on the Siam Railway. If we had known it, his chances of survival in July 1943 were very poor indeed.

... My second card [from Tam on Christmas 1943] and the best Christmas present I could have had. I was rather cast down to hear that Tam had received no letters, but then I never wrote with any confidence that my letters would get to him. I somehow could not see the Japanese bothering with POW mail. However, I maligned them there because an awful lot of my letters did get through. From Tam's remark that he hoped the English climate was agreeable it was obvious that he got some news of me – which was, of course, from the radio message I had sent through the BBC.

While on the subject of correspondence, it reminds me that once a week I stayed in the office at lunchtime and typed my letter to Tam. I had the office to myself, it was quiet and peaceful, and although it was often baffling to know what to say, in case the conditions in which the letter was received were so awful that what I wrote jarred with Tam's feelings at the time, still I enjoyed my quiet half-hour communing with him. It was a great deprivation when, in the summer of 1943, we were told that we could no longer send letters, but only 25-word postcards. Twenty-five words! What could one possibly say of interest in so few words? I sent a card a week from the middle of 1943 till the war ended in August 1945, but Tam says he only received about six of them; just as well perhaps as I fear I tended to repeat myself. It is very hard not to in such brief messages.

... The Christmas of 1944 we spent once more with Aunt Mabel and Joan in Harpenden. Round about that time another batch of cards from Far East POWs came through and several of my friends heard from their husbands, but this time I got no card from Tam. Not only was I bitterly disappointed, but I was also desperately worried, as the last card I had received had been the typed one with the spidery signature, that had set me wondering about Tam's health. Also the papers had carried articles about Japanese ill-treatment of POWs, particularly on the railway in Siam, about which news had been trickling through. A lot of people got cards headed 'Camp No ... Siam', but as none of Tam's were so headed I had no idea at that time that he had been in Siam. So I was feeling heavy-hearted that Christmas, though still nursing a dim hope that perhaps there were a few more cards to come through.

SIAM (THAILAND)

Sapper Edgar Whincup, Royal Engineers
POW from February 1942 to August 1945
Camp 242, Non Pladuk, Burma–Thailand Railway
At intervals over the years we were issued with two or three special prisoner-of-war postcards to send home. These buff-coloured cards had standard messages printed on them such as a) I am well b) I am not well c) I am working d) I am not working. When sending them home, we crossed out the statements which were not applicable to our condition at that particular time.

Lieutenant-Colonel Philip Toosey, 135th Field Regiment, Royal Artillery
POW from February 1942 to August 1945
Camp 249, Tamarkan
After two years we received the first letters from home. Many of us found these to be a reminder of a forgotten life, disturbing or even unwelcome.

In my camp I encouraged and in fact assisted black market activities but I made it a condition that those who made money out of it had to give 50 per cent to the hospital for the sick men. They deserved the 'rake-off' because they took the most enormous risks by wandering around the countryside at night.

Corporal Charles Kinahan, Straits Settlement Volunteer Force
POW from February 1942 to August 1945
Camp 250, Chungkai
One of our principal tasks in Kanchanaburi was to go to the store of a Siamese station contractor named Boon Pong, who also ran a canteen in Chungkai camp where small items such as bananas, peanuts, tobacco and duck eggs could be purchased with the pittance which we earned for working. I struck up a relationship with Boon Pong, who acted as an important underground channel between us and the British civilians who were interned in Bangkok, and had access to money and much-needed drugs, which were passed to our camp via Boon Pong and our party. This was an immensely valuable contact. Because of it Colonel Owtram kept me on the parties for over two years, so that I was never put on any of the parties which were sent up-country – sometimes to their deaths.

The Boon Pong contact involved risks. Thanks to the indolence of the Korean guards in charge of our party we got away with 'murder'. Boon Pong even cashed a £50 cheque for me and others. It was duly presented after the war and I still have it as a family memento. Boon Pong was the source of supplies which must have saved the lives of many prisoners. In particular he was the source of medical supplies and torch batteries which enabled Max and Donald Webber to operate their radio receiver. Occasionally I took out an empty torch case and brought it back with three fresh batteries in it. This kept us in touch with the progress of the war and was of immense help to our morale. We had to be careful about the extent to which we released the news to the main body of prisoners. Careless words in the hearing of our captors could have cost lives. Sadly we had a few men from amongst the British and Dutch (largely Eurasian) prisoners who were quite capable of passing on the word to our captors in order to ingratiate themselves.

Major R C Laming, 3rd Indian Corps
POW from February 1942 to August 1945
Camp 240, Non Pladuk, and POW Camp 248, Kanchanaburi
While I was in Non Pladuk POW Camp in December 1943 Lieutenant-Colonel Toosey asked me if I could read Thai newspapers. I replied that I could.

Between December 1943 and June 1944 we received Thai newspapers intermittently. I would translate them and pass the news verbally to certain selected officers, who passed it on to the officers' hut. At that time nothing of major importance was happening and it could be done verbally.

After the landing in France we had very good contact with the Thais through a Dutch NCO who went out on a work party and brought in papers nearly every day. He was a brave and clever man and although he had one or two narrow escapes from the Japanese Military Police he was never caught and he never took an unnecessary risk.

During this time the news was so much fuller that it had to be put on paper. I received much assistance from Lieutenant Colonel Pargeter, Royal Corps of Signals, and Captain Coombes, 137 (A) Field Regiment, RA, who had been studying Thai while a POW.

The papers would come in at about 1800 hours in the evening and they would be translated and destroyed by roll-call next morning. All notes were destroyed as soon as read and all precautions were taken.

As a result we were able to avoid discovery entirely by the Imperial Japanese Army, who had no idea what was going on.

After 23 December the Dutch corporal was sent up-country and we lost our contact and got no more Thai newspapers.

On several occasions air-dropped pamphlets were picked up and brought into the camp and were dealt with in the same way.

There was a separate contact for Chinese newspapers, which were trans-lated by Captain Grice, and Nippon papers when found abandoned or collected from the Nippon officer were translated by Captain Escritt, Royal Army Service Corps.

The same precautions were observed throughout.

After our transfer to Kanburi Camp we were more strictly watched and contact with Thai was practically impossible.

Tobacco wrappings were translated, old wrappers, scrap thrown away from the Nippon offices ...

The Commandant of Camp I JA himself unknowingly brought us the news of the German capitulation on the wrapper of a parcel.

In August Lieutenant Colonel Pargeter, who was out on a grass-cutting fatigue, managed to secure a Chinese newspaper and a pamphlet dated 18 July; this was our last news until 15 August when we were allowed to send a party to Kanburi to buy Thai newspapers and to listen to the radio at the shop of a Chinese merchant.

JAPAN

Lieutenant Stephen Abbott, East Surrey Regiment
POW from February 1942 to August 1945
No 7 Despatch Camp, Chi
The receipt of mail from home in this camp seemed to be fairly good except in the case of several men who received no mail at all when it had been apparent that their families would be writing to them. During our two and a quarter years in this camp we were permitted to send six letters or postcards and each month five per cent of the camp were allowed to send wireless telegrams. In the later months cables were received by about 100 men.

THE DUTCH EAST INDIES

Aircraftman Frank Deakin Jackson, Royal Air Force
POW from March 1942 to August 1945
Liang Camp, Ambon (Amboina), the Moluccas
Every prisoner's thoughts were with our loved ones back in England. Very difficult to describe those feelings. Did our relatives and friends know we were still alive? Did they know we had been taken as prisoners of war? We just did not know the answers. It is true that while in Java we had been given cards

to complete with messages for those at home. Four brief sentences had to be selected from ten composed by the Japanese themselves. Sentences so unimaginative. A few examples: I am very fit, The Japanese treat us very well, We are very content, I am very happy, etc, etc. Four of these innocuous phrases were to be chosen after which 25 words of one's own choice were to be added. Of course, extreme discretion had to be employed when composing these. We were very sceptical of these leaving Java, let alone arriving in England.

In the event, two of my cards reached my parents about two years later. A little before, they had received the information that my name had been 'picked up' as being a prisoner of war by the Australian Broadcasting Corporation.

Pilot Officer Erroll David Shearn, Royal Air Force
POW from March 1942 to August 1945
356, Sourabaya, East Java
The Japanese, for some reason or other, authorized a mass visit to the prison camp by civilians from Sourabaya. I and another of the RAF got into conversation with two English-speaking Dutch girls. One of them told me that she was on a trip to Java when the Germans invaded Holland and she had decided against going back home. She had obtained employment in Sourabaya. She and the other Dutch woman, so she said, were left unmolested by the Japanese soldiers. Indeed, she had been given a telephone number by a Japanese officer which she could ring in the event of her being annoyed by any of the troops. She and her friend gave us some small but welcome gifts in the clothing line.

An amusing incident occurred when 'closing time' came for the civilian prisoners. The Japanese pushed them all out, shouting and gesticulating at them. There was in consequence a tremendous scramble to get out of the gates. In the turmoil one of the prisoners got caught up and swept through with the departing civilians. He battled his way back, but was denied entrance by a Japanese guard. He was heard protesting: 'But I'm one of the prisoners, I live here!' I imagine he was eventually given permission to re-incarcerate himself.

8
HEALTH

'...I can remember one man who was so thin he could be lifted easily in one arm. His hair was growing down his back and was full of maggots. His clothing consisted of a ragged pair of shorts, soaked with dysentery excreta. He was lousy, and covered with flies all the time. He was so weak he was unable to lift his hand to brush away the flies which were clustered in his eyes and on the sore places of his body.'

– British officer POW, Siam

J ust as captors were obliged to house and feed their prisoners, so they had to provide them with medical treatment – often an urgent necessity considering the circumstances in which the men were captured. Soldiers, even if not wounded or injured, might well enter captivity suffering from exhaustion and shock; sailors might well suffer anything from wounds, injuries and burns to frostbite, hypothermia, exposure and dehydration. Almost all airmen entered captivity after sudden and violent action, and as many as 10 to 15 per cent would reach the ground burnt, wounded or injured – perhaps all three. Medical treatment would have to be quick and effective, and might well continue throughout the duration of a serviceman's captivity.

According to Article 14 of the Geneva Convention, each POW camp had to have an infirmary where prisoners could receive medical attention of all kinds. Isolation was recommended for patients suffering from infectious and contagious diseases. The cost of such treatment was to be borne by the detaining power. By mutual agreement all sides could retain, rather than repatriate or exchange, captured doctors and medical orderlies to care for their compatriots.

Prisoners who had serious illnesses or who needed vital surgery were entitled to be admitted to any military or civil institution qualified to treat them – again, at the expense of the detaining power.

Articles 13 and 15 ruled that prisoners should attend a medical inspection at least once a month to monitor their general state of health and cleanliness and to detect infectious and contagious diseases, particularly tuberculosis and 'venereal complaints'. Thus prisoners should be provided with baths, showers and toilets (including night latrines in their barracks), which should at all times be clean and well maintained. They should also be allowed fresh-air exercise and sports equipment.

To be fair to Germany and Italy, there was no shortage of hospitals in either country, but keen as they might be to fulfil their prisoners' medical needs, they did not share the same enthusiasm for general hygiene. Most POW camps, especially those for other ranks, were unsanitary and some were uninhabitable. Almost all camps in all theatres of war were at some time infested with lice and fleas, which seemed equally impervious to heat and cold and which caused skin infections and spread disease.

As usual, it was the International Committee of the Red Cross in Geneva, the British, American and Canadian Red Cross, and various other relief agencies that did the most to promote the physical and mental health of prisoners of war, providing medical equipment and special food. Their many activities on behalf of Allied POWs in Germany and Italy can be looked upon as one of the great success stories of the war. The death rate among British POWs in Europe was only 5.5 per cent for the Army, two per cent for the Royal Navy and 1.5 per cent for the RAF – and that includes those killed trying to escape. Thus, there is hardly an ex-POW who has not at some time or another expressed undying gratitude for the help the relief agencies provided.

Articles 68 to 74 of the Geneva Convention provided for the repatriation of prisoners of war who were seriously ill or seriously wounded or had been captive for a long time. The decision as to who qualified was arrived at by a Mixed Medical Commission, consisting of two neutral doctors and a medical officer of the detaining power, who examined patients put forward by each camp's medical officer. Although one of the neutral doctors acted as chairman it was often the detaining power who had the last word, and it was a sore point among prisoners that many men who should have been sent home were forced to remain captive and died as a result. Bad faith on all sides was also to blame, with the result that no prisoner of war was repatriated from Italy until April 1942, none from Germany until October 1943 (by which time 50 prisoners selected for repatriation in 1941 had died) and none from the Far East (and then nearly all civilians) until September and October 1943.

But physical and mental health was one thing – spiritual health another. No matter what facilities were provided either by captors or relief agencies, and no matter how many friends surrounded him, a prisoner might still feel hollow inside, an emptiness not entirely accounted for by inadequate food. At such times he could only find solace in religion. Inevitably, with entire armies surrendering to the Germans and the Japanese, chaplains found themselves behind the wire, too, and although they were strictly speaking Protected Personnel and were entitled to be repatriated or exchanged, in practice most stayed with their flock, either voluntarily or under duress. These men not only, on the whole, gave comfort to their parishioners but also proved a thorn in the enemy's side, and were often moved at short notice from camp to camp. One was even sent to the *Sonderlager* – 'special camp' – at Colditz for allegedly possessing a 'jemmy'. Another reason for transferring chaplains was that there were never enough of them to fill the spiritual needs of the millions of POWs. Although there were seven chaplains, Catholic and Protestant, in Stalag Luft III alone, they had to spread themselves amongst 15,000 men. Only one armed forces rabbi was ever captured, and that was in the Far East, where there were in fact few Jewish prisoners.

GERMANY AND OCCUPIED POLAND

Despite the terms of the Geneva Convention, the burden of providing medical treatment and sports equipment for POWs in German hands fell largely to the Red Cross (which already provided the bulk of prisoners' food), along with army medical officers and orderlies who found themselves captive after the campaigns in France, North Africa, Greece and Crete.

The Red Cross sent a variety of medical parcels and sports equipment, much of the latter supplied by the YMCA. Standard medical parcels – containing disinfectant, soap, bandages, gauze, lint, drugs and aspirins – were sent from London to Geneva every week. Meanwhile, the Invalids Comfort Section of the Red Cross Prisoners of War Department supplied special parcels for the sick. One was a 'milk parcel' and the other an invalid parcel. A typical milk parcel contained such items as creamed rice, lemon curd, custard, tomatoes, cheese, dried eggs, tomato sauce, barley sugar and chocolate. The invalid parcels contained more solid food – minced beef or sliced meat, tinned fruit, tinned salmon, meat and vegetable extracts, cod-liver oil and malt, glucose and honey. At Geneva there was usually a balance of 40,000 milk parcels and another 40,000 special food parcels. This was calculated on the assumption that 5 per cent of POWs at any one time would need medical attention. From Geneva they were sent to senior medical officers at prison camps and POW hospitals to use as required.

Anything that was required urgently – such as special drugs, trusses, spectacles and false teeth – was sent by air, usually by the Invalids Comfort Section. A request would be sent from Germany by cable and the item was packed in London, if possible, on the same day. Once packed, the item was immediately flown by 'Clipper' to Lisbon, where it would be collected by a post-office official who took it across to the office of the German airline. The supply of artificial limbs was more complex. Amputees were examined by an International Orthopaedic Commission, which had permission to investigate every single maimed British prisoner. Those in Germany who needed artificial limbs were sent to Lazarett IXC, a military hospital at Obermassfeld attached to Stalag IXC at Bad Sulza. The prosthetic limbs were made by a team of Swiss experts in Geneva, who travelled to Obermassfeld to fit them.

Ironically, one of the worst German camps, Stalag VIIIB at Lamsdorf – where there were repeated outbreaks of typhus and where POWs suffered from dysentery, diphtheria, tapeworm, lice and fleas – also had one of the biggest and best infirmaries.

The cause of much illness amongst prisoners in German hands was poor sanitation. The most offensive and noisome part of any camp was usually the latrines, which were primitive to say the least, and even 'showcase' camps like Stalag Luft III were no exception, while one wag at Schubin was moved to scrawl on the lavatory wall: 'It's no good standing on this seat/The crabs round here can jump ten feet'.

GERMANY

Flying Officer Michael Heriot Roth, Royal Air Force
POW from May 1940 to May 1945
Oflag IXA/H, Spangenberg, May–June 1940

The castle's sanitary facilities were less than adequate: two flush toilets for the whole company. At a pinch we could have got by with these had it not been for the French, who compounded their unpopularity by squatting on the seats with their boots. The result: seats caked with mud and turds, for which the French made no apology and no effort to clean up. No habit could have alienated them from the British more effectively. 'Some G— d—d effing French b—d' was mild reportage, and invariably related to the latest excrescence in the toilets. From birth, the French had been conditioned to believe they catch some dreadful disease if their precious derrières touched the seats. Nothing could convince them otherwise. The Entente Cordiale was doomed by superstition.

Committee of the International Red Cross
POW Hospital Report, May and June 1942

OBERMASSFELD HOSPITAL contained, in January, 356 British prisoners, including nine medical officers, one dentist, one chaplain and 36 medical orderlies.

The hospital is not far from Meiningen. It is a large modern building, standing beside a stream in a broad valley.

The patients are mainly orthopaedic cases, but there were also 15 blind prisoners of war. Its chief defect was that it was overcrowded. This matter was being taken up with the German High Command. The wards were airy and well lighted and the beds of a comfortable hospital type. Red Cross food parcels were arriving in ample quantities. (Visited 22.1.42.)

STADTRODA. – The hospital for British prisoners at Stadtroda is part of the civil hospital of the town of Stadtroda, ten miles SE of Jena. It stands on a hill, from which there is a pleasant view. It contained, in January, 56 patients mostly Australians and New Zealanders. There were four British medical officers and about 15 British medical orderlies. The hospital deals mainly with minor surgical cases.

The normal weekly issues of Red Cross food parcels was being made, and the prisoners were fairly well off for clothes. The wards were well ventilated and each bed was provided with at least two blankets.

HILDBURGHAUSEN HOSPITAL, which was also visited, stands at the edge of a small village, in a wood, in the same region as Obermassfeld. In January it contained five British medical officers, 28 medical orderlies, and 70 British patients, who were in comfortable single beds, with two or three blankets and clean bed-linen. In spite of the cold weather at the time of the visit, the rooms were well heated.

Clothing was in a satisfactory state, and one food parcel per man was being issued weekly.

Pilot Officer Idrwerth Patrick ('Paddy') Bentley Denton, Royal Air Force Volunteer Reserve
POW from July 1941 to May 1945
Oflag VIB, Warburg, October 1941–September 1942
In this camp an interesting physiological characteristic made itself evident. Those with more or less salty skins (nothing to do with cleanliness) were either bitten remorselessly by bed bugs or fleas or left strictly alone. I was one of the former and the bloody things poured out of the old woodwork of the hut and attacked me and others like me until we were a mass of bites and some sores. The others, like Derek [Pilot Officer C D Roberts], regardless of whether they were on upper or lower bunks, were quite untouched. It is fascinating that these creatures had lain dormant for years but, as soon as the requisite human flesh presented itself, came together in their armies to attack. Watching a bed bug at work on your body requires a certain degree of detached interest. The predator is initially small and partly translucent. Having once got a grip on the situation and the mandibles or whatever securely anchored, the hitherto translucent

214

body slowly distends as the blood is transferred from the victim. One would have thought that after so delicious a gorging they would have tottered off, like obese clubmen after a delicious lunch and vintage port, to find a comfortable chair and snooze away. Not so. They stick like billy-ho and are always ready for another go. This is the moment to counter-attack. A precise pincer movement between finger and thumb produces a satisfactory squelch. Regrettably this causes the blood to splash about a bit. This is not a battle that you can win as they always have enormous reserves lying in wait to renew the offensive.

Fleas are different and not so prone to being caught and destroyed so that was just an unending scratch.

One night, whilst fitfully sleeping, I awoke to feel what I thought was a gentle hand on my chest. I assumed that someone had another marvellous illusory idea for escaping so, somewhat drowsily, I asked 'What gives?' or words to that effect. There was no response. As the warm pressure was still there I put my hand down to my chest and found a very large rat indeed, quite peacefully kipping. I was, I am afraid, a little unkind in the way that I rejected his presumed advances and threw him to the floor. As the light in the corridor was kept on by the Germans I felt an obligation to follow the progress of this rat. He proceeded quickly under the door and into a large elongated hole in the floorboards of the corridor. From this point of advantage he gazed at me with a look combining dislike and mortification. As I had no suitable weapon to hand that would fit into the slot I did an awful thing. I found some old bits of paper which I lit and stuffed them quickly either side of him. I went back to bed. He did not disturb me again and presumably he learnt a sharp lesson to recount to his offspring.

Lance-Corporal Jack Sollars, Queen's Royal Regiment
POW from 1943 to August 1944
Stalag IVA, Hohenstein-Ernstthal, January–August 1944
Unfortunately, while a prisoner in Italy, I had contracted some spinal trouble, although this was not diagnosed until I got into the hands of the Germans in January 1944.

Stalag IVA, where I finally arrived in Germany, was a POW hospital and, I believe, a former mental home. It was right out in the country and it became pleasant with the warmer weather. TB cases were placed outside on a balcony to benefit from the sun and the fresh air. Food was the best we had had for a long time.

There were Russian prisoners in the place but they were in a special compound and very poorly treated.

We had books from the Red Cross at Geneva, some of them of excellent quality.

Practically all the Allied forces (with the exception of the Americans) were represented in the camp.

An international medical commission arrived around May or June and seemed to be composed of Swiss Army doctors whose uniforms reminded me of French gendarmes or General de Gaulle.

I was taken in to them on a stretcher and they looked though my records and asked a number of questions. Later I learned that I had been recommended for repatriation.

The great day came about the end of August 1944 when we were moved to another camp (run by the French) and eventually (in the middle of a moonlit night) put on flat four-wheeled horse-drawn trucks and taken to a huge hospital train (adapted from International Wagons-lits sleeping cars), pulled into a siding which seemed miles from anywhere.

On the train conditions were, to us, quite luxurious. We had German orderlies and the medical care was of the best.

On our way to the Baltic we saw a good deal of war damage (once, in a forest, we passed a highly camouflaged factory which had almost been flattened by our bombers). In Berlin the damage we saw was vast. Many streets, even with houses standing, seemed deserted. Gardens of better-class houses were full of fruit trees from which unwanted apples and pears were hanging.

The Metro was still running but, as we passed through one marshalling yard, we saw hundreds of smashed rail vehicles of one sort or another.

In one big station our train was put under an armed guard but we were able to see the crowds greeting other trains bringing wounded from the Russian front.

From Berlin we ran though fine open country with many trees and lakes until we reached Sassnitz, the ferry-train port for Sweden.

I saw German guards giving up their arms before we set out and, after sailing three miles, Swedish attendants came and told us we were free. Shortly afterwards I was seasick; my stomach could not cope with the erratic motions of the open stern of our train ferry through which, from my cot, I could see the turbulent waters of the Baltic!

Private Stanley John Doughty, 12th Royal Lancers
POW from December 1941 to February 1945
Stalag VIIIB, Lamsdorf, 1944–45
My stomach was giving me more trouble now, and problems were also arising with my bowels, and eventually I remember vomiting blood, on quite a

substantial scale I think, whilst down at the lavatory. I must have passed out, and don't remember much about the next few weeks, but I was in the *Revier* (the Stalag hospital) with difficulty of sight, terribly weak, and with a headache to end all headaches. I was given two large blood transfusions by the old system whereby the donor had to lie on a bed beside you, at a higher level, and I suppose his heart pumped the blood into you. I have every reason to be grateful to the dozen or so donors from the UK and NZ who gave me blood, which I'm sure they could not spare, and to the doctors who bothered under those circumstances, especially when I continually vomited again and again and the whole process had to be repeated.

The news from both the Russian and Normandy fronts was encouraging, and I eventually made good progress, especially when I heard that the 'Mixed Medical Commission' was coming and that I was to be included on their lists. This Commission was made up of German, Swiss and British doctors who, if they agreed, had authority to exchange prisoners who could play no further part in the war. The catch was that you had to be an in-patient if you were to be considered for repatriation, and as things were going it seemed as if I would be discharged back into the camp by the time they had arrived. I had been feeling sore ever since the desert sand first caused trouble, and circumcision seemed to be a relatively painless price to pay for the promise of repatriation, and so it turned out to be. With the connivance of the British Medical Officer I suggested circumcision, to which he agreed, and this minor operation was delayed and delayed until the Commission had arrived. It must have been 4–5 weeks, I suppose, and if the Commission had been further delayed perhaps we would have thought of something else.

They did arrive, and on the great day I, and some 20 others, passed. I had never felt so glad to be ill. In view of the scarcity of food most of my sustenance came from liquid food contained in the Red Cross medical parcels, mostly Ovaltine, with the result that I can't even face one cup or the smell of it today. I was able to hold this down by now, and it kept me going. Men with open wounds had to be dressed in paper bandages and drugs were non-existent. Tooth extraction, for instance, was done without any painkillers. Christmas came and went and we waited anxiously until at last the German doctor in charge gleefully told us that 'Tomorrow is the day'. Few slept that night, and in the morning sure enough the long process began. Identification, counting, more identifications, and so on. Body searches, and the last farewells from the medical staff, and we were outside the gates, on a horse and cart, with a guard. I remember thinking: 'What do we need an armed guard for now?' during our trip to the station, but I suppose orders had to be followed.

There we sat, in a draughty hut on the station, for what seemed hours before our train came – and what a train. It seemed to be composed of coaches, not trucks, from all the railways of Europe, in various stages of disrepair. Unfortunately, too, some of the heating couplings could not be made, so that the travelling turned out to be rather cold. Some prisoners were already on board from other camps, and I suppose we made the number up to about 200. Quite a number of stretcher cases, travelling on the floor, and the rest of us 'walking wounded', as we were termed, on seats that had undoubtedly seen better days.

The atmosphere was electric, only dampened somewhat by our companions saying that they had already been two days on the train. We were soon to discover the truth of this when eventually the train jolted and jarred its way to the Swiss frontier. We collected one more lot of prisoners and were about ten days on the train altogether, being shunted onto sidings in remote places on single-track branch lines, as I suppose the main lines were either bombed or required for military use. We were endlessly counted and checked until even the guards saw the funny side of it all. This travelling menagerie pulled into the German Konstanz station one morning early amidst great excitement. Hopes were high and eyes bright. Some of our companions had already cheered us up by saying that they had been on the last exchange, last year, which was supposed to take place through Sweden, but that at the very last minute – they had actually seen the Baltic – it had been cancelled, they thought because the Germans had been insisting on a 'two-for-one' instead of a 'one-for-one' and the Allies wouldn't have it. You can imagine what this did to our spirits.

However, there were obvious signs that something was about to happen. The platforms were decked with bunting and a military band was tuning up. Both seemed incongruous in the Germany we had seen during our trip; bombed and wrecked railway systems; smashed towns, and shortages of prac-tically everything. To this day, I think it is incredible that the Wehrmacht could even think of this trip, with all its supply problems, under these circum-stances. It says much for the organizational efficiency of the nation, but also the mixture of cruelty and kindness that makes up their national psyche, which I can so little understand.

Within half an hour, without any fuss or noise, an electric train pulled in, and such a train that it could only be a dream. Clean, externally and inter-nally, like a vision from another world, and from it descended, or were carried, the German prisoners which were to be our passport to freedom. They looked well enough, apart from their injuries. The military band struck up; there was a speech of welcome; they were all given something in a paper bag, and were then carried away in a fleet of horse-drawn carts. Now, we thought, it would be our turn. We would all be moved into this splendid, unreal palace, and move quickly through Switzerland.

To our dismay this did not happen. Minutes dragged by. The band packed up and moved off and to our horror the train silently moved off back to Switzerland without us. The despondency and fear could be felt, as solid as a brick, but luckily we were not long left in doubt. Just as silently as the other, a new train came into the same platform as the last, again like a vision from a world long forgotten, and into this, after final counting and identification, we were helped ... Our guards left us, and without a sound the train moved off across a bridge, and pulled up again very shortly with the station sign reading 'CONSTANCE (Suisse)'. We had made it.

Sapper Don Luckett, Royal Engineers
POW from July 1941 to May 1945
Arbeitskommando 951 GW, Hieflau, Austria

The *Kommandant* was asked about our proposal to burn the straw from the flea-ridden mattresses, and he readily agreed, adding that only the straw could be destroyed. So a fire was started some distance from the house, and watched over by a guard who stood at a discreet distance. After a while the whole palliasse was thrown on the fire, and when discovered by the *Kommandant* what we were doing, we were screamed at by him, as it was 'an act of sabotage', and cursed at for not obeying orders. If it had been possible to have burned the blankets we would have done so, but we knew that there was not a chance of a further issue.

In the course of time we managed to wash the dirty articles in some sort of fashion, though marred somewhat by the absence of soap or powder, but at least it gave us a little satisfaction to know that the blankets had been in water, and henceforth we slept on bare boards.

There was one redeeming feature, however, that arose from the flea situation, that being that some weeks later we found that we were also free from lice, and as one sage put it, 'You don't get the two together' – what truth there is in that pearl of wisdom is uncertain, but the lice had gone, for which we were most thankful. We eventually did rid ourselves of the fleas, but it took many weeks of relentless pursuit and hard work, which did pay off in the end.

Lieutenant A F ('Junior') Powell, 13th Light Anti-Aircraft Regiment
POW from April 1941 to May 1945
Oflag VA, Weinsberg

Before I was captured I weighed 170 lb and I have a record of my weight from August 1944 to March 1945, and see that I was down to 147 lb in January.

During that winter on some occasions my fingers would lose all their blood and the only way to get it back was to swing my arms around.

Flying Officer Oliver Philpot, Royal Air Force Volunteer Reserve
POW from December 1941 to October 1943
East Compound, Stalag Luft III, Sagan
An unpleasant thing in the summer of 1943 was the shooting of Lieutenant Kiddell. This officer was clearly unbalanced, the British authorities had strenuously applied for his removal to a home, the Germans had said it was a sham and then taken no action. Kiddell quietly left the camp sick-bay one night and was later, near the wire, killed by a sentry. He was wearing pyjamas.

POLAND

Telegraphist Herbert Edgar Elliott, Royal Naval Volunteer Reserve
POW from August 1940 to May 1945
Fort 17 (Stalag XXA), Thorn, October 1940
There were two Belgian doctors here, and I went to see them one morning, not feeling too good, and was told to come again the next day with my shirt off. Such was the medical treatment meted out then.

I attended two funerals but the identity of the deceased was not disclosed to us. It was a strange sight, in this Polish cemetery: a dozen Englishmen singing 'Lead Kindly, Light' and 'Abide with Me' from memory. Most of us had not sung them for years. Polish people gathered about the railings of the cemetery and showed much sympathy.

We were put to work unloading railway trucks and various other jobs.

Lack of food, unspeakable living conditions, no clean underclothes on top of my recent experiences were pulling me down fast. Many of us dropped from sheer hunger.

I was very pleased when I was told I was being moved with 500 others.

Lieutenant David Lubbock, Royal Naval Volunteer Reserve
POW from July 1941 to April 1945
Oflag XXIB, Schubin
When we were shot down I received metal splinters in my eye. Those sticking out of the eyeball were very carefully and well removed by a young German doctor in the front line, but one or more within caused a weakness in my vision

such that I could only read the first couple of lines of a book before it all became blurred. Flight Lieutenant Dowdeswell, who was an oculist and whose father had an optician business, examined my eyesight and made a prescription for me. We got the Protecting Power to get father Dowdeswell to make a pair of spectacles and had them sent out to me. They were superb and I could read and write over long periods. As a result for a hobby I started to write a book. Other activities were teaching a group of erstwhile medical students about nutrition, and giving talks to the camp on 'Food is good for you!' Also taking a class to learn Scottish Country Dancing till one foot went through the floor and I damaged my ankle!

Some people had home worries – matrimonial – and others must have found adaptation to POW life extra hard. While at Sagan I was called in to help an attempted suicide recover, at Schubin I unconsciously tipped the balance of a friend by telling him to make up his mind while he was dithering in the washhouse, getting in the way. 'Yes, David, I will' he said. An hour later (in broad daylight) he was climbing up the perimeter wire, not stopping when called by the guards to do so. They consequently opened fire and he was killed on the spot. He used to play wind instruments and was a fine musician.

ITALY

Prisoners in Italy were somewhat disadvantaged compared to their compatriots in German hands. Since the climate in Italy was more extreme, and most camps were either very temporary structures – some merely rows of tents surrounded by barbed wire – or ancient buildings such as castles and monasteries, prisoners were much more prone to illness and even at the best of times felt pretty low. Italy was also at first unprepared for receiving POWs, which meant that for months decent medical treatment barely existed. However, as time went on prisoners in Italy enjoyed a Red Cross and YMCA service comparable to that of their brethren in German, as well as fairly good medical facilities, with POW hospitals usually run by religious orders. The fact that they got more fresh fruit and vegetables than prisoners in Germany was also beneficial in the long run.

Lance-Corporal Lawrence Bains, Middlesex Yeomanry
POW from June 1942 to August 1944
Campo PG 66, Capua
When I arrived here in August 1942 I was not at all well, suffering from acute diarrhoea and general weakness, and so reported sick at the first opportunity.

Sick and wounded prisoners repatriated from Italy in the war's first POW exchange arrive at Alexandria, April 1942 (*IWM A8622*)

British, Australian, New Zealand and South African prisoners repatriated from Italy in 1942 broadcast messages home from Alexandria (*IWM A16087*)

The medical supplies were practically non-existent, but they had plenty of little brown pills which, with avoiding all liquids for a day, helped me to achieve some control over myself. The food in the camp was the best we had yet experienced, and with the addition of Red Cross parcels, I could feel myself gradually pulling round.

In September I had another bout, and an acute headache lasting several days, but the same treatment again worked a partial cure. I gradually increased the amount of liquid soups, etc, until I had reached normal rations.

The only epidemic was a slight diphtheria scare, and we were all examined, but very casually. Three people went down in our tent of eighteen until the carrier was found when everyone had a throat infection test. We had two inoculations against this; the first hardly affected me, but the second, much stronger, laid me out for a day and I hardly troubled about my food!

Corporal Eric Barrington, Royal Air Force Police
POW June 1942 to April 1945
Diary kept in Campo PG 73, Carpi (Modena)
Friday, 8 January 1943. Our miserable little 11 o'clock tiffin over, I decided to do some long-delayed dobying, but when I got down to it I found it was all I could do to wash a shirt, and then I felt so weak and giddy I had to lay down for half an hour to recuperate besides 'bashing' half a bar of chocolate; that was delicious anyway. One of the chaps in the opposite row of bunks was reported for being lousy – a quite true expression – he was taken away and came back bathed and with all his hair shaved off all over. Serve him right. We have too many lice, try as we do to keep them down. It seems to be a rule of the Eyeties that all their POWs must have so many per square foot. I never saw a country so destitute of the elemental necessities of disinfection and sanitation. We applied for some sulphur in our last camp to burn in the tents and keep down the flies and the lice, but as usual nothing doing. Here at any rate the winter has killed off the flies. May the Lord help us if we are here for another winter. None of us is fit after six months' captivity.

THE FAR EAST

The outlook for prisoners in the Far East was much less rosy than it was for those in the Western theatre of war. Most FEPOWs suffered from beriberi, diphtheria, dysentery, malaria and tropical ulcers; thousands were injured labouring on the Death Railway and in copper mines; all were starved, and

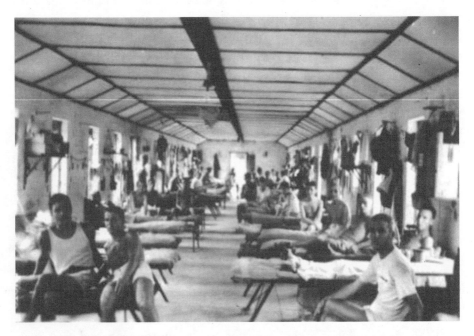

The hospital in Shamshuipo prison camp, Hong Kong (*author's collection*)

almost all were overworked. Yet although the Imperial Japanese Army had captured Allied medical supplies in abundance as it swept south-eastwards, it refused to issue them to prisoners of war. The British suffered most of all. They were new to the tropics and did not have as strong a resistance to tropical illnesses as the Australians, New Zealanders or the Dutch, who had a much tougher upbringing along with a healthier diet. Thus, it was the British who died in the greatest number. Of the 3,400 who had left Changi to work on the Burma–Thailand Railway 2,036 were dead by April 1944 – a 60 per cent death rate. Of the 3,662 Australians, 1,060 died – a death rate of 28.90 per cent. Even so, many of these deaths could have been avoided had it not been for the attitude of their captors.

POW doctors in such camps as Changi, Sonkurai and Tarsao were forced to make do with whatever drugs and medicines could be smuggled, in small amounts, into the camps, and often had to perform surgery – including amputations – with worn-out or improvised instruments.

During the 'Speedo' period one doctor at Kanyu was seeing 500 patients a day. Even when the railway was finished, death and disease were never far away. Between July 1942 and January 1945 the hospital at Non Pladuk admitted 25,000 patients.

Those prisoners who were transferred to Japan might have found the climate cooler but in winter this was a distinct disadvantage, as their thinly walled unheated huts provided inadequate shelter against the bitter Japanese winter. Men already weakened by malnutrition, malaria, dysentery, diphtheria ('the dip'), beriberi, tropical ulcers and overwork now found themselves suffering from frostbite and circulation problems. An examination of prisoners liberated from Hong Kong in 1945 revealed that 68 per cent were still suffering from beriberi. It is no wonder that the slogan 'never forget – never forgive' is often used by former FEPOWs.

SINGAPORE

Captain Arthur Geoffrey Threadgold, Royal Artillery
POW *from March 1942 to August 1945*
Selarang Barracks, Singapore
It was from Selarang Barracks that I went into Roberts Hospital with acute beriberi, where I was fed a diet of rice polishings – a sawdust-like husk off the rice, rich in Vitamin B, which was hulled off the rice grain in order to present it a white appearance. This sawdust, if eaten with sugar, took one hour to eat, but I obeyed medical directives and within about ten days had a skin like a

baby and the beriberi had gone and, what is more, I was really physically active again – I really felt well.

SIAM (THAILAND)

Sapper Edgar Whincup, Royal Engineers
POW from February 1942 to August 1945
Camp 241, Ban Pong (Burma–Siam Railway)
As we progressed as far as the cutting the Japs suddenly brought in a large number of Tamils from Malaya to supplement our workforce, which was becoming seriously depleted owing to lack of food and overwork. The Tamils, not having the same interest in and concern for hygiene as we had, soon became victims of cholera, and we found ourselves surrounded by camps the occupants of which suffered from this dreaded plague.

This forced us to take special care in our camp, and resulted in our taking extra precautions against contracting this disease. As each small tent accommodated six men, special arrangements were made by the six to make the tent as hygienically clean as possible. So we arranged that each morning one of our number would 'report sick'. He would stay behind and was therefore responsible in our absence for sterilizing all our eating and other utensils before our return 'home' for the day's work. Also he was to make sure all water, be it for washing, drinking or general use, had been boiled – because the water came from the river and because the river was a carrier of cholera it was, therefore, subject to the full treatment. We were convinced that all these precautions helped to keep the number of victims in our camp down to single figures. By contrast, in the Tamils' camps, where hygiene was practically nil, the occupants were dying in large numbers. This made us all the more careful.

Lieutenant-Colonel Philip Toosey, 135th Field Regiment, Royal Artillery
POW from February 1942 to August 1945
Camp 249, Tamarkan
The sick were in an appalling condition. Approximately 75 per cent of the parties were stretcher cases and men frequently arrived dead. They were brought in cattle-trucks or on the railway and there may have been 30 or 40 per truck. No arrangements had been made for food or treatment on the journey by the Japanese. On one occasion a party of 60, mostly stretcher cases, were dumped off the railway in a paddy field some two miles from the camp in the pouring rain at 0300 hours. They were left without a guard and a search party had to go out

from the camp to locate them. It is impossible to describe adequately the condition of these men. As a typical example I can remember one man who was so thin he could be lifted easily in one arm. His hair was growing down his back and was full of maggots. His clothing consisted of a ragged pair of shorts, soaked with dysentery excreta. He was lousy, and covered with flies all the time. He was so weak he was unable to lift his hand to brush away the flies which were clustered in his eyes and on the sore places of his body. I forced the Japanese staff to come and look at these parties, which could be smelt for some hundreds of yards, but with the exception of the Camp commandant, they showed no signs of sympathy and sometimes merely laughed.

During this time we saw scenes of misery which will live for ever in the memories of all of us. We always managed to give new parties a meal whatever time they arrived. This normally consisted of a rice cake and a cup of hot, sweet tea. Many men burst into tears at receiving help and food.

Chaplain M Cowin (RC), Royal Army Chaplain's Department
POW from February 1942 to August 1945
Camp 240, Non Pladuk

All that could be done to assist me in my work was done by the British Camp Commandant and his Staff, whilst I was at the above camp. The obstructive attitude of the Japanese, however, made it impossible to aid me much.

The Japanese policy regarding religion was much the same at Non Pladuk as at other camps in which I had been stationed. There has never been any question of freedom of worship; that has been forbidden. Services for the most part have been restricted to once a week, and Sunday was not allowed as a camp holiday. For long periods and with no explanation services were forbidden, and when, with the greatest of difficulty, permission was obtained to recommence them, sermons were prohibited.

No classes for religious instruction were allowed. Morning and night prayers could not be said. Permission to build churches, more often than not, was refused, and even when granted, no material was supplied by the Japanese. Interference by individual guards at such services as were allowed was not infrequent. No difference was made by the Japanese in the treatment of chaplains to that of any other prisoner, but I must add that owing to the efforts made by the British Camp Commandant and Staff at Non Pladuk I was always protected from the indignities and humiliations to which other officers were often subjected.

Although I made supplication scores of times to be allowed to visit adjoining camps where there were no Roman Catholic chaplains to minister to the men, such permission was always refused, with no explanation and often rudely. With the result that hundreds of Catholics died denied the Sacraments, the supreme consolation of their faith, and burial by a priest.

No transport was allowed for the bodies or burial parties, and the former, sown up in sugar sacks, had to be carried to the cemetery on stretchers. In the case of Non Pladuk, the cemetery was about a mile distant.

At a time when morale was low and full freedom of worship would have been of incalculable value, the Japanese went out of their way to obstruct chaplains in their work. They were completely indifferent to every kind of pleading. Throughout their captivity the prisoners of war were starved – starved of food, starved of clothing, of medical supplies, of news, of letters from home – and starved of spiritual consolation.

SIAM AND SINGAPORE

Sergeant William McDonald Innes-Ker, Straits Settlement Volunteer Force
POW from February 1942 to August 1945
Sonkurai No 2 Camp, Thailand, and POW Camp 330, Changi
18 June 1943. God what a place this is – no one knows its name. Sanitation foul – open shit pits with shit not only inside but all around as well, where dozens of poor fellows couldn't make it. Everyone has festering sores – which are covered in flies – we have no bandages and little antiseptic. Flies are terrible. Rain and ankle-deep mud for weeks – no one has any socks left and many no boots. We are not allowed to bathe in the river and of course all drinking water must be boiled – we have to carry it 200–300 yards up a slippery slope.

Cholera is said to be a little better and total deaths now 206 – out of 1,400. The next camp (Aussies) has 190 out of 700. It's sheer bloody murder – I imagine that out of some 7,000 troops on this section of the road there can only be 1,000 working and 5,000 of the rest sick. No exaggeration. How long we can endure I don't know. Two parties already have beat it but nothing further is known of them. An Aussie camp 60 kms away has been bombed by our planes and some lads killed – also some Nips!

2 July 1943. Cholera has abated – we hope for good – fevers have increased instead – weather is very showery and mosquitoes away from our hut fires are bad, on the road they are maddening. Food a bit better in that we get more meat and rice, but no veg at all bar a bean or two in the stew. Beriberi is rampant and in general health poor; out of 1,250 men we can only raise 160 a day for Nip work! Latest news is that the sick and infirm may be shifted 60 miles on to a base hospital camp. I am on the list for it, as are most men of 40 and over. It

'Cholera Hill', where sufferers at Sonkurai No 1 camp were isolated from the rest of the inmates (*author's collection*)

may or may not come to anything and likewise may be for the better or worse, one never knows.

4 July 1943. Nips getting tough, beatings and kickings fairly common. Forcing people out on to their precious road which is in a dreadful state, sick and all. Fevers and dysentery our main sickness now. God, what a country! Bamboo and jungle, elephants and yak cattle – poor starved beasts, no fat on them at all. Mud. Hot sun at times, night mists – few thunderstorms, dryish atmosphere. We ourselves are filthy – no soap for weeks, no wash for days – no clothing except shorts and boots all covered in mud. We pray for Wavell [Viceroy of India] to do something and do it quickly, else hundreds more must die, and personally I do so want to live and come back to you and home, Dearest.

... I had very bad goes of malaria in Siam, with shivers, shakes and rigors, the bouts coming regularly every few days, but after a few months back in Changi the bouts suddenly stopped and I never had malaria again. No known reason, for we had no treatment or drugs in those days; you just sweated it out under a blanket for 24 hours and arose as weak as a rat.

Dysentery was also said to be a hundred per cent for the Siam crowd, but while I did from time to time have goes of what the Aussies called 'trots', I never suffered acutely as so many did – suffered and died from it ...Tropical ulcers, another great killer, also passed me by. I had a half-crown-sized one on the joint of one big toe, and one on a finger, which were a bit troublesome, but they healed eventually. Paul Pancheri has a hole in his shin the size of a saucer to this day, and he nearly lost his leg from it. A popular form of treatment when these ulcers were growing was to introduce fly maggots into the putrid flesh round the edges of the hole, the idea being that these would eat away the bad stuff, and if you were lucky and could control them you then had a chance for the edges to heal, but often the bone got exposed and went black and then gangrenous – and that was that. The burning *ghat* was not long away for you.

Another one hundred per cent trouble for us all was scabies; this was caused by lice and raised festering sores all over our bodies, especially at pressure points, like pelvic bones and elbows. I had it pretty well all over, off and on – everywhere, including the very tenderest parts of my body. Searching for and catching lice was an all-time occupation in Tanabaya camp in Burma (Thanbyuzayat), and at one time when I was reduced to only a small towel round my loins (my clothes, such as they were, having been pinched while I slept), I made a practice of standing in the sun and catching 100 lice off my towel every morning! While later on when I was back in Changi I once gave an evening lecture on lice and the methods of catching them, for many of the Changi boys, who had never moved from there, knew nothing about them!

I have omitted to mention cholera in the list of our Siamese afflictions; why I do not know, for it was the biggest actual killer of them all, though if any treatment or proper hygiene had been possible it might have taken less toll. In our camp at Sonkurai, where 900 out of 1,200 died, I suppose it would not be wrong to guess that 400 of those deaths were from cholera. We had a separate cholera camp made about half a mile away in an abandoned bamboo clearing, just next door to the burning *ghat* where our dead were burned every night.

THE DUTCH EAST INDIES

Aircraftman Frank Deakin Jackson, Royal Air Force
POW from March 1942 to August 1945
Liang Camp, Ambon (Amboina), the Moluccas
We were barely three months at Ambon when our first death occurred, and the cause was dysentery. This disease was to be the principal factor in the many deaths to follow. We were allowed a cemetery on the hillside facing the camp. I was on a few grave-digging parties and the experience was a frustrating nightmare. We would remove an inch or so of soil and then have to hack away at the coral. Spades were useless in this procedure so we burrowed away with either chunkels [a kind of large hoe] or pickaxes. (I am not too sure whether or not we had pickaxes.) I doubt that most graves were more than two and a half feet in depth. Come the monsoon rains and coffins were exposed, having been denuded of the little covering we had shovelled over them. Soil and rocks would be restored at the earliest opportunity.

The only material available for the making of coffins was bamboo. Experienced woodworkers would make strips of the bamboo and then fashion utility coffins. It was dreadful but little else could be done.

It was customary for friends of the deceased to form the burial party and act as bearers. Having no Padre in the camp the burial service was recited by whoever felt capable of the duty. Thankfully we had a very able bugler in Larry Hinchley of the Army, who sounded 'The Last Post' at every burial. Larry was a great stalwart who added much-needed dignity to every ceremony. At every remembrance service I have attended or witnessed on television, vivid pictures of Larry and the sad scenes on the hill return and the tears begin to swell. I understand Larry was a member of the Salvation Army and I am very happy to record he survived and lives to this day [1992] in Bristol. His emotions must be greater than my own.

Because of the intense heat and prevalence of disease, burials had to take place as swiftly as possible. It often happened that a friend died and was buried before one had returned from a working party. In such cases men [who had been] left in the camp for some reason or other would assist in the committal.

Most deaths occurred overnight and in these cases friends were given the opportunity of attending the funeral in the morning. It was under these circumstances that I attended the third, I think, burial to take place at Ambon. The usual guard accompanied the cortege, as did the Japanese commandant. This officer placed fruit and vegetables on the grave, giving every sign of being very respectful. We could be little other than cynical about his offering coming too late to help our comrade. As I observed his impassive face at the graveside I did not then have the satisfaction of knowing this character was to hang in Changi Prison some four years later. Deaths were to become so frequent that Japanese officers chose to forgo attending the funerals. Their absence was welcomed.

Pilot Officer Erroll David Shearn, Royal Air Force
POW from March 1942 to August 1945
Camp 356, Sourabaya, East Java
It was then that I had to have – as we all did – some inoculation or other. Mine went bad and I had a poisoned left arm – swollen from shoulder to wrist. I was removed from our room to a part of the school set aside as a 'hospital'. It was here I had the advantage of treatment by Wing Commander (Medical) Cornelius William ('Con') Coffey. We had become fairly friendly from the days at the aerodrome at Tasik Melayu. He viewed my arm and left me some pills. On his rounds he was accompanied by a Flight Commander (Medical) who had, before the war, been in private practice. After Coffey had left the pills with me and departed with the Flight Commander, the latter reappeared very rapidly and said: 'For Christ's sake give me those pills Con Coffey gave you – they'll bloody well kill you if you take them.' He substituted some different pills. I feel they must have been a better choice. Anyway, I survived. I was, though, extremely unwell – temperature 105 or thereabouts. When I went to the latrine I fainted on the way back and hit the deck with a bump. I did the same the following day, but this time I was more on my guard and was able to lower myself more gently to the ground. On the third day I asked one of the orderlies to accompany me. I passed out as usual but he carried me to my bed and I have no recollection as to how I got there. One moment staggering towards the 'hospital', the next conscious moment lying in bed. After some two or three weeks my arm got better and I returned to the room I had left to go to 'hospital'.

Shortly after this dysentery broke out in a big way. About 1,000 cases out of the total population of 2,000. The Japanese got scared of the outbreak spreading into the town and the order came through that all who were free of dysentery were to go to a different camp. This turned out to be an old wireless station a few miles out of Sourabaya.

JAPAN

Lieutenant Stephen Abbott, East Surrey Regiment
POW from February 1942 to August 1945
Official Debriefing Report on No 7 Despatch Camp, Chi
When our party left Changi [in May 1943] it was specifically stated that no doctor was required. As a result there was no qualified medical attention during the voyage to Japan, and until November 1943 there was no prisoner doctor in the camp. Between May and November of that year a Nippon doctor would occasionally visit the camp and examine the sickest personnel. For the first five months the supplies of medicine, dressings, etc, were almost negligible, but in the latter half of our time these supplies were reasonable. From the outset the policy of the Japanese has been to send every possible man to work. Many deaths and serious illnesses, such as pneumonia, have been caused by this policy. During the first eight months it was a common practice for the camp commandant or one of his staff to send men out to work without the authority of the doctor or even of the Nippon medical orderly.

At the beginning of November 1943, Commander Cecha of the United States Navy was sent to this camp. At this time there were approximately 150 sick in camp and the Japanese were commencing to worry about the bad state of health. However, the authority of Commander Cecha to decide whether a man was fit to work or not was very scantily recognized. In March 1944, Captain Pizer, United States Army Medical Corps, arrived and started a policy of cooperation tempered with firmness which eventually resulted in his obtaining almost complete control of the sick parades. In order to do this, however, Captain Pizer himself was forced to send to work many sick men who should have been resting. From the time of his arrival onwards there were only five deaths in the camp and one of these was caused by a quarry accident. With the arrival of Captain Rizzoli, United States Army Medical Corps, and a party of 200 men from Osaka in May 1945, further control of the sick situation was obtained by our own doctors.

9
EDUCATION AND ENTERTAINMENT

'Regularly the Japs would search our quarters, ransacking our beds and equipment, looking for pens, pencil and paper. They possibly feared that any notes we might make would be used against them in the future.'

– Far Eastern POW

While thousands of prisoners between 1939 and 1945 were forced to work for the enemy, there were almost as many who were exempt from working under Article 27 of the Geneva Convention. Officers and senior NCOs were two such exceptions. In Germany others, such as Royal Air Force NCOs and other ranks, were barred from working in any case because they were bent on sabotage and escape. No such restriction on employing the RAF applied in Italy, but in both Germany and Italy there was an admirable number of soldiers and seamen who were fit to work but who swung the lead and thus denied the enemy cheap labour, instead using their abilities for the benefit of their fellow prisoners by helping with internal camp administration. However, once the twice- or thrice-daily roll-calls were over; the three pathetic meals a day had been cooked, served and eaten, and any other obligations and duties had been fulfilled, the empty hours stared back at the prisoners like a yawning chasm.

Once again the Geneva Convention came to the rescue, with Article 17 exhorting captors to encourage intellectual and sporting pursuits. Article 39 permitted prisoners to receive consignments of books, either individually or communally, from sanctioned suppliers and relief agencies.

In September 1939 the leaders of the world's religious alliances – mainly Christian – met in Geneva to determine which bodies would perform what tasks throughout the war. The Young Men's Christian Association (YMCA) was given the job of attending to the spiritual and cultural needs of POWs and civilian internees. This included supplying books (including bibles), musical instruments and sports equipment. The YMCA also produced 'The Prisoner of War Log', a hardbound commonplace book in which prisoners could record their thoughts and impressions of camp life. The warring nations allowed many of these items to be sent free of charge, and most countries, even Nazi Germany, viewed this work sympathetically, even going so far as to agree, in 1942, that vocational examinations could be held in the camps. Textbooks were sent by the Educational Books Section of the Prisoner of War Department of the Red Cross, which also sent out exam papers to some 17,000 prisoners in 88 different camps.

Prisoners also mounted arts and crafts exhibitions, and held sports days, and those in Germany even took vocational courses and sat examinations, using equipment allowed them on parole.

While most of what the prisoners produced was lost when their camps were abandoned at the end of the war, much written and photographic evidence survives as a tribute to their remarkable spirit and ingenuity.

GERMANY AND POLAND

As the war progressed, more and more 'hostilities only' servicemen who in peacetime had been engaged in commerce, education, the arts or competitive sports found themselves behind the wire. Educational and cultural activities flourished – particularly once the flow of Red Cross food parcels improved and prisoners were better fed. Former journalists, printers and bookbinders, and those with literary aspirations, banded together to produce newspapers and magazines, which came out either daily, weekly, or monthly. In 1940 a group of army officers in Oflag IXA/H at Spangenberg produced *The Quill*, which they continued when they were transferred to other camps. This contained poetry, reminiscences, 'think pieces' and humorous articles, all laboriously hand-written, and cartoons, drawings and paintings using materials provided by the Germans (on parole), the YMCA and the Red Cross.

Another group of officers, in Oflag VIIB at Eichstätt, produced a literary magazine called *Touchstone*, which was professionally printed locally. British and Commonwealth Air Force officers in the Belaria satellite of Stalag Luft III produced *The Log*, while their NCOs in Stalag Lufts III and VI produced *The Daily Recco*, a far more modest effort that was pinned each day to the camp noticeboard. Perhaps the best-known camp magazine is *Flywheel*, started by a team of motor-car enthusiasts in Stalag IVB, at Mühlberg on the Elbe, which was published in book form after the war.

At *Arbeitskommandos*, owing to lack of materials and free time, magazines took the form of newsletters written in pen and ink on exercise paper and passed from hand to hand (one such was *Snips*, produced by Signaller Frederick William Daniels of the Queen's Royal Regiment).

One-off novels, volumes of poetry and miscellanies were also produced, the manuscripts sometimes being sent home via the Red Cross and published while the war still raged. One of the first was *Backwater*, a selection of poems, articles and illustrations by army officers in Oflag IXA/H, selected and edited by Lieutenant-Colonel Guy Adams of the East Surrey Regiment and published in England in 1944. Another officer, Captain R K Montgomery of the Royal Engineers, lectured on English Literature in Oflag IVB and at Oflag IXA/H and had his lectures published as a book, *Reading for Profit*, in early 1945 while he was still a prisoner.

Such talent and enterprise was also to be found in the Stalags. Sergeant Ron Mogg, who left journalism to join the RAF and was shot down early in the war, discovered he had a gift for poetry. In Stalag Luft VI, Heydekrug, his verse was transcribed and illustrated by fellow sergeant J W Lambert and published by Basil Blackwell in 1945 as *For This Alone*. Others kept diaries and made entries in their wartime logs, not only to pass the time but also as a record to show their parents, sweethearts, wives, children and grandchildren.

Almost all camps had their professional and aspiring actors, musicians and impresarios who staged shows and concerts for their fellow prisoners. Through the good offices of the YMCA, prisoners were sent musical instruments and many camps in Germany were able to form full classical orchestras, jazz bands and massed choirs. Recorded music was also sent on 78 rpm shellac discs and certain men were appointed as keepers of the camp gramophone, visiting each room in turn to play requests. Many camps boasted a theatre, often built by the prisoners themselves by removing the partition walls of several rooms in one of the huts. The best theatres were probably in Stalag Luft III's North Compound and Oflag VIIB, Eichstätt, where it was not unknown for a new play, written by a professional playwright in England, to have its world premier. Props and costumes were usually made by the prisoners, although sometimes ready-made costumes were hired from theatres in Berlin.

Officers in these and many other camps, including Stalag Luft VI, also established what became known as 'The Barbed-Wire University' and sat examinations accredited by professional bodies back home. Many an ex-POW forged a successful postwar career as a result. Lectures were also given on a wide variety of subjects without reference to structured courses of study – there was even one on whale hunting.

The Germans sometimes showed films, but these had such obvious propagandist intent that prisoners howled with derision and barracked their captors until they were forced to scuttle off with their screens and projectors.

GERMANY

Telegraphist Herbert Edgar Elliott, Royal Naval Volunteer Reserve
POW from August 1940 to May 1945
Marlag Nord, Sandbostel, January 1941–June 1942
We were given fairly comfortable rooms and beds, and naval officers and men began to arrive fairly frequently. Eventually we had about 900 men including some merchant seamen and 100 naval officers. We had very little to do and as soon as possible we had soccer going strongly and converted a hut into a theatre. Football was first-class and most enjoyable. The shows put on were really the most enjoyable I have seen anywhere and the ingenuity displayed in making theatrical effects is beyond all praise.

Boxing shows were frequent and good. Dances and fancy dress parades were held, some men dressing as females. A lot of good fun was made in this manner.

Squadron Leader Herbert Douglas Haig Cooper, DFC, Royal Air Force
POW from July 1941 to May 1945
Oflag VIB, Warburg, October 1941–September 1942
Earlier on when Red Cross [musical] instruments started to arrive, a consignment came from the USA consisting of violins, saxophones, clarinets, etc, and included an American instrument known as a Sousaphone ('oompah! oompah!') – a huge thing which seemed to wrap around the body. Nobody wanted to play this, except one – no names no pack drill – so I will call him 'Charlie'. But where to play and practise this instrument? It was decided that the only place was the *Abort*, a hole in the ground in the far corner of the field with a shed over it. Here Charlie practised.

Morning and night the Germans would have a parade for us to be counted, but bloody-minded German officers would hold a parade at any time just to annoy. It so happened that one such German came into the camp, blew the whistle, and shouted: 'On *Appell!*' Having assembled us, they started to count – '*Eins, zwei, drei, vier, fünf*', and so on until the end of the line. One short! Pandemonium – panic – and we looked at each other wondering who was missing. Someone remembered Charlie over in the bog practising. 'Charlie! Charlie! On *Appell!*' and Charlie came running across the field, still with his instrument slung over his shoulder, and stood on the end of the line.

But the methodical Germans had to count again, and when the guard arrived at Charlie, he blew him a RASPBERRY down the Sousaphone! Can you picture the situation? The German whipped out his pistol and would have shot the first one to move, and here we were standing stiffly at attention with tears of laughter streaming down our faces.

Major Elliott Viney, Oxford & Bucks Light Infantry
POW from June 1940 to May 1945
Oflag VIIB, Eichstätt, Bavaria

Books, smokes and gramophone records could be sent in any number. At the end we reckoned there were 80,000 books in the camp; before the end we packed some 2,000 of the more important library books, all of which eventually reached England. I had been a librarian [in several camps] from the beginning in 1940, but with an excellent staff I did not need to spend much time on it by 1943.

Being, as Tim Munby said, Vice-Chancellor of our 'University' was a more important but rewarding job. Of course, we had many dons and schoolmasters. Edward Ree, for instance, was headmaster of Chesterton, a Seaford prep school (opposite my own), whilst C J Hanson was a most distinguished Cambridge law don. Classes in every conceivable subject went on every day, but fitting them into the limited room space was always a difficulty. Here I was helped by Arthur Fleet, later Registrar of Bristol University.

All the teaching was leading up to the exams of the English examining bodies – the Law Society, the Bar, all the Engineering Institutes, Civil, Electrical, etc, the Chartered Accountants, the Insurance, Bankers and several others. The exam papers came from England (via Switzerland of course). My German book censor glanced at the papers and the exams went ahead, though sometimes interrupted by an air raid, then more censoring and back to Switzerland; three or four months later we got the results. Altogether nearly 1,000 passed their intermediate or final professional exams during the last four years.

Pilot Officer William ('Bill) Greenaway, Royal Air Force
POW from November 1941 to April 1945
Stalag Luft I, Barth, and Stalag Luft III, Sagan

In the early days our classroom was the sand outside the hut, which we used for a blackboard, writing and drawing with a piece of stick for chalk. We had no textbooks – we relied on memory.

Eventually, with the aid of the Red Cross, this evolved into the finest university in the world, with degrees taken. It was the proud boast that it was impossible to mention a subject to be studied and not be able to find someone in the camp who could teach it. Our Education Officer, Tim Penn, later joined the Ministry of Education.

POW drawing of barracks corridor, Stalag Luft I (*Nicholas G D Craig*)

Sub-Lieutenant Maurice Driver, Royal Navy
POW from August 1940 to April 1945
Stalag Luft III, Sagan

Stalag Luft III, whether in the East or North Camp (to which I went when it was opened) was immensely rich in the best things of civilized life. There were many who had gone straight from university into the armed forces and were both pleased and willing to discuss and teach on all manner of topics, and in particular the humanities. The camp was a university for me, and when I returned to England in 1945 I was a very different person to the one who had left in 1940. I could not say that this was a universal experience, but it was certainly so for me. I had been very good at school in science and mathematics and took part in the education programmes in the camp, lecturing and tutoring many who were interested in furthering their prospects after the war. Some were interested in getting permanent commissions in the RAF, but the most popular future was farming in one of the colonies – and especially Rhodesia or Kenya.

I was very pleased in 1989 to receive a call from Australia from a man I had not seen or heard of since 1944. He had heard that I had been killed in an air crash shortly after the war, but had learnt otherwise at a reunion in Australia. He telephoned me to tell me how grateful he was for the chemistry I had taught him, which had been a great help in his career in the wool industry. I felt immensely pleased, not only because I felt I had achieved something, but also because it brought back memories of those who had helped me in the camp.

Lieutenant David Lubbock, Royal Naval Volunteer Reserve
POW from July 1941 to April 1945
East Compound, Stalag Luft III, Sagan

It is remarkable how much talent, and how varied, there was in the camp. Apart from the brilliant forgery folk working for escape and escapers, one of whom had been a bank teller, there were the radio experts who could make sets out of scraps. One, Wing Commander Roger Maw, made a wooden clock, which woke him up in the morning and shut the window!

Pilot Officer Hugh Edward Lance Falkus, Royal Air Force
POW from June 1940 to April 1945
East Compound, Stalag Luft III, Sagan

I lived in the same block as Robert Kee and next door to Aidan Crawley. The two were always chattering about politics. I helped construct camp theatre and produced and acted in loads of shows – plays, revues, concerts. We ripped out two partition walls and built a stage at one end with a proscenium arch. We also had a piano. Everything in the theatre was on parole and we also gave our word that no one involved with theatrical activities would escape from that block. We got lots of little perks from the goon who supervised us. We had two stage carpenters – one called Mackenzie – he was a keen angler, and the other was McKechnie. The Sagan theatre – and the war – reshaped my life because it led me into show business. I was determined thereafter to go into filming and writing.

Aidan Crawley was among those who acted in the camp theatre and I put on a pantomime that he choreographed. Crawley was a good tap-dancer and ran a tap-dancing school in the camp. Bruce Organ, an impresario from Stratford-upon-Avon, also acted and produced. Among our plays were *Gaslight* – June 1943, *George and Margaret* – May–June 1944, *Thunder Rock* – October 1943, *French Without Tears* – November 1943, a Christmas Panto – December 1943, *Blithe Spirit* – February 1944, *Hamlet* – May 1944, *Arsenic and Old Lace* – June 1944, and *Robin Hood*.

I also read Negley Farson's book *Going Fishing* in 1943, while surviving a term of solitary confinement following an escape attempt. A guard smuggled the book into the cell. It was the only literature I had access to for about two months and was a revelation as well as a solace. It was the best fishing book I ever read. It was reissued later as a result of my praise for it.

Pilot Officer Jack Kenneth ('Tiger') Lyon, Royal Air Force
POW from June 1941 to May 1945
North Compound, Stalag Luft III, Sagan

Every new theatre performance was eagerly awaited and I think the standard was very high. Many performers went on to become professional actors. What follows may not be so well known. POWs were once asked to audition for a new show and each competitor asked to take part in an excerpt from a play by (I think) Eugene O'Neill. The action takes place on a freighter and one character has the words 'Bleedin' Dutch hog'. This phrase was duly voiced with great gusto by each participant. There were some Germans in the audience who applauded each time, apparently quite unaware that 'Dutch' is colloquial American for German.

Musical talent seemed far less evident than the histrionic, possibly because practising with instruments was decidedly unpopular with room-mates. Jules Silverston played the cello, 'Kit' Carson the violin. Roland Stamp had quite a good voice. His 'Adelaide' was worth listening to. Pianists I cannot recall and neither can I remember a specific concert, although there must have been some. I am a devotee of classical music, and most appreciated were the record recitals by those fortunate enough to have received records

Prison camp dance orchestra at Oflag IXA/H, Spangenberg (*author's collection*)

from home in a usable condition and a gramophone. Former Battle of Britain pilot Squadron Leader Macdonell had one, I recall.

Private Harry K Swann, Queen's Regiment
POW from June 1940 to April 1945
Letter home from Stalag VIIIB, Lamsdorf, April 1942
Life continues much the same, though it's been more eventful lately, though of course events here are small happenings that gain importance from their rarity. Post has not been very good lately, but a few days ago I got a book parcel, with the Shakespeare, Shelley, Aristotle, etc, which is a great joy. These few classics will last me for a long time to come, and as for other books we really do have as many sent out as we can use.

This week we had a party from another camp joined to ours, and they've brought with them a complete orchestra, including a piano. This is what we have been wanting for a long time, though we had a harmonium and a violin, and have usually been able to borrow a piano for concerts.

Last night we had a second performance of a musical comedy, *Windbag the Sailor*. You'd really be amazed by how much can be produced by so little; scenery and costumes as well as acting compared favourably with a lot I've seen in amateur performance in England.

Sapper Don Luckett, Royal Engineers
POW from July 1941 to May 1945
Stalag XVIIIA, Wolfsberg, Austria
An incident that caused a degree of mirth amongst us was that a party of German officers had visited the compound and had asked our boys to sing the song about 'Hanging the washing on the Siegfried Line' – a group of 40 or so obliged, and sang it with such fervour that the officers stalked off, and the performance wasn't asked for again.

POLAND

Pilot Officer Idrwerth Patrick ('Paddy') Bentley Denton, Royal Air Force Volunteer Reserve
POW from July 1941 to May 1945
Oflag XXIB, Schubin, 1942–43
Winter in Poland is beautiful, austere and bitterly cold. 30°F frost, 30°F below inside our huts. Chilly to say the least. It was therefore sensible, as the camp

was built on a steep incline, to build from snow a toboggan run. This was looked on by the Germans as a good, healthy and harmless occupation. At the top of the camp, adjacent to the block where we lived and separated from the American blocks, were two flights of steps with wall balustrading which, presumably, in the former glory days of the house and gardens, were ornamental and useful and good viewing points. Surmounting these lay a flat stone platform from which descended one flight of steps to another platform and then the second flight. It took little time to cover these quite deeply in snow and by a variety of means lead this snow path down to the bottom of the hill where we constructed, quite futilely, what we hoped might be a launching ramp. It was a silly idea and never worked. However, by pouring water and other liquids onto this slope it became totally glazed. Down this, on a luge which the goons helped us to construct with bits of wood and steel for runners, a variety of people hurled themselves, intrepid, to what seemed nasty accidents. None actually occurred.

Inevitably, we had Canadians amongst us. One enormous fellow, Bob, who was earlier at Warburg, had been an Olympic swimmer and decided that this was a bit tame. One way or another he managed to get made by one of the engineers some skates. With these in place he then proceeded to attempt the impossible, which he achieved on many occasions, by skating down the balustrade of the steps, jumping onto the run and ending up base over apex at the bottom. Most exhilarating to watch and he never broke a thing.

ITALY

Camps in Italy were likewise blessed with men of talent. It could, indeed, be fairly argued that up until the time of the Italian armistice and the removal of Allied POWs to Germany in September 1943, there was a greater concentration of prewar artists, writers, journalists, actors, teachers, craftsmen and budding geniuses in Italy than in Germany or even the West End of London. The camp magazines, theatrical productions, sports days and art and craft exhibitions were of comparable quality to those in Germany. Among the most notable prison-camp magazines produced in the Mediterranean Theatre were *The Benghazi Forum*, *The Rezzanello Revu* and *The Tuturano Times*. Unfortunately, their producers were twice cursed – losing their precious artefacts when they were evacuated from Italy and again when they were liberated in Germany in 1945. But many diaries and even full-length novels (such as *The Trap* by Dan Billany) survived to be published later.

Lance-Corporal Lawrence Bains, Middlesex Yeomanry
POW from June 1942 to August 1944
Campo PG 66, Capua

Another item that helped keep up our spirits was the Concert Party, organized by RSM Rowe, and produced mainly by Sergeant Blackett. These concerts took place, usually on a Saturday, at about 1800 hours, the stage being the parcel-distributing platform. Sketches, songs, community singing – all the usual stuff, and not to a very high standard, but very welcome all the same and a real help to flagging spirits. Normally I would not have troubled to attend such a show, but it was a relaxation and helped us to forget our circumstances, and I was very grateful to the artists, amongst who were several South Notts Hussars favourites. All the performers and stage-hands drew 'buckshees' afterwards at the cookhouse, but although some murmured against this, I thought they deserved it ...

...Closely connected with health is exercise, and this was the first camp where we had any facilities at all, even though these consisted only of solid ground to walk on. Every evening some time after our evening brew, I and most of the camp would walk round the perimeter, at varying speeds, for varying numbers of times. At the beginning it was as much as I could do to stroll round slowly about twice, ie, approximately half a mile, but towards the end of our stay I enjoyed going round a dozen times, and at quite a reasonable speed, although it was nearly always an effort to start this measure of self-discipline. My partners in these walks varied, but after Lance-Bombardier G Joyce became my pudding partner [mess-mate] I always went round with him.

The only official sport was boxing, which started about a month after our arrival and took place on most evenings. It was always attended by a large crowd (even I went as it afforded a distraction), and sometimes the Italian officer in charge of the compound paid a visit. It was a marvel to me how fellows could stand up to the blows, for some of them were obviously not very fit. All entrants afterwards drew 'buckshees' at the cookhouse, and occasionally odd articles from Red Cross parcels were given as prizes. We also had a more or less compulsory contribution of Italian cigarettes towards a prize fund. These displays made me feel very inferior and strengthened my determination to keep myself fit by constant walking exercise.

British prisoners in Italy having a flutter. Gambling was a popular pastime in the camps (*author's collection*)

Private Maurice Newey, Royal Army Ordnance Corps
POW from June 1942 to April 1945
Campo 54, Fara Sabina (Rome)

Musical instruments had been sent to the camp and a band was formed. There was an empty tent near us and they practised in that. They nearly drove us barmy as they practised playing 'Frankie and Johnny' over and over again. They were terribly amateurish. I don't think they ever got that tune right.

The concert party from the other compound was allowed to come over and give a performance. The band set off with their signature tune, 'The world is waiting for the sunrise', and it sounded very impressive after listening to 'Frankie and Johnny'. We were treated to a trombone solo by Fiery Fred, a former member of the famous Black Dyke Mills Brass Band. He could make that trombone almost talk.

Their compère was a tall sergeant and a great comedian. He was one of those people who, by merely standing on stage and twitching an eyebrow, could have an audience in stitches. We thoroughly enjoyed that concert and gave them a great ovation.

On their second visit the compère had to pay a visit to the bog. He had slipped on a greasy plank and his right leg plunged into the foul mass underneath. Undeterred, he removed his boot and sock, cleaned his trousers and rolled them up to his knees. A howl of laughter greeted him as he appeared on stage, but when silence was restored he announced: 'Well, lads, I've got some shit-hot news for you from bog number one.' This really brought the house down. The bog was well known for spreading rumours.

On another occasion he asked us to be serious for once, as he would like to give a rendering of 'The Floral Dance'. He had a very pleasant bass voice, but he couldn't get past the second line, as everybody just exploded with laughter. He tried once more, but it was no good, he just looked so comical trying to be serious, that we could not stop laughing.

Lieutenant William Bompas, Royal Artillery (Field)
POW from December 1942 to April 1945
Campo PG 21, Chieti

I suppose a good point about being a POW is that one could read books one wouldn't normally do – we had a camp library of 1,000 books and I ploughed through *The Conquest of Mexico* and *The Incas of Peru*.

Lieutenant A F ('Junior') Powell, 13th Light Anti-Aircraft Regiment
POW from April 1941 to May 1945
Campo PG 17, Rezzanello

In September 1941 I had the idea of producing a camp magazine, partly to occupy and amuse ourselves and perhaps for publishing '*dopo la guerra*'. A fellow POW, (Nobby) Clarke, though this a good idea and came up with a format – editorial, news, gossip, and whatever else we could think of. We solicited contributions for a first issue and struck a rich seam. The text was typed in two copies and all covers, advertisements and cartoons done in triplicate, usually by me. There were unpaid advertisements at the front and the back of each issue. Each article started at the top of a page and any space on its last page was used for a cartoon or an advertisement. The covers, different each month, were in colour, as were a lot of the cartoons. We then had a lot of loose sheets and these were bound together in book-like form by [Lieutenant] Ken Whitworth [Royal Artillery], who was in the bookbinding business.

The magazine tells a lot of how life went on and who were the charac-ters. The 'social' articles, by Joe Fishbourne (Staff Captain), were written as if from a hunt, a school, a society reporter and recorded highlights of each month. New arrivals, departures, illness, accidents, who had what responsi-bilities, escapes and comments on personal habits. The news articles, written by Brian Ashford Russel (London journalist), gave not only the news from the Italian newspapers but also an analysis of what was really happening and possible future events. And there was always a review of any play or lecture. At first the other articles were on outside, prewar activities, but as time went on there were more and more on in-camp affairs. Some were in verse, some-times parodies of well-known poems, and often with a message for someone. Similarly with the cartoons – some were based on actual events, some on outside happenings.

The magazine was well received, but we always had to solicit some of the contributions to keep it going. In January 1943 we increased the press run to four copies. Distribution was on an honour system, one officer passed it on to the next until it was returned to us. We never lost one.

Nobby and I each kept a copy of each edition and the spare other copies were sold to contributors for one pound paid to a bank in England, the proceeds to be used to help printing costs after the war. In fact the money, some £30, was donated after the war to the Earl Haig fund for ex-servicemen.

Lieutenant David Dowie, 4th Battalion, East Yorkshire Regiment
POW from June 1942 to September 1943
Memoir written in Campo PG 49, Fontanellato, near Parma

At Rezzanello I had found what were the best places and times for study; I never settle down to work well if there are distractions – Henry's violin regularly drove me out of the ante-room. All that routine has been destroyed by coming to Fontanellato. We are very crowded, and there is no place whatever for work. The Italians are making unnecessary difficulties about everything – Red Cross parcels, water supply, blackout regulations, lights out, etc. Roll-calls take ages. There is too much organization, which doesn't work. The *Carabinieri* have searched our room twice in one week, which may be smart from their viewpoint; and so far they have not returned the notebooks they confiscated when we came, so work is held up even if there were any place for it.

Corporal Eric Barrington, Royal Air Force Police
POW from June 1942 to April 1945
Diary kept in Campo PG 73, Carpi (Modena)

Wednesday, 27 January 1943. During the afternoon I got in a spot of exercise on a three-mile route march along the Via dei grilli, through the marshland, now being cultivated by State farms. Very cold and muddy, but when my circulation was working it did me a world of good. I arrived back at camp at 4 pm to a feast of half a dixie of rice skilly; could I have done justice to a mixed grill! Also very tired so I dozed off afterwards for an hour. What would Eileen think if she knew a three-mile walk on a straight road had knocked me up? I shall indeed need some training before I cross Blackstone Edge again, and may it be soon.

Lieutenant John Pelly, Coldstream Guards
POW from June 1942 to April 1945
Diary kept in Campo PG 21, Chieti

23 August 1942. Sunday today. Got myself into French and Italian classes in the educational programme, and also Agriculture. There is unlimited talent in the camp, and one can take nearly any language from Russian to Zulu to Sesuto. Also engineering of all types, all sides of business management, history, literature, shorthand and Bible study, etc, etc. There is a very complicated programme worked out, and all starts tomorrow. I have got four periods of French per week, two of Italian, and one each day for

251

Agriculture (which I hope may be of some practical use to me at Pershaw one day), the rotation of lectures in the Agriculture is Mondays: Estate Management. Tuesdays: Livestock. Wednesdays: Chemistry. Thursdays: Soils, Fertilizers and Crops. Fridays: Genetics, or the art of breeding, etc, and each Saturday we have a general interest talk about farming in various parts of the world.

I am hoping to get moved to the 'C' Bungalow tomorrow. [Lieutenant] Tony Maxtone-Graham (Scots Guards), who is head of the Dramatic Society, asked me to write up any sketches I know, as they are short of scripts. I hope I do a lot of acting here, as I love it.

Extract from POW newspaper, *Tuturano Times*, 19 March 1943
Campo PG 85, Tuturano
On Thursday 11 March Tuturano Camp was inspected by Colonel Pallotta, representing the Chief Commandant of POW Camps in Italy.

Despite inclement weather, the Colonel carried out a thorough inspection of the camp, and showed an active interest in the prisoners' welfare.

The inspection was an independent function, unconnected with the recent visit of M Iselin, representative of the protecting power. Colonel Pallotta, tall, smart, and bemonocled, toured the camp area accompanied by the Camp Commandant and his Staff of Officers. His imposing military figure attracted much attention. Making it clear that he desired no formalities, he took notice of all aspects of camp life, and his questions showed a sympathetic interest in the prisoners as individuals.

Barrack huts 12, 9 and 1 were inspected by the Colonel, and the Infirmary visited. The evening meal was being served at the time of the inspection, and he spoke to the carrier and satisfied himself as to the quality of the food.

Colonel Pallotta confirmed the earlier statement regarding personnel in tents, ie, that the problem would shortly be solved by the exodus of working parties.

He commented on the condition of the camp, as a result of the preceding extremely bad weather, and, in concluding his inspection, promised a number of improvements as, and when, possible.

In the evening, the Colonel attended a performance by the band and concert artists in the Camp theatre, and expressed himself highly pleased with the show and the high standard of talent exhibited by those taking part.

Midshipman John Franklin Dalgleish, Merchant Navy
POW from August 1942 to April 1945
Diary kept in Campo PG 35, Padula

Padula Exhibition and Fête. 12 June 1943. An exhibition of work done whilst in POW camps was held in the Mess today. Contributions included water-colour sketches, oils, pencil and black and white sketches, embroidery and knitting, stuffas [home-made stoves], posters, dress designing, stuffa plans, architecture and cakes. There was some really first-class stuff shown though, in my estimation, not enough original painting and sketching.

In the afternoon the garden fête was held. Aunt Sallys, darts, coconut shies, horse racing, shove ha'penny, and all the other similar sideshows at a garden fête in England were distributed about the court. Conjuring, in the hut, by Brend was very good and a replica of a destroyer's firing turret with spray and noise and flashes in attendance during firing in rough weather were represented. This sideshow was enthusiastically attended and was perhaps the most popular of the afternoon.

'Guess Your Weight' did very well and I found I still weighed 10st 4lb. The Fareblueswells under the leadership of Artie Graham played during both dinner sittings.

It was intended to have the New Concert Orchestra playing on the lawn, but this was not allowed by the Italian authorities who, it is believed, feared that the villagers would think we were celebrating the fall of Pantellaria [a Italian island south-west of Sicily], which good news we received today.

'The Open Door'. 25 June 1943. A comedy thriller. Very good acting, scenery and costumes but the story was rather dry and took a lot of explaining in the first act. Padula Theatre Orchestra played throughout the intervals. The girl in the play, his first appearance, made-up extremely successfully. Even his legs looked passable after all this time 'in the bag'.

THE FAR EAST

Even in the Far East hundreds of prisoners took incredible risks by keeping secret journals, recorded on any scraps of paper they could find. Indeed, many accounts published after the war by such well-known authors as Russell Braddon, Terence Kelly and Sir John Fletcher-Cooke were based on notes hidden inside bamboo shoots or buried in the soil under their huts. Far Eastern prisoners of war were also able, occasionally, to stage shows and plays,

Kampong at Changi, from a
drawing by Signalman John Stanley
Walker (*Mrs Jean Carpenter*)

Barracks interior, Changi, by Signalman
John Stanley Walker (*Mrs Jean Carpenter*)

Room with a view, Changi, by Signalman
John Stanley Walker (*Mrs Jean Carpenter*)

a remarkable achievement considering that many were sick and starving, and that they received few or no facilities from the Japanese or from the Red Cross, the YMCA or any other relief organization, and had little free time.

Sergeant William McDonald Innes-Ker, Straits Settlement Volunteer Force
POW from February 1942 to August 1945
Camp 331, Changi Prison, Singapore
Naturally, in such a large camp we had numberless 'experts' in various subjects, and a sort of University Course was started, lectures being given nightly on all sorts of subjects. I attended some: one I remember on bee-keeping ...

Pilot Officer Erroll David Shearn, Royal Air Force
POW from March 1942 to August 1945
Camp 346, XVth Battalion Barracks, Bandoeng, Dutch East Indies
It was in this camp that, encouraged by the exhortations of the Japanese commandant, we formed what we humorously dubbed the 'University of Bandoeng'. Now, it should be known that this was a very modest effort with classes for officers, numbering in each 'faculty' at the most ten or twelve. We had an architect; a former lecturer of a Welsh university on the French language; Van der Post, who, having acquired a Chambers Encyclopaedia of Literature, held forth on Literature, and I, who lectured on English Law. There may have been others but I cannot recall any such. There was to my knowledge no Java-wide educational effort as is depicted in one of Van der Post's books concerning life in Japanese prison camps in Java. The grandiose picture he there draws is very much a figment of his extremely fertile imagination. Life apart from the 'University' was reasonable. It was here I decided I would write a novel. I did so, and produced between 100,000 and 120,000 words in about six weeks. Wightwick, who had written ten novels of which he had had six published, read my 'masterpiece' and told me he thought I could find a publisher for it. Alas! There came a time when the Japanese got 'windy' about plans for escape or some other nonsense, and all written matter had to be handed in for their inspection and destruction. I decided to bury my literary effort. I wrapped it in a waterproof cape and put it in a tin box, which I buried in the garden of our house.

Sapper Edgar Whincup, Royal Engineers
POW from February 1942 to August 1945
Camp 242, Non Pladuk, Burma–Siam Railway

We made many games from a variety of materials obtained in the camp and 'borrowed' from the Japanese – chess, draughts, ludo and other board games – all in an attempt to relieve our boredom.

Regularly the Japs would search our quarters, ransacking our beds and equipment, looking for pens, pencil and paper. They possibly feared that any notes we might make would be used against them in the future. I lost my first pages of notes in one of these searches but later I made further notes and hid them in a length of bamboo with the open end always visible. The Japs would have become suspicious if the closed end had been facing them on their search. My second set of notes were written on a Japanese issue notepad 'acquired' from them, although my method of hiding my notes was very risky, because if caught I would be subject to very severe punishment. I still managed to keep my notes and notepad – I brought them home with me and still have them in 1988.

Remarkably, one of our number had obtained an old typewriter and one day, caught unawares by one of these searches, he was unable to hide it. The Japs ignored it, the possible reason being that they were only looking for pens and papers, and typewriters were not included in this category.

Back at Non Pladuk, 'Ace' Connelly, the camp bugler, formed a four-piece band, the instruments, as with other things, appearing as if out of thin air. Major Cheeta, the camp commandant, was so enamoured with the band that he decided that it would stand outside the guardroom every morning and play to the railway working party as they left the camp. Believe it or not, the tune he demanded was 'Hi Ho, Hi Ho, it's off to work we go'. Nobody felt or looked like the Seven Dwarfs.

Also at this time a concert party was formed called 'The Harboured Lights', and again material for outfits and props appeared as if from nowhere, obviously by courtesy of the Japs but unknown to them. Although working long hours we still managed to put aside one or two nights a month for a show. I frequently wondered if the Japs recognized any of the materials used in these shows, or, more importantly and ironically, whether they understood the import of many of the sketches, which we devised solely for the purposes of 'taking the mickey' out of them.

Lieutenant-Colonel Philip Toosey, 135th Field Regiment, Royal Artillery
POW from February 1942 to August 1945
Camp 248, Kanchanaburi, Burma–Siam Railway
On one occasion we were told that some high-ranking officers were coming
from Tokyo to inspect the officers' camp and we were told we might stage our
concert party, which had been stopped for some time, which we did, and the
famous tune 'Colonel Bogie' was played as the Japs marched into the camp
and that verse we all know so well was sung by all. They stood firmly to attention and saluted as we cheered: they thought we were cheering them!

Lieutenant Stephen Abbott, East Surrey Regiment
POW from February 1942 to August 1945
Official Debriefing Report on No 7 Despatch Camp, Chi, Japan
During the first eight months at this camp no entertainment of any kind was
permitted with the exception of card-playing after 12 noon on rest days. After
this time we were permitted to have a concert on rest day evenings. A few
musical instruments were supplied, and a gramophone. Lectures or debates
were not permitted. There were approximately 100 books in the camp library,
supplied by the YMCA and the American Red Cross. In the summer of 1944
a few swimming parades on rest days were conducted.

10
ESCAPE

'...escape was never really on the cards. We were many hundreds of miles from the Allied units in North Burma. You could not disguise yourself as a Siamese or a Burman and would be entirely dependent on the native peasantry. The few who did try were quickly handed back to the Japs for a cash reward.'

— British prisoner in Siam (Thailand)

E ver since the Enlightenment it has been accepted by warring nations that prisoners of war, as they have been trained and are being paid by their government, have a duty to try rejoining their units and so carry on the fight. Never has this duty been so strongly impressed upon prisoners as it was during the Second World War, especially after the fall of Dunkirk.

Undoubtedly the best time to escape was soon after capture and while in transit. However, at this early stage the prisoner was almost invariably either wounded, or in a state of shock, or relieved at having survived violent action, or – as was the case in France in June 1940 – simply swept up in the tide of men marching towards prison camp. Only a man of extraordinary character and determination would have taken the initiative and escaped under such circumstances. Some of those force-marched towards Germany in 1940 did indeed make a break for it, and most were recaptured and either shot or given a good thrashing; some escaped, were recaptured and escaped again and again until finally reaching neutral Spain and then being repatriated to Britain. Even so, it might take up to 18 months or two years to reach home.

A number of escape routes existed in France and the Low Countries, set up by local patriots and at first operating independently of any organization from Britain. However, thanks to the efforts of a small band of determined army and air force officers, the War Office overcame its usual tardiness and in December 1939 the organization that became known as MI9 (short for Military Intelligence Department No 9) was officially established to foster escape and evasion, first throughout Western Europe and later in the Middle East and Far East. As well as supplying escape lines with money, equipment and personnel, it lectured servicemen on evading capture and provided them with escape kits; it sent equipment such as maps, compasses, saws, files and clothing (disguised as blankets) to prisoner-of-war camps, and established a system of coded letters by which escape information and military intelligence could be exchanged. The results of all this activity have always been notoriously hard to assess (even one of its own operatives, Airey Neave, who had himself escaped from Germany, had difficulty untangling the complicated and contradictory statistics), and most of the escape equipment never reached its intended destination, but there is no doubt that the knowledge that the War Office was for once 'putting its money where its mouth is' did much to increase morale amongst prisoners.

GERMANY, AUSTRIA AND POLAND

No one can escape from a prison camp in enemy territory without knowing the lie of the land and without having some form of cover story. This was particularly so in fascist Europe, where you couldn't break wind without showing a fistful of documents. Usually escapers posed as itinerant foreign workmen, millions of whom had been pressed into service on pain of death or reprisals against their family. The donning of the disguise itself was dependent upon the initial achievement of getting out of the camp, escape from which experts broke down into three methods: 'over' (cutting through or climbing over the wire); 'under' (tunnelling) and 'through' (walking through the gate in disguise).

When the first escape by tunnel was made by a party of British officers from Oflag VIIC, Laufen, in September 1940, MI9 was informed by coded letter. Unfortunately, the escapees were recaptured and sent to the fortress at Colditz, which the Germans were now using as a special camp for escapers and troublemakers. Unfortunately, too, letters could take as long as three months to reach their destination, which somewhat retarded the usefulness of the information contained therein. The counter-escape section of the Abwehr, Germany's military intelligence service, soon caught on to MI9's various ploys to disguise escape aids, and escape and counter-escape activities developed into a duel of wits.

Almost from the beginning and throughout most of the war, would-be escapers had to fall back on their own resources, and most escapes took on an amateurish and gimcrack quality. However, Stalag Luft III and other RAF camps were unusual in being highly geared towards escape activities. From

1941 onwards all RAF camps were declared 'operational' by their SBO. In other words, although without weapons, the prisoners were still to wage war on the enemy by other means. During the period 1941–44 as many as 75 per cent of the prisoners were involved in either making escapes, providing the backing for escapes (gathering intelligence, bribing guards, making disguises, forging papers, laying on diversions) or sending home information in coded letters. This activity culminated in the 'Great Escape' from Stalag Luft III on 24–25 March 1944. That this ended in tragedy, with the slaughter of 50 of those recaptured by the Gestapo, and effectively put an end to escaping for the rest of the war, is now well known.

GERMANY

Pilot Officer Harry Ryland Bewlay, Royal Air Force
POW *from November 1939 to April 1945*
Oflag IXA/H, Spangenberg
My wife was due to have a baby in February 1940 and I could not bear the thought of not being there to see it. I made my own escape reconnaissance and became the first prisoner of the war to start a tunnel, which meant chipping my way through 300 feet of solid limestone rock. With an improvised hammer and a chisel, I began to attack the foundations of the castle.

A few days later the commandant, von Meyer, and Helmboldt, his interpreter, paid a rare visit to the SBO, Wing Commander Day. 'Could you please tell the officer who is trying to dig a tunnel to desist,' said Helmboldt. 'The noise is disturbing the commandant's sleep.'

And that was the end of my first escape attempt.

Gunner Cyril George King, Royal Artillery (Territorial)
POW *from May 1940 to April 1945*
Oflag VIB, Warburg, 1941–42
One of the members of our room, a fine Welshman from the Welsh Guards, had managed to get himself into the ranks of an escape party of officers. This meant that he spent quite a lot of time assisting in the digging of a tunnel and would be entitled to take his place in the queue when the work was complete. More often than not he arrived back covered with filth and we assisted by providing hot water, both for washing himself and washing his working clothes. No evidence must be left lying around the hut.

Pilot Officer Harry Bewlay at Spangenberg. Bewlay attempted
to tunnel out of the castle in February 1940 (*H Bewlay*)

One tunnel had been constructed underneath a recreation room at the lower end of the camp, but there had not been enough wood to support its walls and one officer was buried alive beneath the fallen earth. On another occasion the Air Force officers managed to extinguish the main lights, including the searchlights at night, and an exodus was attempted over the barbed wire, but this time the officers concerned were quickly recaptured and brought back to solitary confinement for a while. Christmas came once again and passed with its usual forgetfulness and misery – just another day in actual fact.

Wing Commander Joseph Robert Kayll, DSO, DFC, Auxiliary Air Force
POW from June 1941 to April 1945
Oflag VIB, Warburg
Regarding the opening of Red Cross parcels after escape attempts, the original reason for this was that the German security department realized that escape equipment was being sent from the UK and getting into the camp – such as maps, money, compasses, etc. Their reasoning was as follows: The Red Cross had given their word that no contraband of any sort would be allowed in Red Cross parcels. The security thinking was that if the UK were sending stuff, they would put it in Red Cross food parcels.

So all the tins, etc, were opened and of course nothing of any kind was found. The small amount that was sent was in individual clothing parcels, about which no promises had been made, and in some rather infantile games sent by a phoney welfare organization. Also new uniforms for Fleet Air Arm pilots, sent I think from Gieves', were very cleverly made so that the removal of buttons and some stitching made a very good business suit.

Lieutenant-Commander William Lawton Stephens, Royal Naval Volunteer Reserve
POW from March 1942 to October 1942
Oflag IVC, Colditz
I found Colditz a great change after the other camps I had seen. The morale and spirit of the prisoners was very high indeed and I suppose that almost every prisoner who was there was trying actively in one way or another to escape. This made things a little difficult with so many nationalities, but a very good system had been worked out to give everyone a chance. Each nationality had an escape committee of five or six officers, who entirely controlled the escape attempts of that nationality; then, in addition each nationality appointed a representative for an international escape committee,

who decided which country should be the next in turn to try a scheme. I think there were only one or two British who did not want to try to make a break, and as a result our escape committee worked on a rota system, which took into account how long one had been in the camp and how much value one would be to the war effort if one succeeded in getting home. The only means of short-circuiting this rota system was to think of a scheme for getting out, and if this was approved by the committee one would then be given the opportunity of trying it oneself. Naval officers were fairly high priority, but even so I was well down the list and it looked as if it would be many months before my turn came around.

Acting Squadron Leader Norman Edgar Canton, Royal Air Force
POW from November 1941 to April 1945
East Compound, Stalag Luft III, Sagan, 1942–1944

It was chaos when we arrived from Stalag Luft I in April 1942 and later I went to see Lieutenant Commander Buckley, then in charge of the 'X Organization', to help plan escapes, but not until Roger Bushell arrived later that summer did I become involved as Adjutant. But I attended meetings as Block 65 representative and helped get things organized. I made one escape attempt from East Compound, cutting through the wire with another British POW named Johnson.

Along with another chap who eventually pulled out we planned to cut through the eastern stretch of wire, between the two goon boxes near the main gate, at night. We were equipped with forged papers, mine claiming I was a Hungarian peasant labourer, our uniforms were adapted slightly to resemble civilian clothing, and we had wire-cutters made by another POW, Johnny Travis I think. The escape took place on 16 September 1942 – my birthday and not long before the first 'purge' to Oflag XXIB, Schubin. We sneaked out of our barracks at about 12 midnight and everything went off without a hitch. It took us 35 minutes to crawl to the wire, which we cut through without cutting ourselves or being disturbed.

Both of us had planned to head for the Balkans and link up with the partisans, but we'd decided to travel separately. So after cutting through the wire we split up, went to Sagan railway station, caught the same train and sat in different carriages at opposite ends, me at the back, Johnson at the front. I was out two days. I got picked up when my train went into a siding and a woman cleaner reported me. Three soldiers came and picked me up. Johnson got further but after four days he, too, was picked up by the Wehrmacht at another railway station.

Private Kenneth ('Kim') Stalder, Royal Army Medical Corps
POW from May 1941 to April 1945
Stalag IIIE, Kirchhain

There I dug a tunnel with Flight Sergeant Jock Alexander, the camp leader, a Kiwi Sergeant called 'Red' Breckon, and a team of Canadians and Yanks. We broke out on 11 May 1942. I was fifth out of the tunnel after the two Canadians, who were the main diggers, and Jock and Red. I snaked along for about 50 yards on my stomach to a copse and then crawled on hands and knees to another copse where Jock and Red were waiting. We headed for Stettin on foot but only got as far as three-quarters of the way. We had made a rule not to walk by day, but we broke our own rule because when we laid up during the day we were constantly getting bitten by mosquitoes. So we walked by day, and three or four days after our escape were spotted and questioned by a Hitler Youth. We pretended we were French, but our French wasn't good enough and he fetched a local policeman. He aimed his gun at us but his hand was shaking. He chained our hands together, and had so much left over that in the end we were festooned with chains. We were marched at gunpoint to the local jail – a typical country police jail right next door to the policeman's own house.

In the house on the other side of the jail lived an old woman, and she smuggled fags into the cells for us. Back at Stalag IIIE there were so many prisoners waiting for their term in the cooler that we didn't get sentenced.

Lieutenant David Lubbock, Royal Naval Volunteer Reserve
POW from July 1941 to April 1945
East Compound, Stalag Luft III

After returning from Schubin I became a member of the escape committee with responsibility for security through to the end. Wing Commander Joe Kayll was the head, followed later by Lieutenant Commander Peter Fanshawe. Aidan Crawley was in charge of intelligence. I don't remember from whom I assumed the task, which involved such functions as a constant watch being kept on the gate so that we knew at all times what 'goons' were in the compound, keeping escape equipment and helping would-be escapers from being caught. When Mike Codner and Eric Williams proposed to tunnel from under a vaulting horse the idea seemed to us practically impossible but so fantastic and novel that it might be worth a try. Its success is well known. Secrecy was so important, and we never knew if there was a 'mole' in the camp, that except those actually working on it no one was informed. The secret held.

The most unpleasant task for the security officer was having to let other tunnels be found from time to time. This had to be because the earth being brought up could not always be hidden completely. Hence the goons could tell that tunnelling was taking place. To safeguard the Wooden Horse, therefore, other tunnels had to be sacrificed periodically to account, falsely, for its sub-soil appearing under the huts where all tunnel sub-soil was distributed and hidden as far as possible with top-soil. The ferrets, who were privy to this, were frequently crawling under the huts.

In escape attempts in the past I found that people took as much fat as possible for their food, realizing that it had more than twice the energy (calories) for weight as protein or carbohydrate. That diet would make them sick. I devised two balanced replacements, a dry powder to be taken with water and a slab, both made up from ingredients of Red Cross parcels. These proved good but it was inevitable that some stores of them would be found and confiscated by the goons. I discovered that at Christmas time it was distributed to the local children.

Flying Officer Percy Frank ('Red') Eames, Royal Air Force
POW from July 1940 to April 1945
East Compound, Stalag Luft III, Sagan

The day after the Wooden Horse escape – a Saturday – we were being bustled out of our rooms by soldiers armed with Tommy-guns and into the hut corridor, which was full of lockers. I shouted: '*Raus!*' to the prisoner in front of me. He was so scared out of his wits that he leapt sideways and ended up squeezed between two lockers, which were only about four inches apart!

Major Elliott Viney, Oxford & Bucks Light Infantry
POW from June 1940 to May 1945
Oflag VIIB, Eichstätt, Bavaria

Escaping was a very tight closed shop; probably not more than 50 out of 1,800 were involved at any one time. Most of us never knew if and when an escape was planned; all you knew was that every now and then you had to walk or read outside one of the blocks and give a prearranged signal if a sentry was seen approaching.

Telegraphist Herbert Edgar Elliott, Royal Naval Volunteer Reserve
POW from August 1940 to May 1945
North Compound, Stalag Luft III, Sagan, March 1944

The officers were very daring and the Germans used one guard for every two prisoners to run the camp. On one occasion an officer dressed as a German

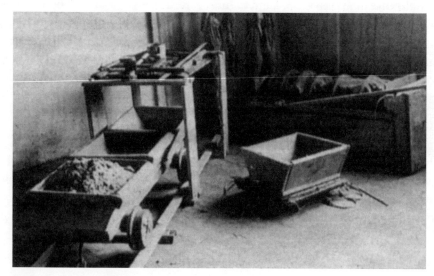

Section of the 'underground railway' and the air pump from tunnel 'Harry', Stalag Luft III, March 1944 (*author's collection*)

marched a party of 26 officers out of the compound, past sentries and all were away for several days before being recaptured. Several tunnels were dug, but all with one exception were found before being completed.

This exception was very cleverly hidden and took nearly a year to complete and was really a very clever and hazardous piece of work. The final episode was a great shock to us in the camp and the people back home.

The tunnel actually started from the block in which I lived and went down to a depth of 36 ft (or so I was told) and had to travel quite a good distance and the exit was a few feet inside a wood outside the camp. A large-scale escape was planned, 250 men to go through in one night. I saw these men dressed in all types of clothes enter the block and I can only say that the organization was on a large scale and excellently planned. Owing to an air raid and two men becoming stuck in the tunnel a considerable amount of time was lost and only about 80 men got through before they were discovered at 4.50 the next morning. Then of course everything was in an uproar with guards armed with Tommy-guns running about everywhere. After a day's hard work, the Germans found out who had escaped and continuous broadcasts were made to the public to the effect that these men were desperate and dangerous and must be arrested at all costs.

Hannelore Lewerentz (née Zöller)
German mail-censor at Stalag Luft III, Sagan, from January 1943
I shall never forget the night of the great escape 24–25 March 1944. A friend and I had been in Sagan town to see a film and when we left the cinema an air-raid alarm was sounded. It was between 11 and 12 pm when we left the air-raid shelter. On our way to the camp we had to go through the railway station building. There we noticed two or three little groups of strange-looking men who seemed to be waiting for a train. They were extraordinarily dressed and looked somewhat nervous. Knowing that in our camp kriegies had self-made clothes from their variety shows we had a fair idea that these men could have escaped from the camp. We waited for a moment and observed them and then some of them disappeared. We went to see the station policeman and told him of our suspicion. He asked one group to identify themselves. They produced some documents to prove that they were 'Fremdarbeiter', which meant foreign labourers. My friend and I then continued our way to the camp and at the gate asked the guard whether anything was going on in the camp, escape or so. 'No, everything is quiet,' he said. In our rooms we told this event to some other girls and discussed whether we should phone the Commandant. However, it was past midnight and we thought we probably would make a fool of ourselves.

Next morning we were shocked by the news that some 80 kriegies had escaped that night. For a long time, and keeping in mind the dramatic consequences of this escape, we often wondered whether we had done right.

Pilot Officer Hugh Edward Lance Falkus, Royal Air Force
POW from June 1940 to April 1945
East Compound, Stalag Luft III, Sagan
I had been close to Roger Bushell, having been with him in Stalag Luft I and Oflag XC. He came to see me before he led the big break and I begged him not to go. I grabbed him by the shoulders. Bushell said he spoke good German and had good clothes – he wouldn't get caught.

The events have since been glorified as 'The Great Escape'. A mass escape at that stage of the war was stupid and showed a lack of perception. It was a gross mistake by those in authority. The bombing campaign had made the Germans bitter and on edge. Conditions in Germany were dodgy. To escape in large numbers was asking for trouble. It made no sense and there was no glory in it. It was a miserable affair.

The number of men going out should only have been half a dozen. It happened so patently near the end of the war it was a mockery, a stupid venture, meaningless in the context of the war. As though they mattered to its outcome! Bushell was vain, conceited, assertive and very over-confident. Dear God, the mystique of authority! Men who wield it and men who follow – they're like children.

POLAND

Pilot Officer Maurice George Butt, Royal Air Force Volunteer Reserve
POW from August 1940 to May 1945
Fort 15 (Stalag XXA), Thorn (Toruń)
First attempt mid-September 1940 en route from Dulag to Stalag Luft I Barth. Four of us planned to jump the train at the best opportunity as far north as possible. As twilight came on the second day the moment arrived and we dropped out whilst the carriage was stationary in a siding awaiting coupling up for the final leg of the journey to Stralsund. Unfortunately we were spotted crossing the marshalling yard and recaptured lying in the ditch at the side. Our first night at Luft I was in the cooler.

When we left Barth for Spangenberg in January '41 all hope of jumping en route to the station at Stralsund were dashed by the security measures employed by the guards who were spaced at 100-metre intervals, sub-machine guns at the ready. The goons had been listening to the plans for escape it was revealed later when microphones were discovered under the western hut and sabotaged immediately (we learned two years later!).

Second attempt occurred at Thorn in mid-May '41. Strong rumours persisted that evacuation of the camp, a semi-underground fortress of pre-WWI vintage, was imminent.

Dickie Troward and I decided to team up and schemed to go to Russia. Our attempt was coordinated with another scheme involving six others who were to walk out of the front gates and we two were to become 'ghosts', ie, to disappear into the unused half of the camp and therefore assumed by our captors to have escaped with the six. Then after the camp was evacuated during the next week, with no guards around we were to walk out and head east to Russia. All too simple.

The six, who presented themselves at the main gate immediately after a guard change, claimed they were required at the *Kommandantur*, the camp commandant's quarters about one mile down the road. The ruse worked, Ray Milner was a very fluent German speaker and acted as escorting interpreter, the other two RAF were 'Pissy' Edwards, who later committed suicide at Schubin, and Geoff Dodgshun; while of the three army types Airey Neave and his partner actually crossed the border into Russia but were brought back at rifle point by the frontier guard. This was days before Germany attacked Russia and they would have been lucky indeed to have survived the turmoil of that period.

For our scheme Dickie arranged maps, compass, routing and clothing and my part was to acquire sufficient rations and learn some useful Russian phrases. This latter was accomplished by the patient tutoring of an army type whose mother had escaped from Russia after the revolution. There were only two dozen phrases, some of which were simple words, but my tutor was appalled by my efforts at longer phrases. One of these was 'Take me to Sir Stafford Cripps the British Ambassador, he is my uncle', which was quite untrue of course.

The night before we were to disappear I decided to visit the Senior Officers' room to top up our larder. There had been a distribution of Red Cross parcels earlier that week, the second lot to reach the camp. I was confronted by a most extraordinary situation on entering the room. There was a Luftwaffe pilot complete with his yellow lapel tabs, accompanied by the German commandant in deep discussion with the roomful of senior RAF and Army officers. Germans seldom came into the camp in the evening – unless there was a crisis of some sort. I listened for fifteen minutes and decided to look elsewhere for spare rations. Later we learnt that this Luftwaffe officer was Von Werra, the one that got away from British captivity on his third attempt, by jumping ship down the St Lawrence River in Canada. He had been sent by Goering on a tour of inspection of RAF camps and happened to visit our reprisal camp that evening whilst house-hunting in the area. He was a man of short stature but very alert and strutty, posturing and demanding the full attention of everyone around. Typical extrovert fighter boy.

I went to the Padres' room as an alternative source of supplementing food. There were two in the room and they seemed to think a Bible was suitable equipment to carry, but I left with an extra tin of corned beef instead.

The next morning after watching the six leave through the front gate Dickie and I scrambled through a gap in a barred window, made by removing two one-inch-diameter pre-sawn bars stuck back into position by a glutinous mix, and these were re-stuck by our supporters after our exit. The sawing had been done the previous week.

We lay up in the doorway to a bunker into which we had a skeleton key. Unfortunately neither of us could unlock the door so we lodged in the doorway, which was about half a metre deep. The balloon went up and we heard the prearranged signal that the escape had been discovered, which meant our taking maximum concealment for the inevitable search.

Despite dogs employed in checking the unused half of the camp we survived two searches. At one stage I well remember hearing the heavy breathing of the fat *Hauptmann* standing a metre above our heads, his silhouette reflected by the sun onto the wall two metres in front of us. We had taken great care to comb and 'preen' the grass and wild growth littering the approach to our hide and it had paid off.

The third search on the second day was a much more toothcomb affair and the *Feldwebel*, known as 'Scarface', approached our position from in front of us and drawing his Luger he fired two shots to signal his satisfaction of our discovery – or perhaps to frighten the lives out of us, which it certainly did. He fired into the air above our heads but the experience was hair-raising.

ITALY

Even with a super-efficient organization at their disposal, escapers found Germany and Poland tough nuts to crack – but Italy was even tougher. There were a number of reasons for this, the main one being that most Britons were fair-skinned and even the most Celtic-looking could not convincingly pass for Italians because their demeanour was a dead giveaway. Neither was help forthcoming from the civilians until the Armistice was declared on 3 September 1943 and suddenly hundreds of friendly peasants appeared, having been 'anti-fascist' and 'pro-Allied' all along. Furthermore, British prisoners constantly underestimated their Italian captors, who by dint of their peasant culture were curious – and very observant. Many an escape plan came to grief because prisoners failed to grasp this elementary fact.

Although 602 prisoners had escaped from Italian POW camps up to the Armistice, only two had made home runs via Switzerland – Lieutenant Anthony Deane-Drummond of No 2 Commando, who posed as a German soldier on leave, and Lieutenant M E Stewart of the Intelligence Corps – while another four were hiding in the Vatican. But in September 1943 thousands of prisoners in Italy woke up to find their guards had disappeared and, despite receiving by coded radio messages a fatuous War Office order to remain in their camps, the bold ones walked out and took to the hills. With the help of Italian peasants, more than 5,000 escapers and evaders reached neutral Switzerland and another 12,000 crossed the front line to link up with Allied troops. Thus, in defiance of all the odds that had been stacked against them in the previous three years, two out of every three British and Commonwealth escapers and evaders who made it home were from Italy. Had more SBOs disobeyed the War Office order, thousands more would have made it. Instead they were entrained for Germany.

Lieutenant A F ('Junior') Powell, 13th Light Anti-Aircraft Regiment
POW from April 1941 to May 1945
Campo PG 17, Rezzanello
Occasionally someone tried to escape – no one got clean away or even very far. In September 1941 the Italians found a tunnel had been started from the cellar, the outer walls of which were outside the barbed-wire fence. My battery commander was at that time in charge of the cellar so was punished. I was not allowed to help in the tunnelling as I was too big!

In January 1942 an 'other rank' got away and the rest of us were kept out in the courtyard until the authorities assured themselves that they had us all back under control. In March 1942 three officers tried to escape during an evening lecture and we were kept there for hours, but it gave the speaker extra time. After an escape attempt there was usually a search of our rooms and some copies of the *Rezzanello Revue* were taken, but never mine.

Lieutenant John Pelly, Coldstream Guards
POW from June 1942 to April 1945
Diary kept in Campo PG 17, Rezzanello
13 September 1942. Sunday. An officer escaped from the camp this morning. He got out by hiding under the daily fruit cart which comes in each morning, but

by the worst of bad luck he was seen by a civilian in the village, who chanced to look under the cart. On him were found 18 unopened tins from food parcels. The Commandant was simply furious; the Italians opened every tin left in our parcels and closed the rooms for good. Everybody furious in the camp, but apparently the Commandant is within his rights.

Lance-Corporal Lawrence Bains, Middlesex Yeomanry
POW from June 1942 to August 1944
Diary kept in Campo PG 53, Sforzacosta
15 September 1943. Today the general atmosphere of the camp was quieter than for several days and we were settling down again. Nevertheless, Bill Brookes and I kept our kits packed for any emergency. About 1430 hours there began to be felt an uneasy slackening of discipline, and crowds of POWs clustered round the main gate in *Settore* 1, and the sentry seemed undecided as to action. The locks were removed and the gate left slightly ajar and the sentry started shouting and pressing the alarm, but nothing happened. Meanwhile, groups of POWs entered the Italian stores, which were out of bounds, and returned with haversacks and water bottles. The sentries could stand it no longer, and passing a sign round the camp soon disappeared and were later seen legging it for all they were worth across the nearby hills. Evidently they had some rumours of a German column, so despite orders of Captain Frewen (the senior MO) over the amplifier, the canteen, etc, were raided by hordes of POWs – I have never seen anything like it, looting and destroying everything in sight. Bartlett, Brooke, Goodfellow and myself had decided to act in concert and so we thought to have a meal (it was now 1600 hours) and then leave. The confusion, and the numbers leaving the camp, was such that we could eat as much as we wanted, but after I had had a good feed, Captain Frewen appealed over the amplifier for guards for the gate, so we thought it a good time to go.

It was a wonderful feeling to be outside the camp after eleven months, but we were really too excited to appreciate it. We headed along the road to the west, passing several grinning *carabinieri*. I soon found even my scanty kit heavier than I had expected but daren't leave anything behind.

After walking a few hundred yards we stopped a cart and the four of us clambered on and jogged along, merrily jesting as we passed others still walking. When we had put sufficient distance between us and the camp, at a side-track leading south, we dismounted and were immediately pounced upon by some peasants who gave us several pieces of bread, each bigger than our daily camp ration. This was a pleasant surprise and we thought boded well for the future.

Lieutenant Richard Gordon Clover, Royal Artillery
POW until September 1943
Campo PG 49, Fontanellato

There are plenty of others who had a more exciting time but what happened to me was quite exciting enough. I got clear of the camp the day after the Armistice without incident. The Huns came to take us over but we had wind of their approach and got clear with a few minutes to spare, and they hadn't enough men to comb the whole countryside for us.

That was in northern Italy within a week's walking of the Swiss frontier, which I was much tempted to make for. However, I set out to walk south with another officer. We walked and walked and then some, always in the mountains, never on the roads, nipping over main roads and railway lines and walking across country roughly south-east. We swapped uniforms for some filthy, ragged civilian clothes, begged food as we went from the peasants and lived mostly on bread and grapes.

After about six weeks we must have covered over 500 miles, and with a zigzag, cross-country course it took some hard walking. Food was not plentiful nor very sustaining, and we slept and shivered by night in stables or barns or in the open. On the whole the peasants were friendly and helpful, though fearful (penalty for helping ex-POWs was death). I could speak the language fairly well but of course with my accent and appearance could not very well pass for a Wop!

Then, 20 miles from the line, we got caught by the Huns. They were getting more and more numerous as we got closer to the line and it was very hard to dodge them, and the line being stationary made it still harder to get through.

We spent some very unpleasant days starving in a dungeon well south of Rome and of course got covered with lice. Then we were put on a train for Germany, locked in cattle-trucks with a bucket and a bale of straw. We took a poor view of that, a poorer view still when the RAF came and bombed the train. However, there was a spot of confusion and, watching all chance, I managed to nip off and hide in an air-raid shelter with a lot of civilians. Then I got into the mountains again alone and spent a couple of months on a pile of bracken in an old shack high up in the mountains, hoping for the line to move a bit. With the winter it was getting terribly cold there so I contrived, through a Wop I had met, to get into Rome. There I wandered from refuge to refuge till I found a permanent billet where I hid for four months like a troglodyte until the Allies arrived in Rome.

That time in Rome was the worst off all. I had a bed but food was scarce and I had to stay hidden almost the whole time. Spies and informers were numerous and the reward for capture of an escaped prisoner was high.

Lieutenant Jimmy Day, The Worcestershire Regiment
POW from April 1941 to September 1943
Campo PG 41, Montalbo, and Campo PG 49, Fontanellato

I had previously escaped from Crete by boat, after the surrender there, to land ten miles behind German lines, and then got out of the Water Tower camp at Ben Chasi to be recaptured at Barco ten days later. I then spent the best part of two years at Montalbo, from which no one could escape, for it was a Colditz, built on rock with guards and floodlights every dozen yards apart.

Our opportunity came when they decided to close the camp down and move us to Fontanellato, for a Flight Lieutenant John Hall and I discovered a priest hole which the guards would never have found, and we had it all prepared and water laid on, ready to disappear an hour before the move-out time, and stay there a week or more if necessary until the guards left, and then break out.

Our friends frightened us and told us they would shoot us like dogs if there was no one to witness the discovery – I am sure we would have got away with it, but fear is a terrible thing as you know, and I allowed myself to be influenced.

It was this idea, of staying behind when all the others had left, which I applied to the Fontanellato field, and the escape committee did a good job of arranging for the picks to level the ploughed field, and the diversion to keep the prowler guards from us, whilst we dug a section hole and covered it with bed-boards; under guise of a game of cards, where all but one were watching whilst I trowelled out the small hole, and covered it with a blanket when danger approached.

After my Montalbo funk, I needed a brave companion, so I asked 'Pip' Gardiner, VC, MC, who told me that he did not relish being shot. So I settled for Mike Ross, who was the only officer from my regiment in the camp, and when I undid both wires at the end of the field and propped them up with grooved sticks, Mike made a good job of re-covering the hole, so that Tony Roncorroni, Toby Graham and Joselyn could go again three or four days later.

Roncorroni died of a heart attack shortly after the war. I had a lot of time for him and he insisted we got physically fit, but why he needed to do this I cannot guess, as he went by train, whilst we walked.

Whenever you fail, you tend to blame someone else, so on my last venture I decided to go alone, although I met people on route but never stayed longer than a day with anyone unless it was to repair my boots, which I had done three times.

I have forgotten most of the villages, but I remember the southern village of Fratura, high above Lake Scano, which was full of POWs and Italian soldiers wishing to cross the line, which they thought was ten miles away, when it was at that time 60 miles ahead.

I crouched down and eventually marched all day, to arrive at nightfall where the flat, high mountain plain dropped down to the Sangro, and I would have stayed the night, but I just missed a German patrol looking for POWs at a sheep-farm tent by seconds, and decided to continue down the mountain to the river below, and it was on this slope that they must have been building the Cassino line, but because it was dark I could not see, which was just as well.

It was then that my second bit of luck occurred, for the heavens opened … and I walked in my stockinged feet past German bivouac tents at the bottom who were meant to be guarding the entrance to the village, from which I heard many screams and had visions of rape and pillage.

I was so wet that I avoided the bridge, which had to be guarded, and waded across the Sangro, to find myself in the darkness around German gun emplacements surrounded by sandbags.

I walked on until dawn, when I heard and saw the church bells of a village, and I was so exhausted, wet, cold and miserable, that even if the whole German army was there, I was going to find a house with a fire. Fortunately, I was met outside the village by a cow boy who took me to a carbon-burners' hut in the hills where we slaughtered a sheep, fed, and then I slept for two days.

The name of the village I do not know – but one day I will find it.

It must have been four days after this, with the villages and roads crawling with Germans, that I crossed the line, and my first indication was when a *contadini* gave me a packet of Lucky Strike, an appropriate word, and told me an American patrol had arrived and returned to a village five miles away.

I walked along the *strada*, not realizing until I made contact in the village that four people had been blown up there by mines the Germans, in retreat, had laid on the path. It had to be a question of luck!

Lieutenant-Colonel Sydney Charles Fane de Salis, King's Royal Rifle Corps
Captured November 1941, escaped 1943
Campo PG 29, Veano
September 1943. Before the Armistice there were 200 officers at Veano. Most of us were Lieutenant Colonels and Majors. There were a few very young officers and one or two RAF.

All kinds of schemes had been prepared to meet various eventualities when Italy came out of the war but none of the schemes foresaw the actual happenings.

Lieutenant-Colonel Sydney Charles Fane de Salis, DSO (*Lucinda Brooks*)

The camp was unluckily situated no more than ten miles from a German-owned aerodrome, which was used for training young Germans. The town of Pialesya was also about this distance away and had a fluctuating number of Germans from week to week.

The British Senior Officer, throughout the day of the Armistice, and the succeeding days, was quite convinced that our camp would not be taken over by the Germans. Why he was of this opinion it is hard to say.

8 September 1943 dawned, as far as we knew, the same as any other day for us; with the usual roll-call before breakfast and the usual poor coffee, but the breakfast made palatable by the excellent foods sent by the Red Cross and received by us weekly. It was not until dinner (noon) that the terrific news of the Armistice reached us. The first indication was the troops in the yard throwing their hats in the air and their rifles on the ground, and almost immediately after this one of the interpreters told us the news, while we were at lunch. We all stood up and fairly shouted the National Anthem and I for one felt a lump in my throat. It MIGHT mean so much to us. Freedom – home and everything we had waited for so long.

That night we were told by the Senior British Officer that the Italians were quite aware it was their duty to prevent the Germans taking us away and that they would fight to prevent it, etc. Some poor fools believed this.

The next day was one of conferences; and steps were taken to give us warning if the Hun came up any of the three roads leading to our camp.

Orders were issued that no one should leave the camp, though we would be allowed to sleep out if we wished it. This meant sleeping in the fields.

'Tishy' Lister [Lieutenant-Colonel Martin Douglas Bathurst Lister, Royal Tank Regiment] and I decided that, as the Hun might come to the camp early next morning, we would sleep in the open air. We did so and it was the first of many nights spent under the stars.

Next morning, 10 September, the SBO was going to tell the officers at 11 am that, although he considered it unnecessary, and even unwise, any who wished could leave the camp that day.

Luckily, just before we met, the Italian commandant sent for the SBO and said that as his instructions were to let us scatter if he could not look after us, we must all go by 2 pm, as by now most of the Italian guard had deserted and he could do nothing to stop the Germans taking over the camp. This message was therefore given to us and the fun began.

Very few other camps were as lucky as we were. At one camp the SBO said that any officer who left the camp would be court-martialled, with the result that the Germans took the whole camp, and only those who jumped out of the train escaped going to Germany.

Our party consisted of Lister, Gordon de Brayne and self, and we decided to go as soon as possible.

None of our party had made any serious plans and so everything was rather a rush.

We had to decide whether we should hide in the hills and wait for the English to make a landing near Genoa; whether we should try and walk south and join our troops near Naples (600 miles); whether we should try to cross to France; whether we should go straight to Switzerland; and to make things more difficult we had no idea what the attitude of the Italian peasants would be as regards feeding us, or reporting our whereabouts to the German troops.

The SBO advised everyone to wear uniform, which was an unfortunate decision as we all eventually had to try and look like peaceful Italian civilians. We decided to carry as much tinned food as possible, a change of underclothes, a blanket and greatcoat. (The weather at this time was beautifully hot – like a hot summer day in England.) When we put the stuff together we found we should have to make double journeys as we each had over 100 pounds weight of kit.

We managed to get some cold food at about 11.30 am and we were about a mile clear of the camp by about 1.30 pm, clear of the main road.

We struggled on and, pouring with sweat and out of breath, we were well in the hills by 3.30 pm. Later on we heard that the alarm was sounded in the camp at 2.15 pm, which alarm soon spread to the hills and forced us all to hurry even more to areas we felt would be safe from German patrols who might come to look for us.

At about 4 pm this alarm reached us and we decided we must move on and leave everything we couldn't carry with us. In my case I left under a bush a costly Fermanagh rug, a kitbag, a dozen tins of food (Red Cross and private parcel from Egypt), thick underclothes, 12 cakes of soap, and I carried on with me a load of about 60 or 70 lbs.

By about 6 pm we felt we could go no further and lay down in the bushes. All this country is ideal for hiding in. Hilly, no motor roads, chestnut trees, continental oaks, hazel bushes and one or two other types. Plenty of water in streams and pools. We now sorted out our food and found we had enough for a month on fairly short rations, which would consist roughly of a half-pound tin of meat or fish, a very small tin of cheese and a tin of biscuits between the three of us.

At about this time Henry Rogers, the camp Padre, came by and asked to join our party, as he had failed to find his companion.

We now had our first meal of biscuits and tinned salmon but were really too exhausted to eat it – though we did our best.

Lieutenant William Bompas, Royal Artillery (Field)
POW from December 1942 to April 1945
Campo PG 21, Chieti

It was a curious situation after the Italian Armistice. Our guards at Chieti had pushed off home and we could have walked out of the gates; but, alas, our Senior British Officer, a pretty useless ex-Indian Army colonel, had had instructions from the War Office that we were to stay in our camp, guarded by the Italians until Monty arrived in a few days. (The story is that Monty thought we would go out and rape the Italian women.) It was pretty obvious after a day or two that our Italian guards were not around to protect us from the Germans, and that Monty would not be arriving shortly. However, the SBO did not use his initiative, and we young subalterns obeyed him. (He was court-martialled after the war but got off.)

Once the Germans had taken over the camp – we got those paratroopers who had rescued Mussolini from the Gran Sasso as guards – we felt free to try to escape. I got out once dressed as a German private in charge of a working party of British other ranks – actually four junior officers suitably dressed – but didn't get far. The German commandant put us in the cooler for a few days. (I read after the war that he was in fact quite amused by this episode.)

Another attempt, getting out of a cattle-truck, was thwarted when we picked the lock too soon. But such is life.

THE FAR EAST

The Far Eastern theatre presented even more obstacles to British and Commonwealth escapers than did Italy. Escaping from the camps was not in itself impossible or even difficult: few camps in the Far East were built along the lines of those in Germany and Italy and fewer still with security in mind, and some did not even have fences. But the terrain beyond the camps was vast and often thick with impenetrable jungle. Moreover, it was almost impossible for a white European to blend in with the natives, and in any case one could not always rely on their help, as some of them were pro-Japanese. The greatest obstacle, however, was the attitude of the Japanese and Korean guards themselves, who would just as soon shoot an escapee as kill a rat. Recaptured escapees were beaten, tortured, and shot or beheaded, according to the captors' whim, and sometimes other prisoners were selected at random for similar punishment. In 1942 prisoners in Changi, Singapore, were made to sign a declaration that they would not attempt escape, thus giving their guards an additional excuse to mete out extreme punishment.

However, against all odds, some did escape successfully, the most notable being Colonel Lindsay Ride, who with several companions escaped from Shamshuipo camp in Hong Kong and reached Free China, where he set up the British Army Aid Group (BAAG) and helped liberate some 2,000 others from Japanese captivity.

Commander R S Young, Royal Navy
POW from December 1941 to August 1945
Shamshuipo Camp, Kowloon, Hong Kong
There was barbed wire fairly thickly all round, left over by us, and the number of Japanese guards was much increased. Even here, however, one could easily have got out, chiefly through the large drainage pipes which led into the sea, the barracks being on the harbour's edge. Colonel Ride, a civilian Australian doctor in Hong Kong who had many Chinese contacts and plenty of money, did get out. He was to play an important part later trying to arrange escapes. He set up an HQ in China to effect this. Most of the attempts proved disastrous.

For myself, I thought it better to wait for a more opportune moment later. It was obviously no good escaping except with a well thought-out plan, some food and plenty of money. Some of the local Hong Kong POWs were managing to get a little food passed in through the wire or by Chinese girl-friends or by their ex-servants. With money all might be possible. Our Naval Paymaster had brought out from the dockyard some months' pay packets running into thousands of dollars. This he thought it wise not to dish out at this stage. It was a pity he didn't, as later it was of no use to us at all.

Sapper Edgar Whincup, Royal Engineers
POW from February 1942 to August 1945
Camp 330, Changi Barracks, Singapore
The Japanese issued their Imperial Japanese Army Order No 17 on 24 September 1942, requiring each POW to sign a declaration stating that we would not try to escape. This was contrary to King's Regulations and so we refused. Consequently, after numerous attempts to persuade us to carry out this order, and a multiplicity of threats, as a punishment we were told to move to Selarang Barracks, another peacetime British Army depot. All we were allowed to take was bedding and eating utensils. As far as I can remember

15,000 men, plus all Aussies, were billeted in four barrack blocks which, in peacetime, would house 1,500! Then, shortly after our arrival, another crowd of POWs arrived. In an attempt to force us to sign the declaration the Japs surrounded the barrack blocks with barbed wire and posted machine guns on each corner and on the roofs of the buildings. As we were covered in this way and with so many POWs housed there, we were forced to sleep in shifts. Can you imagine the chaos? No, you can't.

Every man was given one pint of water per day for cooking, washing and drinking. The medics were sited at one corner of the square and the only protection for the sick were large, communal mosquito nets, under which the MOs had to perform minor, and sometimes major, operations. Part of the barracks square had to be dug upon to make latrines, but most regular soldiers always had the ambition to do this to most barracks squares.

Then, on 5 September, we were told that all the sick from Roberts' Hospital were to be brought in, adding enormously to everyone's discomfort (this is an understatement). We now suffered two deaths and dozens of dysentery cases, so, under duress, we signed the declaration.

Sergeant William McDonald Innes-Ker, Straits Settlement Volunteer Force
POW from February 1942 to August 1945
Sonkurai No 2 Camp, Burma–Siam Border
During our first, despairing months at Sonkurai we had three escape efforts; parties of six or ten men slipped away in the night in an effort to reach more civilized parts. The first two parties were never heard of again; they probably died in the jungle or were killed by gangs of Nips or Thais. I have not explained that there was no question of barbed wire round the camps: they were completely open to the countryside around, which was all dense jungle and very mountainous in parts, so escape into or through it was not possible without tools, food and some idea of where to go.

The last of our escape parties, some 12 men led by a couple of officers, did manage to struggle through to the coast, or at least half of the party did. The rest died en route of exhaustion, ulcers and fevers. We learnt this when a couple of months later we spotted some of the escapees coming back, in chains, guarded by Nip soldiers. It seems the few that lived got through the jungles and ravines to the coast at Ye, progressing sometimes only a few hundred yards in a day, so dense was the terrain. Here, near Ye, they holed up in a Burmese village, where, when their money ran out in a few days, they were handed over to the Nips. They were beaten and tortured and eventually sent back to Singapore and placed in Outram Road Jail (the Kempeitai headquarters). A year later one survivor was brought back to Changi and our medics nursed him back to life. The Outram Road Nips did not like their prisoners to die on them, and they often brought back to us wrecks of men who really had no chance and usually died in a few days.

On the occasion of the last escape party, the next day, when it could no longer be concealed that men had fled (one in fact was the Quartermaster Officer in charge of all our supplies and grub – the one who survived Outram Road Jail), we were all paraded by our furious Nip guards – all twelve of them! One junior officer, one *gunzo* (sergeant), and ten men. The guards were split up into two search parties, given rations for a day and ordered, in front of us, to load their rifles and depart north and south to search for the escapees. Blow me down, there they were, ten bedraggled Nips fumbling uncertainly with their rifles, with which, being ex-British captured stock, they seemed unfamiliar. In the end, after much shouting and face-slapping by the officer, he ordered one of our sergeants to instruct the guards in how to load their rifles!

Corporal Charles Kinahan, Straits Settlement Volunteer Force
POW from February 1942 to August 1945
Camp 241, Ban Pong, Siam (Thailand)
The camps were surrounded by high bamboo fences, which were easily penetrated. In fact escape was never really on the cards. We were many hundreds of miles from the Allied units in North Burma. You could not disguise yourself as a Siamese or a Burman and would be entirely dependent on the native peasantry. The few who did try were quickly handed back to the Japs for a cash reward.

Lieutenant-Colonel Philip Toosey, 135th Field Regiment, Royal Artillery
POW from February 1942 to August 1945
Camp 249, Tamarkan, Siam (Thailand)
In early January 1943 four private soldiers of the East Surrey Regiment came to me and said they were going to try to escape. I warned them of the difficulties but nothing would stop them and so we did our best to try to give them supplies and keep their absence hidden as long as we could. But they were caught the very next day and brought back close to the camp and shot.

11

PUNISHMENT AND REPRISALS

'...in view increasing German ruthlessness and lack of regard to Geneva Convention chiefs of staff rule that under present circumstances it need no longer be considered duty of P/W to escape ...'
— message from MI9 to Senior British Officers

The 1929 Geneva Convention devoted no fewer than 22 articles to 'Penal Sanctions with Regard to Prisoners of War' – on the face of it a good index of how fractious prisoners had been punished in previous conflicts. The sum of these 22 provisions was that prisoners of war should not be punished any more harshly than the captor's own troops, the usual penalties being confinement to barracks for petty offences, 30 days' solitary confinement for major offences – such as escaping, in the case of a POW – and fines for damaging property. However, these rules failed to take into account the civil and military cultures of the prospective belligerents. Verbal and physical abuse, for instance, had long been common in the German, Polish, Czech, Russian and Japanese armed forces, while being unacceptable to those of Britain and the Commonwealth. It was nothing for an Eastern European army officer to shoot on the spot soldiers who had abandoned an untenable position. NCOs and other ranks were routinely slapped, punched, kicked and hit with rifle butts not merely for breaking the rules but simply for appearing a bit dim and uncomprehending. Such punishment was common in Italy as well. When Italy and Germany went fascist, such incidents increased in number and severity. If these punishments were considered the norm in their armies, then they would also be applied to errant prisoners of war.

GERMANY AND OCCUPIED POLAND

As well as the conventional armed forces (the Wehrmacht) Germany also had its secret state police – the *Geheime Staatspolizei*, or Gestapo – plus the

Sicherheitsdienst (SD, security and intelligence service) and the SS (*Schutzstaffel*), all of which tried at various stages of the war to run POW affairs and finally, after the 'Great Escape' in 1944, succeeded. Up to then, prisoners had been relatively safe from Gestapo and SS interference, but even so were subject to individual and collective acts of punishment, officially sanctioned and random, that violated the terms of the Geneva Convention. After escape attempts food, personal and clothing parcels were sometimes withheld and tampered with. In addition to the shooting of the 50 after the Great Escape, hundreds of prisoners were sent to 'comparative' camps at Posen (Poznan) and Thorn (Toruń) in 1941 as a tit-for-tat reprisal for alleged ill-treatment of German prisoners in Canada, and between autumn 1942 and the end of 1943 more than 4,000 British and Canadian army officers and men in seven different camps, as well as RAF NCOs in Stalag VIIIB, Lamsdorf, were shackled after German soldiers killed by commandos in the raid on Sark on 7 October 1942 were found with their hands tied behind their backs. As Germany began to feel the impact of Allied air raids, random acts of spite resulted in prisoners being shot for very minor infractions and newly downed airmen being hanged by vengeful civilians. As the tide of war turned against Germany, only the fear of punishment by the victorious Allies prevented the Gestapo and SS from slaughtering prisoners – especially bomber crews – outright.

GERMANY

Flying Officer Michael Heriot Roth, Royal Air Force
POW from May 1940 to June 1945
Oflag IXA/H, Spangenberg, May 1940
As we trudged from the village towards the castle road, the guards kept shouting for us to hurry. Eventually, this harassment became so irksome, so uncalled for, so stupid, we started shouting back telling them to lay off and shut up. The commotion reached its height as we passed an orchard where some schoolgirls were playing catch. A couple of chaps gave good-natured whistles. The girls stopped their game, gawked and giggled, and one waved at us. We cheered. This fraternization was too much for the *Feldwebel* in charge. Halt! Those who had insulted the citizens of the Reich would step forward immediately! Someone translated. More cheers, whistles and catcalls. What could he do? His orders were to deliver 30 POWs to the castle. Unsure of themselves, his guards unslung their rifles and threatened to club the nearest prisoners. As a body we yelled we would resist any

violence. We were Field Marshal Goering's prisoners and we guaranteed that the Field Marshal would hear about any brutality. This gave them pause. It was a messy situation, unexpectedly resolved by the girls, who, having gone back to their game, accidentally threw their ball among us. The guards were nonplussed. So they turned on the girls in their anger, reprimanding them for being friendly with the enemy. None of the girls was more than ten or eleven, and they probably didn't know or even care who we were, so when the guards stupidly pointed their rifles at them, they froze a second, then, squealing hysterically, dashed into the depths of the orchard.

We at once demanded that the *Feldwebel* send a runner for a German officer so we could report this cowardly, unmilitary-like behaviour of his guards against the innocent youth of the Reich. We said we were entitled by German Army Regulations to air our grievances before an officer, and further, we refused to even discuss the matter either with him or with his bullying squad. The *Feldwebel* was speechless. No one had ever spoken to him in such terms. He stood transfixed, legs apart, hands on hips, and literally frothed. At long last, unable to find words, he suddenly about-faced and gave orders for the march to continue. From then on there wasn't a sound, nor indeed any further reference to the incident.

Pilot Officer Idrwerth Patrick ('Paddy') Bentley Denton, Royal Air Force Volunteer Reserve
POW from July 1941 to May 1945
Oflag XC, Lübeck, 1941
After a few days, being British, we made a football out of bits of palliasse cover and some filling. I suppose there were only about 50 of us in the camp.

On the Lübeck side was a fair-sized sand patch and there we played our football games. One day the ball trickled over the tripwire. We made a pointing gesture to the guard and one of us stepped across to retrieve it. The guard shot three rounds at him only one of which hit, a simple nick on his leg. Nothing serious but we thought a totally unnecessary and unfair piece of goonery.

It was a useful lesson again since the sound of the shots brought everyone off their bunks and out of the huts and we surrounded the goon box of the offensive little man. We expressed ourselves and our opinions of his forebears in perfectly explicit, grammatical English language, the purpose of which seemed to make some impression.

Flight Lieutenant Joseph Edmond Tobin Asselin, Royal Canadian Air Force
POW from September 1941 to May 1945
Tunnel escaper from Oflag VIB, Warburg, October 1941
The treatment I received after my capture on this occasion was the roughest of any of my escapes. It included face slapping, assorted kicks, a bayonet jab, stealing of personal belongings and on my return to camp, being made to stand, facing the wall at attention without food or water for about 14 hours, with a guard standing over me. The reason for the latter was that the German security officer was furious at my unwillingness to answer questions on methods used in building and engineering the tunnel. Also, the fact that he was unable to find any German money, maps, compasses and other escape paraphernalia, which I had disposed of while being marched back to camp.

Lieutenant David Lubbock, Royal Naval Volunteer Reserve
POW from July 1941 to April 1945
Stalag Luft III, Sagan
March 1942. Sagan. Pete Gardner and I shared an end room of one of the huts with Douglas Bader until after the *Kommandantur* had had more of our 'goon' baiting than they could stand, he was escorted off to Lamsdorf under platoon escort which he formally inspected! Knowing about my prewar experience as a nutritionist, the *Kommandantur* at this same time, 1942, asked me to join a scientific research group working on production of vitamin concentrates from various sources when I would no longer be kept behind the wires of POW camps. When I refused I was purged with a group of about 40 including Lieutenant Commander Buckley RN (superb head of our escape committee), Wing Commander Hull and Squadron Leader Aidan Crawley to Schubin, Oflag XXIB, in Poland.

Gunner Cyril George King, Royal Artillery (Territorial)
POW from May 1940 to April 1945
Stalag VIIIB, Lamsdorf
Generally speaking each compound held a particular nationality: Indian, Palestinian, South African – mainly Afrikaners – Australian and New Zealand and, at the time we arrived, Canadian – for this was at the date of the Dieppe raid. As it was maintained by the Germans that their own men captured at this time were put in chains, the Canadians had their hands bound behind their backs all day long until it was time for the Germans to lock the barracks and force the men to their miserable beds. They were not allowed to go on working

parties and thus other men were in great demand in order that identity could be exchanged. Very rarely was this obtained, for freedom of movement was very sweet and it was only very lazy men who would take on the exchange and manage to have themselves filtered into the compound.

International Red Cross Representative
Oflag VIIB, Eichstätt, Bavaria, 1942–43
Prisoners who are handcuffed are quartered in Block I of the Upper Camp. The number of these prisoners remains fixed, and if for any reason, such as illness, a prisoner of war is un-manacled, another takes his place. The men are freed from time to time during the day and night. They are able to see and converse with others in the camp. The Camp Leader reports that they have been well treated and receive special kindnesses, such as the use of a larger space for exercise and a higher basic food ration. Their morale is said to be excellent.

In the Lower Camp accommodation is not quite so good, lighting is inadequate, only acetylene lamps are provided. Brick stoves provide the heating, but are said to be of better quality than those in the Upper Camp. The orderlies' Section was very overcrowded. Sanitary installations are bad.

Miss Christine Knowles, OBE
Chairwoman of meeting of next of kin of officers
Discussion with members, London, 6 October 1943
MISS CHRISTINE KNOWLES: OBE: Shackling is going on in certain camps, but it is much less rigorous than it was. The chains are longer. I saw a prisoner repatriated quite recently, and he told me that his guard said to him: 'I am not shutting them [the manacles]. Go inside; you can get your hands out then. But when you get outside the camp put your hands in again, because otherwise I shall catch it.' I think there is no doubt that there is far more freedom in cases where the use of shackles continues, because we hear of people playing baseball and hockey. It may be difficult, and it may not be so good a game, but it is something. A number of officers I have heard of say they can do everything except undress, and of course shackles are always removed in the evening.

A MEMBER: Might I add just as a footnote that my own son and his friend were released from further shackling on 17 June. They have not been shackled since. I was wondering whether you had news of all of them being released in this way?

MISS CHRISTINE KNOWLES, OBE: Unfortunately not all. But I think that what you say is an indication of what may happen. After all, the shackling was done for a definite purpose, and that purpose had manifestly failed. The Germans do not go on interminably with a thing they feel is a failure. They must know by now. The only idea in the German mind was to humiliate our men, and if you refuse to be humiliated and nothing more happens, they see it becomes more or less – as some men have written – a farce.

A MEMBER: My son was in shackles from October 1942 until August this year. Then he was in hospital for a month, and another man volunteered to take his place.

MISS CHRISTINE KNOWLES, OBE: That, I think, is very common. I know one young officer who has never been out of his shackles, because he continually volunteered in that way. He has never been out of shackles because whenever someone else was ill he volunteered to take his place. He has been in shackles from the beginning, and is continuing. He was the same officer who said that one can do everything in shackles except undress.

THE MEMBER: Oflag VIIB.

MISS CHRISTINE KNOWLES, OBE: In that camp at the same period when the shackles were being used very extensively they were having dramatic performances, and certainly the Commandant had given them a great many facilities. I think it is more a case of continuing the order. As you know, the Germans always carry out any order given. This order came out, and until it is reversed they will go on doing it.

A MEMBER: They do not shackle the men at night, do they?

MISS CHRISTINE KNOWLES, OBE: Never.

Telegraphist Herbert Edgar Elliott, Royal Naval Volunteer Reserve
POW from August 1940 to May 1945
North Compound, Stalag Luft III, Sagan, March–April 1944
After the mass escape all huts and blocks were surrounded by armed guards and then the commandant tried to check us up in each hut.

This took the Germans all day, as we were all in the wrong huts to cause confusion and delay Jerry.

After he got us all sorted out, which necessitated looking at a photograph of each man, a list of names was broadcast over the German radio that about 80 dangerous officers were at large.

Much could be said about this episode of prison life; but let it suffice to say that precisely four [*sic* – in fact, three] got home, 50 were shot and the remainder returned to the camp. Those who returned to the camp told us they had seen the others taken from Görlitz prison by the German Gestapo, six at a time in private cars.

Whether they tried to escape again we do not know but we could not understand why all were killed and some not wounded.

The German Air Force officer [*Hauptmann* Hans Pieber] said: 'I hope not one of you Englishmen will even think that the Luftwaffe had anything to do with this terrible deed.'

Gertrud Koppenhöfer (née Böttcher)
German mail-censor at Stalag Luft III, Sagan from October 1943
After the big escape of British prisoners in March 1944 investigations by SS took place and many persons in camp were suspected having supported the escape efforts of the prisoners. The German camp commandant, *Oberst* von Lindeiner, several other officers and some Luftwaffe soldiers of '*Postüberwachung*' who were allowed to enter the POW camps and had personal contact to the prisoners were interrogated by the Gestapo; some were imprisoned and sentenced.

As from then we were all watched by the Nazi authorities in the camp more than ever before and we had to take precaution in what we said. Suspicion increased because we could not know whether there was a spy in the barracks or walking around our living quarters listening to our conversation or watching where we went.

Sigrid Haase (née Moritz)
German mail-censor, Stalag Luft III, Sagan, from October 1943
When the mass escape took place in March 1944, I was on leave at that time at home and had heard the news on the radio. We then noticed patrols looking for the escaped prisoners. When I returned to camp there was deep mourning and grieving about the shot ones, especially with those censors who had lost one of their 'customers'. For explanation it should be said that by the time you got to know your POWs whose mail you had to censor although you never saw or spoke to them. I do not think that I was interrogated by the Gestapo on account of the escape.

From: IS9 (Intelligence School No 9)
To: Senior British Officer, Stalag Luft III, Sagan

IN VIEW INCREASING GERMAN RUTHLESSNESS AND LACK OF REGARD TO GENEVA CONVENTION CHIEFS OF STAFF RULE

THAT UNDER PRESENT CIRCUMSTANCES IT NEED NO LONGER BE CONSIDERED DUTY OF P/W TO ESCAPE BUT IT IS NOT FORBIDDEN TO DO SO.

DO NOT LET GERMANS KNOW.

POLAND

The Camp, German Propaganda Newspaper for Allied POWs, published in Berlin from 7 July 1940 onwards

According to a report received here, German officer prisoners of war were transferred in November 1940 to Fort Henry, near Kingston.

The report contains the following details:

The fort, which was built in the year 1832, is surrounded by ramparts so that it is impossible for the prisoners of war to see anything of the country beyond their camp area.

Within the area of the camp there is neither grass, bushes nor trees.

The ground is covered with fine gravel.

The prisoners of war cannot but have the intolerable feeling of being in confinement, almost really being imprisoned in a gaol.

The report expressly refers to the gaol-like character of the camp, and states it is suitable for the accommodation of criminals but not for prisoners of war, least of all for officer prisoners of war.

According to the published camp regulations the German officers in Kingston have only three times a week, for two-and-a-half hours, the opportunity to use the sports ground outside the camp.

In Fort Henry, the senior German officer has to share a casemate with three other officers.

All other casemates have to accommodate ten officers each, who are thus closely packed together in a small space.

In spite of the heating, the dampness in the walls and ceilings is still visible.

Cracks in the ceilings are only temporarily filled up, so that dust, dirt and water penetrate through them.

Each casemate has only two windows, which look onto the courtyard.

The daylight entering through them is so dim that it is impossible to read or write without artificial lighting.

During the day, only nine latrines are available for the use of the German officers.

There is no canalization; buckets must be used with chloride of lime as disinfectant.

The latrines lie in a little shed on the courtyard, in the immediate vicinity of the dining rooms.

The report further states that all prisoners of war in Fort Henry are locked up in their casemates at eight-forty-five pm.

The doors are not opened until seven-thirty am on the following morning. Buckets are placed in the rooms for emergency relief during the night.

All guards at Fort Henry are equipped with rubber truncheons, which do not form part of the regulation outfit of the Canadian troops but are used only for the guarding of convicts.

Pilot Officer Maurice George Butt, Royal Air Force Volunteer Reserve
POW from August 1940 to May 1945
Fort 15 (Stalag XXA), Thorn (Toruń)
The sending of 400 Army and RAF officers to Toruń (Thorn) and a similar number to nearby Poznan (Posen) was an act of minor revenge or reprisal so typically dear to the German outlook.

In the autumn of 1940, when the numbers of Luftwaffe personnel shot out of the skies and taken prisoner by the British became a real security problem, it was deemed expedient to ship them to Canada. In their turn one group of these Fliegers decided the best contribution they could make for the German war effort was to burn down their hutted camp. This happened near Fort William (now Thunder Bay), Lake Superior, and when the Canadian authorities issued them with canvas tents as a protection against wind and rain, the Luftwaffe were well pleased with themselves. They had not, however, realized the severity of a Canadian winter. Canvas did not keep out the cold, and it is reported that the prisoners were reduced to begging on their knees for alternative accommodation. When the protecting power was brought in, the only option on offer was a disused penitentiary at Fort William.

This was accepted in desperation, and the *Herrenvolk* took their treatment with bad grace. The news got back to Germany via the protecting power and Hitler ordered similar treatment for British POWs. Hence the assignment of 400 to Toruń.

Considerable attention to detail was paid to synthesize comparative treatment – windows blocked up to limit daylight to 15 inches square for a room of 14, locking in rooms at night with a jam tin for a loo. A ten-minute burst of water from a long pipe over a trough with holes of one-eighth of an inch diameter at 24-inch intervals along a pipe, ensuring that only about one third of the inmates had any form of ablutions. And the most charming loo arrangements, a six-holer in a circle with our backs to a central pipe from the ones similarly situated one floor above.

Other constraints included limited access to fresh air, two one-hour breaks per day for exercise in an area confined on all sides by the embankments of earth covering the semi-underground fortifications which ensured living in a cloister-like environment of underground corridors and rooms.

The novelty factor helped to cushion despondence, indeed on our arrival we were herded into the main semicircular tunnelway, about 15 feet wide, to be greeted by a reading of the riot act. A *Hauptmann* addressed us stating that this was a punishment camp in response to the bad treatment of German prisoners, etc, etc. This harangue was treated with derisive remarks and a few cat-calls. The tension built up quickly and the *Hauptmann* drew his Luger from his holster. The POWs responded by a rousing cheer. Fortunately for everyone, captors and captives alike, no shooting started, as in the confines of the long tunnel, ricocheting bullets could have killed guards with equal impartiality, the guards being at intervals both sides along the group of prisoners.

The *Hauptmann* visibly recognized with amazement that the British prisoners before him were a most unusual lot, refusing to be cowed by threats, and changed his posture by calling on the interpreter to state the orders for the day (even though it was well into the evening). We were to be marched off in groups of 14, and locked up in our rooms for the night etc.

The Senior British Officer, General Fortune, got to work to appraise the position and insisted that our protecting power be called in. The protecting power is a war-neutral country whose representatives were responsible for conducting the non-military affairs of a combatant nation. At this particular time the United States was our Protecting Power, and Argentina was that for Germany. Later Switzerland took on the role when the USA became embroiled in the war.

So one bright morning after roll-call, a delegation appeared comprising a group of German officers in their best uniforms and a few civilians. The latter group was the American Ambassador in Berlin complete in long overcoat, Homburg hat and brolly, some say with spats too, but I don't remember that. Anyway this elegant group went round the various corners of the camp block to see the evidence with their eyes. The main points at issue were being locked up in our rooms at night, the unnecessary obstruction to natural daylight ie the boarded-up windows, and the limitation to washing which was in part necessary as all the water had to be pumped up by hand to storage tanks, a task done by orderlies, British Tommies captured at Dunkirk. Lack of exercise was to be adjusted by unlimited access to the confined area plus a promise of occasional parole walks outside the camp in order to be able to kick a football about on an open area nearby. All points were agreed in the only place where there was room to move – the area where we were counted, and the Germans were displaying a feeling of magnanimity to the point of swaggering, when General Fortune suddenly turned round to say: 'But Gentlemen, there is one other point – this camp is lousy, the bedding provided is creeping with fleas.' Whereupon a deep hush fell on all the group, a monocle dropped off the face of one German officer and General Fortune spun round and commented: 'Lieutenant, fleas please.' Two junior officers sprang forward each with a match box and in unison poked the trays of the boxes to release scores of fleas which, on sudden exposure to bright light, leapt in all directions. So too did the decorous assembled group of inspectors. It was hilarious to see.

With the new deal in operation, life was comparatively much better. What was most missing were books to read and Red Cross parcels. To feed the mind, all sorts of talks were given by different people on subjects ranging from Beekeeping to Selling Bananas, Greyhound Racing to the Tombs of Egypt. The diversity of the army types was most apparent as they were older men, and consequently had so much more worldly experience. One ex-Hong Kong policeman related the problems of crime in China, which were quite different to the unlawful activities of POWs, in particular combatting the gambling woman we found an intriguing subject. Life on Assam tea plantations compared to work on the Stock Exchange were worlds apart too.

A form of Rugby was played on the parole walks but it proved ridiculous because of lack of energy – indeed it was extraordinary to behold a man running with the ball and then suddenly to stop completely for lack of stamina, the result of the steady reduction of spare fat since capture, on a starvation diet. Injuries such as simple bleeding from scratches usually became septic, and this was seen to be an avoidable hazard to survive. Hence rugger was out.

ITALY AND THE MEDITTERANEAN

British and Commonwealth troops taken prisoner in North Africa were strictly speaking under the jurisdiction of Italy and so even if captured by the Afrika Korps were generally handed over to Italian soldiers (although occasionally an exception was made for airmen, who tended to be retained by the Germans and sent to Germany). There was a great deal of difference between the behaviour of the two armies toward their prisoners: the Afrika Korps tended towards chivalry whilst the Italians inclined towards brutality. However, in the aftermath of the invasion of Greece and Crete the German treatment of prisoners, especially during transit, was unaccountably harsh, and many brutal atrocities were committed for minor breaches of the rules. Away from the front line, however, Italy's regime was a good deal less strict, and punishment and reprisals were as often as not merely nominal.

Sapper Don Luckett, Royal Engineers
POW from July 1941 to May 1945
Dulag 185, Salonika (Greece), 1941

It was well after curfew, that first night in our new 'camp' and quite some time after it had gone dark, when the sounds of automatic- and rifle-fire shattered the stillness of the night, coupled with shouts and screams, with more than a few loud voices shouting: 'Murdering bastards!' – it was some time later that we discovered that some of the men had been shot using the latrines, and at that time it took some believing. Slit trenches had been dug on one side of the square for that very purpose, and the probing searchlights had picked out the men using them and the sentries had opened fire on the unfortunate souls. When daylight eventually came, several bodies could be seen close to the slit trenches, and there was much chatter in the long lines of men that spanned the square on that first morning parade. A commotion broke out at the end of one line, and it appeared that our senior NCOs had attempted to make some sort of protest to the *Kommandant* about the previous night's shooting, and were beaten up for their trouble.

Lance-Corporal Lawrence Bains, Middlesex Yeomanry
POW from June 1942 to August 1944
Campo PG 66, Capua, Italy

These notes about Capua would not be complete without a passing reference to the 'Mush' or prison. This was a single tent some distance from all the rest and enclosed in some dilapidated barbed wire. Qualification for entry was usually damage to Italian property, which meant breaking or stealing wood either from the cookhouse, latrines or barbed-wire supports, and offenders had the sympathy, in fact the support, of most on the camp. Another crime was lighting in the tents. A few of the inmates had taken items from Red Cross parcels or other people's kits, and these of course were universally condemned. The Mush in any case was rather a farce, and the occupants had to leave it for washing, etc, and also for drawing food from their groups, and as there was no guard they went about practically without restriction and with little risk of detection.

Lieutenant A F ('Junior') Powell, 13th Light Anti-Aircraft Regiment
POW from April 1941 to May 1945
Campo PG 17, Rezzanello, Italy

The usual punishment [for escaping] at one time was '*Rigoroso*', which meant being confined to one's room. This was not much of a punishment as it meant not having to attend roll-call or get up for meals. After some of the 'Revues' had been taken [and the Italians saw caricatures of them] the punishment was changed to so many days in a cell in the outer courtyard. This showed the power of a cartoon, but no one complained. Persistent offenders were transferred to another camp, usually Chiete – a punishment camp.

Lieutenant John Pelly, Coldstream Guards
POW from June 1942 to April 1945
Campo PG 17, Rezzanello, Italy

1 September 1942. We had a punishment roll-call at 0330 hours (very cold it was, too), as three officers were not in their Bungalow at 2130 hours last night. The officers also got five days in the 'cooler' for insulting the Italians.

14 September. Big mutiny in the morning. We had an extra roll-call in which the Commandant tried to drill us by a bugle. Everybody simply furious and refused to move or respond to any orders from the Italians. One officer marched off to the 'cooler' by the Italians for refusing to obey an order from the interpreter, amid the ringing cheers of the whole camp. All the guards in the place were turned out and surrounded the parade, while machine guns were brought out down by the gate. A stalemate then set in, neither side making a move, and after a couple of hours, the SBO and the Commandant came to some compromise, and we were dismissed by the SBO. A sitrep [situation report] was given to us after the parade by the bungalow commander (Lieutenant-Colonel Kilkelly, 8th Hussars).

16 September. Four roll-call parades today. The Commandant's getting his own back by collective punishment for the escapees, etc.

17 September. An extra roll-call this morning nearly led to a serious incident between the POWs and the Italian guards. My bungalow was surrounded by guards as is usual in a hut search, one of the guards was tripped by an officer, this led to a fight and general mêlée, and Dick Finch (Frontier Force) was hit over the head with a rifle butt and taken to hospital unconscious. There is little doubt that it was entirely our fault. It was very lucky that the guards had not got their bayonets fixed, as I am sure they would have used them with relish. Anyway, we were all surrounded and ourselves and the bungalows given a good searching.

Lieutenant Dan Billany, 4th Battalion East Yorkshire Regiment
POW from June 1942 to September 1943
Campo PG 49, Fontanellato, Italy

We soon discovered that the sentries here are much quicker on the trigger than at Rezzanello. If you look out of the window after dusk, they do not waste time writing out a report about it. They shoot. And after lights out, if they see or hear anything they don't like, they shoot again – at random, anywhere into the building. It would have seemed strange in England to go to bed and sleep calmly whilst men outside were firing rifles in at the building, but you very soon got used to it. So far nobody has been hit, though there are holes in the bedroom walls. It sounds much more alarming than it is.

THE FAR EAST

The potential for extreme penalties was much greater in the Far East, where the Japanese were prosecuting a war of racial hatred and revenge against the West. Human Rights had never really cut much ice with them, and from the mid-nineteenth century onwards were eroded by the military's perversion of the Bushido code, under which all foreigners (with the exception of Jews, whom they admired) were subhuman; even their own civilians were treated with contempt. Since Imperial Japan did not expect its own troops to become prisoners – suicide was preferable – and had not ratified the Geneva Convention, it felt at liberty to treat Western prisoners as badly as it saw fit. The command structure also encouraged ill-treatment: soldiers were given to understand that any order given, even by a lowly sergeant, originated with the Emperor, who was there by divine right. If a sergeant told you to stick your bayonet in a prisoner's belly, you obeyed.

Far Eastern POWs were doubly unfortunate in that the Japanese equivalent of the Gestapo, the Kempeitai, had a much greater influence over prison camps, from interrogating newly captured prisoners to questioning them after escape attempts or any minor violations of the rules. As is often the case, the men who were most fond of quoting the rulebook were those who themselves most often flouted the rules that governed decent human behaviour. Rare indeed was the errant prisoner who got away with no more than thirty days in the cells.

The Imperial Japanese Army's 'Penal Regulations for Far Eastern Prisoners', drawn up at the end of 1941, read as follows:

The following Regulations shall come into force on or after the date of Promulgation:

PENAL REGULATIONS FOR PRISONERS

Art. I   The present Regulations are to be applied to those Prisoners of War who commit a crime:

Art. II   When a number of prisoners in a group act outrageously or intimidate, the ringleader will be sentenced to death, or penal servitude or imprisonment for life; the rest will be sentenced to penal servitude or imprisonment for life or for a period of a year or longer. Those who made preparations for or plotted for the same, will be sentenced to penal servitude or imprisonment for a period of a year or longer.

Art. III   Those who kill the man who is on duty of superintending or warding or escorting will be sentenced to death.

Those who made preparations or contrivance for the same will be sentenced to penal servitude or imprisonment for a period of two years or longer.

Art. IV   Those who injure or give a blow or menace those who are on duty of superintending or warding or escorting will be sentenced to death or penal servitude or imprisonment for life or for the period of two years or longer.

When a group of men commit the same, the ringleader will be sentenced to death, or penal servitude or imprisonment for life, and the rest will be sentenced to penal servitude or imprisonment for the period of three years or longer.

Those who commit the foregoing two crimes and cause death will be sentenced to death.

Art. V   Those who resisted or did not obey the command of one who is on duty of superintending, or warding or escorting will be sentenced to death or penal servitude or imprisonment for a period of a year or longer. When a number of men in a party commit the foregoing crimes, the ringleader will be sentenced to death, or penal servitude or imprisonment for life and the rest will be sentenced to death or penal servitude or imprisonment for the period of two years or longer.

Art. VI   Those who insult the man on duty of superintending or warding or escorting in his presence or openly, will be sentenced to penal servitude or imprisonment for the period of five years or less.

Art. VII   When a number of men escape in a group, the ringleader will be sentenced to death or penal servitude or imprisonment for life or for the period longer than ten years, and the rest will sentenced to penal servitude or imprisonment for life or for a period of a year or longer.

Art. VIII   An attempted crime of the first item of Article II, the first item of Article III, the first and second items of Article IV, and the previous article, will be punished.

Art. IX   When those who are released on parole break the parole they will be sentenced to death or penal servitude or imprisonment for the period of seven years or longer. When the preceding man takes arms and resists, he will be sentenced to death.

Art. X   Those who swear not to escape and break it, will be sentenced to penal servitude or imprisonment for the period of a year or longer and those who break other paroles will be sentenced to penal servitude or imprisonment for a period of ten years or less.

Art. XI   When a number of men form a party with the purpose of disobedience the ringleader will be sentenced to penal servitude or imprisonment for a period of a year or longer amounting to ten years; the rest will be sentenced to penal servitude or imprisonment for the period of six months or longer amounting to five years.

Art. XII   The regulations of Article VII will not be applied to a crime of those taken captive a second time, which was committed while they were captive on the first occasion.

SINGAPORE

Sapper Lionel Morris, Royal Engineers
Captured February 1942
Camp 330, Changi Barracks

Shortly after 'lights out', without warning all hell broke loose. It appeared that someone had relit the guardhouse lamp and this had been spotted by a passing Jap patrol. Armed with staves, and rifles rattling, the guards, yelling and shrieking like demons, arrived in our midst. We knew nothing of the Japanese language, but it was evident from their grunts, hisses and gesticulations that we had committed a sin.

The guard commander booted the offending light to extinction for all time, then we were all lined up and our faces roundly slapped, after which performance the patrol marched off into the night. Thus the sleepers in the guardhouse were left in peace in body if not in mind. I smiled wryly to myself. Thus came the New Order! Sixty or more men could have their faces slapped and no one seemed anxious to do anything about it, nor was it prudent to vex the guard, whose power was absolute.

SIAM (THAILAND)

Sergeant William McDonald Innes-Ker, Straits Settlement Volunteer Force
POW from February 1942 to August 1945
Sonkurai No 2 Camp, Burma–Siam Border

I have been asked if we were tortured. Well, yes, at times I suppose you could call it that. For example, I have seen one of our men tied to a tree in crucifix fashion, and there he stayed for four days without food or water; until, in fact, he died. And all because he raised his arm to protect his head when an irate Nip Engineer started beating him because he had dropped a rope he and a lot of us were hauling on to raise a bridge timber. Beatings, all over the body and head, with bamboos, rifle butts, iron bars – anything – were daily occurrences, and if you were lucky and you could remain on your feet and did not make any retaliatory move, you could get off with only bruises and cuts. Many, however, were beaten senseless and left to lie until time to knock off, when we would carry them home and attend to their wounds.

Rations were cut or withheld totally for a day or so at the slightest pretext. Sick men, even those who could not work, were made to work, and we had to carry them to the job piggy-back and put them down in the shade, if there was any, where they made some attempt at cutting logs or doing something. You have seen the film *Bridge on the River Kwai*. We had a 'Hot Box' like the one shown in the film, where prisoners were occasionally incarcerated for some misdemeanour. Most who went in came out only to die. We had a Jap commandant at Changi who was exactly like the one depicted in the film, and I think whoever directed the film must have had very good advice from an ex-POW.

THE DUTCH EAST INDIES

Aircraftman Frank Deakin Jackson, Royal Air Force
POW from March 1942 to August 1945
Liang Camp, Ambon (Amboina), the Moluccas

An odious form of punishment was to make the culprits punch and slap each other's faces; light blows were rewarded by being clubbed with the rifle. This procedure occurred many times and was sickening to both victims and witnesses. We learnt to be careful and discreet, particularly as our officers were not immune from this harsh punishment. Often they paid the penalty for the sins of their men. Officers were generally treated as badly as we, and while we paid for our own misdeeds, they suffered for those of the multitude.

Pilot Officer Erroll David Shearn, Royal Air Force
POW from March 1942 to August 1945
Camp 353, Xth Battalion Barracks, 'Bicycle Camp', Batavia

An order came through that that the prisoners were to surrender all article of gold. I had some evening studs and cufflinks with gold backings. I decided to bury them so that they would not fall into the hands of the Japanese. After I had done so the Japanese issued a further order to the effect that their first order had not resulted in many gold articles being handed in and they were certain quite a lot had been retained by the prisoners. They therefore extended the time for compliance with their requirements. If an appreciable quantity of further gold articles was forthcoming all would be well and no action would be taken against those who had disobeyed the first order. If, however, there was not a satisfactory response to the second order, collective punishment would be inflicted on the whole camp. After reflection I mistakenly decided to dig up my hidden evening studs, etc, and to hand them in.

Shortly after having done so, despite the indication that no further action would be taken, I found myself towards the end of a longish queue down which an infuriated Japanese was battering his way with an iron rod. I experienced that uncomfortable sensation of my heart and stomach changing places as this sadistic lunatic got nearer and nearer my place in the queue. However, to my relief, before he actually reached me he apparently became exhausted with the efforts he had been making. After taking a swipe or two at the unfortunate interpreter (I think he was E M MacDonald, a friend from Malaya who had taught himself Japanese), he dismissed the remaining potential victims.

Lieutenant-Colonel Philip Toosey, 135th Field Regiment, Royal Artillery
POW from February 1942 to August 1945
Camp 249, Tamarkan

I remember an occasion when a certain Corporal Lawson, a regular infantry soldier who, on my instructions, had been stealing Japanese tools and selling them to the Chinese outside the camp to raise money for our hospital, was caught. He was interviewed by the Kempeitai, and I heard the most awful groans and screams and could hardly bear it. In the end I was given permission to go in and see if I could intervene in any way, and there was Corporal Lawson, standing completely naked, facing the Japanese officer, who had a drawn sword on the table, and his back was raw with wheals from a whip, from his neck to his heels. I asked him what the trouble was and he said: 'Well, sir, I have told these little brutes the truth and they won't believe me and I am not going to lie to please them.' I said: 'Now, Lawson, don't be a fool. Do you know what they want you to say?' and he said: 'Yes, sir.' I said: 'Well, say it, and if your conscience is in any way hurt, I will take full responsibility when we get home.' This he did and the beating-up stopped immediately. This had included other tortures, like cigarette burns and matches under his fingernails. He was a very brave man indeed. Fortunately, when he told them what they thought was the truth, the beating-up stopped and he was confined in some prison or other until the end of the war, but he lived through it and came out quite fit and well. It taught me the lesson that torture does not necessarily bring out the truth; it merely brings out what the other side wants to hear.

Sapper Edgar Whincup, Royal Engineers
POW from February 1942 to August 1945
Camp 239, Nakhon Pathom, Burma–Thailand Railway
At the time when the planes were passing over our camp at night, Taffy Davies (a veteran of the 1914–1918 war) and myself were ordered to clean out all the ashes from the incinerator and spread them out on the ground, at the same time making certain there were no glowing embers left which would attract the attention of aircraft. Unfortunately, one night a small pile burst into flames again, the fire was noticed by the guard on the outside of the bamboo fence, and he immediately sent for both of us. Knowing there would be trouble, we asked our RSM MacTavish, senior NCO, to accompany us.

After putting out the fire, the Korean guard told Taffy to fetch a box. When he had obtained one, Taffy was ordered to stand in front of the box, while the guard stood on it. This was the usual procedure, as the Korean guards were naturally too short to deliver their favourite punishment, that of beating us about the head. Poor old Taffy received this punishment and, in addition to the bruises, also in the process had his false teeth knocked out, the guard immediately stamping on them and breaking them into small pieces.

Now it was my turn. The guard knew I had a bad leg, so he decided to beat the shin of my good leg with his rifle butt. This was extremely painful but suddenly he decided to stop. When he had left us we both realized we had been let off very lightly. On being dismissed, we hobbled back to bed, vowing not to let such a thing happen again.

Next morning the guard came up to us while we were working near the incinerator and said how sorry he was for the beating, at the same time telling us to be more careful in the future. What strange people they were.

JAPAN

Lieutenant Stephen Abbott, East Surrey Regiment
POW from February 1942 to August 1945
Camp 13B, Aomi
June 1943. Lieutenant J P Burrough, Royal Corps of Signals, misunderstood the Japanese orders regarding the method of cleaning the rooms. The Japanese interpreter, Private Hanga (29th Regiment), struck him with his closed fist and knocked him down. When he regained his feet he was further struck, causing bleeding of the face and bruises. A few days later Lieutenant Burrough failed to see an approaching lance-corporal and did not call a group of men to attention. This same interpreter took him into the middle of the yard – in full view of all the men – and struck him several times causing his nose to bleed.

Some Japanese soldiers took a photograph belonging to Sergeant Warren, 1st Manchester Regiment, from his shelf. Lieutenant N J Turner reported the matter to the Japanese interpreter, Hanga, and was later severely beaten by him because he had done so. The beating lasted about 15 minutes and Mr Turner was badly bruised.

War Ministry, Tokyo
'Kill-All Order' issued by Kempeitai to camp commandants, 1 August 1944

When the battle situation becomes urgent the POWs will be concentrated and confined in their location and kept under heavy guard until preparations for the final disposition will be made. Although the basic aim is to act under superior orders, individual disposition may be made in certain circumstances. Whether they are destroyed individually or in groups, and whether it is accomplished by means of mass bombing, poisonous smoke, poisons, drowning, or decapitation, dispose of them as the situation dictates. It is the aim not to allow the escape of a single one, to annihilate them all, and not to leave any traces.

12
EVACUATION AND LIBERATION

'The guards came to move us on and both companions on either side of me did not move. The guard poked them and said to me: "How is it that your friends are not moving?" A close look showed that they were dead, as were several others in the field. The bodies where left were they were, and we were on the march again.'

— British prisoner evacuated west from Poland, January 1945

No one watched the progress of the war with a keener or more critical eye than the prisoner of war. Only an Allied victory could bring his release. Each Allied advance brought the day of liberation that little bit closer; but each defeat, setback and delay could mean postponement of that long-awaited day by weeks, months or even years.

Almost all POW camps had a 'War Room' in which maps were pinned to the walls. As news of Allied movements reached the prisoners, specially selected men, usually those with a background in intelligence, planning, logistics and signals, interpreted the news and amended the maps accordingly – moving a piece of red string (the Allies) here, a piece of black string (the Axis) there. They had to be careful about this, of course, as the alterations had to be in line with what their captors believed they knew; and the prisoners, with their secret radios, coded letters and ability to read between the lines, knew more than their captors suspected. They were also inclined to overreact, sinking into deep pessimism when the news was bad, and showing great exuberance (perhaps even cracking open a 'brew') when it was good.

For the first three years of the war the news was almost always bad – defeat in France and the Low Countries; defeat in North Africa; defeat in Greece and Crete; the fall of Hong Kong and Singapore. Never, it seemed, had Britain been so determined to suffer so much military humiliation for so long.

When Germany attacked the Soviet Union in June 1941 prisoners knew that even if the German army might initially make spectacular gains, the Nazis were doomed; an Allied victory was not now a matter of 'if', but 'when'. But the Japanese attack on Pearl Harbor that December, and the subsequent fall of Hong Kong, Malaya, Singapore and many of the Dutch and American territories in south-east Asia burst the bubble of such optimism, as well as dooming the world's biggest army to years of captivity in the Far East. Prisoners of war, particularly those in Europe, began to wonder if their leaders had any commitment at all to the war effort. An indication of how they felt was best summed up by the results of a poll conducted in several POW camps asking: 'Which *neutral* country would you prefer to live in?' The favourite was England. A new arrival at Stalag Luft III an summer 1942, when asked when the invasion was likely, replied that Hitler had 'probably lost his chance by now' – a clear indication that Britain was still on the defensive rather than thinking in terms of taking the war to the enemy.

ITALY

The victory of the 8th Army at El Alamein in October–November 1942 was the first nail in the Axis coffin. On 10 November Winston Churchill made his now-famous pronouncement: 'This is not the end. It is not even the beginning of the end. But it is, perhaps, the end of the beginning.' His speech resonated with prisoners of war, in particular those in Italy, who now foresaw an Allied invasion and reckoned that it was just a matter of 'sitting it out'. Great was their rejoicing when on 10 July 1943 British and American troops landed in Sicily, a momentous event followed on 3 September by a British and Canadian assault on the toe of Italy, the Italian capitulation, and the joint British and American landings at Salerno on the 9th. Joy turned to consternation, however, when a War Office directive reached the camps telling prisoners: 'In the event of an Allied invasion of Italy, officers commanding prison camps will ensure that prisoners of war remain within camp. Authority is granted to all officers commanding to take necessary disciplinary action to prevent individual prisoners of war attempting to rejoin their units'. The order had originated with General Bernard Law Montgomery, commander of the British forces, who did not want the campaign in Italy jeopardized by thousands of POWs roaming the countryside bent on sabotage; in any case, he expected the campaign to be over in a matter of weeks. Most SBOs obeyed the directive, but in the meantime Lieutenant-Colonel A C Simonds, a former SOE operative now in MI9, was ordered by Allied Forces HQ in Algiers to rescue as many Allied prisoners in Italy as possible. While all those involved were still reeling from the confusion, and 70,000 prisoners were awaiting the arrival of the Allies, the Wehrmacht stepped in, resulting in more than 53,000 officers and men who ought to have been freed being transferred to Germany to remain as prisoners for another two years.

Corporal Eric Barrington, Royal Air Force Police
POW from June 1942 to April 1945
Diary kept in Campo PG 73, Carpi (Modena)
Saturday, 2 January 1943. Churchill is reported to have said in a Christmas speech that all POWs and overseas troops will be home in six months, probably just another rumour but I hope it is true. Any more of this life will be just a waste as we have tasted the best and the worst it has to offer.

Lieutenant A F ('Junior') Powell, 13th Light Anti-Aircraft Regiment
POW from April 1941 to May 1945
Campo PG 19, Bologna
The war news was getting better and better and on 3 September the Allies landed in Italy. No one had any idea of how things would turn out, so the escape committee drafted Plan A and Plan B to cater for the various possibilities. I don't remember being given any details of any plan and neither was put into effect.

But at 7 pm on 8 September the Italian commandant entered the camp and announced to the SBO that an armistice had been signed between the Allies and Italy. The softball game that was going on stopped and we all went wild. Several beards came off, as the Armistice was their death-knell. The Italian guard disappeared and we were on our own with an open gate. We had been issued with a normal issue Red Cross parcel that day but then got an unopened one that evening – we were no longer on the Italian ration strength. Some keen escapers put their possessions on their backs and walked out.

At 4.30 next morning those of us who had delayed our departure were awoken by the new word 'AUS!' delivered by an armed German soldier. Although the Allies had hoped that under the Armistice the 70,000 Allied prisoners would be repatriated, General Rommel thought otherwise and Italy found itself an occupied country with no authority. Those prisoners still in the barracks were put between the double barbed-wire fence with the new guards while other guards searched the countryside for the missing prisoners.

Unfortunately someone had told the Germans that some prisoners were armed, but this was untrue. When it was seen that the Germans, rounding up the missing, were about to shoot, one officer shouted: 'Schiesse hoch' ('Shoot high'). Even so, one officer was hit in the wrist and died later and another was wounded.

As the would-be escapers were caught they were brought back to camp to join us between the barbed-wire fences. Eventually the Germans were satisfied that they had all the prisoners back and we were allowed back into the main camp. We had been retaken by General Rommel.

Private Erik G Laker, The Royal Sussex Regiment
Prisoner from October 1942 to May 1945
Diary kept in Campo PG 70, Monturano
16 September 1943. A daily roll-call had been held at 0900 hours. On Thursday 16th we dismissed, turned round, and saw a German in the sentry box. When I saw that sinister-looking steel helmet I felt as if I had received a violent blow in the stomach which fell to the region of my knees. I thought bitterly that it was much too much to hope for that we should have attained our freedom. It was all going to start all over again in a different country. We were now prisoners of the Italian Republic Fascist Army. Things went on as before the Armistice except that no German roll-calls were held.

GERMANY AND OCCUPIED POLAND

When the D-Day invasion took place, those who had previously been prisoners in Italy were, naturally, a good deal more cautious than most in their predictions as to when they would finally taste freedom. Every year around Boxing Day prisoners would remark gloomily: 'Home or homo by Christmas.' Now Churchill was predicting they would be home 'by the time the leaves begin to fall'. This news received a very low-key response, and for several months life in POW camps in Germany and Poland went on pretty much as normal, except that closer attention than ever was paid to the war news and prisoners began to face up to the possibility that their German guards might force them to evacuate westwards, or simply abandon them to the advancing Russians – or massacre them. In many camps secret squads were formed to resist any attempt to wipe prisoners out, to man sentry towers, to secure rations and to take over important local amenities and installations in the event of the enemy retreating. One camp, Stalag IIIB, at Fürstenberg an der Oder, had even secured a cache of weapons and ammunition bought using chocolates, cigarettes and coffee for barter.

Unknown to POWs and to the Allied authorities, commandants of prisoner-of-war camps in Germany and Poland were warned by the OKW as early as March 1944 that at the first sign of an imminent invasion they were to evacuate all POWs from border areas and invasion zones. The first accurate glimpse of what the future held came in June and July, when in a matter of only five weeks the Russians advanced 450 miles (720 kilometres) into Poland and the camps there were closed down and the prisoners force-marched to camps in Germany. The further west the Russians advanced, the further west the prisoners were moved. Evacuations began in earnest in September, but most took place during the very severe winter of 1944–45, with millions of prisoners and refugees marching in columns, on starvation rations, through snowstorms to such camps as Fallingbostel, Lückenwalde, Nürnberg, Moosburg and Westertimke in the south-west and the north of Germany. To those prisoners who had read Tolstoy's *War and Peace*, the snow-covered landscape with its black, winding columns of evacuees reminded them of Napoleon's 1812 retreat from Moscow. Between September 1944 and January 1945, nearly 2,000 British and American prisoners died 'on the road'.

When the survivors finally arrived at their new camps they found a reversion to the conditions that had prevailed earlier in the war – overcrowding, squalor, hunger, cold, fleas and lice, and, sometimes, brutal treatment by guards who were uncertain of their futures and dead scared. They also encountered new prisoners – such as the 6,642 captured at Arnhem, the failure of which dashed hopes of ending the war by Christmas, and those taken in the Battle of the Bulge.

POLAND

Private Alfred Charles Bryant, The Royal East Kent Regiment (The Buffs)
POW from July 1940 to May 1945
Arbeitskommando attached to Stalag, XXB, Marienburg (Malbork)
During the latter half of 1944 there were rumours of a Russian offensive against the German front. Christmas came and went with no bonus, such as our release. Then one day in January 1945, when we were still working on the farms, the guards came running around and told us that we had to move out of the area as quickly as possible. The rumours had been true.

On 21 January we and the thousands of other prisoners in the area started to walk, but the guards would not tell us where to, as they did not know themselves. All they could say was that the Russians were coming, and it would be difficult to estimate which of the two sides were most afraid of this, us or them.

After the snow which had fallen the night before it was well below freezing and we walked for the entire day, stopping at intervals but getting nothing to eat. We joined thousands more POWs from various camps, until we formed one long mass of darkness against the white snow.

That evening we were herded into a very large field, where the snow was about seven feet high and five feet wide round the edge, the column winding round like a python until all POWs were within the barricade.

Those that were able to lay down in the snow to sleep under the stars; the rest had to do as best they could standing up. Frostbite was one of the worst complaints as the only clothing most of them had was battledress and a pair of clogs, in a lot of cases home-made. Often, one clog would be bigger than the other and would have to be stuffed with paper. The small one would be difficult to put on and remove, and cause the foot to swell and throb.

Being one of the lucky ones able to lie down I did get some sleep that night, but in the morning I was not even sure that that had been the wise thing to do. The guards came to move us on and both companions on either side of me did not move. The guard poked them and said to me: 'How is it that your friends are not moving?'

A close look showed that they were dead, as were several others in the field. The bodies were left where they were, and we were on the march again.

Again we had nothing to eat, and that night we were pushed into a large barn, packed like sardines. The lucky ones could squat, and I was one of them; the unlucky ones had to stand up and sleep if they could. The next morning the guards came again and those of us who had managed to survive were again marched away. The dead were left behind in the barn.

We had little food but the weather had improved a bit by this time.

We were still walking in March and even the guards were tired of marching. We slept in the open and those that died were left. Regular rations of food were non-existent, and to keep alive we scrumped in any fields we came across. Carrots, turnips, potatoes, anything was hoarded and then shared when we stopped for the night.

The six of us who had been together for almost five years decided to take turns to get the food for the others. We were getting weaker each day and many of the young lads lost heart. By this time we were desperate for food. One evening after we had stopped it was my turn to go and see if I could dig for vegetables.

The guard saw me and while he was shouting at me – telling me he'd shoot me if I went – a young lad from the column made an attempt to get into the field and the guard shot him in the back and he was left in the field.

We found we were only a few miles from the Russian lines. As we made our way back down the road a German convoy was going the opposite way and we found out we were being used as a cover. Back we walked to Berlin, still having very little food.

At the end of April the guards were changed to older men who were ex-WWI veterans who had been in the trenches and they allowed us to go into the fields to scrape for food. But by that time we were very weak and were almost too scared to sleep in case we did not wake up again. The lads were dropping like flies. One day a young lad was on his knees praying when a guard came along the road. The lad fell on his face and the guard picked him up and put him on his cycle and pushed him about two miles along the road to a house, but before he could reach the house the guard pushed the lad off and said he had died.

We were still walking in May. We had lost two of our group, as they had not been strong enough to carry on. One day we heard the Germans had been defeated and we wondered when we would get back home. By this time we were walking skeletons, and I think that if we had been left another day we would all have been dead.

The Americans liberated us and took us to a town called Halle in Germany, where we stayed until we were strong enough to fly home. It was then about the middle of May. We were overjoyed when the day came for us to return to dear old England.

The way we got our back on the Germans was to mimic Hitler and the Hitler Youth. When the Germans were finally rounded up, we thought: 'That's one to us.'

GERMANY

Squadron Leader George Dudley Craig, Auxiliary Air Force
POW from November 1941 to April 1945
East Compound, Stalag Luft III, Sagan
Towards the end of 1944 it became quite apparent to everyone that the end of the war was in sight and naturally there was much speculation as to how this might affect us in the camp. Many theories were put forward, including the complete liquidation of all POWs by the Germans. The most popular theory was that the Germans would either hand the camp over to us or else that they would simply go off without saying a word, and that we would wake up one day and find no guards on the wire. In view of these undeterminable possibilities, the Senior British Officer formed a Planning Committee whose

terms of reference were to prepare various Defence Schemes to meet every possible contingency, including that of liquidation.

This Planning Committee was made up of representatives of the Escape Committee and the Intelligence Organization. So Joe Kayll, with whom I was sharing a room, was involved in the former capacity and I was involved in the latter capacity. Each compound (there were five compounds) having evolved schemes of their own, it then remained for the senior officers of each scheme to dovetail them all together.

In East Compound, in which I was, we took particular care that nothing should be written down, and our security was, I think, very good. Imagine our horror when we were presented with the North Compound Scheme in writing to the last detail. They had been training 'shock troops' whose job it was to assault the guard boxes and seize the machine guns, etc, and eventually overcome the Germans guarding the camp. For weapons they had made and hidden cudgels, etc. In addition there was a party detailed for parachutes inside the compounds. Their scheme also included the organization of all members of the compound into Czechoslovakia, and maps were prepared and lectures given to the group leaders.

Naturally, with a plan of this nature, it was virtually impossible for all members of the compound not to know all about it, with the consequent security risk of careless talk. We in East Compound were quick to disassociate ourselves from such a scheme and our SBO had several heated interviews, under the guise of official finance talks, etc, with the SBO of North Compound. In the end he succeeded in persuading the North Compound planners to destroy all written evidence of their schemes and to soft-pedal with their shock troops, etc.

In the meantime our plans were taking shape and were based in the main upon the assumption that the Germans would either hand the camp over to us or leave us without warning. The possibility of liquidation, we felt, was one which could not be adequately guarded against.

My own job was in regard to Intelligence and I had to be prepared to have full details of such things as the water supply, the whereabouts of the power station, the local armoury, any perimeter defences like pill-boxes; also the numbers of guards and local garrison troops, etc, etc. In addition the names of any 'friendly' Germans who would be prepared to help us. Details of all local aerodromes, the length of runway, type of surface and local obstructions like wireless masks, factory chimneys, etc, in case any of our own aircraft wanted to land, etc. Details of local wireless stations and that we could take control of to make WT contact with England. All these details had to be pinpointed on the map of the local surroundings, but naturally nothing was marked on the map – all details had to be memorized for security reasons.

As our Defence Plans were nearing completion and lists of various trades of all members of the camp were compiled so that butchers could take over the supply of meat, plumbers the water supply, electric engineers the power stations, etc, etc, reports came in of the possibility of the Germans marching us away from the camp. The Planning Committee at once turned its attentions to this new angle and issued advice with regard to the secret making of haversacks, etc, which were prohibited by the Germans. The camp soon got busy sewing, and when the time arrived that we were pushed out onto the roads, everyone was fairly well equipped.

Squadron Leader David Malcolm Strong, Royal Air Force
POW from September 1941 to April 1945
Stalag Luft III, Sagan, Belaria satellite compound
As adjutant I was the first to be told that we were being evacuated. The *Lageroffizier* entered my room at one am, shone a torch at me and said: 'We march to the vest.' I replied: 'You can march to the vest if you wish, but as the advancing Russians are our Allies, we think we'll stay here.'

But the Huns had Tommy-guns and therefore the last word.

Lieutenant David Lubbock, Royal Naval Volunteer Reserve
POW from July 1941 to April 1945
East Compound, Stalag Luft III, Sagan
When word of our imminent departure (a few hours) was announced we started to prepare, making sledges and selecting what to take. Aidan Crawley made a pair of bellows, which proved a life-saver on the freezing march. I took the draft of a book I had been writing. When we reached Muskau, where the contingent was split up to proceed different ways, I got a French priest to take the book to get somehow, some time, to the UK for me. He was as good as his word and years later it turned up in the Ward Room in Portsmouth Barracks, and was sent me by Peter Fanshawe. At one of our previous halts a Russian girl, forced to work on an adjacent farm, slipped me a fresh egg, my first for nearly four years. She might have been shot if noticed. I swallowed it with delight and eternal gratitude. When proceeding through one cold clear moonlight night I felt I could not walk much further when suddenly all pain and exhaustion left me. I walked to the back of the column, picked up some exhausted straggler compatriots' belongings for them and forged ahead with them to the front of the column.

The night seemed the most beautiful I had ever experienced. This episode lasted about an hour I should think, until we came to a place where we stopped for the night (akin to the ecstasy of flagellation?). Another day I continued walking in the same direction; the column had turned a corner. I was asleep.

Pilot Officer Patrick Greenhous, Royal Air Force
POW from May 1940 to May 1945
North Compound, Stalag Luft III, Sagan
Eventually when the Russian guns could be heard as they approached the Oder we were told that we had to move out at a few hours' notice taking only what we could carry. There followed a very unpleasant three days' marching through the snow – it was January, I believe – at darkness we either slept in fields or in barns. I had one warm night lying next to a cow in a cowshed and had some warm milk for breakfast. Whilst at a place called Muskau we were quartered in an old school – and the Hermann Goering Panzer Division pulled in, having been heavily engaged against the Russians. The tanks and crew were filthy and shot-up. However, by next morning the men were showered and in clean uniform and the tanks had been patched up and repainted white – and they went back into action. Quite impressive.

We ended up at Milag Nord, between Bremen and Hamburg. Eventually the guards disappeared and we were told by the CO to stick together. Ken Mackintosh and I found two German cavalry horses all saddled up and very weary in a field, whilst we were scavenging for food. We rode up to a farmhouse, and the farmer and his wife were terrified – because the horses were still carrying carbines and sabres. They found some ham and eggs and fed us. Suddenly there was a noise at the door and it flew open to reveal a British para in full gear. 'What the bloody hell do you think you're doing here?' he said. 'You're right in the front line – bugger off!!' So we did!

Gisela Moody (née Vorhoff)
Mail-censor in Stalag Luft III, Sagan, from August 1944
After the POWs were evacuated in January 1945 the roads were strewn with left-over mementoes, food and cigarettes. So the censor-girls went into the camp stores and gathered as much food and as many cigarettes as they could manage. But I couldn't bring myself to join in. It seemed like robbing the dead.

Craftsman Maurice Newey, Royal Electrical and Mechanical Engineers
POW from June 1942 to April 1945
Arbeitslager E3, Blechhammer, and Stalag VIIA, Moosburg
Up until 1943 I was in the Royal Army Ordnance Corps. In July 1943, whilst
a POW in Germany, I received a letter from the War Office saying that I was
being transferred to the REME, and my rank would be known as Craftsman.
The technical side had been separated from the Ordnance side.

Personally speaking, I was pleased we were separated from officers. The
sergeant majors are the backbone of the British army and I was fortunate to
find one in E3. He was Sergeant Major Hobbs of the Gloucester Regiment.
On the long march from Upper Silesia to Stalag VIIA in Bavaria, he and the
German sergeant major, together with some of their staff, went round
German villages foraging for food and distributed to us when we were almost
in dire straits.

The sounds of artillery fire coming from the west could now be plainly
heard. When it began to sound as if we would be in the line of fire, an officer
was let out of the camp to meet the advancing Americans. I was of the
opinion that they were bound to know of the existence of this Stalag. It was
a main Stalag, not a working party camp. However, when the advance
reached us, the artillery stopped short and kept firing all night over our heads.
We cheered as the shells screamed over, glad that somebody else would be at
the receiving end.

When we were liberated Sergeant Major Hobbs was given the option of
choosing to go anywhere he wanted. He said: 'Where can I go? No, I'll stay
with my men.' Many years later I read a book about Korea and learnt that
Sergeant Major Hobbs of the Gloucesters had been captured by the Chinese.
I hope he survived that ordeal.

A group of us clubbed together and from somewhere we obtained some dry
lentils. We had found a large cooking pot, so into this we put in the lentils,
potatoes and tins of stewed meat, made a fire in the compound, and sat round
it while it cooked. We polished that off, cleaned the pot, and threw in some
ears of rice. When they were cooked we threw in some raisins and sugar.
When it was dished out we covered it with Nestlé's milk. Ah! That was
living.

Next morning was spent cleaning ourselves up. It was great to have a hot
shower and a shave in hot water. We soon had fires going and making our
favourite beverage. Feeling more like human beings once again, we went on
a tour of the camp. It was full of American GIs. Most of them had only been
in captivity for a few months. We were appalled at their lack of morale. They
were lying around, unwashed and unshaven, and seemed to be full of self-

pity. They were not short of food and we were soon busy using our bartering techniques.

Lieutenant William Bompas, Royal Artillery (Field)
POW *from December 1942 to April 1945*
Oflag 79, Brunswick
11 April 1945. 0930 hours: Two Jeeps with American troops arrived at the camp. Place went mad, but not too mad. They say there'll be truckloads of food this afternoon. A few very loud bangs in the area – God knows what they are. Now give me food, home, and security.

2130 hours: all under control. I'm not really excited; it was really expected, so is now more or less an anticlimax. But the food! We went into the German stores, and have had half a loaf each, double stew ration, and get more tomorrow; for the first time in two and a half years I have a full stomach and no worry about the future. We should be on American rations inside three days, too, and leave here fairly soon after. I've definitely eaten well – got hold of a 2lb tin of Jerry peas and bashed the lot!

19 April. This last week we have been doing very well. We have gone out and scrounged at all the nearby villages – eggs, milk, bread, asparagus, honey, spinach; and our official camp providers have raided stores of tinned meats, fruits, etc. Everyone has over-eaten, had diarrhoea, been sick, etc; we have also drunk red and white wines, brandy, sherry, gin, and queer Russian drinks; about 20 chaps have pinched cars, and most rooms have bikes; everyone is completely fed up, and nearly 200 have gone, though it is hoped to get 2,000 away every day. I'm fed up with being a bloody Boy Scout on an hour's notice to leave.

Squadron Leader George Dudley Craig, Auxiliary Air Force
POW *from November 1941 to April 1945*
Stalag IIIA, Lückenwalde
The last six weeks before getting home were probably the most interesting and exciting weeks of my life and, looking back on them, I wouldn't have missed them for anything.

After our march in January, we from the East Compound ended up at Stalag IIIA at Lückenwalde, about 30 miles south of Berlin. It was a huge camp with about 17,000 to 20,000 POWs of about 25 different nationalities! We were housed in long open stone barrack huts divided into two rooms – we had about 200 in one room and 250 in the other. We had three-tier beds, about two tables per room and a few stools; no cupboards or cooking facilities. It wasn't too bad as we had no clothes to put into the cupboards and very little to cook!

Things began to happen on 11 April when the Huns suddenly marched us down to the station at Lückenwalde and put us 50 men to a cattle-truck with a view to taking us to near Munich as possible hostages. Well, we stayed in the station on a siding for two days and nights and they failed to get an engine for the train, thank goodness. So they then decided that it was unlikely we would get through without interception by the Americans, so we were marched back up to the camp!! There we stayed till the end. It was very noticeable how the attitude of the Huns changed towards us; they couldn't do enough for us, the slimy —! Not that they actually did very much.

We then waited, hearing gunfire from both East and the West fronts, and we wondered which side would win the race to us. About the 18th it became clear that the Russians would win and the result on the German guards was comic to watch. They all became jumpy, and each night we used to see small parties of them slinking off in civilian clothes carrying suitcases! They were all terrified, to a man, of the Reds. By the morning of the 21st there was a mere handful of them left and at 1200 hours they handed over the camp to us and all the German officers and remainder of the men marched off to their certain deaths!

Luckily we had prepared a very thorough defence scheme for just such an eventuality, as we had in the camp, as I've said, about 17,000 men of 25 different nationalities who needed controlling quickly to stop them breaking out of camp and looting the neighbourhood. So a police force of British, American and Norwegian officers marched out to prearranged places and picketed all the food, ammunition and clothing stores. Our greatest difficulty was 5,000 starving Russian POWs. We managed to get them under control by giving them Red Cross parcels and letting them make themselves sick with overeating!! Things went very well and we got control of the camp OK, except for the odd Russian POW who would go out fully armed and bring in German soldiers as prisoners. We were naturally frightened of jeopardizing our position as POWs and giving the Huns an excuse to come in and wipe us all out. The Russian POWs also set up an ambush on the road outside the camp and shot any German civilian they saw. Things weren't made any easier by the presence of a strong SS gun battery just nearby who threatened to open up on the camp and flatten it completely if they found any German prisoners in the camp or any arms or if the activities of the ambush didn't stop! It was a bit awkward, because the camp was full of German prisoners (brought in by the Russkies) and arms, and it was very difficult to control the Russkies. Luckily the SS battery retreated without carrying out their threat.

At 6 am the next morning a Russian armoured car appeared in the camp and was followed shortly by a tank spearhead – some enormous tanks which simply crashed the camp gates and wire down amid enthusiastic cheering. It was certainly a very stirring moment indeed. There were some Russian women fully armed with Tommy-guns sitting on these tanks. So we were liberated!!

Telegraphist Herbert Edgar Elliott, Royal Naval Volunteer Reserve
POW *from August 1940 to May 1945*
Diary kept on the march from Marlag und Milag Nord, Westertimke
Tuesday, 10 April 1945. Ordered to pack our kit, served out with two Red Cross parcels and fell in 3 pm and left camp. Of 680 men only 170 of us fell in, the others had broken through the barbed wire with the aid of German guards, and hid themselves. The 170 of us however marched off and during the first hour were shot up twice by our fighter planes, killing two horses, wounding another. One civilian driver (Russian) was killed and a guard wounded. We were only able to march six kilometres and had to hide up in a village owing to being strafed so much. The night was spent in a wood outside the village and we could hear artillery near Bremen all night, also our night fighters kept shooting up the roads. During this short march we became experts at diving in ditches and any other available cover. We did not feel too happy. We woke up wet through.

Wednesday, 11 April 1945. Got up at 5 am. Made fairly quick march of ten kilometres and rested for two hours, having caught up with RAF and RN officers who were also on the move. Supplied with hot water in a field and Spitfires were shooting up the roads around us. We were all very nervous when they were near us. Artillery fire could be heard in the distance. The march was continued, but owing to strafing by the fighters, we were forced to put up in another wood at 4 pm. Here we spent the night, whilst flares were dropped and strafing of the roads continued.

Thursday, 12 April. Recommenced walking 6.20 am – covered 16 kilometres by 10.20, passing RAF and naval officers on the way, lying up in fields. Were informed three naval officers had been killed and two wounded by our fighters. Life now was a great uncertainty to us all. There was no opposition from German planes and we passed dead horses and wrecked lorries as we passed along. We had no means of letting our planes know who we were. We remained in a field for the remainder of the day and all night and were issued with one cube of sugar per man for three days' rations. We slept well in the open and had no trouble from aircraft.

Friday, 13 April. Remained another day and night here. Very cold wind. Boiled some potatoes and had a stew. Water was difficult to obtain but washed the feet of my socks in a small tin. As weather was very doubtful, some German soldiers were turned out of a barn to enable us to sleep under cover. We were well supplied with bread. Many aircraft were over during the night.

Saturday 14 April. Got up at 5 am, made some coffee and on the march at 7 am. Stopped at 9 am and spent day and night in an orchard. We were now used to this country life of living and sleeping in the open and on the ground in a blanket. In spite of dampness we appeared to take no harm. Shortage of water but managed to have a wash down in some muddy water and washed out my underclothes (or tried to). A lovely sunny day and we were getting as brown as berries. We placed out POW signs made with towels and the planes appeared to come down and recognize it for they left us unmolested. There were about 2,500 spread about in fields and the planes must have got wind that prisoners were being moved. This however did not prevent them from shooting up any lorries that happened to be near us and we had several narrow escapes. Heavy bombers passed over us during the night.

Sunday, 15 April. Up at 5 am and began march 7 am. Marching all day except for periodical rests. Hid up in wood for half hour because of aircraft. Crossed River Elbe north of Hamburg about 4 pm. Saw several small German aircraft. Billeted in barn next to a dairy and by a stream. Stripped off and bathed in stream and washed underwear.

People very friendly wherever we went and we were able to exchange things for eggs, etc. Good weather.

Monday, 16 April. Rested here all day and managed to obtain a boy's barrow to put some kit in for bar of chocolate. The day enjoyed by all.

Tuesday, 17 April. Walked another ten kilometres and berthed in a field but owing to showers most of us crowded into a small barn. Quite good here but the village was badly off for food and we could do no exchanging. Several Polish girls here living in a cottage where we were and the boys 'had a good time'.

Our aircraft were over strafing and blew up an oil dump a quarter of a mile from us.

Wednesday, 18 April. Dull weather. RAF and RN officers billeted in fields near us. 2,000 Belgians passed us on the march. Visited RAF camp. Issued with American food parcel.

Thursday, 19 April. Walked about 25 kilometres and rested up in a farm. Leg swollen and blistered feet but very fit otherwise. Aircraft over during night.

Friday, 20 April. Grand weather. Left 7.30 am. Walked 15 kilometres and slept in barn by railway. Strafing a few yards from us during night. Fred sick with dysentery.

Saturday, 21 April. Raining. Left at 7.30 pm and walked about 17 kilometres. Rested for night at farm. Frequent showers. Seven kilometres from Lübeck. Strafing during night.

Sunday, 22 April. Remained here for day resting. Leg swollen.

Monday, 23 April. Left 9 am and marched through Lübeck and saw results of air raid in 1942. Berthed in German barracks on edge of town. Fine buildings and good quarters but crowded. RAF remained outside Lübeck and berthed on farms. No barbed wire around us here, and women and children are also here.

Tuesday, 24 April. Settling in. Visit of German General. Our fighters very active. Red Cross parcel.

Wednesday, 25 April. Resting and cleaning up.

Thursday, 26 April. Lovely weather. Six men from Stalag XIB, Fallingbostel, arrived and reported 38 killed and lot wounded by our planes. Also number of German guards killed.

Friday, 27 April. Overcast. No aircraft.

Saturday, 28 April. Showery weather. No aircraft over. Played Poles at soccer, won 4-1. (About 6,000 Poles here.) News of our previous camp being released by Guards Armoured Division. Heard Heavy Artillery fire during night.

Sunday, 29 April. Showery. Belgian and French officers drifting in from the Roads. Heard 2nd Army crossed Elbe north of Hamburg and are 50 kilometres from us. Also news of Himmler's request for peace.

Monday, 30 April. All Red Cross stores being brought in. Protective Organization announced. Low flying German aircraft over all day.

Tuesday, 1 May. Our aircraft over shooting up. Columns of smoke seen near camp. Red Cross wagons in and out all day.

Wednesday, 2 May. German aircraft flying very low. Our aircraft very busy and fires observed all round Lübeck. Reports of our patrols in Lübeck. Excitement in camp. Polish girl came into camp trying to find brother. Many refugees moving—

5 pm. Swarm of our aircraft over.

5.15. British Armoured 11th Division arrived. Cheers. All Germans shut in barracks. We are no longer POWs. Marine POWs took over camp guard. Units of armoured columns packed around us. Many explosions and fires. Sent letter to wife. Little sleep this night.

Thursday, 3 May. Hoisted White Ensign with ceremony. Three cheers. 'God Save the King.' Armoured column moving along road. Gangs of German prisoners march by, some without escort. Camp hive of activity. German vehicles being brought in. Prisoners brought in, searched and marched off.

Pilot Officer C G Lythgoe, Royal Air Force
POW from December 1941 to May 1945

We were camped just outside Lübeck and the day before we were liberated we had more German POWs than British POWs.

We were liberated – a scout car came across us by accident. The major in charge (or was it a colonel?) spoke to us, and it brought tears to the eyes of most of us. We were moved on by the army and got friendly with a captain who entertained us in his Mess, and we got tight and told him the army had not a clue on how to get us out and said: 'Take us to an aerodrome and we will get home'.

Lieutenant A F ('Junior') Powell, 13th Light Anti-Aircraft Regiment
POW from April 1941 to May 1945
Stalag VIIA, Moosburg

Then we heard a rumour that we were to march to the redoubt in the mountains and then that Bavaria had asked for a separate peace.

I have learnt since that the German commandant arranged to have the area declared a neutral area but that the nearby SS units broke the agreement by blowing up the bridge over the River Isar. On 29 April we felt that the end was very near and then we could see tanks coming across the fields. One prisoner, who got onto the roof of a bungalow, was hit by a bullet and died. US soldiers looted Moosburg village as a reprisal for the destruction of the bridge over the Isar.

When the German guards disappeared some ex-prisoners cut the outer wire and joined in the looting and we, British and American, officer ex-prisoners mounted guard at each hut to direct any returning prisoners to the main gate. Here they were searched to find any weapons. Anything else they could keep.

THE FAR EAST

Most Far Eastern prisoners of war had to wait until August and September 1945 to taste freedom. In the meantime, the fear that they would be massacred by the Japanese, who would then commit mass suicide, was very real – and even more so after the bombing of Tokyo, Hiroshima and Nagasaki.

Unlike POWs in Germany, whose situation had been tenuous enough, prisoners in the Far East would have been too weak and ill to offer any resistance. When Japan surrendered at midnight on 14 August, the number of prisoners stood at approximately 140,000 British and Commonwealth, 20,000 Americans and nearly 60,000 Dutch (including civilians).

Some 37,000 were in Japan alone. During the next two weeks only 1,000 of these prisoners were recovered. On 21 August as many as 36,000 were still in their camps, factories and mines waiting for freedom.

SIAM (THAILAND)

Mrs Enid Innes-Ker
Wife of Sergeant William McDonald ('Tam') Innes-Ker (prisoner from February 1942 to August 1945)
Now that the fighting in Europe was over we longed to hear news of victorious action in the Far East, while realizing, of course, that it would take time to mount any action against Malaya. We had been fighting the Japs in Burma for some months, and I think by this time in 1945 our forces had retaken Rangoon. I found myself that summer possessed by an almost unbearable feeling of impatience as I wondered how much longer we would have to wait. I feared long-drawn-out and hard fighting in Malaya, wondered what the Japs would do with their POWs under these conditions, and rather dreaded to think how they might treat them. One of the things that made me sad during the war was the thought of good years of our youth being wasted apart, and I wondered when, if ever, we would be able to start a family.

…The moment of truth lay not very far ahead; had Tam survived, how was his health, and how had these years as a POW changed him? Fortunately, the card I had just received, dated 21 March 1945, gave me great hope; I felt that surely if he was alive in March he would have survived through to August. My mind churned with both happy thoughts and doubtful ones at this time, as I waited impatiently through the longest four weeks of my life before I got news of Tam.

Corporal Charles Kinahan, Straits Settlement Volunteer Force
POW from February 1942 to August 1945
Camp 244, Tha Muang base hospital camp
As the Allies' advance in Burma progressed the Japs made plans to move the prisoners further east through Bangkok to Eastern Siam and French Indo-China

(now Cambodia and Vietnam). By the early months of 1945 the officers were assembled in Kanchanaburi camps and the rest of us went to Tha Muang camp (between Kanchanaburi and Ban Pong).

By the spring of 1945 the Allies were advancing fast in Burma towards Rangoon. We knew this, and realized why the Japs were moving parties of prisoners through Bangkok to eastern Siam and Cambodia. We had visions of long route marches, which the weaker prisoners were unlikely to survive. We were worried as to what might happen to those of us still in camps on the railway should the Allies overrun our area. We feared that the Japs would simply kill us before themselves retreating east. We had ideas of bursting out of our camp and taking to the jungle to await the Allied advance – a grim prospect.

Thanks be to God we were saved from such horrors by the Japanese surrender following the atomic bombs on Nagasaki and Hiroshima. At that time the Allies had reached Rangoon and the banks of the Salween River, still several hundred kilometres north of us.

On the day the Japanese Emperor agreed surrender I was out of camp on a working party. As we boarded the lorry to return to camp, Boon Pong walked past us and, looking straight ahead and not at us, shouted out the news of the surrender. How to keep this news quiet! There would be major excitement amongst the prisoners, which the Japs were bound to notice, resulting in forceful enquiries. Fortunately, shortly after our return to camp we were called out on parade by the Japanese camp commander, who told us himself. He told us that his men were to keep their arms and were responsible for our safety. This was a sensible decision. Goodness knows what would have happened to the Japs/Koreans had they been forced to give up their weapons! The excitement amongst the prisoners was tremendous. My personal feelings were relief and thankfulness to have been spared. We had built a little camp chapel, where many of us repaired to give thanks.

A Royal Signals NCO had been parachuted into our area and he was able to radio reports to Allied HQ in Rangoon as to our numbers and condition of health, etc. Subsequently, Allied transport aircraft came over and dropped supplies of food and medicines.

We remained in Tha Muang camp for about two weeks before our repatriation could commence.

I have two recollections of this period. In the nearby small town there was an Italian RC missionary unit. The members of the order got home leave after ten years. If they returned from leave they remained at the mission for the rest of their lives. A party of prisoners who were Roman Catholics marched out to mass in this church. This was a tremendous event for the native Christians as well as for our boys. It must have made a lifelong impression on all concerned.

28/8/45

レンゴウグンノホリョヘ
ALLIED PRISONERS

The JAPANESE Government has surrendered. You will be evacuated by ALLIED NATIONS forces as soon as possible.

.Until that time your present supplies will be augmented by air-drop of U.S. food, clothing and medicines. The first drop of these items will arrive within one (1) or two (2) hours.

Clothing will be dropped in standard packs for units of 50 or 500 men. Bundle markings, contents and allowances per man are as follows:

BUNDLE MARKINGS | | | | BUNDLE MARKINGS

50 MAN PACK	500 MAN PACK	CONTENTS	ALLOWANCES PER MAN	50 MAN PACK	500 MAN PACK	CONTENTS	ALLOWANCES PER MAN
A	3	Drawers	2	B	10	Laces, shoe	1
A	1-2	Undershirt	2	A	11	Kit, sewing	1
B	22	Socks (pr)	2	C	31	Soap, toilet	1
A	4-6	Shirt	1	C	4-6	Razor	1
A	7-9	Trousers	1	C	4-6	Blades, razor	10
C	23-30	Jacket, field	1	C	10	Brush, tooth	1
A	10	Belt, web, waist	1	B	31	Paste, tooth	1
A	11	Capt. H.B.T.	1	C	10	Comb	1
B	12-21	Shoes (pr)	1	B	32	Shaving cream	1
A	1-2	Handkerchiefs	3	C	12-21	Powder(insecticide)	1
C	32-34	Towel	1				

There will be instructions with the food and medicine for their use and distribution.

C A U T I O N

DO NOT OVEREAT OR OVERMEDICATE   FOLLOW DIRECTIONS

INSTRUCTIONS FOR FEEDING 100 MEN

To feed 100 men for the first three (3) days, the following blocks (individual bundles dropped) will be assembled:

3 Blocks No. 1
(Each Contains)

2 Cases, Soup, Can
1 Cases Fruit Juice
1 Case Accessory Pack

3 Blocks No. 2
(Each Contains)

3 Cases "C" Rations
1 Case Hosp Supplies
2 Cases Fruit

1 Block No. 5
(Each Contains)

1 Case Soup, Dehd
1 Case Veg Puree
1 Case Bouillon
1 Case Hosp Supplies
1 Case Vitamin Tablets

1 Block No. 7
(Each Contains)

1 Case Nescafe
1 Sack Sugar
1 Case Milk
1 Case Cocoa

1 Block No. 3
(Each Contains)

1 Case Candy
1 Case Gum
1 Case Cigarettes
1 Case Matches

1 Block No. 10
(Each Contains)

3 Cases Fruit
2 Cases Juice

Notification of the Japanese surrender: leaflet dropped to Far Eastern POWs in August 1945 (*via Imperial War Museum*)

The second memory is of trouble which we had with prisoners breaking out of camp at night and going to the nearest village, getting drunk on local spirit and then molesting the local girls. They were lucky not to get a knife in their backs. To avoid further trouble and possible loss of life we arranged to bring the native hooch into the camp where they could get drunk safely.

Sapper Edgar Whincup, Royal Engineers
POW from February 1942 to August 1945
Camp 239, Nakhon Pathom, Burma–Siam Railway

And now our red-letter day – 18 August. On this day Major Cheeta, the Jap commandant, announced that the war was officially over! This was the moment we had waited for all these long years, the day for which we had endured the interminable suffering, the day the armies had fought for, the day we immediately remembered our lost comrades, while we lived – and it had arrived! Almost immediately we received all the Red Cross supplies that had been held back by the Japanese – cigars, soap, clothes, food and much-needed medical supplies. We had a concert that night, the first for a very long time. This time Nippon music was not played and we, sentimentally, finished the evening with a noisy but happy rendering of 'God Save the King' – an end to our unhappy, long-drawn-out relationship with Nippon.

Next day we held a Thanksgiving Service and even went for a walk outside the camp – that sounds a very ordinary occurrence – but we went on our own, as comparatively free men. We also held a cricket match (with strange equipment conjured out of thin air after three years), England v Australia. Blast it! Australia won. When a plane appeared over our camp it was a change not to dive for cover – in fact, we stood up and waved, like excited schoolboys – and why not? Actually it dropped some leaflets telling us the war was over, to look after ourselves, and indicating that our people would try to get to us as soon as possible. Soon, the next day, another plane flew over but we never knew what it dropped, if anything.

A dramatic change in our supply of food occurred when Sergeant Sherring went into Ubon, obviously to conduct some negotiations. The result was that we are to have twenty head of cattle, eggs, fruit and other comestibles, rather different from the Nippon rations. Yet, after seven days, we are still waiting for someone to arrive from Bangkok. Our breakfasts were now almost like the ones we were used to having in England, fried egg and bubble-and-squeak, while for tea we are getting used to fried chicken.

Still, days went by without any news of our own people arriving to look after our interests, even though the Korean guards have gone and the

American prisoners of war have left. Even more frustratingly we were told that planes would fly over on the 9th day to drop supplies but nothing happened.

Sunday, 26 August was a better day. Colonel Toosey and 30 officers arrived bringing news of other POWs and the conditions they lived under. His statement that we had been among the lucky ones, even though our life had hardly been a bed of roses, made us wonder what our other comrades had gone through in Jap hands. He gave us some hope of early release – we knew Colonel Toosey as a go-getter and trusted him implicitly – but two days went by and our frustration increased. There was, however, a change in the fortunes of 20 of our sick comrades, who left at last for Bangkok.

Then on 28 August our hopes of early release were raised when not only did planes drop food, clothing and medical supplies, but some 'special service' officers arrived (American, Thai, Chinese and English), together with two sergeants from the Parachute Regiment. One of the sergeants even told us he had been in Edinburgh four weeks ago. But at least things were moving. Yet it's strange how seemingly minor occurrences annoy us, such as when we read a copy of *Picture Post* for May 1945 announcing that they were writing articles dealing with the awful experiences of POWs in Germany. What about us? Are we the forgotten Army?

The next events which encouraged us were when four RAMC men dropped from a Liberator aircraft, when 300 men were allowed to go to the races at Ubon, and when I sent a real letter home – the first since January 1942. We were also given a concert, the main attraction being some Thai dancing girls, a fact which guaranteed a full house. We still wondered when we were going to move, especially when we heard on the BBC news that POWs are being released.

It is very difficult to explain our frustration as day upon endless day went by and we remained where we had been for so many years. Let me just tell you of some of the events which partly relieved our boredom but were minor irritants when all we wanted was to get away. We saw ancient silent films starring old-time favourites such as Monty Banks and Chester Conklin, we played football against a Thai team, we held a sports day when the prizes were presented by the Governor of Ubon, we wrote home, we welcomed the supplies dropped from friendly planes – but not the plane which dropped rice – hadn't we existed on rice for three years? The ludicrous statement that annoyed us most was contained in a letter to Colonel Toosey, received from Bangkok, complaining that he was spending too much money on food. His reply was brusque and to the point: 'I do not think so and I will increase the expenditure'. Fancy the authorities wanting to cut out our rations after we had been on restricted rations for so long! You may be surprised that I use the term 'minor irritants' when some events, such as concerts, etc, were organized for our pleasure, but we were not exactly interested in pleasure – they seemed to be time-wasting activities in the long wait to get home.

Rumours abounded as to how and when we would be going home, but nothing material to our condition occurred. I sent a cablegram to Edna, parties went into Ubon (I was not among them), 'Timber', a friend, was picked up by the local constabulary being the worse for drink, Lady Mountbatten was supposed to be coming to see us but didn't (as we thought she was coming much cleaning of the camp ensued), we were allowed a 'wet' canteen one night (a noisy party, too), planes dropped food regularly and the days went by.

Thirteen days have now disappeared into a morass of boredom and inactivity and we are thoroughly 'browned off'. Why should I bore you with minor incidents? You must realize that we still felt like prisoners, but no longer of war but of the unbending, regulation-bound British Army.

THE DUTCH EAST INDIES

Pilot Officer Erroll David Shearn, Royal Air Force
POW from March 1942 to August 1945
Camp 353, Xth Battalion Barracks, Batavia

Early in 1945 we moved back from the prison at Bandoeng to the Cycle Camp in Batavia. Conditions here were as bad as they had previously been, but not quite so terrible as they had been in the prison at Bandoeng. There was a little more space, so overcrowding was not so intense. One sinister requirement was that the prisoners had to dig trenches across the parade grounds. Wightwick and I were firmly of the opinion that these trenches were dug so that the prisoners could be herded into them and machine-gunned in the event of the Americans landing in Java. I was told after our liberation that plans had in fact been discovered in the Japanese HQ, which confirmed our joint surmise.

In August 1945 we learnt through our wireless that the atomic bombs had been dropped at Hiroshima and Nagasaki and that the Japanese had surrendered. Wightwick and I did not immediately throw our hats (metaphorically) over the windmill. We had a fear that the Japanese general in command in the Far East might decide to carry on the good work and fight to the finish. We decided that if we were going to be liberated, the probability was that the Japanese would improve our food allowance. In consequence we kept anxious eyes on the intake at the camp kitchen. After some forty-eight hours or so, to our immense relief, we saw large carcasses being brought into the camp kitchen – far in excess of what, up to that time, had been delivered. We reckoned that this was indicative of a 'change of heart' on the part of our captors and that we might now reasonably rely upon survival.

Early in September Harold Maguire, who was a Battle of Britain pilot and a Wing Commander, asked me how soon I could get ready to leave Java for Singapore, as Group Captain Francis had signalled that he was landing a flying boat at Priok (the port of Batavia) and would be able to fly out a very limited number of prisoners. I answered that I was ready to leave that very moment and as far as I remember I did so certainly before an hour had elapsed.

We landed at Seletar – an RAF station in Singapore – and were most hospitably welcomed by the people there. I had my first whisky and soda for over three years, and wisely made it one, and one only, that night. Some of the ex-prisoners who beat it up suffered for it more than a little the next day.

JAPAN

Gunner Frederick Hawkes Thompson, Royal Artillery
POW from March 1942 to August 1945
Icuno copper mine
16 August 1945. Well, it's happened – what reaction? For some reason or other – none – absolutely nil. Is it because we just can't believe it or what? Perhaps it's because we have been told nothing by the Nips. We went on parade this morning and we were simply told – no work. Then we knew that something was up – although we all thought that it was because of the rumoured invasion we heard about last night of the Northern Island. Then came the news from the paper (translated by the Major) about the end of the war. Actually everyone is cool, calm and collected – maybe the reaction will set in later when we realize that it means the end of this existence of misery – hunger – humiliation and everything else is over. Thank God that I have survived, and my friends here with me – On the food and the threat of approaching winter, things would have been terrible for the fortunate ones who would have survived – Still, it's over – Let's see how we go – I still can't realize it – we have been disappointed so often – It's been a long grim period which I would not do again – but once more Thank God – I am alive and kicking.

13
REPATRIATION

'A great placard was hanging up bearing the words "Welcome Home", but I am afraid I could not see it very well. My eyes were too misty. The kindness of these people seems to get you somehow. An end to bombing and the barbed wire, guns and Germans. It seems to be too good to be true that it is all over, that I am in England again at last.'

– returning prisoner of war

For men who had been prisoners for as many as five and a half years – and in Germany in 1945 there were more than 30 who had been captured before the end of 1939 – liberation was a long time coming. But even a few weeks or months is a long time to spend in captivity, and those men captured at Arnhem and in the Ardennes in 1944 were likewise impatient to get home. Relief and jubilation soon turned to boredom, frustration, impatience and anger when liberated POWs – now ex-POWs – found themselves once more bound by red tape to remain where they were until arrangements could be made for their repatriation.

As the ex-POWs saw it, their superiors back home knew roughly how many prisoners there were to repatriate, and where the camps were located; with the war now winding down they easily had the manpower and transport available to ship them home on the double. However, although the war was coming to an end in Europe, it was still raging – and raging viciously – in the Far East, and men and equipment were being transferred to that theatre of operations. Things were also grim for those operational personnel who were not sent to the front and who therefore believed they would soon be stood down and sent home: they now found themselves retained on active duty liaising with former prisoners of war and organizing transportation, welfare and rehabilitation.

The War Office had in fact prepared provisional plans for the repatriation of liberated prisoners in Europe and the Far East as early as July 1942. Two months later the Imperial Prisoners of War Committee began refining the plans and broadly agreed the main points. MI9 and the Red Cross also took a hand. Yet, when it came to putting these plans into operation, the nations who had mounted no fewer than five massive inter-Allied invasions – of North Africa, Sicily, Italy, Normandy and the South of France – since November 1942 let red tape, contradictory orders and international and service rivalries delay the repatriation of liberated prisoners.

WESTERN EUROPE

The order went out to MI9 officers in Western Europe that the speedy return to the UK of 'any British or American prisoner of war' should not be delayed by long-winded debriefings. Yet each MI9 interrogator was allowed 60 lb of personal baggage and 100 lb of stationery, while another nine tonnes of stationery were held in 'forward reserve'. As ex-POWs arrived at staging camps in Antwerp, Brussels and Reims, each was issued with a short questionnaire, which he had to complete before being allowed home. No one could board an aircraft home without first filling in this form. Predictably, such reimposition of service discipline was not welcomed by frustrated ex-prisoners and only about 54,000 completed the forms, some answering the questions with simply 'Yes' or 'No', others scrawling obscenities. Of the rest, some, with their acquisitive POW habits still deeply ingrained, stole the pencils, others went AWOL, while still others 'escaped' from their liberators and hitchhiked back to England. Most troublesome of all were those who used the forms as an opportunity to vent all their pent-up grievances against the War Office, MI9, fellow prisoners, their SBO, their 'Man of Confidence', etc.

The job of recovering POWs in Western Europe fell mainly to the British, as there were more British, Commonwealth and nation-in-exile (such as Czech, Polish, Dutch and French) prisoners in that sphere of operations than there were American. However, America was the senior partner in the Allied coalition, and also had the most equipment, such as jeeps, lorries and aircraft; had penetrated farther into Germany; and had administrative responsibility for a wider area. Thus, although prisoners at Lübeck had been liberated by the British, those in Colditz, Frankfurt am Main, Moosburg, Nuremberg and Wetzlar had been freed by the Americans – usually by Patton's Third Army, hell-bent on getting to Berlin and shooting 'that paperhanging son-of-a-bitch' Adolf Hitler. At Stalag Luft I, Barth, and in camps to the east of the river Elbe, such as Stalag IIIA, Lückenwalde, matters were even more complicated. Their Russian liberators were reluctant to let Allied ex-POWs out of their hands until White Russian renegades held prisoner by the British were repatriated. In effect, the Allied ex-prisoners, many of them highly trained RAF officers, were being held hostage. However, by 4 June 1945 a total of 166,650 British and Commonwealth prisoners had been repatriated from Germany. They found that although they had at last shed the abbreviation 'POWs', they were now 'RAMPs'. 'What the hell are ramps?' they wondered. RAMPs were 'Recovered Allied Military Personnel' – one impersonal military term had replaced another.

Lieutenant A F ('Junior') Powell, 13th Light Anti-Aircraft Regiment
POW *from April 1941 to May 1945*
Stalag VIIA, Moosburg

The relieving force deloused us (DDT?) very effectively. We were each given a V-mail form to write home, but I got there first, but otherwise we were left very much on our own. Our senior officers tried hard to find out when we would leave and to speed up our departure. While we were waiting I met another ranks prisoner from Banbury, my home town, and we agreed that the first one home would tell the parents of the other to expect him soon. By 5 May some 3,000 prisoners had left the camp but we heard that only 500 had been flown out. My turn came on 7 May, and we walked over the fields to another road where US army trucks awaited us. Someone had collected a German steel helmet and was wearing it. The senior officer present said that if he wished to look like a German he would be treated as such.

The trucks took us to an airfield at Landshut, not far away. No planes arrived that day so we slept there, I think on gravel, by a road roller. Next day the system started to work. The advanced US forces were being supplied by air, and, as the planes came back empty, a ground controller called them to land. Quite a large number responded to the call and lined up near the runway while we were arranged into groups of the right size for a load.

When one Dakota started down the runway in its take-off a wing touched the wing of a parked aircraft and it was swung round – this damaged several aircraft. Progress was halted until all the parked aircraft were well away from the runway, and then we took off. It was a lovely sunny day and it was interesting to try to recognize the places where we had been from the air.

We landed at Reims on 8 May and were taken to a special camp where we showered and were fed. Canned peaches! Next day we were taken to a large airfield where we waited until some Canadian bombers landed. We were soon airborne, and took turns looking out from the gunners' turrets at France, the Channel, and then England. We landed at Wing in the afternoon, where we were given a warm welcome, tea and cakes.

Private Kenneth ('Kim') Stalder, Royal Army Medical Corps
POW from May 1942 to April 1945
Stalag 375, Fallingbostel

I was flown back in a brand-new Lancaster. Then I was sent to Newcastle and a rumour flew around that we were being sent to the Far East.

One night me and my mates were pulled up by Redcaps and I threatened to shoot one of them. I was sent to a hospital in Southport, but was allowed out for three days to get married to Irene, who I'd met when she was 16 and living a few streets away from me in London.

Pilot Officer Patrick Greenhous, Royal Air Force
POW from May 1940 to April 1945
Marlag-und-Milag Nord, Westertimke

We were sent back from the camp in empty ammo trucks and when passing through Rheinau I looked down at a jeep with an RAF Wing Commander in it and recognized him as a Volunteer Reserve Pilot Officer who had joined No 264 Squadron in 1940 – his name was Barton – and he survived to command the squadron, re-equipped with Typhoons. I called to him and he looked up and said: 'Good God, it's old Greenhous! Jump in with a couple of chums and we'll fly you back tomorrow. We have an aircraft going to the UK for spares.' So, taking Laurence Reavell-Carter and John Casson with me we went up to the squadron on an airfield just outside Rheinau. We sent a combat report into Group – five years late! – had a meal and lots of wine, and next day took off for England. We landed at an aerodrome somewhere in the south, got out of the aircraft, the three of us, and wandered into a vast hangar inside which were lines of trestle tables and piles of food and tea. A lady came to greet us and said: 'Where are the others?'

'What others?' we replied.

'Well, you're supposed to be 300 POWs,' she said!

It would appear that the famous communications network had failed again!

Squadron Leader George Dudley Craig, Auxiliary Air Force
POW from November 1941 to April 1945
Stalag IIIA, Lückenwalde, April–May 1945

Actually, for the next week there was a good deal of mopping up in this area and shells flew over the camp and one landed on the camp, luckily on the sports field and hurt no one. And one night a German fighter shot up the camp with cannon but, here again, though he peppered one hut he didn't hit anyone.

Then a full-scale battle started just outside the camp when about 11 surrounded German divisions tried to break through in order to surrender to the Americans. We had a couple of stormy days and nights but still no casualties!

By this time a so-called Administrative Staff of Russians had appeared to run the camp. Actually the British and Americans ran the whole outfit and the Russians just put spokes in the wheels by issuing contradictory orders which they never committed to writing (probably because hardly any of them could write). Our relations with the Russians were of the friendliest and their behaviour was very correct indeed. They are just like children – very uncultured and easily amused. What they love is something that goes off bang and they fire their Tommy-guns into the air as their greatest delight!

Then one day an American jeep, with war correspondents, appeared and people became very restive because the Russkies seemed in no hurry to repatriate us and the American lines were only about 40 miles away. The result was that hundreds of fellows just walked off on their own towards the American lines. Then the Americans were rather naughty and sent to the camp about 80 empty lorries and hid them in the surrounding woods, while parties of men were marched out through holes in the wire to these lorries, before the Russkies realized what was happening. When they did realize, they put armed guards on the wire and many shots were fired over the heads of would-be escapees! Anyhow, the next day our numbers were down by about 5,000.

The Russkies were very angry and I think this episode delayed our eventual repatriation quite a bit.

However, things were smoothed out after a very stormy meeting with a Russian General Famin and, on 20 May, they produced 100-odd trucks and took all American and British to Coswig on the Elbe where they were detrucked and walked over a pontoon bridge and en-trucked in waiting American trucks. A grand moment indeed.

Before we left the camp, we had had to handle thousands of French, Italian, Serbs, etc, civilian slave workers of both sexes. We had over 550 women in the camp by the end. We also had a lot of German rats who claimed British and American nationality and wanted to come back with us. These people we handed over to MIS (the American Military Intelligence Service) so that they would have their hooks on them before refusing them admission.

And so to Halle-Leipzig aerodrome under the Americans, who treated us excellently and most efficiently. We were delayed there by bad weather for five days and then brought by American aircraft to Brussels and there handed over to the RAF. The party of 25 in which I was left Halle about 9 am and got another plane straight away at Brussels and landed over Guildford for lunch. The others spent the night at Brussels before coming on.

The thing that sticks in my mind as the most wonderful is the fact that the Huns never set foot in this country and made the mess of it that they did in Europe. You would never think, from looking at the English countryside, that we had been at war – the shop windows actually have goods in them; the houses are not pockmarked with shell holes like those in that part of Germany through which we travelled by truck.

Telegraphist Herbert Edgar Elliott, Royal Naval Volunteer Reserve
POW from August 1940 to May 1945
Diary kept at former German barracks, Lübeck
Friday, 4 May 1945. Deloused. Told off for No 8 Group for proceeding home. All German women moved from barracks. Germans are now doing working parties for us.

Admiral Carter now in charge of Lübeck. He visited my room and told us that a German ship full of refugees had just been sunk by our bombers who were not aware of the refugees and nearly all were burnt to death. He also told us of Germans turning machine guns on some people 200 yards from a ship and killed 200. British, Polish, French and Belgian flags are flying everywhere. Our POWs are guarding stores on wharf sides.

Saturday, 5 May. Today we left Lübeck in army transport wagons at 1.30 pm and arrived Luneberg 6 pm. It was an interesting but unpleasant trip as we had frequent showers and no covers over the wagons. Lübeck and Luneberg were undamaged but villages in between showed signs of hard fighting. We crossed the Elbe by the pontoon bridge north of Hamburg and it was evident a hard fight had taken place at this crossing. We passed fields full of German soldiers who were now POWs and saw many groups marching without escort. Some were mere boys about fifteen years of age.

Our billets were German barracks in the outskirts of the town and had suffered in a small way from a/c attacks. We found the RAF officers already here and many soldiers awaiting planes to fly home.

Sunday, 6 May. RAF officers moved off in lorries to a 'drome about a day's ride away. Weather too bad for flying.

Ex-POWs keep arriving. Food and entertainment good. Went to a cinema in the town.

Monday, 7 May. Went to another cinema and still waiting for news of leaving for home.

Tuesday, 8 May. Went to aerodrome but no planes available.

Wednesday 9 May. Returned to Lübeck by lorry where Lancasters were waiting for us. Left 2 pm, arrived Wing, near Leighton Buzzard, 5.20 pm without incident and had a most comfortable trip. Left here 8 pm by lorry (RN), arrived London 11 pm, caught special train to Havant 12.15 pm, arrived Havant 2 am and taken to Stockheath naval camp.

Thursday, 10 May. Had two hours sleep. Completed routine and home at 5 pm. Now all's well.

Mrs Vivien Johnson (née Symonds)
Pen-pal, later wife of Pilot Officer Theo Faire Storrier Johnson, New Zealander in the RAF (POW from August 1940 to May 1945)

When the great march ended and POWs were released Theo thought that I was still in the Women's Land Army as no mail had arrived for six months. But the heavy labouring work had caught up with me by the end of 1944 and I had been invalided out for five months; then I put my age forward by a few years and became a driver of a mobile canteen to go to Italy for a year. Theo just had time to go to London from his uncle's home in Harrogate to meet me in King's Cross station and spend a few hours with me before I left for Liverpool with my group to board a ship for Naples. Theo's train held probably every aircrew and ground crew from all the aerodromes up the east coast to celebrate the peace thanksgivings. He waited until everyone else had swarmed out and came down the platform all alone, so we finally met up after so many years sight unseen: then it was another year before we met again – this time for another 25 years.

Mrs A E M ('Wendy') Fleming (née Weeks)
Welfare Officer, St John Ambulance Brigade

It was most exciting being in Brussels for VE Day.

Actually on VE night a great number of us were helping at a Canadian Depot. We were issuing comforts to returning Prisoners of War until about 3 am.

Working for Prisoners of War was terribly thrilling and a queue of ex-POWs is a queue the end of which no one wanted to see. We had many Depots of Distribution but I think the most popular was the one at the airfield. It was here that we could watch for the planes coming in from Germany [and go] out to the windy landing ground and help the men out of the planes. I cannot tell you how humbling it was to greet these men and take them across to the sheds where the YMCA gave them tea and we gave them warm woollies, cigarettes, chocolate and toilet requisites. There had been knitting parties all over England making comforts for the troops.

Cheers filled the air when these men were told to be ready to go in the waiting lorries to planes waiting to take them to Blighty.

In most cases these men spent a night in Brussels and went to England the following day. So much suffering and anxiety seemed to reach its climax in the sight of the planes full of happy soldiers taking off on the last stage of the homeward journey. We humbly concealed our emotions and turned to deal with the next queue.

There was one amazing characteristic about these men – British soldiers – None of them complained, and if we said: 'Have you had a bad time?' the reply would be: 'Oh, it's all over now, it wasn't too bad'. Usually they asked if we had come from their home town.

Private Erik Laker, The Royal Sussex Regiment
Prisoner from October 1942 to May 1945
Diary kept in Stalag IVC, Wistritz bei Teplitz (now Bystrice, Czech Republic)
Wednesday, 23 May 1945. Kolumbus Zweitlager, Lindau. After three days of lying about eating, drinking, smoking and chewing, we moved today. Boarded the plane and took off at 1400 hours. Plane was a Dakota. Trip took three hours dead and we landed at Reims at 1700 hours. The weather was very rough, making the plane bounce about a lot, and I felt a bit groggy. Got into wagons at Reims and were taken to an American camp called Tent City No 3. Had a grand meal and were then moved by trucks again to Tent City No 1. I saw English, or rather American, white bread here for the first time in two and a half years, and I thought I was eating cake. At Tent City No 1 we were deloused, had a shower, and a complete change of clothing, all American.

Thursday, 24 May 1945. Had another marvellous breakfast, dinner, and moved off about 1200 hours. Not back to the same aerodrome, but one about fifteen miles from Reims. A great many Lancasters on the 'drome and we boarded one at 1615 hours. One engine failed to start, however, and we had to wait an hour and a half while repairs were done. We were dancing around with impatience and I almost got to biting my fingernails.

All other planes had gone and we finally took off at 1805 hours, arriving at Oakley at 1950 hours. A fairly smooth journey, part of which I made in the midships gun turret. Great fun moving the guns up and down and spinning the turret round. Went over a wood, part of which was torn and blasted in an indescribable manner. One of the crew told me it was a V1 site. The boys had certainly given it the bizz.

When we landed at Oakley we trooped into a hangar with tables set out containing stacks of food. Everybody, however, was I believe, too full up with excitement to eat much. I know I was.

A great placard was hanging up bearing the words 'Welcome Home', but I am afraid I could not see it very well. My eyes were too misty. The kindness of these people seems to get you somehow. An end to bombing and the barbed wire, guns and Germans. It seems to be too good to be true that it is all over, that I am in England again at last.

Miss Margaret ('Peggy') King
Sister of Gunner Cyril George King, Royal Artillery (POW from May 1940 to April 1945)
We had heard he was being repatriated and the day came when we heard boots coming down the back passage. Could it be? – and it was! I cannot remember how long he had at home but he was far from well and found life a problem.

It is hard to believe but eventually he was posted up north with the possibility of being sent overseas! My father wrote to the government about this, and he was given a posting nearer to us.

THE FAR EAST

The Far East was largely an American sphere of operations, and it was to the Americans that the task of locating and evacuating POW camps fell. They also air-dropped supplies. However, as British and Commonwealth prisoners were in the majority, some British, Australian and New Zealand presence as liaison and welfare officers was deemed essential by their respective War Offices. Each nation sent out well-qualified and well-briefed personnel. But MI9 and MIS-X (the American equivalent of MI9) had never been fully integrated in the Far East, and there was a breakdown in communications. Each nation sent either too few or too many personnel and failed to keep each other informed, especially the Americans in charge. As it was, top MIS-X officers whom the British had been used to dealing with had been replaced with others who wanted to do things their own way. British and Commonwealth recovery personnel found themselves allocated tasks they were not briefed for and not competent to do, or wasting their time on pointless jobs. In addition, as the ships transporting ex-POWs home would be supplied almost exclusively by the British, Australian and New Zealand navies and merchant shipping lines, prisoners had to wait several weeks for the ships to become available.

Another reason for the hold-up was poor knowledge by the Allies of the exact location of Japanese camps. However, 'E' Group – MI9's advanced base in New Delhi – had compiled an astonishingly detailed map, with the help of the British Army Aid Group (BAAG), of the whereabouts and strength of all the camps in Burma and Malaya. This was handed to Lord Mountbatten when he was accepting the Japanese surrender. Only now could the real work of repatriating the prisoner begin.

In the meantime, welfare officers from all three services, men and women of the Red Cross, volunteer nurses, members of the St John Ambulance Brigade and ENSA did their best to keep the liberated prisoners occupied and to fatten them up for the long journey home.

SINGAPORE

Signalman John Stanley Walker, Malaya Command Signals
POW from February 1942 to August 1945
Camp 331, Changi Prison, Singapore
For three and a half years we had been slaves of the Japanese. We were forgotten men, so we thought. Relief came quickly, clothes were issued and we were on a ship, a British ship, the first ship to leave Singapore for the United Kingdom since the Japanese occupation.

For five days we sailed through a glass-smooth sea. Apart from the ship's complement all on board had known, and shared, the trials of incarceration. Were we free? It was hard to realize the truth. We were still all together, as we had been before.

In the late afternoon we sighted Ceylon, then came the lights of Colombo, and, after darkness had fallen, we slowly moved our way past the mole into the gigantic harbour, a harbour crammed with troop transports and naval craft of all kinds. All was silent. Then a lone searchlight came flickering across the water; we were recognized, and our ship's mission instantly became apparent. A hooter blew, then more hooters; the sky, the water, the ship, were all illuminated with searchlights.

The silent entry into the harbour now became a triumphant procession as we passed ship after ship on our way to the mooring. Each vessel's crew cheered as we passed; ships' bands played; all expressing the one word, 'Welcome'!

Only one ship was silent. True, our hooter was replying, but we couldn't cheer. This was beyond our expectations. As officials came aboard, as the noise died down, we gradually realized that once more we were in a British-owned

Jubilant prisoners at Changi, Singapore, cheer their liberators, August 1945
(*IWM ABS 87339*)

port, in a country that had not been overrun, and we were free men returning to our home country.

Pilot Officer Erroll David Shearn, Royal Air Force
Prisoner from March 1942 to August 1945
RAF Seletar, Singapore

I got fitted up to an extent with the necessary gear and clothing and then started to organize my return to the UK. I soon realized that unless I did something personally about my repatriation I was likely to remain in Singapore for quite a while. I heard that there was some organization at Sime Road (the ex-civilian internment camp), which could be of use. On going there I found in charge an ex-government civil servant whom I knew fairly well. He held out the possibility, but by no means the certainty, of an air passage in a week or so, or a berth on the SS *Sobieski* leaving the next day. I opted for the latter. First because of the fact that I would definitely be on my way, and secondly because I thought the sea voyage would have the result that I would land in better condition than if I went by air. It was, I think, a wise decision. By the time I arrived in Liverpool at the end of October I could easily have been taken for a normal healthy individual.

The voyage on the SS *Sobieski* was very pleasant, and daily I felt I was getting stronger and more normal. A highlight was stopping off at a port near Suez, where there were enormous sheds through which we passed collecting gear from a counter extending the whole length of the shed. We started off with a bright yellow leather bag, made, I think, locally, of camel skin; next, battledress, underclothes, pyjamas and everything one could think of, down even to campaign medal ribbons. Subsequently the RAF sought to bill me for this enforced issue of necessities. The demand came a few days before I was due to fly to Kuala Lumpur in April 1946. I took no notice of the charge, but as a precautionary measure I closed my banking account with RAF bankers and transferred the balance to my account with the Chartered Bank. I heard no more of what I have always considered an attempt at daylight robbery.

On reaching Liverpool we were transferred by bus to Cosford, an RAF station near Wolverhampton. After twenty-four hours or so there, during which medical examinations took place to see that we were free of the more communicable diseases, we were allowed home on leave, pending a further and more intensive medical scrutiny and discharge from the RAF. I got back before the end of October. I felt considerable amusement at the sight I must have presented as I got out of the taxi outside the flat Kathleen had rented in Vincent Square. My luggage was, to say the least, assorted. I had a small tin

Prisoners at Shamshuipo, Hong Kong, await the arrival of the Royal Navy on 15 August 1945. The Union Jack fluttering overhead was made by the prisoners, and was the first time they had seen their national flag flying since December 1941 (*Mrs E M White*)

box, rather like the large cash and document container favoured by Chettiars [an Indian trading community]. This had been acquired in Singapore and was the nearest I could get to a uniform case. I had a wicker basket bought in Colombo and largely filled with oranges, which I had heard were scarce in London. There was my yellow leather camel-skin bag handed to me at the port near Suez, and an airman's kitbag obtained at Cosford. All I needed was a parrot in a cage!

SIAM (THAILAND)

Mrs Enid Innes-Ker
Wife of 'Tam' Innes-Ker, Far Eastern POW since February 1942
So time passed until I got word of Tam on 9 September. This came from Mr Topham of Blythe Green, Jourdain [a shipping company], who had had a cable from another [ex-POW] saying he and Tam were homeward bound on the *Monowai*, and fit – only Topham was such a stutterer that what I heard was 'sick'. My thrill that Tam was actually on his way home was somewhat tempered by the thought that he was sick. I rang Anthony Sampson in the BBC News Room and asked if he had any information about the *Monowai*. He came back later with the information that she was a hospital ship, and he understood that she was the first one out of Singapore with POWs. He was quite wrong about her being a hospital ship, but at the time we both thought that probably, as the first ship out, she was bringing those who were most ill. After that you can imagine my relief the following day when I got Topham's letter and a copy of Brandon's cable, and saw that the operative word was 'fit'.

Soon after this came Tam's first cable, which once more put the cat among the pigeons. The cable is datelined 'Colombo', but says: 'Arrived safely at Singapore'. It rather looked as though Tam was so confused he did not know where he was. I learned later, after Tam got home, that these cables were written in Singapore, but them carried on the *Monowai* and not sent off until they got to Colombo. Hence the discrepancy between the wording and the place of despatch.

Within a day or so came Tam's first letter, and then everything really was all right. You cannot imagine the joy that letter brought. To be in touch again, to receive a proper letter after those four brief cards in four years, and above all it was the Tam I knew writing. He obviously had not changed and said he was quite fit, and all my fears were put at rest ...

During the next few days letters and notices poured in from the Colonial Office and the Red Cross, announcing that Tam had been released, and giving me addresses to write to – in many cases different addresses. In the event, as Tam had already left Singapore, nothing I wrote ever reached him, and though I wrote to various addresses to catch him on the way home he received none of my letters. I have sometimes wondered what happened to all these ecstatic outpourings of mine. They were certainly never returned to me, though I did get back, some weeks after Tam arrived home, a whole bunch of 25-word postcards that I had sent off in previous months.

Meanwhile I gave in my notice to the BBC and left by the end of September …The couple of weeks I had between leaving the BBC and Tam's arrival home was a very fraught time. I spent hours on the 'phone to various people in Norfolk trying to find a cottage to rent for the winter, and then later, when I had an idea of Tam's arrival date, trying to book us in to a hotel for a couple of days after his arrival. I must have tried about forty hotels in London before someone at the BBC put me on to the bed-and-breakfast place just opposite Claridge's where I was finally able to book a room. I think it was probably not a reputable hotel, but it suited us admirably.

One minute I was on cloud nine and writing reams to Tam, and the next I was either worrying about accommodation, or cast into the depths because I was sure that he would meet and fall for someone on the way home after all those years of never seeing a woman – there were bound to be nurses and other women on the ship and we all knew how quickly shipboard romances could flourish; or else I was very distressed because Tam's letters kept coming in saying he had not heard from me. I also became very depressed about my clothes, and suddenly came to realize how tatty my underwear was.

There were two ships racing each other home, the *Monowai* and the *Corfu*. For a long time we thought the *Monowai* was going to be first home but the *Corfu* just beat her and docked at Southampton a few hours before the *Monowai* docked at Liverpool. Tam sent me a cable saying that they were arriving at Liverpool on 11 October – the same date as that on which he died 37 years later.

Tam was due at Euston at about 1 pm. There was no question of having lunch. I just grabbed a taxi and dashed off to Euston. There was a great crowd of waiting wives and we were not allowed on to the platform but were kept back by barriers till the train came in. And then from every door there burst men with bright yellow faces (they had been dosed with mepacrine on the way home). I frantically leaped over the barrier and made my way along the platform amidst this sea of uniforms and yellow faces, wondering whether I would recognize Tam, and then I saw him – fighting off the well-meant attentions of a WVS lady who was offering to carry his kitbag. He had spotted me vaulting over the barrier and could not shake off the WVS lady quickly enough.

Well, of course, Tam's first evening in London the cost of stamps and bus fares was not exactly a subject of prime importance and did not figure in our conversation. Then the next morning I emerged from my bath to find that Tam had disappeared. He was away such a long time that I was beginning to get quite worried. When he did appear he was bearing a bouquet of flowers for me.

We were so very happy during those following weeks that I felt nothing could ever touch us again; now that Tam was well and safely home what could ever be as bad as what we had each been through?

Corporal Charles Kinahan, Straits Settlement Volunteer Force
POW from February 1942 to August 1945
Camp 244, Tha Muang base hospital camp
About the end of August 1945 we began our journey home – by train (partly on our railway) to Bangkok, then by air to Rangoon and ship to Liverpool. As we boarded the train the excitement and exhilaration was terrific. We were in metal freight boxcars such as we had come in from Singapore more than three years before. Many of the troops climbed on to the roofs of the boxcars, waving and shouting to the field workers and residents as we passed through villages and rice fields. It was safe enough to ride on the roofs in the early part of the journey, as we knew there were no bridges to pass under, but once we joined up with the main line to Bangkok discretion prevailed.

At Bangkok we were taken by lorry to the racecourse, where a tented camp had been set up. We stayed there for just one night before boarding aircraft to fly to Rangoon. The planes were twin-engine Dakotas, which had been employed in the supply of the Allied advance through Burma. They were not fitted out to carry passengers in any comfort – no heating and passenger seats, just tin seats which folded into the wall. The noise was deafening, there being no sound insulation. As we gained height it got colder and colder and we were really glad of the blankets provided. Our pilot flew due west out into the Indian Ocean and then due north to Rangoon. Other planes flew north-west along our railway to let the troops view from the air their handiwork where they had left so many dead comrades. Sadly, two of the aircraft crashed. One was lost with all hands, the other managed to put down in a rice field with no casualties. It was terribly sad that lives should be lost in this way having survived three and a half years as guests of the Emperor of Japan. I imagine that the Dakotas which brought us out had been pushed to the limit on their work in supplying the British advance, and flying 'over the hump' into Yunnan Province in China.

Landing at Rangoon airport (Mingladoon), we were thrilled to be greeted by WVS ladies with hot 'cuppas', etc. And, thrill of thrills, a good measure of American Bourbon whiskey! Having had no alcohol for three and a half years, the sensation was marvellous! We were glad that we did not have to drive.

We were accommodated in tents in the University precinct, where we spent several days in comparative luxury. We were visited by the C-in-C, Lord Mountbatten. No bullshit parade, just chatting informally with groups of men.

We sailed from Rangoon on a fast Dutch freighter, *Boissevain*. In peacetime she sailed between Durban and Hong Kong, carrying passengers and freight. The holds had been converted into troop decks, with rows and rows of hammocks.

Rather than sleep (?) in hammocks in crowded troop decks many of us slept on the decks in the open. Under normal troop-ship conditions this would not have been allowed, but the OC troops on the ship took a lenient attitude towards returning POWs and I managed to sleep on deck all the way to Liverpool.

The *Boissevain* stopped at Colombo for fuel and food supplies but we were not allowed ashore. Next we called at Port Tewfik near the south-west end of the Suez Canal near Port Suez. Here we were issued with temperate climate clothing and footwear, and were even issued with medals – four in my case: 1939–45 Star, Pacific Star, Defence Medal and Victory Medal! The passage through the canal to Port Said was a great experience, as most had never been that way before (or since). From Port Said we went direct to Liverpool. The arrival and landing on English soil was an emotional experience for us all.

We tied up on the Prince's Landing Stage in Liverpool immediately beside the Liverpool–Belfast ferry. What a temptation to jump on board. Sadly, we were taken to a dreary transit camp outside Liverpool, there to kick our heels for several days. At last I was given a rail pass to travel to Belfast via Stranraer/Larne. It was a long, dreary journey in a crowded train – standing room only. The only bright spot was a message on the ship's Tannoy – 'If there is a Corporal Kinahan on board would he please report to the Purser's Office', where I was informed that a private single cabin had been reserved for me!

My prewar firm Lyle and Kinahan had been doing their stuff through John Morrison, a former director of the company, resident in Larne. I (and three or four other returning prisoners) were met at Larne by John and the local Mayor.

Dad met me at York Street station. Mum felt that the emotion of the occasion would be too much for her. She had saved up her rice ration to give her dear Charles a nice, rich rice pudding – little realizing that we had been living on rice (sometimes little else) for three and a half years!

My parents had had no news of me since the fall of Singapore. They knew from a Danish friend, who was on an official evacuation party on the day we surrendered, that I was alive and well at that point. Otherwise only an official Japanese printed card signed by me early on saying that I was 'working for pay'. We were not allowed to add anything, but at least the signature was a message in itself. My father came to the conclusion that I was dead, though Mum never gave up hope. It was fortunate that Dad survived to change his will back again after my return!

Telegrams which I sent via the army network from Rangoon, Colombo, Port Tewfik and Gibraltar never reached them. The first news they had of me was a telegram from Liverpool.

Sapper Edgar Whincup, Royal Engineers
POW from February 1942 to August 1945
Formerly at Camp 239, Nakhon Pathom, Burma–Siam Railway
I can now joyously announce that it's 24 September and I am writing this in Ubon – we are on the move at last!! We leave here at 4.30 pm tomorrow by train, in coaches (comfortable travelling for the first time since January 1942), and should arrive in Bangkok in two days' time.

Actually we had a typical Far-Eastern send-off, ie, a monsoon storm as we entrained, one hour late, at 5.30 pm, but who cares now? As we journeyed to Korat we were greeted at every station by a reception committee of Thais with flags, cakes, as much as we like to eat, and a guard of honour of Thai schoolchildren. On we went to Bangkok and left almost at once by air for Rangoon. I went straight to hospital and luxuriated in clean white sheets, ate roast beef, potatoes, peas and my first real bread for three years. It was only for one night, as the following day we were moved to a transit camp, where I met up with quite a number of my comrades, including 'Timber'. We spent a few more days here, being fitted out with clothes and going to the pictures. I personally received a knotted scarf from the Red Cross.

The day before we boarded our ship, the *Chitral*, we were entertained to a party held in Rangoon by the WVS. It was held in a hotel, and the lads played tennis, danced, and swam in the pool. It lasted all day and we behaved like kids let out of school.

Next day was the one we had waited for all these long years, so I will just simply say: 'On Monday, 1 October, we boarded the *Chitral* at 12 o'clock' – we were on our way, away from rice, boiled seaweed, boiled cucumber, tropical ulcers and everything that had beset us for so long. England was a long way away but it was there, waiting for us, and, under our feet we had moving steel and timber, not Far Eastern dirt and mud.

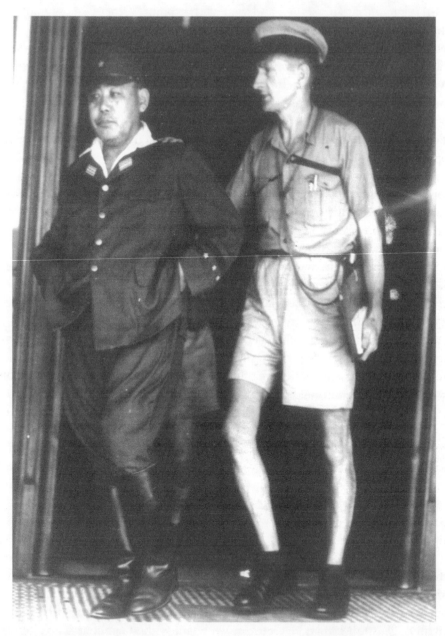

Colonel Takanuda, former commander of POW camps in Hong Kong, is led to prison, August 1945 (*IWM A30752*)

JAPAN

The Reverend G Bower, Royal Navy
Letter from HM Hospital Ship Tjitjalengka, Yokohama, 12 September 1945
My Dearest Margery

At last there seems to be a little respite and a short time to write a few lines. The last week or so has been extremely hectic. I could write a book about what has been happening lately, but unfortunately there isn't time for that so I'll have to give you a very brief and condensed idea of what has been happening.

We were cruising up and down off the coast of Japan when we heard the glorious news that they had surrendered and could see the top of Fujiyama towering above the clouds very clearly. We were anchored in the bay just outside here on VJ Day and the surrender was signed only a few yards away from us, and we saw this boat with the Japanese officials coming by.

I am almost certain I was the first British Padre to set foot in Japan after the surrender! Some of our chaps had to go ashore to make arrangements for ex-POWs and I went with them. I have never seen such utter desolation in all my life. Yokohama is certainly a desert city and the carnage caused by the bombing is terrific. There were very few Japs about and the ones I saw looked utterly dejected and were just lolling about looking very sulky and miserable. We saw queues of them filing out of the city, women overburdened with luggage and babies and men shuffling along beside them carrying nothing. I felt rather sorry for the Japs then, but I certainly don't now. I have heard and seen too much evidence of their fiendish atrocities. We are now tied up alongside a quay and for the last week we have been just about as busy as we can be. But it's certainly glorious work, which we all enjoy. In this last week, altogether 1,500 ex-prisoners and internees in Jap hands have passed along this quay, been de-loused, etc, and medically examined by our doctors and those who need urgent treatment came on board here. Every now and then a ship comes alongside us and takes off a few of the less serious cases.

I have been struggling to keep them all supplied with cigarettes and all the other little comforts of life. What these poor chaps have been through is almost unbelievable and their cheeriness and sanity is just amazing. I cannot imagine how they managed to survive at all. The vast majority are either British or Australians who were captured at Singapore or Hong Kong. Most of them are suffering from beriberi, a revolting disease caused by undernourishment, which makes them look hideous and swollen up like a balloon. Many with TB. All the rest give you a real shock when you first see them – they are so ghastly thin with their bones standing out. Their gratitude for the

Survivors of the naval vessel HMS *Jupiter* after liberation in Batavia (*IWM A30800*)

tiniest little thing you do for them is deeply moving, and their joy and excitement at seeing simple little things like an English cigarette or a piece of bread and butter is terrific. They can't eat much as their tummies are not used to good food, although their hunger and weakness is terrible. Most of them for the last three and a half years have had to work in coal mines, copper mines and blast furnaces for fourteen hours a day. Their rations, two small bowls of rice and beans twice a day. Occasionally they got a piece of stinking fish, which was a luxury.

The hundreds of stories I have heard of their torture and punishment are too revolting to describe. All of them without exception were frequently knocked down by their Jap guards and beaten unconscious. I have seen distorted fingers with no nails, as it was a regular punishment for minor 'offences' for a chap to have a finger broken or his nails torn out. Hundreds died in all the camps. Yet there seems to have been quite a number of pro-Allied Japs who smuggled food and news.

Gunner Frederick Hawkes Thompson, Royal Artillery
POW since March 1942
Writing on American Red Cross Form 539A, 14 September 1945

Well – here we are at last on that long-discussed and long-yearned-for dream that at times seemed would never materialize – the boat. At present we are sailing under blue skies and the atmosphere all round [...], which in plain American means 'the goods'. Quite a few interesting things have happened since the war finished – but we are now definitely in a Yankee atmosphere. It really started with the 'air drop' when a B-29 sailed over the camp and dropped us food and clothing by 'chutes. They thought of everything – complete clothing kits from briefs to hankies – even toilet requisites – food (naturally mostly canned) and then chocolate, candy, stacks of chewing gum – cigarettes, tobacco and matches.

The train journey to Yokohama was one glorious 'nosh'. I think my mate and myself ate a good meal every two hours on the average – while 4 oz of cheese in a roll with coffee was considered just a snack! We didn't consider ourselves greedy – I guess we've got a few tons of food to put away to make up for our slimming diet we've had in the last three and a half years.

One pleasant memory that will always remain – is the sight of our first white people since we left Japan. We had a long wait in the train just before we entered Kobe (?) and there we picked up the League of Nations, or so it seemed. We had Romanians, Dutch, Spanish, South Americans and Swiss, amongst others, on board the train. All spoke perfect English and in the hour or so that they spent on the train we had interesting chats with them and loaded them up with food and clothing etc.

The biggest surprise, however, was on our arrival at Yokohama station when I looked up on hearing a soft lazy voice asking men: 'Would you like some candy?' and seeing a beautiful blonde American girl. She was only one of many, and what with them and a brass band playing 'California Here I Come' like mad, it was all rather overwhelming – and [...]

Junior Purser Edward Cadwallader
Canadian Pacific Coast Service, September 1945

I was a Junior Purser on the Canadian Pacific Coast boats (the 'Princess' boats) running up and down the Canadian/American west coast. My ship was on the 'Triangle Run', ie, Vancouver, Victoria and Seattle, every second day running in one direction, and in the reverse direction the next.

My ship made two pick-ups of repatriated POWs, which for us began at Seattle, where we picked them up; we put them ashore at Victoria that same afternoon for hospitalization in a former army camp at Gordon Head, just outside Victoria proper. Here these men were intended to get such hospital treatment as necessary before being eventually released or shipped further on toward their homes. Quite a considerable number, as I remember, were Englishmen who had still a journey ahead of them of some 6,000 miles. Many were brought aboard as stretcher cases. I could not help wondering if many of them would ever make it home.

At that time I don't think many Canadians knew much about Japanese atrocities and treatment of prisoners. (This subject to correction from those who know better!) My station in harbour in Seattle was ticket collector. To watch the men coming up the gangway and over the side was most difficult. I was on duty and there was no possibility of conversation. That came later.

When we cleared harbour and I was off duty I decided to go walkabout. I managed to engage a few of the ex-prisoners in conversation. Among them was one man who was more robust than his companions. I forget where he was taken prisoner, but he was shipped to Japan and made to work in a large factory which, among other things, was engaged in some ship-building. Of course, I asked about their treatment there. He told me that for even the slightest infraction of the rules they were beaten severely. Often it would be from the butt of the guard's rifle. This was commonplace, and he did say that as best they could they were able to shake it off. Of course, to survive they had to. He told me that if anything went wrong the guards would go berserk, which in reflection I think was from fear, something from inside the nature of the Japanese. (My own thoughts on this.) If and when things did go wrong the order of the day would be beatings all round.

The above was the first of two contingents. The second a few days later was like unto it. This contingent of men consisted of some Canadians, who had sailed from Victoria for Hong Kong shortly before Japan went to war against us. I remember one of them, Ray Squires, because he had been visiting a family in Esquimalt I knew well and the son of whom, Robin, was a contemporary at my school. Again I was on the gangplank as the repatriates came aboard and, shortly after, when the ship was on her way towards Victoria, I was on the upper deck when I noticed a familiar face, which I recognized as that of the lady Ray used to meet at Robin's home. In a moment I twigged why she was on board – to meet her husband or fiancé (whichever it was). So, not seeing Ray, I looked about for him. Nothing for a few moments, but then, scarcely distinguishable for whom he was I recognized him. But it took a few moments to sink in that it was he. He had become so emaciated and like all of them had the most ghastly pallor of dirty green-grey. Also his pallor seemed to me deep set, not something that could ever be washed out.

When I recognized them I went over to them to say 'hello' and 'welcome home'. Ray's wife was nice enough but Ray, I think, did his best to stay away from me. I know that he had a very sour look in his face as though resentful of everything and everybody. Well, I took the cue from what I thought I saw and withdrew.

Nearly all the men suffered from beriberi, dysentery, or malaria, and possibly all three.

When we reached Victoria, Ray went ashore and into the military hospital at Gordon Head and I lost sight of him for a time. Later he did re-emerge, and worked in the grocer shop of Robin's father, where he undertook light duties, gradually regaining his strength.

HONG KONG

Lieutenant John Gordon Pelly, Royal Naval Volunteer Reserve
HMS Tyrian, September 1945
A day or two after our return from Hong Kong we sailed for Kiirun [Chilung] in Formosa [Taiwan]. The object was to remove the surviving prisoners of war. We sailed to Kiirun and I have never seen a place quite so badly bombed, with every building apparently down and sunk ships all over the harbour. And there on the jetty were fully armed Japanese.

Lieutenant John Gordon Pelly, RNVR (*Mrs John Pelly*)

All the time we were there (7–11 September) we felt most uncomfortable as there was nothing definite and we were a force of two cruisers and two destroyers in contract to [overseeing] 300,000 fully armed Japanese. However, nothing untoward happened and we cleared the jetty for the arrival of the hospital ship. Various doctors went inland to the camp and eventually the improvised hospital train arrived bearing its grim cargo. I just can't describe the scene – a boiling hot humid day with the sun beating down, the frightful smell of rotting human flesh and the lack of any breeze. The train was brought alongside the ship and the surviving prisoners of war were carried aboard. Pictures of the Belsen camp were heaven compared with these remains of men – too weak to lift a fleshless arm, let alone smile or usually even open their eyes. It was the most ghastly sight and made one realize just how inhuman the Jap has become. Apparently the camp was too indescribably sordid and thousands of men had died or been executed.

I talked to a lot of the Stanley Camp (Hong Kong) people in the hospital ship and they were better off, though horribly emaciated and weak – there they were mostly civilian prisoners.

I walked around the town and found every building bombed – the smell atrocious and every disease in the world prevalent. It used to rain nearly every day as we lay alongside this stinking jetty. I organized a wardroom relay race against the Petty Officers, which we won; otherwise there was very little doing excepting keeping watch day and night with our sentries and the Jap sentries, both fully armed, staring at each other. The Japs used to bow and scrape and salute every time any officer passed and they looked very ridiculous.

Having seen to the embarkation of the prisoners we sailed from Kiirun in howling wind, running into heavy seas outside – and we set course for the mouth of the Yangtse Kiang.

THE PHILIPPINES

Brigadier Hugh Wrigley, CBE, MC, Australian Imperial Force
Commander, No 3 Australian POW Reception Group, Manila, Philippines
Writing in News Of The Empire, *magazine for reception staff, 13 October 1945*
Our mission is well-nigh finished. Thousands of our countrymen of the British Commonwealth have been sent homewards after years of tortuous living in Japanese Hell Camps. I am sure each of us feel some honour in being allotted this task of playing some small part in restoring to them the good life of free peoples that they have missed for so long.

The SS *Chitral* arrives at Southampton laden with prisoners repatriated from the Far East, October 1945 (*IWM HU87338*)

As Commander of this Group I desire to pay tribute and offer thanks to all who have shared in full measure in the attainment of our goal.

The successful accomplishment of our Mission, the comfort and service we were able to render have only been attainable because of the magnificent assistance of the Army of our Great Ally – the United States. All Officers and Enlisted Men of the 5th Replacement Depot – without exception from the Commanding Officer Colonel George L Smith to each private performing his job – have set a standard of friendly service mere words can never acknowledge. Undoubtedly the basis of this cordiality was laid in past days when inch by inch we stood together and mounted the great offensives; the fruits of which gave us our present job in Manila. I want every member of the US Army who has been associated with us to know the appreciation of every recovered prisoner of war and myself and my entire staff for all they have done for us.

The great servants of the Australian soldier – our philanthropic Organizations attached to our Armed Services – have been joined in a most worthy manner by the American Red Cross and all have endeared themselves to all they serve so well.

To my own staff – I will not mention ranks or names and I include the Reception Teams from other British Commonwealth countries and members of Navy and Air Force – I tell you never before in my Army career have I commanded such a hard-working team. For the enthusiasm and cheerfulness with which you accepted this huge and worthwhile job I express my grateful appreciation.

And now, our task over, we turn to the future; we will all shortly proceed in the ways of our individual bent. I hope we will all hold fast to the friendships we have made in our long association during bitter war and will ever be generous in acknowledging the great efforts made by all peoples to bring these glorious days of peace. The characteristics displayed by all associated with the work of this Group augur well for a bright future of friendship and prosperity in the eras now opening before us.

From: British Army Delegation, Washington
To: Commander-in-Chief, British Pacific Fleet, October 1945
Major General Lee of the British Army Staff in Washington who has just returned from the inspection of the RAMPs [Recovered Allied Military Personnel] reception camps on the West Coast informs me that RAMPs who were sent back in *Implacable* arrived in far better condition than any others that have yet been received.

He attributes this to the steps taken by the Captain and officer and to the presence of the 25 VADs [Voluntary Aid Detachments] of *Implacable* who did all in their power to assist these RAMPs to return to normality.

The condition of these men was in such marked contrast to others who have not had similar advantages that General Lee is of the opinion it would be very much in the interest of RAMPs if special arrangements could be made for an officer or officers to accompany them on their passage to America with the particular duty of giving them individual attention.

General Lee is, however, somewhat concerned at the fact that these men were issued with dollars by *Implacable* far in excess of the authorized amount, since this must inevitably cause heartburn among others who only receive the stipulated amount.

14
POST-WAR

Some of the 'Returned Allied Military Personnel' had been prisoners of war for as many as five years, some for only a few months. But all found they had lost out in some way by being captured. After initial leave – usually of about two weeks – and a medical examination, the next question was: 'Where do I go from here?'

Career officers found they had a great deal of catching up to do. In the first place, an officer once captured did not rise beyond the rank of army captain, naval lieutenant or air force flight lieutenant, and those already of higher rank received no further promotion. Most were, however, promoted one rank higher once resuming their duties after the war. Those liberated from Western Europe, keen for further advancement, volunteered for service in the Far East, but by the time leave was over, medical boards passed, paperwork done and training undertaken, it was too late – the war in the Pacific was over. Besides, other problems beset ex-POWs. First, they had to readjust to a much more rigid service discipline; second, men used to firing pea-shooters were now at the dawn of push-button warfare, and had to familiarize themselves with the new technology; third, soldiers now had to be politicians as well as warriors, not an easy adjustment to make for men whose politics were normally conventional and rarely thought out; finally, the British Empire was being dismantled and the armed forces were being downsized, making competition for promotion even fiercer. Disillusion soon set in, and many never achieved the seniority required and therefore took early retirement. A few, however, rose to giddy heights, with some becoming generals, admirals and air marshals, but they were few indeed.

Many of those who had only joined up for the duration, expecting that their wives and their jobs would still be waiting upon their return, also found their hopes dashed. The rate of divorce amongst ex-POWs was exceptionally high, not only because their wives had met other men in the meantime, but also because ex-prisoners were often difficult to live with. They weren't exactly digging tunnels from the bottom of their back gardens, but they had developed habits in the camps that could only be shaken off with immense willpower – hoarding useless bits of wood and rusty nails, insisting that every scrap of food on the plate be eaten, having peculiar tastes (spooning condensed milk from the tin was one), being argumentative and restless – and all contributed to marital breakdown. Finding work also proved difficult, as younger, fitter men had taken over their jobs in their absence. Those who did find work were often depressed at how selfish, cynical and irresponsible civilians had become. They who really had suffered starvation and deprivation in all its forms found it very difficult to feel any sympathy towards civilians who grumbled about their lot, especially as rackets and the black market were flourishing.

British ex-POWs had it harder than their brethren from the Commonwealth and the Unites States. Some of these countries showed their appreciation by striking a medal for ex-POWs, and almost all gave them a pension, an additional disability allowance, free medical treatment, retraining and the opportunity to go to university. As they had technically served abroad during the war, they had also paid less income tax and had thus accrued some savings. The British, on the other hand, were well and truly shafted. Officers had had a third of their salary deducted to pay for the hospitality they had received from their captors; the Treasury pocketed the money. NCOs and other ranks, who had been systematically underpaid – if they were paid at all – while undertaking forced labour for the enemy, likewise received no recompense.

Such was their disgust with the postwar dispensation that some retreated into a kind of pastoral idyll – one of Britain's most gallant and decorated air aces retired to the coast and ran a mushroom farm; a once inveterate escape addict bought a stone cottage in a bleak and remote part of Cumbria, there to observe nature, and to write and paint. Another turned to writing and illustrating quaint children's books.

Lucky were they who either gained qualifications whilst a prisoner or developed literary, artistic or theatrical talents. Among those who qualified as an accountant was Flight Lieutenant Anthony Barber, of the RAF Photographic Reconnaissance Unit, who went on to become Chancellor of the Exchequer and a Peer of the Realm. Others learned languages and found their linguistic talents in demand by British Intelligence in a divided Cold War Europe.

Many were they who had written novels and short stories in captivity and found that after the war they could turn their talent to profit. Among the books written in captivity and published after the war were *The Guarded Years* by Douglas Bader, *Yes, Farewell* by Michael Burn and *The Pitcher and the Well*, narrated by a New Zealand airman from his bed in a POW hospital as he lay dying from his wounds. Hundreds of ex-POWs, some in dire financial straits, found in the 1950s that the public was hungry for accounts of prison-camp life, especially if they involved escape endeavours, and were able to turn their misfortune to pecuniary and career advantage by writing popular memoirs, some of which were turned into highly successful stage plays, radio serials, films and TV series. Of the actors who appeared in these dramatizations, dozens had themselves been prisoners of war and had learned their craft in improvised camp theatres.

The art classes that flourished in prison camp included a number of outstanding illustrators and commercial artists, among them Ronald Searle – who created the St Trinian's schoolgirls – Robert Buckham from Canada, and Ley Kenyon, who illustrated Paul Brickhill's bestseller *The Great Escape* (and, without a credit, Eric Williams' *The Wooden Horse*).

Much of this success was achieved despite – rather than because of – captivity, and for most the 'stolen years' (as one described them) robbed them of physical health and undoubtedly caused some psychological damage; early death was not an uncommon phenomenon amongst ex-POWs, and for those who lived to a ripe old age every day was a bonus.

But captivity did give them two important things: gratitude at still being alive, and comradeship from the other lucky ones who escaped death with them. Confronted by a government and a public largely indifferent to their experiences and their fate, former prisoners formed ex-POW associations. They have been an essential mutual support society not only for ex-POWs but also for their widows and orphans. Surprisingly, few of their members have borne any deep-seated grudge against the Germans and the Italians; and some have also come to understand – if not forgive – the Japanese. But the indifference of the British government and the failure of the Axis countries to publicly acknowledge and apologize for their treatment of prisoners of war remains a very sore point to this day.

Miss Christine Knowles, OBE
Chairwoman of meeting of next-of-kin of officers, 6 October 1943
I wonder if you would care to write to me and say in your own words what are the things that you are thinking about for when they return at the end of the war. What do you feel will be necessary? What do you think you personally will want to do? How do you feel about it all? Do you think you are going to find the same man that you said goodbye to? Do you think you are going to find somebody immeasurably better, or do you feel that you are worried? Are you thinking how you are going to readjust yourself, and how are you going on into the new world that is coming? Because there is no question about it,

we have all got to begin to think, and to think very seriously not only about the big planning but the small planning too. Here again I come back to something which has been very evident in the letters from prisoners, and in the visits I have received from prisoners who have either escaped or been repatriated. It matters very much indeed what happens in their own homes. It matters very much more than anything that any public body, or private body, or anybody can do. It does really depend upon their own relations.

Lance-Corporal Jack Sollars, Queen's Royal Regiment
POW in Italy and Germany from 1943 to August 1944
I was taken to a hospital at Birkenhead, then, some time later, moved by train to a military hospital at Swindon near Cheltenham. Eventually I became a patient at Standish House, Stonehouse, where I was kept quiet and well cared-for until fit enough to undergo a massive spine-graft operation at Cheltenham General Hospital.

The surgery was a success and, a year or two later, I was able to pick up the threads of my civilian life and settle down to the less exciting task of earning my living.

All went well and I was able to carry on normally and in reasonably good health until retirement came in 1976.

Pilot Officer Laurence Edwards, New Zealander in the Royal Air Force
POW in Germany from September 1940 to May 1945
Since the war I have rarely heard our own men speak disparagingly of the German frontline troops. We noticed the difference when guarded by a unit on rest from the trenches. The respect which one soldier holds for a worthy antagonist was evident.

I find it difficult to recall the periods of hunger, the unpleasant incidents, the denial to us of normal society, but I have vivid memories of the tolerance and understanding shown to those in trouble, of the desire always to help the other fellow, of the supreme optimism and the irrepressible sense of humour which could always produce a joke out of the tensest of situations.

Private Alfred Charles Bryant, The Royal East Kent Regiment (The Buffs)
POW in Poland and Germany from May 1940 to May 1945
Occasionally I feel a little bitterness against the Germans. But I often told my wife that if the Germans and the English were to become one race, it would be the finest fighting force in the world.

Lieutenant David Lubbock, Royal Naval Volunteer Reserve
POW in Germany and Poland from July 1941 to April 1945

Except that it appeared later that I had developed paralysis of one vocal cord (permanently) my physical health seems to have been unimpaired. Mentally, coming 'out of the bag', I no doubt had a number of defects, some of which I probably have never realized. For some people at first they had difficulty to decide about crossing a road. I was not as bad as that, but I was for months very impatient. For a short time I had a 'pica' for sweet little tea-cakes which I never had before nor have had since. Permanently it distresses me to see a plate of food not fully finished up.

Vivien Johnson (née Symonds)
Postwar wife of Pilot Officer Theo Johnson, New Zealander in the Royal Air Force (POW from August 1941 to April 1945)

He had left New Zealand fit in the A1 category but returned with a scar on one lung and a permanently weakened constitution for the remaining 26 years of his life. Like so many POWs he died young, 51, of stomach cancer.

He never ran down or hated the Germans, though he had little time for some of the non-active service guards. He had enormous natural integrity, which was strengthened by the way in which some of the guards were bribed, then blackmailed. He would never accept anything remotely like a bribe! He once told me that, if our children were starving he would steal food; no one, he said, who hadn't starved, as he had done before the Red Cross organized food parcels, could blame anyone for stealing food.

He said that the Germans had taught him never to get angry, but I fear that this self-discipline was partly responsible for the endless stomach ailments that afflicted him. However, he rose to the top of his profession in the New Zealand Public Service, having gone to Manchester University in September 1945 to study Town and Country Planning. He was the only New Zealand serviceman that I know of who was allowed to stay in the UK to study without going home first, and then returning. When he died on 6 March 1972 he was Director of the Town and Country Planning Division, Ministry of Works. He loved his work, though Government stupidity had the ability to drive him crazy.

Air Commodore (formerly Squadron Leader) David Malcolm Strong, CB, AFC, Royal Air Force (Retired)
POW in Germany and Poland from September 1941 to April 1945

I had married on 29 March 1941 and on release went back to my wife, a WAAF stationed at Joint Headquarters in Plymouth. She got a phone call from her aunt in London that I was back in England, and sat all day at this aunt's home waiting for me. When I finally appeared in officer's jacket and cap, airman's trousers, army boots and a kitbag, she thought: My God! Is this the man I married?

We were like complete strangers – but we went on to have three children!

Sapper Edgar Whincup, Royal Engineers
POW in the Far East from February 1942 to August 1945
Monday, 29 October 1945. I arrived at Midland Station during the early evening and saw a lone figure standing on the platform – it was Edna. I'll just skip over our excitement at seeing one another after three years and just mention that Edna expected to see a thin, anaemic, emaciated Edgar, but, thanks to the medics and the extra food I had recently consumed, I looked reasonably well. In fact I had lost between two and three stones in weight. Interestingly, although there were four other sappers due to travel to Nottingham, I was the only one on that train. A St John ambulance came to pick me up, so within 15 minutes of arriving I was home for the first time in four years – and with a three-month leave pass.

At this stage there had been no mention of my demobilization, but, of course, the notice soon arrived, and in typical army fashion. I was ordered to report to Weston-super-Mare, hardly a short distance from home. There I was kitted out with my civilian suit, had my final medical, and received my pay minus, ironically, the cost of one greatcoat, which I had lost before leaving England in 1941. I stayed one night and quickly returned home, determined to make up for five years which, had it not been for the war, could have been my best years.

Craftsman Maurice Newey, Royal Electrical and Mechanical Engineers
POW in Italy and Germany from June 1942 to April 1945
I enjoyed the postwar POW/escape films very much, as they were high on entertainment. Colditz was of course, officer class. They had all the advantages, a much better education than the rank and file, better food and were able to buy things they needed to help their escape. They were brave men, however, who did escape.

The Wooden Horse was a very good film. It showed the best of British character and gave a true reflection of their perseverance and ingenuity in digging those tunnels. *The Great Escape*, as usual with the Americans, was blown up out of all proportion, portraying Steve McQueen as a great hero. He would have been given short shrift by the Germans. He would have been shot or sent to a criminal prison, as some of our lads were. The shooting of the escapees was a real war crime and it was a constant threat we were all under. 'You are *verboten* to do this or that, or you will be shot,' was often reiterated when we were on roll-call. Not that it stopped us doing our little bits of sabotage.

Lieutenant (later Lieutenant-Colonel) William Bompas, Royal Artillery
POW in Italy and Germany from December 1942 to April 1945

I got to England in April 1945 whilst the war in Europe was still on, and I felt guilty that I had done so little to help beat the Germans. I was more than ready to get a bit of retraining and go out to the Far East – I had had a brother and a cousin killed by the Japs (as well as three other cousins killed elsewhere).

Career-wise, I wasn't held back as much as I thought I would (or should) be. I took a regular commission in 1946, and became an Acting Major when 29 and a local Lieutenant-Colonel when 35 (and happily resigned when just 39).

My love-life never really settled down, as I had missed out on some years when I should have been chasing young women. After three unsatisfactory marriages, I was at last lucky enough to meet the perfect wife.

Corporal Charles Kinahan, Straits Settlement Volunteer Force
POW in the Far East from February 1942 to August 1945, writing in 1990

As I look back on my war experiences, 45 years since VJ Day in 1945, and in my 75th year, I realize how blessed and incredibly lucky I was to survive in such good shape. My memory of those times is still extraordinarily bright. I can remember scenes and individuals as if it was yesterday. I can remember the names of many fellow prisoners whom I have never seen since – and can't remember the names of people I met yesterday!

We British Malayans survived the experience extraordinarily well. We were acclimatized to the tropics; we knew how to look after ourselves and we knew a bit of the local languages. Of the group of 2,000 (Group 2), which formed the first contingent sent to Siam, about 100 were Malayan Volunteers. To the best of my knowledge over 90 of these survived, though not all in the best of health. Amongst those of us who returned to Malaya in 1946 there was a great camaraderie, a sense of being an elite. Anyone who had been in prewar Malaya and had not been one of us was somehow looked down on. Some had, of course, left their units under doubtful circumstances prior to surrender.

Three and a half years spent as a guest of Emperor Hirohito were lost years in the career of an ambitious young man in his late twenties, but no more wasted than those of millions of young people of many nations caught up in Hitler's war. Looking back on those years of long ago, I am sure I certainly gained in maturity and in knowledge of my fellow men. Three and a half years of living in confined quarters, deprived of creature comforts and necessary drugs, often existing on an inadequate diet, and subject to Japanese brutality, one learnt to appreciate the many fine qualities of the British working man from whom I had, up to our surrender in Singapore, been virtually isolated. I had a privileged background and English public school education. The horrors of the early thirties had largely passed me by, whereas most of my fellow prisoners came from humble homes which had suffered all the privations of that ghastly period in our history. Under prison conditions, with all their horrors, with so many comrades dying horrible deaths (16,000 out of 60,000), one learnt that real quality did not depend on a comfortable home background and a public school education. So the experience taught me many valuable lessons; it taught me to appreciate my many blessings and, I hope, the consequent obligations to society. It has left me with a deep sense of gratitude to Almighty God that I was spared in such good health to start a new life in marriage to my beloved Kathleen and our dear children and grandchildren.

Flying Officer Erroll David Shearn, Royal Air Force
Prisoner in the Dutch East Indies from March 1942 to August 1945
At RAF Cosford in the course of my medical investigation I was examined for deafness. A medical officer stationed me some distance from him and murmured some word which I could not make out. He then in the same voice said: 'Whisky and soda.' These words registered at once and I repeated them. The MO told me that his first utterance had been 'Zambesi'. We laughed a bit over my immediate recognition of 'whisky and soda'.

Ultimately, with all my reports completed, I went before the medical board. The officer in charge told me that the board was passing me 'fit for active service'. I protested that I did not want active service, but as an ex-POW wanted an immediate discharge. I was assured I would get an immediate discharge, but that nonetheless my medical category was 'fit for active service'. That, I considered, was reasonably satisfactory at the age of over fifty-three and after three and a half years as a guest of the Japanese.

I was in Java again in 1957 as an adviser to the Malayan Government at the Rubber Study Group. I had in mind to go to Bandoeng to retrieve my draft novel. Unfortunately there was at that time a shooting war being ranged around Bandoeng. I felt I had had all I wanted of that kind of entertainment, so decided not to embark on my contemplated journey to Bandoeng. The novel of the century remains buried there.

Brigadier Sir Philip Toosey, CBE, DSO, Royal Artillery (Retired)
POW in the Far East from February 1942 to August 1945, writing in 1993
The postwar years have been very interesting and I have been very fortunate in my career with Baring's Bank.

The only setback I have had is that I had both tuberculosis and a bad heart attack as a result of my experiences in Siam, but I have recovered from both of them and am now semi-retired and an extremely happy man and can look back on these memories with very considerable pleasure indeed. All the time remembering how much I owe my wife, who brought up my family herself alone through at least four years when I was away from her and then, when I was sick after the war, looked after me in a most splendid manner and has been responsible for saving my life.

Mrs Enid Innes-Ker
Wife of Sergeant William McDonald ('Tam') Innes-Ker (POW in the Far East from February 1942 to August 1945)
(Letter to author, 2006)
Tam came home out of the bag remarkably normal and unchanged. He was older and greyer and had lost the youthful bubble that was previously his, but he was still the same steady, well-balanced, straightforward man he had always been, with his sense of humour undimmed. He never minded talking of his POW days as some men did.

When we retired from Singapore and came back to England he was always very insistent that in the winter months I should keep the larder well stocked up so that we took no risk of ever being frozen in with no food.

Tam did have what I thought was a slightly abnormal dislike of going out when it was raining. This stemmed, I think, from the awful long march from Ban Pong to Sonkurai Camp, when they marched at night and rested during the day in open areas without cover and in pouring rain. He spoke of sitting and making runnels each side of him to let the water run away.

Tam was forty at the end of the war and he never had the same stamina that he had enjoyed before. He was easily tired by physical effort, and I think the heart-trouble that struck him when he was 56 was a result of those POW years.

Mrs Dorothy Threadgold
Postwar wife of Captain Arthur Geoffrey Threadgold, Royal Artillery
(POW in the Far East from March 1942 to August 1945)

Geoff went through a great struggle to overcome his dislike for many things from the Far East, the relentless nightmares that continued right until the time he passed away, and the helpless feelings he had over the loss of so many of his men and the feeling that he had somehow failed them by surviving himself.

He continued to try and assist family and friends of people who had been in the camps with him to try and help them find some sort of closure as to what had become of the people that they loved; this he felt was the last act that he could give the men who fought so valiantly to survive the tortures that they endured in the most horrific way.

Which I feel was one of the forces behind him in his quest to have a memorial of some sort placed for all those who lost their lives in Sandakan and Borneo – to let the world know that there were others outside the Burma Railway who also needed to be remembered. The fact that he had finally seen this through was one of the last things told to him on the day that he passed away. The plaque was finally erected on 18 April 1999, only fourteen weeks after he passed away at Larkhill Royal Artillery church, which I was proud to attend to represent the husband of whom I am so proud.

Mrs Marlene White
Wife of Captain Harry L White, Winnipeg Grenadiers (POW in the Far East from December 1941 to August 1945)
(Letter to author, 2006.)

Every one in the Armed Forces who saw action has a horror story. The Hong Kong veterans have theirs. I asked Harry one time how come he never talked about it. 'There's no point if you weren't there,' he said. This is why reunions were so important to them. Harry was away for four-and-a-half years. That is a long, long time. If you had children before you left (which Harry did) all they would know of their father was this man in a picture.

How could any wife even imagine what they went through? Harry, and many others, would have nightmares for years. He scared me half to death one time. He was kicking some Japanese or having a real fight.

He kept a handwritten type of shorthand diary on his person in prison camp. It helped to convict one of the commandants in the trials after the war.

There was a documentary on the Hong Kong veterans and there it said that many of them suffered from paranoia. At least it explained some things to me. Harry trusted next to no one, and it was mentioned that the lack of vitamins over a long period of time can cause this. It was termed 'vitaminosis'. It took a long time for Harry to trust me, and I instinctively knew that if I ever betrayed that trust he would be shattered. I never did.

The doctors in Canada didn't really know too much about malnutrition. The men had been well fed and well dressed for two months before coming home. They had their limbs intact – most of them – so what was the problem? The problem came through in later years. One of the first organs to go in malnutrition are the eyes. Many became blind and then other illnesses developed.

Gunner Cyril George King, Royal Artillery (Territorial)
POW in Germany from May 1940 to April 1945
After a period of leave we went through basic training at Newcastle to get us fit. There was training for Far Eastern warfare at Lydd, and eventually into a holding artillery regiment. I was demobbed at Guildford in the spring of 1946.

I cannot say any more – the war has had its effect upon all of us and in so many different ways. Those years I must try to forget, and not think again in terms of what I should have done. I am alive – that is the point – and can look at this old word with its so many wonderful aspects, and amazing people, too, if you look for them.

Miss Margaret ('Peggy') King
Sister of Gunner Cyril George King, Royal Artillery (Territorial) (POW in Germany from May 1940 to April 1945)
Although he had a very happy marriage and a daughter his health was very poor, despite treatment. From a strong rugby player he was a shadow of his former self, physically and mentally. He took his own life in July 1981. Living was just too much.

Private Kenneth ('Kim') Stalder, Royal Army Medical Corps
POW in Germany from May 1940 to April 1945
I was discharged from the RAMC as unfit and went back to being a meter-reader. The firm had asked me to return under the 'green card' as a way of fitting me in. They said I could move into the office whenever I wanted to. But one bloke said if I couldn't cope with the job I should leave. So I left. One day I saw an Eyetie with an English girl and I went for his throat. It took my brother and two others to pull me off.

Later I joined the packing department of a London departmental store and became a supervisor; then I did pump maintenance at a garage; and then joined Shell as requisition/customer relations manager at its Wandsworth depot until that closed down and moved to Surbiton. At the age of 59 I retired – I'd had a nervous breakdown. I recuperated at my daughters' (two of my own and one adopted).

I once voted Labour to get the Tory bastards out and then switched to Tory to get the Labour bastards out – couldn't stand communism.

Major Mick Wagner, The Welch Regiment
POW in Italy from January 1942 to September 1943
(Letter to author, 2006)

My experiences as a prisoner of war have had no serious adverse effects on my life over the last 60 years or so. As a 14-year-old I was sent to a boarding school in Switzerland where I met boys from many different countries and backgrounds and made friends of many of them, including Italians from whom I acquired a smattering of Italian. I also travelled a bit in Italy during school holidays and became enamoured of the country. Later, back in England during the Italian invasion of Abyssinia (Ethiopia), and again when Mussolini declared war on the UK after the collapse of France in the late spring of 1940, I was a bit of an 'Italiophobe' at the least.

I was captured in Libya by Rommel's troops, who on that occasion treated me impeccably, but was not particularly impressed by the treatment I received at the hands of the Italians to whom I was handed over. It was perhaps mostly because of their incompetence, particularly at the transit camp at Capua, that made me resentful. When I finally got to a permanent POW camp at Padula in southern Italy I got to dislike them a little less.

It was, however, after our escape from Bologna, where we had been moved after the Allied invasion of Sicily, that my attitude changed completely. Almost from the day of our escape, as we travelled south in our attempt to reach the Allied lines way down in the south, we received, in great measure, the help, support and succour of the *contadini* – the peasant farming community with whom we came in contact in the countryside and in the mountainous regions of Italy. These people were extraordinarily generous and shared with us what little they had and did so at enormous risk to themselves. I cannot speak too highly of their courage and humanity. On two occasions during my nine months in German-occupied Italy (for six months of which I was with a partisan group) I was seriously ill and I reckon I owed my life to the care I got (at great risk to themselves) from the families who hid me in their homes and cared for me at those times.

When I finally escaped from occupied Italy in May 1944, I returned to England and after a bit of leave I joined 21 Army Group HQ, then in Brussels. In 1946 after my 'demob' leave I joined the Colonial Service in Northern Rhodesia and contact with Italy was not feasible. However, I was able on my first leave in 1950 to revisit Italy and seek out several of my closest friends from those precarious months in 1943–44. The welcome I received was as warm as ever. I have maintained those contacts ever since – latterly as a supporter of the Monte San Martino Trust, a registered charity that was established some years ago and which originally offered English language courses in this country to the children of those who helped escaping prisoners. Nowadays it is the grandchildren or even the great-grandchildren who benefit – and most of the original helpers are now long since dead.

As I have already said, I have no hang-ups about my days as a prisoner of war. My memories now are principally happy ones associated with my time on the run after I escaped and with the contacts I have maintained right up to the present time.

Flying Officer (later Flight Lieutenant) Michael Heriot Roth, Royal Air Force POW in Germany from May 1940 to May 1945
Letter to the British Prime Minister, the Rt Hon Margaret Thatcher, 3 July 1979

I have the honour to bring before your judicial forum a matter of personal concern. I beg the liberty to do so, as I recall in memoirs relating to the late Sir Winston Churchill how he told a retired service man to write to him at number 10 Downing Street, after all else had failed.

I was commissioned in the RAF (pilot – 39175) in 1936. I was shot down and taken prisoner 10 May 1940 and was a POW until 7 May 1945.

While we were prisoners we had a third of our pay deducted and withheld by Cox and Kings, Lloyds Bank, Pall Mall. I still have an account there. After the war, the Manager of that bank informed me that the amount withheld was in a separate account and could not be released without instructions from the Treasury. We were income-taxed on this third we did not receive as well as the remaining two thirds of our pay!

I hope you can understand my consternation at this breach of good faith. After five years I was, as we all were, not capable of getting involved with the powers that were, and there was the Official Secrets Act and dire penalties for anyone who tried to communicate our concern to the press. Officers were not allowed to discuss service matters with anyone, regardless of the subject.

I have made enquiries regarding this awful and ruthless matter, and have been informed by the bank that all records have been destroyed and nothing can be done. My question was, who received the pay I earned? It was in a separate account at the close of the war. Where did it go? It appears to have been, to put it forthrightly, connivingly filched by the Treasury.

No records? We did have a war. That needs no recording, and I have my personal service record history from the Air Ministry. This destruction of so-called records does not eradicate the debt.

I have not pursued this matter before, because of my respect for the Official Secrets Act, which in this matter I presumed was in force for thirty years. Who could know if one could be charged for a breach of this Act or, indeed, what is classified as an Official Secret?

Other members of the Commonwealth Forces were not so penalized. On a basis of common fairness why were the English?

At the war's end, there was no conceivable way that any records as to what the Germans had paid us or not paid us could have been available. The money held on our behalf by our banks should have been automatically released to us – we had earned it. According to the conditions of service laid down in King's Regulations and Air Council Instructions all officers were in lieu of part of their pay entitled to a ration allowance of six shillings a day if one did not receive food or rations from the Air Force. This, while we were prisoners, was not paid.

The Germans did not give us the equivalent as their 'barrack behind-the-line troops' as laid down in the Geneva Convention. What they did give us would not have supported our lives. We were able to occasionally buy a bulk issue of old potatoes with the token marks in lieu of rations from either the Germans or the British in 1940–41.

For the first year of captivity we were paid once a month token money by the German Accounting Officer. After the first year, there were no more pay parades.

We were in fact, financially penalized for being taken prisoner.

It is surely time this horrible injustice was rectified.

All records have it appears conveniently gone into the shredder. But the debt still remains. Who got the money placed in separate accounts and held by our banks? No one knows. But those who earned it did not get their rightfully earned pay.

Was it for this we endured what we endured?

The question of what happened to our pay has never been answered. Where did it go? Who got it? Someone did.

IMPERIAL WAR MUSEUM REFERENCES

1. POWs in Germany and Italy
Lance-Corporal Lawrence A Bains, CBE, DL, Middlesex Yeomanry: 88/57/1
E Barrington: 88/58/1 (P)
Lieutenant Dan Billany: 96/14/1
Lieutenant-Colonel W M G Bompas: 86/89/1
Captain R G Clover: 94/8/1
J F Dalgleish: 85/24/1
Flight Lieutenant I P P Denton, RAF: 81/6/1
S J Doughty: 95/12/1
H E C Elliott: 88/20/1
E G Laker: 85/18/1
Lieutenant-Colonel M D B Lister, Royal Tank Regiment: 92/15/1
D W Luckett: 90/18/1
Major Sir John Pelly Bt, JP, DL, Coldstream Guards: 91/15/1
A F Powell: 94/41/1
J C Sollars: 85/2/1
Lieutenant-Commander William L Stephens, RNVR: 86/7/1
Major M S Wagner: 90/18/1
Flight Lieutenant Eric Ernest Williams, MC, RAF: 03/11/2 &2A

2. Far Eastern POWs
Lieutenant S S Abbott, OBE: 89/15/1
Lieutenant-Colonel P A Belton: 95/17/1
Reverend G Bower, RN: 90/38/1
Miss M D St B Crawford: 86/56/1
Mrs A E M ('Wendy') Fleming: 87/14/1
CSM P Hall Romney, Machine-Gun Company, Selangor Battalion, Malayan
    and Singapore Volunteer Forces: account 'In the Land of the Free: Life,
    and Death, on the River Kwei': 81/7/1

Mrs E Innes-Kerr: 84/45/1

Sergeant W M Innes-Ker, Straits Settlement Volunteer Force: 84/45/1

Driver F D Jackson, Royal Air Force, *Misadventure*, privately published, July 1992 (IWM, 93/8/1)

Sapper Charles H G Kinahan, Straits Settlement Volunteer Force: 90/15/1

L E Morris: 91/18/1

Lieutenant John R Pelly, RNVR: 91/15/1

Flying Officer E D Shearn, RAF: 92/36/1

Frederick H Thompson: 87/58/1

Captain A G Threadgold, TD, Royal Artillery: 84/10/1

J S Walker: 93/14/1

Sapper E W Whincup, Royal Engineers: account 'Speedo, Speedo: The Beginning and End of an Epic Life of a Japanese POW': 91/18/1

Commander R S Young, RN: 96/5/1

INDEX OF CONTRIBUTORS

GENERAL INDEX